THE LIFE & TIMES
—— OF ——
HENRY COOKE

BY HIS SON-IN-LAW

J. L. PORTER

AMBASSADOR

Belfast Northern Ireland **Greenville** South Carolina

The Life and Times of Henry Cooke
First published 1871
First Ambassador edition 1999

ISBN 1   84030   047   7

Ambassador Publications
a division of
Ambassador Productions Ltd.
Providence House
16 Hillview Avenue,
Belfast, BT5 6JR
Northern Ireland

Emerald House
1 Chick Springs Road, Suite 203
Greenville,
South Carolina 29609, USA
www.emeraldhouse.com

STATUE OF DR. COOKE.

SAMUEL F. LYNN, SCULPTOR, 1871.

THE GRAVE OF DR. COOKE.

PREFACE.

"The life of Dr. Cooke," says Lord Cairns, "was a large portion of the religious and public history of Ireland for the last half century."

Dr. Cooke's boyhood was passed amid the exciting scenes of the Irish Rebellion, and in one of the most disturbed districts of the country. He was led, at an early age, to regard with feelings of horror those wild revolutionary sentiments which had deluged France in blood, and which were, before his own eyes, convulsing his native land. He was then taught to connect purity of religious principles, both in the individual and in the community, with respect for law and order, and with the development of true national greatness. Time confirmed his early convictions; and he held them with unwavering fidelity, and acted upon them with conscientious devotion, to the close of a long life.

When Dr. Cooke entered the ministry he found the Presbyterian Church infected, and almost paralyzed, by a deadly heresy. He found Irish Protestants generally indifferent to the claims of vital religion. He found the public mind deeply imbued with sceptical and infidel opinions. He found the

education of the masses in a state of lamentable neglect.
Seeing and deploring these evils, he resolved to become a
Reformer.

He spent ten years in unceasing and laborious preparation.
Then, during a period of fully thirty years, his life was a continued series of battles for truth. In every battle he was
victorious. He freed the Church of his fathers from Arianism.
He gave a new impulse to religious life and work among the
Protestants of Ireland. He largely contributed to mould the
government schemes of elementary and collegiate education, so
as to adapt them to the wants of the people. And he founded
and consolidated a constitutional party in Ulster, which preserved the peace of the country, and gave a death-blow to
Repeal.

Dr. Cooke's Life, therefore, is not the history of an individual
man merely, it is rather the history of a great work undertaken
on behalf of pure religion, of sound education, and of constitutional government—a work prompted by ardent patriotism,
prosecuted with consummate ability, and crowned with distinguished success.

Dr. Cooke held strong opinions, both religious and political;
and he propagated and defended them with all those extraordinary powers of wit, irony, and eloquence, with which he
was so largely gifted. He bore down opposition with whatever
intellectual weapons came to hand at the moment. I have not
attempted either to cloak or modify his opinions and acts. His
opinions I have given in his own words; and in narrating
the story of his conflicts, I have, as far as possible, quoted
from contemporary documents. When that was impossible,

either on account of the length of the debates, or the absence of trustworthy reports, I have described the scenes and results from information derived from eye and ear witnesses. I was not myself in any way personally interested or concerned in the events recorded. If, therefore, I have revived old controversies, my plea is, they were necessary to a faithful portraiture of the man, and a full historical narrative.

Dr. Cooke's countrymen were not slow to acknowledge their obligations to him. The numerous and splendid testimonials presented to him during his life, and the almost unparalleled honours accorded to his memory, show how high a place he held in the esteem and affection of the nation.

His fame was not confined to Britain. His struggles for truth were watched by thousands in America; and when he triumphed over Arianism, his brethren in that country were among the first to convey to him a tribute of their admiration.

The materials for this biography have been mainly drawn from the voluminous papers and correspondence of Dr. Cooke, all of which were placed in my hands. In the filling in of details I have been aided by the communications of members of his family, and of some of his early friends and associates. I feel bound to record my special obligations to the late Earl of Roden, the Earl of Mount Cashell, the Right Hon. Sir Joseph Napier, the President of Queen's College, Belfast, Professor Witherow, Counsellor Frazer, James Hamilton, Esq., J.P., Dr. Adair Crawford, and Wm. M'Ilwrath, Esq.

The task of writing a life of Dr. Cooke I have found to be one of no ordinary difficulty. Many of the actors in the great struggles in which he took a leading part still survive. The memory of others is affectionately cherished by friends and relatives. Under such circumstances it would, perhaps, be impossible faithfully to record his labours and triumphs, without giving offence or pain to some of his opponents. While entirely sympathising with Dr. Cooke in his views, I can truly say that it has been my constant aim and effort to narrate events with impartiality. If I have failed, it has been unwittingly; and if I should give offence, none will regret it more than myself.

COLLEGE PARK, BELFAST,
    October, 1871.

CONTENTS.

CHAPTER I.

1788—1808.

CHAPTER II.

1808—1811.

CHAPTER III.

1810—1818.

CHAPTER IV.

1818—1824.

CHAPTER V.

1824—1825.

CHAPTER VI.

1825—1828.

CHAPTER VII.

1828.

CHAPTER VIII.

1828—1829.

CHAPTER IX.

1829—1831.

CHAPTER XVI.

1840—1841.

CHAPTER XVII.

1841—1843.

CHAPTER XVIII.

1842—1849.

THE LIFE OF DR. COOKE.

CHAPTER I.

1788—1808.

Birth and Ancestry—Maternal Influence—Schools and Schoolmasters—State of Ireland at the Close of the 18th Century—The Volunteers—The United Irishmen—Loyalty of the Synod of Ulster—Political Principles imbibed in Boyhood—Dangers during the Rebellion of '98—Early Religious Training —Mental and Physical Characteristics in Youth—Incidents of Travel to Glasgow College—State of Glasgow College in 1802-4—First Acquaintance with Robert Stewart and Henry Montgomery—Training in Elocution— Favourite Authors and Studies.

HENRY COOKE was born on the eleventh of May, 1788, in the farm-house of Grillagh, near Maghera, in the county of Londonderry. The house is gone, and there is nothing to mark its site save a rude cairn. The fame which Henry Cooke attained was not owing to the accident of high birth or early scholastic training. His father, John Cooke, was a plain man, of little education and less pretence; but he was one of those industrious, independent, high-minded yeomen, who have mainly contributed to the prosperity and loyalty of Ulster. He was descended from a family of English Puritans, who, early in the seventeenth century, left their native Devonshire, in the train of the Hills and Conways, and settled in county Down.

During the wars which preceded the revolution of 1688, the English and Scotch colonists in Ulster suffered severely. Many of their houses and villages in Down and Antrim were desolated.   Dr. Cooke, when addressing on one occasion a vast assemblage, narrated the following incident in the history of a lineal ancestor:—" At the first outbreak of the Rebellion all his family were murdered except one little child. Driven from a distant part of the county Down, with thousands of starving Protestants, he carried his child in his arms to Derry, and was, happily, one of those admitted into the city for its defence.   When he mounted guard at night, he had no nurse or caretaker for his little one, so he carried it with him to the walls, and laid it between the embrasures where the cannon frowned defiance on James and slavery.   Providence protected the boy in the midst of famine and death ; and when, in after-years, he was asked how he fared for shelter, ' Well, enough,' was the reply ; ' I had the shelter of my father's gun.' Yes, God—the God of battles—protected the motherless and homeless boy; and he who now addresses you is that boy's descendant."   The blood of a hero, humble in station it is true, yet ennobled by patriotism, flowed in the veins of Henry Cooke.

John Cooke was twice married.   His first wife died young, leaving an only son.   His second wife was Jane Howie, of an old and respectable Scotch family.   At the time of the Ulster plantation, one branch of the Howies settled at Killyleagh, in county Down ; another near Bellaghy, in county Derry.   Mrs. Cooke sprang from the latter, and, being an only child, she inherited her father's farm, the income from which materially aided in after-years in the education of her distinguished son.   She had four children, two girls and two boys, of whom the subject of this memoir was the youngest.

Mrs. Cooke was a woman of remarkable energy and great decision of character.   She was well fitted to fight the battle of life during one of the most eventful periods of Ireland's history, and in one of the most disturbed districts of the country.   She was tall in stature, somewhat masculine in carriage and conversation, ready and fluent in speech, keen and unsparing in sarcasm. She had an insatiable thirst for knowledge, and a memory of extraordinary tenacity. Proud of the struggles of her forefathers in defence of faith and freedom, she never forgot fact or legend connected with their history in Scotland and Ulster. Stories of war and rapine, of flight and defence, were transmitted orally in families from generation to generation. Mrs. Cooke's mind was stored with romantic tales and stirring ballads. To her Henry was indebted for most of those touching anecdotes and incidents of Irish history, and scraps of ballad poetry, which in after-years he often recited with such pathos and power.

From early boyhood Henry was the chief object of his mother's careful and anxious training. She soon discovered his extraordinary powers of mind and memory. He wished to know everything, to study every subject. Ballads, songs, legends, tales of border warfare, of Celtic fanaticism, of popish cruelty, were drunk in with keenest relish. Specimens of Irish wit, humour, and smart repartee were highly appreciated and carefully treasured up. At the same time studies of a graver and more profitable kind were not neglected. Henry Cooke, as a lad, was far in advance of his associates. They all felt and acknowledged his superiority. He was a born leader ; and whether at home or abroad, in playground or class, his leadership was asserted.

Mrs. Cooke's means of instructing her son were not, unfortunately, commensurate with her wishes. To send him from home was beyond her power ; and at the close of last century the educational resources of a remote country district in Ireland were very limited. Henry, however, had the best elementary training available. The first school he attended was at Ballymacilcurr, a mile from his father's house. It was a fair sample of the infant school of the country and the period. The house was a thatched cabin. The seats were black oak sticks from the neighbouring bog. A fire of peat blazed, or rather smoked, in the middle of the floor, and a hole in the roof overhead served for a chimney. The teacher was a Mr. Joseph Pollock, or Poak, as he was familiarly called—a tall lanky Scotchman, distinguished by an enormous nose, a tow wig, a long coat of rusty black, leather tights, grey stockings, brogues, and a formidable hazel rod. On occasions of state, such as the hearing of one of the advanced scholars or a judicial investigation of some mad prank, the Master was accustomed to raise the hazel rod to his shoulder, and with a grand air place astride his nose a huge pair of black horn spectacles. Thus equipped, he felt himself a king, and the urchins trembled at his nod.

But, notwithstanding his uncouth exterior, Poak was an excellent teacher, as teachers were in those days. He was a Presbyterian, of the " straitest sect," and religious train-ing was, in his honest mind, an essential part of a boy's education. On Saturdays, he taught the Lord's Prayer, the Apostles' Creed, and the Ten Commandments to the whole school. Psalms were prescribed for Sunday tasks, and had to be repeated on Monday morning. Catechisms were en-forced without exception, and without distinction. The Shorter Catechism of the Westminster Divines, the Church Catechism, and the Christian Doctrine of the Roman Catholics, were taught to the members of the respective sects. No child was suffered to escape. The hazel rod left an unpleasant memorial of every forgotten answer. Poak was a discerner of character. Young Cooke soon attracted his attention. He was then an emaciated, delicate-looking boy, with sharp features, jet-black hair, and piercing grey eyes. His movements were quick; his voice clear and ring-ing; his speech easy and fluent. The ordinary tasks of the school gave him little trouble; he learned them as if by instinct; but his stories kept all round him idle. He easily outstripped his class-mates, and, despite his troublesome habit of story-telling, Pollock was proud of him. Pointing to young Cooke one day, he said, with an air of dignity, to an intimate friend, "I tell you, sir, that lad, if spared, will rival, if not excel myself."

While yet very young, Henry was removed from the care of Pollock, and sent in succession to several teachers. He was at length placed in a classical school, just then established by a certain Frank Glass. It was situated near the village of Tobermore, four miles from Grillagh as the crow flies, five by the road. Of the school-house itself, and the difficulties experienced in getting possession of it, Dr. Cooke has left a graphic account :—" We were compelled to remove five times in search of accommodation. We had flitted like fieldfares in the commencement of bad weather. The house we got at last had two window-frames, but no glass. One was well secured against light by earthen sods ; the other was open, for some light we must have, and it served to admit, in company with the light, a refreshing portion of rain and snow. We were furnished with one table, whereat our Master sat for audience and judgment. Stones were the seats. I had myself the only stool in the house ; but, the master being too tender to sit on a cold stone, I was robbed of the stool, ' to save him,' as he said, ' from the colic.' By a penny subscription and the aid of a glazier, we shut out the snow ; and, in process of time, we substituted for the stone seats slabs of oak from the neighbouring bog. We thus became wonderfully content, for we had the best Master and the most comfortable school-house in all the country."

The direct path to school lay through fields, over a swampy bog, and across a ford of the river Moyola, which often swept down, a swollen torrent, from the Dungiven mountains. Most parents would have thought a daily walk to and from Tobermore impracticable for a boy of Henry's age, and most boys would have shrunk in fear from such a difficult, if not dangerous path. But Mrs. Cooke was not an ordinary woman ; and fear was never a word in the vocabulary of her son. He was of slender make, but wiry and agile. Among other boyish feats, he had learned to walk, and run, and gambol on stilts ;

and he had often astonished the sober matrons of Maghera by
stalking past their upper windows. What he had learned and
practised for amusement was now, by the thoughtfulness of his
mother, turned to good account.

Henry was enrolled a pupil in the new classical school.
His first morning's journey he never forgot. It left an
indelible impress on his memory. Probably, too, it may
have had some influence in fixing his principles, and moulding
his whole subsequent career; for he often referred to the incident. It was in the year '98, one of the darkest in Ireland's
history. The country was convulsed with rebellion. The
neighbourhood of Maghera swarmed with daring bandits, who
found an asylum among the mountains, and lived by rapine,
caring little what party they spoiled. Henry, thoughtless of
danger, strapped his satchel on his back, poised his long stilts
on his shoulder, and set out for school. His mother accompanied him, anxiety filling her heart. On reaching the ford of
the Moyola, they found the river swollen: to pass it on foot
was impossible. Henry mounted his stilts, crossed the torrent
by a few vigorous strides, and stepped safely on the opposite
bank. Carefully concealing his stilts in the heath, he tripped
gaily onward. When at some distance, he chanced to look
back, and saw the tall figure of his mother standing on a
mound with outstretched arm, pointing towards Cairntogher.
Turning his eyes to the place indicated, a scene presented
itself which might well have struck terror into the stoutest
heart. A farm-steading was in flames—the house of a loyal
man fired by the rebels. The sight was not new to Henry.
Young as he was, he had witnessed many such; yet seventy
years afterwards, when narrating the incident at his own table,
he said the whole scene was as vividly pictured before his mind
as the day on which it occurred.

Frank Glass, Henry's new master, formed a striking contrast in appearance and character to Joseph Poak. He was
a pure Milesian, short of stature, fiery in temper, with features
exhibiting a strange combination of cunning, thought, and

humour. He swore at his pupils roundly, and taught them to swear. But he was a good scholar, and a successful teacher. Like many of his countrymen, his love for classic literature amounted almost to a passion; and he had the rare talent of inspiring favourite pupils with much of his own enthusiasm. Among Latin authors he delighted in Horace, and down to a recent period Dr. Cooke often recited, with great spirit and intense enjoyment, some of his old teacher's quaint renderings of the Odes. Henry's progress was rapid. He was soon able, under such an instructor, to appreciate the beauties of classic poetry. While at school, he committed to memory the Odes of Horace and a great part of the Georgics of Virgil. But the eloquence of Cicero and Demosthenes had greater charms for him than the graces of poetry; and, even in early youth, these writers seem to have been adopted as models. His long walks, instead of impairing, improved his health. They gave him greater muscular vigour. Fragile though he seemed, he was soon known as the fastest runner at the school, and the leader in all games which required skill, courage, and endurance.

For two years he continued, almost without a day's inter-mission, to tread the same path and cross the same ford. On one occasion, during the severe winter of 1800, he nearly lost his life. He left school late in the evening, in the face of a terrible snow-storm. Before he reached the Moyola, the snow covered the ground to the depth of several inches. He searched in vain for his stilts: the spot where he left them could not be distinguished among the snow-wreaths. He made up his mind to ford the stream, and plunged boldly into the swollen torrent. He could not swim, and he was carried away by the current. Exhausted and half drowned, he with difficulty reached the bank he had left. He was drenched from head to foot, but he set out homeward. It was a weary round of six miles. His feet sank, at every step, deep and deeper into the snow; the blinding drift blew in his face; night set in; but the brave boy struggled on, and at last, wearied and shivering, he staggered into his home at Grillagh.

Thus was Henry Cooke trained; trained in a hard but wholesome school; trained physically, as well as mentally, for those
gigantic labours which he afterwards undertook on behalf of
Church and country, and which he performed with such distinguished success, not only while in the vigour of manhood,
but even throughout a ripe old age. Thus was he trained for
long and laborious walks over moor and mountain, in the
faithful discharge of pastoral duties, during the early years of
his ministry. Thus was he trained for exhausting journeys
through the province and the empire in defence of truth and
freedom. Thus was an iron frame inured to toil, and made
capable of sustaining the marvellous efforts of a powerful
intellect.

Henry Cooke's boyhood was cast in one of the stormiest
periods of Ireland's stormy history. Some time before his
birth, when the country was threatened with foreign invasion,
and when England, harassed by enemies, was unable to furnish
regular troops for its defence, a native volunteer force was
organized. On its organization, martial ardour suddenly
seized the entire nation. Men of all ranks and sects joined
the movement. Clergymen became captains and colonels
of volunteer corps. The leading minister of the Covenanters
commanded at a review. The minister of the first Presbyterian (Unitarian) congregation, Belfast, published a
sermon " On the Propriety of setting apart a portion of the
Sabbath for the purpose of acquiring the Knowledge and Use
of Arms." At a great meeting in Dungannon, the Bishop of
Derry was present, dressed in the uniform of an officer of
volunteers. For a time it seemed as if the volunteers
would prove a national safeguard. The defence of crown
and constitution appeared to be their sole aim. Gradually,
however, a change came. The government of Ireland was
then, and had been for generations, corrupt and incompetent.
Its policy was partial and crooked; Saxon and Celt, Protestant and Catholic, were alike dissatisfied. All were
smarting under a sense of injustice, and almost despaired of

redress from the constitutional authorities. The Irish Parliament was a mere sham. Three-fourths of its members were the nominees of Irish landlords, not the representatives of a free people; and any measures of reform which they did agree to pass were usually curtailed, and sometimes arbitrarily rejected, by the English Privy Council. Volunteer officers imbibed strong political sentiments, and, conscious of power, became political agitators. In 1783, a meeting of delegates from Ulster, the representatives of two hundred and seventy-two companies of volunteers, was held in Dungannon, to concert measures for reforming the Irish Parliament. It was there agreed that a convention of representatives from the whole volunteer forces of Ireland should assemble in Dublin, in the month of November. On the appointed day (the 10th) the Convention met at the Royal Exchange, marched in procession to the Rotunda, and resolved to remodel the Irish Constitution. Similar meetings were held in 1784 and 1785; and their proceedings were conducted after the American model. The French revolution now took place, and acted upon Ireland like an electric shock. Its pernicious principles found a congenial soil in the minds of men naturally ardent and fickle, and stung, besides, by a sense of wrong. The volunteer force, originally organized for the defence of the crown, became its most dangerous enemy. Gatherings took place in Dublin, Belfast, Dungannon, and other centres. Men, with arms in their hands, demanded reform; and reform now meant revolution. On the 14th of July, 1791, the anniversary of the French Revolution was celebrated in Belfast with indescribable enthusiasm. The volunteers, horse, foot, and artillery, accompanied by a dense multitude of the populace, paraded the principal streets. Banners were carried, inscribed with revolutionary mottoes. The harp without the crown, surmounted by the cap of liberty, was a favourite emblem. The example of Belfast was followed in other parts of Ireland. The wrongs of an enslaved people were depicted by orators in the style of Mirabeau and Robespierre. Tyrants were denounced with tremendous vehemence. The Government was at length forced to interfere. The volunteers were disbanded. Political assemblies were prohibited. It was too late. Disaffection and rebellion already enveloped the land. The people, backed by an army of trained soldiers, refused to obey a royal mandate. As a recognised and constitutional force, the volunteers ceased to exist; but they were still the acknowledged representatives of the vast body of the nation, and the champions of national claims. A number of their leaders met at Belfast, on the 14th of October, 1791, and organized a new society, or, rather, re-organised the volunteers, under the new name of UNITED IRISHMEN.

The avowed object of this dangerous society was to separate Ireland from the British crown, and form it into a republic. France was the model aimed at. Steps were taken by the leaders to secure French aid. The United Irishmen were not confined to any one class or religious sect. Most of the prime movers, such as Theobald Wolfe Tone, Whitley Stokes, Thomas Addis Emmet, the Rev. William Jackson, were Episcopalians. A few were Presbyterians; but the great mass was composed of Roman Catholics. No ecclesiastical body, as such, promoted or countenanced the movement. The United Irishmen may be said to have constituted an unholy alliance of the godless and the reckless of all sects and classes. Most of them adopted the current French views on religion as well as politics. Payne's " Age of Reason " and " Rights of Man" were industriously and widely circulated by active agents. When sober people refused to accept the infidel pamphlets, they were dropped on the road, or left at the door, or thrust in through an open window. Inflammatory speeches and revolutionary ballads teemed from the press, and were distributed in tens of thousands among an ignorant and excitable peasantry. The result was sad and eventful.

Religion, morality, and loyalty suffered in almost equal measure.

The Presbyterian Church, with which Henry Cooke's family were hereditarily connected, was less implicated in the rebellion than any other religious body in Ireland, yet even its professing adherents were not all free from the taint of disloyalty. But the Church, as a whole, was loyal. The members of the Supreme Court, at the annual meeting held in 1793, declared without a dissentient voice, that "They felt themselves called upon explicitly to avow and publish their unshaken attachment to the genuine principles of the British Constitution—an attachment early inculcated by the lessons of their fathers, and since justified by their own observation and experience." And in 1798, when the French troops were at Killala, and when the whole country was in a flame, the Synod assembled specially at Lurgan, on the 28th of August, and in the face of imminent danger, renewed its declaration of loyalty to the crown, and expressed its disapprobation of the treasonable practices then convulsing the country. It did not stop here. It did not restrict its loyalty to empty words. In a spirit worthy of its history, it voted an address to the King, and the sum of five hundred pounds to the Government, "as the contribution of the members of the body towards the defence of the kingdom." It drew up, besides, and ordered to be read from every pulpit a "Pastoral," denouncing the rebellion, and enjoining loyalty upon all its people as a sacred duty. The Government publicly recognised acts so honourable and decided in the midst of wide-spread disaffection. "I am sensible," wrote the Lord-Lieutenant in reply to the address, "that when the public safety has formerly been menaced, either by domestic traitors or foreign invaders, no description of his Majesty's subjects were more active in all the duties of allegiance than the Protestant dissenters of the Province of Ulster. To find this disposition so cordial on the present occasion affords me sincere satisfaction; and your avowing your principles at the moment when the hopes of the disaffected were revived by the actual landing of the enemy, could not fail to have a beneficial influence on the community."

Yet still, while such was the feeling of the Synod, it cannot be denied that some of the Presbyterian people, and a few—a very few, of the clergy, chiefly belonging to the " New Light " or Arian party, joined the United Irishmen. The Rev. John Glendy, of Maghera, by whom Henry Cooke was baptized, and under whose pastoral oversight he and most of his young associates were trained, was among the number of those implicated.   He was, in fact, a well-known if not an openly avowed rebel.   The influence of such a man in a remote locality, at such a period, was necessarily most pernicious.   In the pulpit, in the social circle, by the family fireside, he could inculcate his revolutionary principles without opportunity or power of reply.   The result was that the district became a hot-bed of rebellion.   Club-meetings were held in the farm-houses.   Debating societies were organized in the villages and country districts.   The wrongs of Ireland, real or fancied, were discussed; and the triumphs of liberty in France and America were described in glowing terms.   Paid agents and enthusiastic politicians went from village to village, and from farm-house to farm-house, arguing with parents, and poisoning the minds of children with false ideas of liberty.   When arguments failed, and persuasions were neglected, mysterious warnings were given, and startling threats were uttered. The frequent incendiary fires and midnight murders showed how terribly the threats could be executed when deemed necessary for furthering the cause.

The farm-house of Grillagh was firmly closed against all emissaries of revolution.   Its occupants would neither listen to arguments nor heed threats.   Henry was beset by the boys at school, and by men on the highway.   Glass, his teacher, was a Roman Catholic, and, like all his co-religion-

ists, was an ardent rebel. His political principles oozed
out in the class, and in his occasional intercourse with the
pupils. But Henry was proof against his plausible fallacies.
Even then his information was far in advance of most of
those who tried to influence him. He had read of the
horrors of the French reign of terror, and had to some
extent investigated its causes. He had learned that while
revolution might overthrow one tyrant, it was likely to raise
up hundreds more cruel and bloodthirsty. He had been
informed of the character and principles of the leaders of
the United Irishmen. He had himself witnessed some of
the crimes perpetrated under the name of liberty. He had
seen houses burned, and men, women, and children mas-
sacred. He had discovered that the Roman Catholics only
joined the Protestants to secure by their aid their own
object, and that object was, as Macaulay has well described
it when writing of a parallel epoch, " To break the foreign
(English) yoke, to exterminate the Saxon colony, to sweep
away the Protestant Church, and to restore the soil to its
ancient proprietors." He had become convinced, in a word,
that the self-styled liberators of Ireland were its worst
enemies ; that they neither feared God nor regarded man.
The state of society is fully depicted in a resolution adopted
by the Secession Church at this period :—" Divine Revelation is contemned ; every species of wickedness is carried
on in a most daring manner ; blasphemy, and the most
horrid prostitution of sacred oaths, are now raging abroad
like an epidemic ; the most barbarous murders have defiled
the land with blood ; fraudulence, rapine, and oppression
are some of the leading features of the day. There is a
general violation of the whole law of God." Corrupt as the
Irish Parliament was, weak, and vacillating, and incompetent as the Executive was, the existing state was infinitely
better than any that could be expected under the rule of
United Irishmen. Henry Cooke was thus prepared for the
arguments and misrepresentations that met him on every

side. With a wisdom, an energy, and an eloquence far
beyond his years, he encountered the propagators of revolution boldly, and exposed alike their sophistry and their
crimes.

His own words, in a letter to a near relative, will give the
best idea of his life and experience at this period, and, at the
same time, of the lamentable state of the country, and the effects
produced on his mind by passing events:—"For weeks together
during the summer of '98 I never slept in my father's house :
to have done so would have been almost certain death. All
loyal families were marked and watched by bands of assassins.
When the nights were fine, we went to the middle of a corn-
field or behind a hedge. When wet or cold we crept into some
cow-shed or under a rock. One night we had ventured to
go to bed; but we were suddenly roused, and hurried out
half clothed. On reaching the door, we saw five houses in
flames in different directions. It was dark, cold, and stormy.
We took refuge in a distant barn, and lay till morning behind
a range of pikes that stood against the wall. On the morning
of the 5th of June, when returning home after passing the
night in a cave among the mountains, I saw the soldiers burn
Watty Graham's house. It was then and thus I learned my
political principles. I was taught in a hard school—the school
of care and suffering. Unceasing watchfulness made me pre-
maturely old. In early boyhood I was taught to think and
act as a man. My personal safety required it. Impressions
were then left on my mind which I have never forgotten, and
which I never wish to forget." His political creed was learned
at an early period, and mind and heart were so deeply imbued
with it that it was never forgotten, never changed.

The religious principles of Henry Cooke were as powerfully and as permanently influenced by the events of that
period as his political principles. His mother's religion
was of the old Scotch type. It rested on a broad and solid
basis of Calvinistic doctrine. It was somewhat stiff and
homely in ritual; it was perhaps stern and formal in its

moral code; but it was thoroughly conservative of all that
is pure and noble in intellect and heart. It may have
thrown a needless gloom over the Sunday; it may have
given a puritanical rigidity to the services of the sanctuary
and the family altar, but it effectually checked that wildness
of faith and morals which characterised the age and the
country, and which was leading to such deplorable results.
Henry may not yet have felt the power of the religion of his
fathers, he may not yet have realised its peace, but he
could not shut his eyes to its influences and its fruits. He
saw around him Christian truth in strong contrast to anti-
christian error. Atheism and infidelity were boldly avowed
by the leaders of the United Irishmen; while the loyalists
were, almost to a man, orthodox. His thoughtful mind
could not fail in the face of these facts and observations
to connect purity of faith with respect for law and order,
and to associate laxity of doctrine with revolution and
crime. He was thus, to say the least, favourably disposed
to embrace those great scriptural doctrines which, in after-
years, he expounded with such eloquence, and defended with
such success.

Careful maternal training largely aided the circumstances of
the times in giving a right bent to his faith, and a healthy tone
to his mind. " I received my first instructions in theology,"
he said in after-years, " at my mother's side. The Shorter
Catechism was her text-book; the Confession of Faith was
her Christian Institutes; the Bible was her final and sole
standard of appeal. Her teachings, clear and decided, if sometimes cold and formal, were confirmed by my own observation,
and deepened by a startling and sometimes sad experience.
She taught me that man is naturally corrupt; that Divine
grace alone can quicken and renew; that the Spirit of God,
reigning in the heart and mind, is the only source of right
principles and pure practical morality. She taught me that
while policy may restrain, and the forms of society control the
passions under favourable circumstances, yet, in times of

political excitement or strong temptation, evil will regain its
place and assert its dominion. She charged me to look, to
examine, to compare, and to judge for myself. I did look, I
did examine, I did compare; and I found it impossible to
resist the combined force of maternal teaching and personal
experience. I could not as yet see the grounds or reasons for
all she taught me to believe. I had not opportunity, perhaps
I had not then ability, to investigate thoroughly the foundations of our faith. I was, consequently, not fully established.
But I resolved, one day or other, to study out for myself, and,
if possible, completely to master, the evidences and proofs of
Calvinistic theology, with a view to make it, if approved, the
basis of my Christian character and acts through life."

The mind of Henry Cooke, even in boyhood, possessed
an energy which was irresistible; and his will had a firmness
which no power or influence could shake. A resolution
once formed was never relinquished. The time for the
investigation he proposed to enter upon was delayed, but it
came at last; it came at a period when fundamental truths
were rudely assailed, and when the doctrines of the Presbyterian Church in Ireland required an able, accomplished,
and uncompromising defender. The peculiar training of the
boy—strange, imperfect, rude as it was—was yet, perhaps,
after all, the very best training of mind, heart, and will for a
gigantic struggle. Native courage and force were not dulled
or dwarfed by artificial refinement.

The great ecclesiastical struggle, in which a combination
of circumstances eventually involved him, required, to ensure success, the exercise of many and diverse qualifications.
The battle could not have been waged, much less won,
without them. Intellectual grasp, logical acumen, profound wisdom, consummate tact, unflinching determination,
were all needed. The assaults of open, powerful, eloquent
adversaries had to be met; the flagging zeal, and not unfrequently the secret opposition, of timid friends had to be
sustained and counteracted; the slumber of more than half

a century of religious indifference had to be roused. Stirring eloquence, readiness in reply, an iron will, were essential to the man who would venture on such a task. The nature of the times, and the state of the Church, would have made a mere press-controversy fruitless. The masses of the people of Ulster were interested in the struggle, and they could not then have been reached through the press. The doctrines in which they had been trained from childhood, and which were inexpressibly dear to them, because of their traditional glory, were being insidiously undermined. A mere sentiment was being substituted for the grand dogma of the Atonement. The people must be made to see and realize this. Scripture truth must be placed before them in strong contrast with anti-scriptural error. Discussions on fundamental principles must take place, and, to be effectual upon the minds of the masses, they must be largely oral.   In the pulpit, on the platform, in the church-court, questions great and grave and subtle had to be treated, and treated in such a way as would not only defy the hostile criticism of keen logicians, but carry conviction to popular assemblies. It is well known that, before large audiences, voice and eye and commanding presence make fluent speech and dialectic skill tell with tenfold power.   In these respects Henry Cooke was singularly favoured.   He was a born leader of men.   Nature had gifted him with noble form and features.   His very appearance attracted attention, and commanded respect.   His eye was bright and keen as an eagle's; his gestures were graceful and natural; his voice was deep, mellow, and of extraordinary compass, it was trained, besides, with remarkable skill, under the guidance of an ear of unsurpassed musical delicacy.   But the special training of Ulster's great orator and controversialist must be more minutely described.

After such elementary instruction in classics, and other branches, as the best schools and teachers in his native place afforded, young Cooke entered the University of Glasgow.   Facilities for travel were not so great then as now.

A journey from Grillagh to Glasgow, in the year 1802, was a formidable undertaking for a lad of fourteen. There were no public conveyances on the route, and posting was out of the question to him. He had to walk to Donaghadee, a distance of sixty miles. There he took the mail-packet, which sailed daily, weather permitting, to Port Patrick, whence he walked to Glasgow. This long journey, which he was obliged to make periodically for a number of years, was not always devoid of interest. The University of Glasgow was at that time largely frequented by Irish students. In it candidates for the ministry in the Irish Presbyterian Church were chiefly trained. Before the commencement of each session, groups of young men assembled in different paris of Ulster, and travelled together, enlivening the toil and monotony of the road by anecdote, legend, and sallies of native wit. The Irish students were known everywhere along the route, especially on the Scotch side of the Channel. Every house was open to them. By day or by night their merry laugh and genial humour made them welcome to a seat at hearth or board. Not unfrequently their bed was an old armchair in a kitchen, or a fragment of carpet in an inner room. On one occasion, young Cooke's party were trudging, weary and footsore, along the road to Ayr. One of them became suddenly ill. It was late at night; the town was some miles distant, and the poor young man was unable to proceed. His companions carried him to a farm-house. The people were in bed; but the students opened the door, entered the kitchen, and kindled a fire. The "good man of the house," hearing the noise, popped his head out of the half-opened door of his room, and calmly surveyed the scene. "What's that, Jock?" cried his wife, in half-smothered accents, from within. " Ow, it's jist naethin ava but a wheen Irish collegioners." Then, telling them where they would get milk and bread, and handing out "a drap whisky for the sick laddie," he shut his door, retired to bed, and left them in possession.

Henry Cooke matriculated in November, 1802. He looked even younger than he was, for he was yet small in stature. His face was pale, and his features were sharply chiselled. He had little appearance of youthful buoyancy and vigour. Early trials, and premature anxiety and study, had hitherto retarded his physical development. It was not until many years afterward he attained that commanding stature and dignified bearing for which he became so eminently distinguished. Little is known of his college life ; and that little is unimportant. The change from the pure air and freedom of the country to the confinement and gloom of a large city, appears to have injuriously affected his health. He took advantage of every holiday and half-holiday to make long pedestrian excursions; and he has often told, in after-life, how much he enjoyed the scenery on the banks of the Clyde, and the stirring associations of Hamilton, Bothwell Bridge, and Langside.

At that period there was nothing specially attractive in the professorial staff of Glasgow College. The scholarship was fair, and in one or two cases profound; but the prelections were singularly dull. Cooke, and most of his youthful associates, appear to have preferred the inspiring stories and romantic legends of Scotland to her cold and formal academic training. His visits to those hallowed spots where the Covenanters struggled and died in the cause of liberty left an impression on his mind which time only deepened. Many of the magnificent bursts of eloquence which in after-years thrilled the hearts of the Presbyterians of Ulster, and roused them to a sense of the duty they owed to their Church, were inspired by the memories of his student rambles. He completed his undergraduate course in 1805 ; but, owing to illness, he was obliged to leave before the session closed, and was thus prevented from taking his degree. In the following session he entered the Divinity Hall, and passed through the ordinary course of theological training. The lectures of Doctors Findlay and M'Leod, who then filled the chairs of Divinity and Church History, do not appear to have been particularly edifying. General topics only were discussed. Particular doctrines, especially such as characterise sound Calvinism, were studiously avoided. The impression was left on the minds of thoughtful students that all specific systems of doctrine were unimportant. Of his theological training he thus speaks : — " Although I studied under two professors in Scotland, there was a great deficiency in their system of education in theology. It was a great deal too general. I never heard any doctrine brought forward." Like many another, he left the University with no very exalted ideas of either the efficiency or soundness of its training.

At Glasgow College Henry Cooke met, for the first time, two men with whom he was brought into close connection during nearly the whole course of his public life ;—with the one as a steady, talented, and useful friend and fellow-labourer ; with the other, as a powerful, eloquent, and uncompromising antagonist. Robert Stewart was Cooke's senior by several years. ·He was in some respects one of the most remarkable men of his age. His features were common, his appearance and address unprepossessing; but he had a commanding intellect, a clear judgment, and a logical faculty of unsurpassed acuteness. He had no pretentions to eloquence ; his language was devoid of ornament ; his voice was harsh ; his gestures were awkward ; his accent was strongly provincial. All this, however, was forgotten the moment he grappled with an antagonist in debate. Then his wonderful mental grasp and analytical power were exhibited. With instinctive quickness he seized upon the weak points of an argument, detected lurking sophisms, and, with a few cold but incisive sentences, cut them in pieces, or, in language of stinging sarcasm, held them up to ridicule. It was impossible to excite him. Amid the storms of debate he remained calm and watchful. His imperturbable temper gave him immense advantage over all who gave way to feeling; and many a time, in after-years, he guided with master-hand the impetuosity of Cooke's eloquence. To the wisdom and tact of Robert Stewart, Henry Cooke was largely indebted for his ecclesiastical triumphs, and for the skill with which he led, during well-nigh half a century, the councils of his Church. When they first met, Stewart's keen perception of character appears to have detected, almost at a glance, the extraordinary talents of the pale, sickly-looking boy. The close friendship contracted during college days was only broken by death, nearly half a century afterwards.

Henry Montgomery was, intellectually and physically, widely different from both Cooke and Stewart. He was born in the same year as the former, but, even at the time of their meeting in Glasgow, he was tall in stature, dignified in mien, graceful and insinuating in address. He was an accomplished English scholar. His vocabulary was choice and extensive, his speech fluent and persuasive. He already gave ample promise of that classic purity of language and noble elocution which distinguished him in after life. Cooke and Montgomery were never intimate. Their mental characteristics were too unlike for that. They met at the social board, in the pleasure excursion, in the debating-club, and there they enjoyed each other's society; but the radical difference in their principles and modes of thought, which began to be early developed, prevented the possibility of closer communion, and seemed from the first to excite mutual feelings of distrust.

Cooke, during his college course, devoted special attention to elocution. It appears, in fact, to have been the only subject he thoroughly studied in Glasgow. Under the care of an accomplished teacher his provincial accent was almost entirely corrected; his gestures, naturally graceful, were improved; his splendid voice was carefully cultivated, and brought under the complete control of ear and intellect. He was not satisfied with the mere theoretical and formal training

of the class-room. He followed it up with a system of his
own, suggested by the plan of his great classic model,
Demosthenes.

His father's house stood upon a gentle elevation, commanding a wide landscape. On the south and east the view
extended from the distant summits of Divis and Cave Mountains, over vast reaches of hill and dale, to the uplands
which hide the Giant's Causeway. On the north and west
stretched the Dungivan range, commencing with the bleak
heathy slopes of Cairntogher, and terminating in the
rounded top of Slieve Gallion. Henry delighted in natural
scenery. He loved the mountains : he felt at home among
their glens and solitudes. The leafy dales and " bracken
braes " of Cairntogher were a favourite retreat for study and
thought. An immense natural amphitheatre, in one of the
retired nooks of the mountain, was especially dear to him.
Here, during the long summer vacations of his college life,
he was wont to spend hours together, reading aloud, or de-
claiming to an imaginary audience. Now he read a Psalm
of David, now an ode of his favourite Horace, now a passage
from Shakspeare, now an oration of his own. He occasionally induced shepherd lads to stand at graduated distances, so
as to test his distinctness of utterance, and to determine the
power of his voice. He carefully measured the distances,
ascertaining by repeated trial what effort was necessary,
what mode of utterance was best adapted, what key, so to
speak, was most suitable, to make his words audible at each
spot. No plan could have been better fitted for training an
orator. He gained perfect mastery over his voice. Its
varied tones were studied and practised; its penetrating
power was laboriously tested, until, like a noble instrument, it
at length responded to his will. The experience thus acquired served him in good stead in after-years. Whether in
pulpit or on platform, in church, hall, or open air, he could
measure by a glance the extent of his audience. He could
put forth, as if instinctively, just enough of voice to reach

the most remote. He was thereby saved from the fatigue of unnecessary exertion, and his auditory was saved from the pain of listening to harsh and overstrained utterances. He was able, too, by skilful practice in modulation, to make the rich tones of his voice, now soft and gentle as the summer breeze, now swelling like the roar of a cataract, fall like music on the ear.

To improve and perfect his style, he began, at a very early age, to study the masters of English eloquence. Among divines, his favourites were Tillotson, Howe, Barrow, and Bunyan; among men of letters, Addison and Goldsmith; among orators, Curran, Wilberforce, and Chatham; among poets, Cowper, but above and beyond all Shakspeare. Of the writings of England's renowned dramatist he never wearied. With quick apprehension, delicate appreciation, and powerful memory, he laid hold of every gem of thought or wit, of figure or expression, making it his own. He could recall a passage at any moment, and with rare skill adapt it to the occasion. He could recite whole scenes from some of the plays. He and his friend Stewart, whose tastes in this respect were like his own, often spent long evenings, during their early intimacy, speaking and responding in the language of Shakspeare's leading characters. Cooke's memory was as ready as it was powerful. This was one of the secrets of his success as a popular speaker and controversialist. An apt quotation or flash of witty satire was always at command, and often told with extraordinary effect in reply to an antagonist; often, too, it served to convert the clamour of an opposing audience into a roar of laughter.

The niceties of English grammar, pronunciation, and philology also claimed the attention of Mr. Cooke. He aimed at becoming a finished as well as a powerful speaker. Accuracy, clearness, and force, he considered the essential qualifications of an orator. To attain these, he studied the standard grammars and dictionaries with which his library abounded. He was not satisfied until he had traced each word to its source, and weighed its most delicate varieties of meaning. He selected his vocabulary mainly from Saxon roots. He avoided, as far as possible, Latin words and Latinised constructions. His language, therefore, had not, perhaps, that honeyed rhythm, that grace and softness, which some others have attained; but what it lacked in softness it gained in power. It was keener, if less showy. Terseness, vigour, pointedness, were its chief characteristics. It told upon all classes. It was intelligible to all. It swayed the passions of the crowd, and it carried conviction to the minds of the learned and philosophical.

CHAPTER II.

1808—1811.

AFTER completing a full college curriculum, Henry Cooke was licensed to preach the gospel by the Presbytery of Ballymena. Then, as now, it was the law of the Church that each candidate for license should write certain " pieces of trial." One of the subjects prescribed to Mr. Cooke was " Is vindictive Justice essential to the Character of Deity?" The paper affords some good examples of that acute logical power which he displayed in such perfection in after-years. But what is chiefly interesting in it is, that it developes with clearness and force the doctrine of Christ's substitution as lying at the foundation of the atonement, and it strongly denounces the heretical dogma that an exercise of Divine mercy alone, apart from Christ's sacrifice, could have saved sinners. In his Trial Sermon on the text, " How shall we escape, if we neglect so great salvation?" another fundamental doctrine is discussed in a way which shows that the writer was entirely opposed to the Arian views then so prevalent. " Had an angel," he argues, " or an inferior minister of God been the person commissioned to publish the news of our salvation, to give the offers of the gospel which Jesus gave, then there would have been some excuse for neglect. But the

person commissioned is no angel, no inferior agent; he is the
same to whom the Lord says, 'Let all the angels of God
worship him.' Behold then what a glorious personage holds
forth to you the offer of salvation! He thought it no robbery
to be counted equal with the Father. Him you may trust,
for in Him there is no possibility of deception. Him you may
trust, for He is able to save to the uttermost. He is King of
kings, Lord of lords."

The costume in which he presented himself before the
reverend court, and delivered his pieces of trial, would, if
adopted by a candidate for licence in our more sober days,
shock all propriety, and go far to destroy his prospects of
success and usefulness: it consisted of a blue coat, drab
vest, white cord breeches, and top-boots. At that period it
was not so remarkable as to call forth reproof or comment
from the members of Presbytery. Years previous it had been
no uncommon occurrence for a minister to appear in the
pulpit clad in the scarlet coat, and other trappings, which
indicated his rank in a corps of volunteers; and, after all, a
minister's usefulness is not dependent on the cut or colour of
his costume.

On the 10th of November, 1808, only a few months after he
had received licence, and when he was but twenty years old,
Mr. Cooke was ordained to the pastoral oversight of the congregation of Duneane, near Randalstown, in county Antrim.
The senior minister, the Rev. Robert Scott, was an old man.
He had never been distinguished for energy, either mental or
physical; and his views, if he had any clear or decided views
on points of doctrine, were believed to be Arian. The congregation had been long neglected. Religious indifference
pervaded the whole community. There was still the form of
Christianity, but there was nothing of the spirit. A withering heresy paralysed both minister and people. Mr. Cooke
entered on his work with earnestness. He met with no encouragement; still he persevered. The sermons and addresses
he delivered show that he was determined on reform. The

fundamental doctrines of the gospel are developed in them with rare lucidity, and enforced with an eloquence that must have startled the slumbering Presbyterians of Duneane. In a discourse preached from the text, " So Christ was once offered to bear the sins of many ; and unto them that look for him shall he appear the second time, without sin, unto salvation " (Heb. ix. 28), he says, " No power short of omnipotence was able to accomplish the great work which Christ undertook; therefore in Him dwelt all the fulness of the Godhead bodily. He entered the lists alone ; alone He triumphed, leading captivity captive, and receiving gifts for men." In another sermon on the text, " Peace I leave with you: my peace I give unto you " (John xiv. 27), these sentences occur, " Christ Himself is made our peace, as the apostle hath declared. If then Christ give His peace unto us, He must give Himself unto us. This peace springs from and consists in His union with us. Because He liveth, we shall live also. Hence it is that He prays, That they all may be one, as thou, Father, art in me, and I in thee, that they also may be one in us. And the glory which thou gavest me I have given them, that they may be one, even as we are. For the same reason this peace must be everlasting. Being Himself eternal, His attributes are so too."

At his first communion he thus addressed his assembled flock :—

" Come, communicants, and let us magnify the Lord together. Slaves too long to the world, let us deliver ourselves to Jesus—to His praise, to His love, to His service. There are in heaven this day thousands and tens of thousands praising and adoring the Lord. Are your hearts joining the glorious choir ? Two things are before you—earth and heaven. Earth is perishable ; heaven eternal. Earth is full of sorrow ; heaven is full of joy. Adhere to Christ and His cause ; be faithful, and heaven is yours. When Anaxagoras the philosopher was asked what he was born for, he nobly answered, ' That I might contemplate heaven.' When the Christian is asked what he is reborn for, must he not answer, ' To contemplate Christ ' ? When we contemplate Him, as exhibited in this memorial ordinance

—in His sufferings and in His triumph, in His humiliation and in His glory,—is it possible that our souls could remain insensible to His love, or that our hearts should be untouched by His mercy?"

The words of the eloquent young preacher went like an electric shock through the congregation. The people had never heard such preaching. All were roused: some were deeply impressed; but many were indignant to be thus rudely awakened from a pleasant dream of security. Mr. Scott was highly displeased. The fervent zeal and doctrinal teaching of Mr. Cooke seemed like a rebuke to his ministerial apathy and chilling homilies. Mr. Cooke was treated with coldness. His work was retarded. His fervour was sneered at, and stigmatized as Methodism. Difficulties were thrown in his way which he was unable to overcome. He was almost starved besides. His whole ministerial income amounted to about five and twenty pounds a year, Irish currency. It is not strange, therefore, that he resigned the pastoral charge of Duneane, and accepted a situation as tutor in the family of Mr. Brown, of Kells.

Mr. Cooke's incumbency at Duneane did not cont nue quite two years. On leaving it he was freed from deep responsibility, and from annoyances which he keenly felt. Probably, had he been placed in a similar position at a later period, the energy of his character might have triumphed over all opposition; but he was still almost a boy; he had little experience; and he had no man to sympathise with or aid him. At Kells he had time for reading, and he took full advantage of it. In Mr. Brown he found a kind and generous friend; and of his intercourse with him and his family he ever afterwards spoke in terms of grateful remembrance.

While at Kells, a circumstance occurred which displayed in a remarkable manner his readiness and power as a public speaker, even at this early period of his life. The incident has been narrated by one who was present—the late William Kirk, Esq., M.P. Mr. Brown was a member of the congregation of Connor, then, as now, one of the largest in Ireland. It was a communion Sunday. The communion services at that period were very protracted. In Connor it was customary to have, in addition to preliminary services, seven Tables, at each of which an address of about half an hour was given. The minister, the Rev. Henry Henry, had always two assistants upon such occasions. On the day referred to, however, both of those engaged were unexpectedly prevented from attending. Ere the introductory services were concluded, Mr. Henry himself became ill, and was unable to proceed. The state of matters was most embarrassing. The immense congregation had assembled. The church was crowded in pew and aisle. Every arrangement had been made for the administration of the solemn ordinance. Bitter disappointment would have been felt, especially by the aged and infirm, had it been postponed. It was whispered to some of the elders that Mr. Cooke was present. After consultation, they agreed to ask him to officiate, though they scarcely ventured to hope he would undertake, without preparation, services so solemn, so varied, and so onerous. But he at once consented. With perfect calmness he took up the order where Mr. Henry had stopped. He delivered address after address with ease and fluency. In power and pathos he far excelled their venerated pastor. The people were astonished and delighted. There was a variety, an appropriateness, a depth of thought, a pointedness of reference to the time and the peculiar circumstances, a happiness of illustration, and a tenderness of appeal, which showed a mind not only ready, but amply stored with the richest materials. That Communion was long remembered in Connor, and the impression left on some of the hearers remains to this day.

Mr. Cooke was not permitted to remain long free from the active duties of the pastorate. He resigned the charge of Duneane on the 13th of November, 1810; and on the 22nd of January following he was installed minister of the congregation of Donegore, near Templepatrick. He was now on " holy

ground " of Ulster Presbyterianism. The people of the parish
were the descendants of Scotch colonists, and many of them
bore the well-known Ayrshire names of Shaw, Hunter, Ferguson, Stevenson, and Blair. He had the oversight of upwards of five hundred families, most of whom were in
affluent circumstances, and all shrewd and intelligent. Donegore was one of the first parishes occupied by Presbyterian
incumbents after the Scotch settlement. It was filled in
succession by some of the most faithful ministers of that or
any age. Stirling and Andrew Stewart were its first pastors.
The sainted Josias Welsh laboured in an adjoining parish;
and Donegore was often visited by Livingstone and Blair. The
savour of their earnest ministrations long pervaded the district;
and the fertile valley of Six-mile-water was the scene of the
most remarkable revival of religion ever witnessed in Ireland.
Changed times, however, had unfortunately come to Donegore.
The divine doctrines and duties, so clearly set forth and so
affectionately applied by Welsh, Blair, and Livingstone, were
almost forgotten. Mr. Cooke found the people cold and
destitute of spiritual life, as those of Duneane. His immediate
predecessor was the Rev. James C. Ledlie, who, after a brief
ministry, avowed Arian opinions, and removed to the congregation of First Larne. Previous to Mr. Ledlie, the Rev. John
Wright had been pastor of Donegore for more than fifty years.
His views could hardly be called orthodox. His theology was
negative in its character. Some of the leading families in the
parish had in consequence adopted Arian opinions. The task
before Mr. Cooke was, therefore, a formidable one. But he
resolved not merely to revive gospel truth in Donegore, but,
by unremitting effort and study and by earnest and faithful
prayer, to bring back the whole Presbyterian Church to its
primitive purity and efficiency.

In Donegore, Mr. Cooke's systematic studies as a theologian
may be said to have begun. For the first time he felt so
circumstanced as to be able to arrange and carry out a
thorough course of reading. His fame as an orator was

already spreading over the Church. Sermons preached in Ballymena, Broughshane, Randalstown, and other places, had attracted much attention. It was seen that he was in earnest, and that he was not satisfied to permit the Church of Knox and Calvin to degenerate into cold rationalism. His influence among his brethren was also rapidly advancing. Some admired his genius; some feared his sarcasm; all acknowledged his power. But he felt that if he would effectually combat prevailing error, if he would largely and permanently promote the spiritual interests of his Church, he must himself be profoundly versed in the doctrines of Scripture.

With these views he entered upon his studies at Donegore. The time had come when he could realize the cherished purpose of boyhood. He has left behind him records of the books read, and the subjects investigated, with the view of testing the doctrines in which he had been trained in youth. He kept no regular diary; he never thought of one. He had a dislike to autobiographies in any form. He has often said, " No man can be trusted with a full and honest development of his own character, thoughts, and acts. There are secret springs and motives at work within him, which he dare not reveal—which, indeed, it would be folly to attempt to expose to the world's eye. Without these, autobiographical sketches are fictions: they are not complete, and therefore they are dishonest." Such were his opinions, and he acted upon them. In his letters to members of his family, and in familiar intercourse with a select and very limited circle of friends, he sometimes gave interesting details of his private life and of the inner workings of his heart and mind. All these were characterized by childlike humility and depreciation of self. The records he has left behind him are entirely different. They are not annals of books read, or work done, or subjects investigated. They are thoughts suggested by his reading; or ascertained facts and acute criticisms, designed and laid up for future use. He attached no importance to a mere verbal record of literary activity, whether in the perusal or compo-

sition of books. He wished to have his mind, and not his
diary, stored with knowledge. To be able to produce from
that storehouse, whenever needed, a fact, an argument, or an
illustration, such as might serve to advance truth, or refute
error, was his ideal of a scholar. A mind of extraordinary
grasp, and a memory which never seemed to forget anything,
enabled him to approach to that ideal more nearly than
perhaps any man of his age.

The first theological work he read was Calvin's "Institutes." This was followed, in rapid succession, by Turret-
tin's "Institutio Theologiæ," Stapfer's "Institutiones Theologiæ Polemicæ," and Van Mastricht's "Theoretico-Practica
Theologia." The marks on the copies he used, and the notes
in his Common-place Book, show with what care he must have
studied, and how thoroughly he must have mastered, those
standards of systematic theology. Butler and Paley were
his handbooks on the Evidences. The philosophical works of
Hutcheson, Reid, and Locke were perused, as were also
Hume's famous "Essays." He carefully analysed the controverted points of theology and philosophy developed by these
authors. He next took up Gale's "Court of the Gentiles,"
which became a great favourite; and he even waded through
the ponderous learning and dulness of Warburton, Cudworth,
and Bingham. With a very few exceptions, he had not then,
and he never formed, a high opinion of the Fathers. He
admired Augustine for his philosophical acumen; and in his
copy of "Chrysostom" many of the most eloquent passages
are marked.

One of the first sermons he preached in Donegore was upon
the text, "And the Lord said unto him, Go through the midst
of the city, through the midst of Jerusalem, and set a mark
upon the foreheads of the men that sigh and that cry for all the
abominations that be done in the midst thereof" (Ezek. ix. 4).
His theme was National Infidelity. "Time was," he says,
"when infidelity ashamed—dreading, as it were, to meet the
public eye—skulked into corners, and said in her heart,

'There is no God.' She kept the secret to herself. She dared not avow it openly. That time is gone. Shame and fear have forsaken her. She lifts her voice in the streets; she calls in the high places; she proclaims rebellion against heaven's King; she thinks it possible to dethrone the Omnipotent. It was only a few years ago religion fell in France before the infidel phalanx, led by a Volney and a Voltaire. In our own country a Hobbes, a Hume, and a Paine, with a host of others, organized a crusade against the Cross. Under their leadership infidelity has marched through Britain. She has invaded the sacred precincts of our own Church. Ministers, at her bidding, now boldly disavow alike the nature and the work of the Divine Saviour. Forgetting Him, they forget also Him that sent Him. What base ingratitude have we been guilty of! How have we forgotten God's sparing mercies! How wonderfully has He preserved us as a nation, notwithstanding grievous sins! We are monuments of His love. Whilst the horrors of war have affrighted other nations— whilst its destructive hand has ravaged their cities, and desolated their plains—whilst their fields have been deluged with blood, and covered with mountains of slain,—we have only heard the dread sound roll ominously in the distance : it has not come near our shores. White-robed Peace has continued to scatter olives over our country. Justice lifts aloft her impartial balance. Plenty sheds abundance around. Commerce spreads abroad her wing, and is fanned by the breeze of prosperity. Toleration bids every man worship God as conscience dictates; while the smile of freedom brightens every British home. Let us then turn with grateful hearts to that God who has so signally blessed us."

In the Presbytery to which Mr. Cooke now belonged there was not a man who thoroughly sympathised with him. He stood alone; and he felt the chilling influence of the theological atmosphere which he breathed. Still, though discouraged, he did not despair; though frowned on, he did not fear. In a discourse preached in 1813, on the text, "Can

these bones live ? " (Ezek. xxxvii. 3), pointed allusion is made
to his difficulties :—

"Now, Christians, ye who have contemplated this moral desola-
tion in the greatness of its extent, I ask you, ' Can these bones live ? '
Can sinners, dead in trespasses and sins, be restored to spiritual
life ?   Is it possible that a mind, by nature at enmity with God—a
mind which has a thousand times deliberately sinned against the law
given forth from the throne of the Omnipotent—a mind keenly alive
to the petty interests of time, but dead to the inconceivable realities
of eternity—is it possible that such a mind can be regenerated ?
Brethren, I feel that I am now on the doctrinal ground of the text.
I am now touching on one of the most profound truths of revelation.
I am on dangerous, because on controverted ground.   But, fearless
of the frowns of men, fearless of the sneer of the sceptic, fearless of
the enmity and opposition of false friends and open foes, I this day
boldly avow, on the direct and infallible authority of God's eternal
Word, that no sinner, by his own unaided efforts, can ever regenerate
himself ; and, consequently, that every sinner, who is converted from
the error of his ways, owes his conversion, and all the consequences
of his conversion, to the sovereign, efficacious, almighty operation of
the Spirit of God.   I know the fashionable divinity of the day
denies that man ' was shapen in iniquity, and conceived in sin.'   I
know the feelings of the talkative sentimentalist are outraged at the
idea that the thoughts of the heart are ' only evil continually.'   Yet
it is so."

A remarkable paper, commenced on May 31st, and finished
September 10th, 1811, indicates the nature of his studies at
this period.   It is entitled " Christianity Tried in the Court
of Reason."   It contains a clear outline of the evidences,
dwelling especially upon miracles and prophecy.   The leading
objections of infidels are briefly but ably handled.   The
fundamental doctrines of the gospel, especially the divinity of
Christ, original sin, and the atonement, are explained, and
defended against Deists and Socinians.   In the terseness of
the style, acuteness of the arguments, and incisive clearness
of the replies to objections, there is noble promise of those
splendid controversial talents which Mr. Cooke brought into
play in after-years.   He discusses the genuineness, authen-

ticity, and inspiration of the Bible, showing familiarity with the latest results of criticism. But perhaps the most important part of the paper is that in which the self-evidencing character of Christianity is developed, as exhibited in its doctrinal system, providing for fallen man all that he needs; in its precepts, prescribing to man a rule of thought, speech, and life, pure and perfect; in its promises, holding forth all that heart could wish for, in time and eternity.

Some questions appended to the paper are striking:—

" Is God not equal and perfect in His attributes of mercy and justice?

" Will He not, therefore, punish if our sin is not blotted out?

" Is God not infinite? Then, there can be no comparison between Him and us, with regard to *importance*. Every finite is alike to Him.

" But will God punish such beings as we, who are of so little importance? Is not our destruction of equally little importance to God, if we continue to transgress? Does not every sin increase in proportion to the person sinned against?"

" Sept. 10th. How shall a man make atonement for sins past, since he can do no more than his duty in time to come? Can a man govern his thoughts? Are they subject to his will? How, then, shall he govern his acts by the power of a mind which is itself confessedly ungovernable?

" Can Socinians and Deists keep all the commandments? are they of themselves able? If they say so, then surely of all men they are the most inexcusable when they break them."

Mr. Cooke prepared his sermons with remarkable care. Though a ready and fluent speaker, he never trusted to his power of extemporaneous oratory in the pulpit. He wrote all his sermons, communion addresses, and even his public prayers, and committed them to memory. He also wrote the brief critical remarks and practical reflections which he made on the Psalms and passages of Scripture selected for public

reading. His voluminous manuscripts show that they were
elaborately revised, and in many cases, to a large extent, re-
written. All his discourses were characterised by clear exposition of Scripture truth and earnestness of application. He
closed his first communion sermon at Donegore with the
following solemn words :—

"The minister of the gospel is commanded to preach Christ ; but
he cannot convert one sinner ; he cannot establish the Redeemer's
kingdom in the heart of one man. This is the work not of man, but
of God. God, who at first breathed life into the form of clay, can
alone breathe spiritual life into the sin-dead soul. All we need as
lost sinners must come from God. Repentance is the gift of God.
Faith is the gift of God. Pardon is the gift of God. New obedience
is the gift of God. Peace of mind is the gift of God. The spirit of
prayer is the gift of God. Resignation to the Divine will is the
gift of God. Victory over death is the gift of God. Eternal life is
the gift of God. All these are His gifts, and His only. Our title to
them is Immanuel's blood ; and the result of them is joy in life,
triumph in death, and glory everlasting in heaven."

His communion address is written in the same spirit :—

"Christian communicants, every duty you are called upon to perform has attached to it its own specific promise. The duty of private
prayer has its promise,—'Thou shalt make thy prayer to Him, and
He shall hear thee.' The duty of reading the Divine Word has its
promise,—'I will bring the blind by a way that they knew not.' The
duty of attending the house of God has its promise,—'I will make
my people joyful in the house of prayer.' The duty you are now
called on to perform, in commemoration of Him, who is God with
God, and man with man, has its promise,—'Whoso eateth my flesh,
and drinketh my blood, hath eternal life, and I will raise him up at
the last day.' Now, communicants, lay claim to the promises. In
deep humility, but holy confidence, pray the Eternal Saviour Himself
to grant you, out of His sovereign mercy, fulness of faith, that you
may realise, this day, mysterious, veritable, joyous union with Him,
and God the Father through Him, while partaking of these
emblems."

CHAPTER III.

1810—1818.

THE errors which prevailed in his Church and country,
served largely to direct the studies and mould the discourses
of Mr. Cooke. He aimed at reform. To free the Church
from error, and to raise the people to a higher standard of
morality, were his objects. The rise of Arianism in the Presbyterian Church of Ireland dates from the beginning of the
eighteenth century. At first it assumed a negative character.
A few philosophic theologians, trained in Glasgow and Leyden,
and indoctrinated with the peculiar views of Hoadly and
Samuel Clarke, imagined they might believe and teach what
they pleased, and yet remain ministers of the Church. No
Church, they said, had a right to interfere with freedom of
thought; therefore, no Church had a right to impose a creed
upon its ministers or members. They would acknowledge
God's headship only; they would render account to Him for
their faith and teachings, but not to man. Such arguments
might have been relevant had those who held them been
engaged in organising a new ecclesiastical society; but they
were already members of a Church, one of whose fundamental

laws was subscription to the Westminster Confession. They
had entered it willingly. No man had forced them to enter;
no man forced them to remain. They knew its constitution,
and they had freely vowed to maintain it. Yet now, when
the question was mooted, they refused to acknowledge the
Confession; they even refused to tell the church courts what
doctrines they held, or what they rejected.

A few leading men of this "New Light" party met in the
year 1705, and formed themselves into an association called
The Belfast Society. The society was professedly designed
for mutual conference on the philosophical and theological
questions then agitating the Christian world. Monthly meetings were held, papers were read, doctrines were discussed,
opinions were expressed, which exhibited more of freedom than
faith. Sermons were preached on the unity of the Church,
the mischief of schism, the right of private judgment. It soon
began to be whispered abroad that the views propounded by
the members of the Belfast Society were subversive of
the Westminster Standards. It was alleged that some
held those Pelagian errors then taught from the Chair of
Theology in Glasgow, and that others had imbibed the far
more dangerous views of Dr. Samuel Clarke. These grave
rumours soon excited dissatisfaction and alarm among
the people of Ulster. The orthodox party in the Presbyterian Church introduced the matter into the General Synod,
and carried a resolution to the effect, that all ministers be
recommended to renew their subscription to the Confession
of Faith. The resolution was vigorously opposed by the
leaders of the Belfast Society. They argued that every
man's persuasion of what was true was the sole rule of faith
to him; that error was not culpable, if held conscientiously
after inquiry; that it was unjust and tyrannical for any
Church to exclude from fellowship those who were even pal-
pably in error on non-essential points; that no point could
be held as essential on which human reason and Christian
sincerity permitted men to differ. They went so far as to

affirm that the doctrine of the supreme Deity of Christ was not essential. It might be held, or it might be denied, without at all affecting a man's Christian standing, or exposing him to ecclesiastical discipline. Subscription to any creed was an interference with liberty, and inconsistent with the genius of Protestantism.

The supreme court of the Presbyterian Church was thus divided into two parties—Subscribers and Non-subscribers. The controversy between them could not rest here. Great principles were at stake. The fundamental doctrines of Christianity were involved. The Non-subscribers constituted only a fraction of the Synod, and they had very few adherents among the laity. Only twelve ministers declared themselves *New Lights*, but most of them were able, eloquent, and influential men. They were united besides, and with untiring zeal they laboured to propagate their views. The orthodox party were at length roused to action. Protracted debates were carried on in the Synod; and, at the annual meeting in 1726, the question of Subscription was fully discussed, and a motion carried excluding Non-subscribers from ecclesiastical communion.

But the Church was not thereby altogether purified. Many signed the Confession reluctantly; others declined to sign, though declaring their belief in its doctrines. Absolute subscription was, unfortunately, not insisted upon in the latter case. In after-years subscription was often evaded, and some of the Presbyteries studiously and notoriously countenanced a violation of the law of the Church.

During the eighteenth century the great body of the Irish Presbyterian clergy were educated in the University of Glasgow. The principles there taught were not favourable to evangelical truth. A system of philosophy was propounded which reduced virtue to benevolence, and undermined the whole scheme of Bible Christianity. Dr. Hutcheson, who occupied the chair of Moral Philosophy from 1730 to 1746, was mainly instrumental in developing this view. His celebrity as a meta-

physician, his eloquence, and his enthusiasm attracted young
men to his class-room, and gained for him a commanding influence over their minds.   Being an Irishman, and the son of
an Irish Presbyterian clergyman, he was all the more beloved
by Irish students. In the Theological Chair the great doctrines
of the Trinity, the atonement, and justification by faith were,
during the same period, either passed over or noticed in such
a way as to leave the impression that they were of little importance.   Dr. Hutcheson stepped out of his own sphere to
caution theological students against introducing such doctrines
into their pulpit ministrations.   John Simson, Professor of
Theology from 1708 to 1740, was known to be an Arian.   Dr.
Leechman, who succeeded after a short interval, was strongly
suspected of holding Socinian views.   Under such training an
evangelical ministry could not be produced ; and both Scotland
and Ireland suffered in consequence.

The political and social state of Ireland, during the latter
half of the eighteenth century, unfortunately favoured the
spread of rationalistic philosophy.   The country and the
Church were alike disorganised by rebellion. The people were
impatient of all restraint, whether civil or ecclesiastical ; and
the character and acts of the rulers were not calculated to
inspire confidence, or preserve order.   The country was inun-
dated with infidel and semi-infidel publications.   Under the
guise of free thought, they captivated the minds of an excitable
and excited populace.   The New Light theology, imported
from Scotland, spread at the same time in the Presbyterian
Church.   It does not appear that any considerable number of
the ministers were as yet professed Arians.   Their theological views were somewhat hazy, and most of them, like
their " Moderate " brethren in Scotland, looked with cold
indifference on definite systems of doctrine.   In some Presbyteries subscription to the Westminster Confession was
not required ; in others, grave irregularities in regard to the
Synod's law were tacitly sanctioned.   The Synod itself, by
a vote in 1783, virtually countenanced departure from ancient

rule. A door was thus opened for the admission of heterodox ministers, and the propagation of heretical doctrines; and for nearly half a century the spiritual life of the Church was paralysed.

But gospel light was not yet entirely extinguished in the Synod of Ulster.   There were many among its clergy and laity who longed and prayed for revival in the Church, and reform in the State.   They lamented the errors in doctrine which had crept into the Church, and they deprecated the revolutionary sentiments which were being propagated through the country.   At a meeting of Synod in 1793, they gave expression to their feelings of loyalty in a "Declaration," which, while it advocates reform, "avows unshaken attachment to the genuine principles of the British Constitution —an attachment early inculcated by the lessons of their fathers, and since justified by their own observation and experience."   At another meeting, held in the very heat of the rebellion of '98, an address was voted to the king, breathing the same spirit of devoted loyalty.   They showed a desire for the advancement of personal religion, by resolving, in 1803, that "each presbytery be enjoined to recommend to each member under its care to be exemplary in keeping up the worship of God in his family."   About 1808, vacant congregations in connection with the Synod began to manifest a decided preference for evangelical ministers.   Mr. Cooke, in his testimony before the Commissioners in 1825, says:—"I was ordained in 1808; I believe I succeeded an Arian: another friend was ordained in 1808, and he succeeded an Arian: another friend succeeded a very decided Arian, until in one whole district, which was twenty years ago entirely Arian, I do not know of one single minister you could suspect of Arianism, except one."

In 1810 an event occurred which may be regarded as the first clear indication of a great approaching struggle on behalf of Scripture truth.   A minister of the Synod resigned his congregation.   Hs was subsequently suspended by his Presbytery for immorality.   He appealed to the Synod, and at the same time applied to be reinstated in his congregation. During the hearing of the appeal he avowed himself an Arian; yet his appeal was sustained, and it was carried by a majority that, if re-elected by the people, he might be reinstated. Five members of Synod recorded their protest against this remarkable decision, and in the succeeding year they were joined by twelve others, who assigned the following among other reasons:— "Because the Rev. J. Ker denied the doctrine of the Trinity, which we consider a fundamental article of the Christian faith, the denial of which is utterly subversive of Christianity."

But the time had not yet come for a united stand against Arianism. The leaders of the New Light party were men of great ability. They had the business of the Synod largely in their hands. They were practised in debate, and eloquent in speech. Their appeals for freedom of thought and Christian forbearance made a deep impression on many who had no sympathy with their theological views. Their theology, besides, was not as yet demonstrative: it was negative rather than dogmatic. The chief men studiously refrained from publishing their opinions on the fundamental doctrines of Scripture. One of them was able to boast that he had preached for half a century, and no member of his congregation could say to what party he belonged. Their discourses were in general weak moral essays, with little in them to alarm, and less to instruct the sinner. "Peace, peace!" was their Syren song; and under its influence the Church was for years lulled to a fatal slumber. No voice of power was raised in Ulster to break the spell. No champion of evangelical truth yet ventured boldly to oppose the skilful advocates of rationalism, and to head and inspire a party determined on reform.

Such was the state of the Presbyterian Church when Henry Cooke's name and fame began to spread over Ulster. He was present at the Synod in 1811, when that noble protest was tabled against the admission of a professed Arian. He took no part in the debate, but a profound impression was made upon his mind. The Presbytery to which he belonged, and into which he had only a few months before been admitted, was largely composed of New Light ministers. His predecessors in Donegore were, as has been stated, Arians; and under their training it will not be thought strange that many of the leading families were imbued with Arianism. Some of Mr. Cooke's most intimate literary friends were also Arians. He was still a very young man—only twenty-four. He was not yet prepared for his great work; but there is extant evidence that prevailing errors largely occupied his thoughts, and that he was making careful preparation to oppose them. Among his papers of this date is a summary of Scripture proofs of the doctrine of the Trinity, classified in an original manner, under twenty-seven heads, in each of which the same names, titles, attributes, and works are shown to be ascribed to Father, Son, and Holy Ghost. His manuscript sermons of this period bear evidence of close study, and all discuss more or less fully the doctrinal and philosophical speculations which then agitated the Church. They are carefully written out, and the erasures and corrections are very numerous. Some of them, indeed, appear to have been entirely re-written, and the elaborate notes which formed the groundwork of each discourse contain references to the authors consulted.

Mr. Cooke's mind was undergoing a thorough training for the conflict which he saw approaching. But, so long as he remained in Donegore, he was surrounded by the chilling influence of New Light scepticism. Referring to this at a later period, he says, "I was once a member of a presbytery where Arianism prevailed. During that time I was led to join in Arian ordinations, and in the license of real or supposed Arians. Over this record of my life I sincerely lament. It avails me not to blame the Synod that exposed me to the temptation by its defective or erroneous discipline; it avails me not that other and better men are still in similar circumstances. But while I lament the existence of the evil, and my own share in it, I would labour to warn or to relieve others from similar temptations and errors."

When in Donegore he had no friend to sympathise with, counsel, or encourage him. Perhaps it was better so. Encouragement might have stirred up his impulsive nature, and driven him to conflicts for which he was not ready. It was a critical period in the history of the Presbyterian Church. A weak argument, faltering logic, an unprepared assailant, might have given an impetus to error, which would have stayed the work of reform for another half-century. It was better that the struggle was postponed until the mind of the champion of evangelical truth was fully matured, and his course of theological study completed.

At this period we meet with the first of a series of letters which extends over more than half a century, and throws a clear and mellow light not only on his public labours, but on his inner life and feelings. The letters exhibit the true character of the man—playful, witty, affectionate, humble, yet bold and firm when public duty called, or Christian principle was at stake. The first is addressed to Miss Ellen Mann, of Toome, who soon afterwards became Mrs. Cooke. It was written on the occasion of the death of her young brother :—

"SILVER SPRINGS, 3rd Feb. 1813.

" MY DEAR ELLEN,—However anxious I was to stay a day or two with your father and mother in their present affliction, my engagements with the Presbytery would not permit me; but, though forced to come away, my thoughts have ever since been with them and you. From my knowledge of their fond attachment to their child, I am well aware how great must be their sorrow. Would to God it were in my power to comfort them and you. God alone is able to bind up the wounds which He himself has made; and He is not only able, He will assuredly do it to all who call upon Him through Christ. . . .

" You will forgive me when I say I do not intend to offer consolation. Consolation is in the hands of God only. Seek it from Him; but to instruct and advise is the duty of the ministers of His Son Jesus Christ.

"It is, I believe, generally supposed that the Bible condemns grief for the death of friends. It does not. Neither do I condemn it; nay, I approve of it. The Bible shows us Rachel weeping for her children, and refusing to be comforted. It shows us the mother weeping at the cross when she beheld her Son. It shows us Jacob declaring that he would follow his son to the grave mourning. It shows us David pouring forth his heart-sorrow for Absalom. It shows us the sisters of Lazarus weeping at the brother's grave. And, what is most wonderful of all, at the tomb of Lazarus 'Jesus wept.'

"But, my dear Ellen, do not think that all sorrowing is to be approved. Far from it. We may sin in our grief. How? Whenever we murmur against God. Let every one carefully avoid that danger. Hear the words of God Himself to all the sons and daughters of affliction, 'Be still, and know that I am God. Be still, and learn that I have done it. Remember, that I am God, and do all things well.' Remember the words of Job, 'The Lord gave, and the Lord hath taken away; blessed be the name of the Lord.'

"Our friends in general advise us not to grieve; but I give no such advice. We have never grieved enough until we have amended our lives and repented of our sins.

> 'Why are our friends snatched from us? 'Tis to bind,
> By soft affection's ties on human hearts,
> The thoughts of death, which reason, too supine
> Or misemployed, so rarely fastens there.'

"We seldom think of death while we are happy; but when affliction lays its hand upon us, then we remember that we must die. Oh! how merciful is God. Even by the hand of death He teaches wisdom. . . .

"There is another reason, powerful above all, to teach us resignation to God when He takes away our friends. God can provide for them better far than we can, even though we had the world in our gift."

All his letters to his wife and family, in one part or another, breathe the same spirit of deep piety. With him there was no parade of religion; there was no ostentatious sentimentalism. It was only to those who were admitted to the circle of his inner life that he spoke and wrote in such terms. Strangers, however observant, could not read his true character. Those who met him at the social board, where his wit sparkled, or amid the din of intellectual conflict, where cutting irony and fierce invective scourged his assailants, were apt altogether to misunderstand the man. The childlike gentleness of his nature ever displayed itself in his home; the surpassing tenderness of his heart was revealed before the tale of sorrow; his religious feelings found expression in converse with those he loved and trusted.

Mr. Cooke's power as a pulpit orator was already beginning to be known over Ulster. On the 18th of December, 1814, he preached in Belfast, on behalf of the House of Industry. His text was Proverbs iii. 27: "Withhold not good from them to whom it is due, when it is in the power of thine hand to do it." The sermon made a profound impression. The fervour of his appeals touched every heart, and the power of his eloquence kept his audience spell-bound. The sermon was published by request. It contained some passages of great beauty; but, like all his printed discourses and speeches, it gives no real idea of the orator. So long as the pen was in his hand he was calm, acute, logical. In his study he could analyse a text, arrange a subject with wonderful skill, and illustrate with unequalled fertility of imagination. But in his writings there is a certain degree of stiffness and formality. They leave the impression that the writer was under some restraint. When, however, he entered the pulpit, or ascended the platform, and saw before him the eager faces of living men—when breathless attention, riveted gaze, and waves of emotion passing over the audience, showed him that his words were telling, that they were finding a response in the minds of his hearers—then he cast off all restraint; his frame appeared to dilate ; his face lighted up with a halo of enthusiasm ; his words flowed forth in an impetuous torrent; he gave full play to the genius of oratory. Arguments that seemed, and seem, cold and formal on paper, now, like polished shafts, pierced every conscience ; illustrations, sketched in bare outline, now glowed in the gorgeous colouring of finished pictures ; appeals issuing fresh from a full heart, and delivered with all the impassioned fervour of, manner, look, and voice, carried away both intellect and feelings with a force that was absolutely irresistible. The auditors were overcome with intensity of excitement. They lost command of themselves. They bowed and swayed like a forest before the tempest's blast. They sprang to their feet; they laughed ; they wept. Reporters have been seen to drop their pencils and sit, as if paralysed, gazing on the speaker. The grandest passages were thus lost. The speaker himself could not recall them. Frequently reports of his speeches were sent to him with blank spaces here and there, and a request that Dr. Cooke would " fill up the beautiful passages wanting."

When his sermon was published, those who had heard it were disappointed. It seemed like the cold skeleton of a thing once radiant with life and beauty. Still, it contained some noble thoughts. To illustrate the self-sacrificing zeal of those who devoted valuable time to the management of such an institution, he took the case of John Howard :—

" Mark the benevolent, lamented Howard ! Animated with a spark of God's own love, he compasses sea and land in search of misery, bearing in the one hand the registry of its woes, in the other a cordial for its relief. View him through the grated window of some deep, damp dungeon, as he sits by the side of the captive, and listens to his woe-fraught story. The woes which hitherto had wept in silence, transferred to his tongue, sound in the ears of European and Asiatic monarchs. He opens his mouth for the dumb, and pleads the cause of those who were devoted to destruction. Does

this appear a grievous, an unprofitable task? No; on every step he
trod the eye of Heaven looked down well pleased,—it was marked in
the Book of Remembrance; and when his body, the victim of his
own benèvolence, sank on a distant shore to an untimely grave, his
deeds erected for him the noblest monument—a shrine in every
feeling heart. No less acceptable in the light of Heaven is that man
whose religion, pure and undefiled before God and the Father, leads
him to search out the wretched retreats of poverty, to visit the
fatherless and widows in their affliction, to nerve the arm of industry, and rescue the neglected offspring of the poor from the
seduction of idleness and the fangs of vice."

Mr. Cooke's growing popularity, and decided advocacy of
orthodox views, exposed him to the enmity of the New
Light party. The leaders of this party maintained in the
church courts an iron rule. Any who ventured to oppose
them, especially if young men, were assailed with every
weapon which logic, eloquence, wit, and sarcasm could furnish.
The more timid spirits trembled; even the boldest dreaded
an encounter with the giants of Arianism. It was customary
for the members of Synod to dine together. The wit and
irony of the ecclesiastical despots flashed as brilliantly,
and cut as keenly, at the table as in the council. Soon after
Mr. Cooke's sermon in Belfast, he met his brethren at one
of their festive reunions, and he was made to feel that his
popularity was not without attendant evils.

"Mr. Cooke," said Mr. ———, the most brilliant of the
New Lights, "I hear you are a great preacher."

In a moment the buzz of conversation and the merry
laugh were hushed. The rising orator, it was thought, was
about to be extinguished.

Mr. Cooke bowed to the querist with a pleasant smile.

"I understand the old ladies were in tears, and the young
in raptures, when you preached in Belfast."

Again Mr. Cooke bowed.

"You have evidently formed a high idea of your own
abilities," continued Mr. ———; "and in your case the old

adage does not hold, that 'modesty and genius are twin-sisters.' "

A murmur of applause ran round the table, accompanied by a merry laugh. Mr. Cooke, without moving a muscle, turned his piercing eye upon his haughty assailant, and coolly replied—

"You know, sir, there is no general rule without some exception."

"True," responded Mr. ———, "quite true. You are an exception. As for me, I have a very poor idea of my own abilities, and I always like to form an humble opinion of my gifts and success as a preacher."

"That shows your good sense," replied Mr. Cooke, with cutting irony; "and you will, doubtless, be glad to learn that, in this respect, the public entirely agree with you."

This was a home-thrust, and set the table in a roar; for Mr. ——— was known to be as dull in the pulpit as he was ambitious of popular applause.

Mr. Cooke now exhibited new powers — powers which stood him in good stead in after-years, enabling him to parry many a deadly blow, and turn aside many a venomed shaft. In ready wit, in sparkling repartee, in scathing sarcasm, few could equal him. His conversational powers were very great. He had an inexhaustible fund of anecdote; and he therefore became the centre of attraction in every social circle he entered.

But widening intercourse with leading men in Ulster, and occasional conflicts with the heads of the New Light party, made Mr. Cooke painfully conscious that he was not yet prepared for that struggle which he saw looming in the distance. He felt that his academic training had been incomplete. He had entered the university a mere boy. He had found nothing there to rouse his slumbering powers. He had left ere his mind was fully alive to the advantages of higher collegiate studies. Now he was a new man. He longed to recal the opportunities he had lost. His ardent

mind panted for knowledge. Some departments, for which
he had a natural taste, he had never touched; others he had
merely touched. The branches of study he most desired to
cultivate could not be satisfactorily prosecuted in private,
or in a remote locality, where he had neither books nor
teachers. Prompted by these considerations, and encouraged
by an indulgent congregation, he applied to his Presbytery
for leave of absence, for a time, from pastoral work, that he
might return to the university. Leave was granted, and,
placing his young wife under her father's roof, he set out for
Glasgow, in October, 1815. During that session he attended
lectures on moral philosophy, natural history, and anatomy;
and he also gave attention to several departments of medical
science. Unfortunately, only a few of his letters to Mrs.
Cooke, of that period, have been preserved, but these show
with what enthusiasm he entered afresh on the studies of
the university, and what a sacrifice his tender heart made
at the shrine of duty, in separating for so long a period from
the loved ones at home. After describing, in a long letter,
his almost incredible labours, he thus refers, in soft and
touching tones, to a holiday excursion :—"I have seen
Hamilton Palace, with all its magnificent paintings, and
Bothwell ruins, with all their romantic scenery. How deeply
I felt the truth of the poet's reflection :—

> ' 'Tis not the soft magic of streamlet or rill,'

that can itself afford the most exquisite enjoyment,

> ' Had you, the beloved of my bosom, been near,
> 'Twould have made each dear scene of enchantment more dear,
> And have shown how the best scenes of nature improve,
> When we see them reflected from looks that we love.'

"On the top of the donjon keep of Bothwell my mind was
irresistibly carried to you. The melancholy notes of the
unfortunate Lady of Bothwell seemed to vibrate in my ears, as
she stooped over her forsaken infant, saying :—

> ' Balo, my boy, lie still and sleep ;
> It grieves me sore to hear thee weep.'

" I thought you might perhaps sing so to poor Johnny, and blame his father for leaving him. But no ; my Ellen judges otherwise. She knows the father's heart is with his dear wife and children, and counts with pleasure the shortening days of absence. I will return as soon as possible ; but, you know, I must be guided by the nature of my studies.

"Write soon. I enclose the song I mentioned. Sing it to Johnny ; it will sooth him till his father's return."

He took a leading part, during the summer of 1816, in the business of the Church. He was especially interested in the negotiations between the Synod, the Government, and the Royal Belfast Institution. But still, it is evident from his manuscripts, that his time and thoughts were mainly given to systematic study. In November, he again went to Glasgow, and devoted himself to theology, chemistry, geology, metaphysics, and medicine. On his return to Ireland, in the spring of 1817, the training of candidates for the ministry of the Presbyterian Church occupied his attention. The state of parties in the Church, and the different modes adopted by different Presbyteries, rendered a radical reform necessary. As a leading member of the Synod's Committee of Examination for the Belfast Institution, he had full opportunity of judging what plan would be best for the interests of the Church ; and he was instrumental in framing and passing a law that, in addition to a full under-graduate course in some college, each candidate should fulfil a period of not less than two years in the study of Theology, Hebrew, and Ecclesiastical History ; and further, that no candidate should receive licence until one year after having completed the prescribed course.

In the autumn of 1817, Mr. Cooke obtained leave of absence from his Presbytery, and entered Trinity College, Dublin. He attended, at the same time, some of the medical classes at the Royal College of Surgeons, and walked the hospitals. In the class-rooms and hospitals of Dublin, he first became acquainted with a kindred spirit, ardent, laborious, successful like himself in the pursuit of knowledge. Acquaintance begat mutual esteem, which ripened into a friendship that continued through life. Dr. Adair Crawford, of London, still survives to bear testimony to the mental powers of his early friend and fellow-labourer. He states that Mr. Cooke's capability of sustained work, his intellectual grasp, his delicacy, and almost intuitive quickness of perception, his rapidity of reasoning, his lucidity of expression, were alike the wonder and admiration of all who knew him. His progress was astonishing. He seemed to comprehend the most difficult subjects as if by instinct. Though his health was delicate, and his frame far from being vigorous, he laboured night and day. Dr. Crawford affirms that he acquired more real knowledge of medicine in a single session than many do in a complete curriculum.

He wrote to Mrs. Cooke, a few days after his arrival in Dublin:—" I attend only three classes as yet, but they take up four hours. I attend two hospitals, and will probably attend a third, as I wish to see as much practice as possible during my residence here." A week or two later he says :— " This letter written, I sit down to pore over a skull, and count its bones and joints till midnight. Could you see me through the key-hole, you would take me for an old monk contemplating mortality. It grins horribly, yet 'to this complexion must my lady turn, should she paint an inch thick.' " In January, 1818, he writes :—" God keep you all from fever. We have enough of it here. I visit seventy patients every morning before eight. We have nearly five hundred in our hospitals, and they constitute only a small part of the sick establishment. . . . As to my going home, you know that, according to the most approved doctrines of matrimony, the husband is bound to obey the wife in all points. I am real 'Old Light,' and will not impinge upon sound doctrine. So, name the day, and I go.

" Still, my dear, I must state my reasons for wishing to stay here as long as you can possibly allow me. First, to acquire medical knowledge I must have time. The longer I remain, the more must I be presumed to learn. Add to this, my present opportunities are such as may never return : I wish to make the most of them."

Medical and philosophical studies did not engross the whole of Mr. Cooke's time and energies when in Dublin. He was the first, or one of the first, in the Irish Presbyterian Church to engage in missionary work. In the sixteenth century a number of English Puritans settled in the south of Ireland. Though they had been long deprived of evangelical ministers, many of them clung to the ancient faith, and in the year 1817 began to be supplied again with religious ordinances. Immediately upon his arrival in Dublin, Mr. Cooke entered upon ecclesiastical work, which one would suppose might have been enough to tax his whole strength. "On coming to Dublin," he writes to Mrs. Cooke, " being too late on Saturday morning for the Carlow coach, I officiated in Mary's Abbey at the sacrament of the Lord's Supper. On the Wednesday following I preached a funeral sermon on the Princess Charlotte. I went on Saturday last to Carlow, and am to return and preach there again next Sunday. The Sunday following I go to Stratford. And so on in rotation, so long as God may give me strength, and acknowledge my humble labours."

His sermons in Dublin made a great impression. There are some still living who remember them with admiration and gratitude—admiration of the talents displayed, and gratitude for the saving effects produced. His fame as a pulpit orator was established in the metropolis ; and, at the request of Mr. Horner, he consented to preach before the civic authorities, on behalf of one of the city charities. The service was in every respect a great success : the collection amounted to the munificent sum of £343.

His labours in Carlow and Stratford were so highly appreciated that the Synod of Munster, in July, 1818, resolved unanimously "that the thanks of the Synod are due to the Rev. Mr. Cooke and the Rev. Mr. Stewart, who have recently supplied the congregation of Carlow, for the zeal, prudence, diligence, and ability exhibited by them in fulfilling the objects of their mission ;" and on the 4th of the same month a similar resolution was passed by the Synod of Ulster.

The fruits of the mission were permanent. A congregation was organised in Carlow. Its first minister was the Rev. (now Dr.) James Morgan, who afterwards became, and during a period of forty years continued, the attached friend, the faithful and honoured fellow-labourer, of Dr. Cooke.

CHAPTER IV.

1818—1824.

MR. COOKE's ministry in Donegore was now drawing to
a close. A wider and more congenial field opened up to
him. He felt reluctance to leave a people from whom he had
experienced the utmost kindness and indulgence. They, too,
were unwilling to let him go. They thought they had a
special claim upon him. They had borne long and patiently
with his absence in Glasgow and Dublin; and now they
were grieved and dissatisfied that, when his mind was fully
matured, and his great powers fully developed, he should leave
them. Yet still they felt proud of their minister. His pulpit
eloquence had kindled their admiration, and his pastoral visits
had won their hearts. After the lapse of half a century, the
memory of the earnest young preacher is still cherished in the
cottages of Donegore and the farm-houses of Six-mile-water.
"Dr. Cooke," writes a son of one of his old parishioners, the
Rev. John Armstrong, "adopted the custom of expounding
the Psalms before his morning discourse. His expositions
were most instructive, and his leading thoughts were put before his hearers with such point and clearness that they were
remembered by many to their dying day. The same was true of

his sermons, in which some bright idea or original expression, was sure to come out and take lodgment in the minds of the more godly. In conversing with the older people of Donegore on religious subjects, not many years since, I had proof of this. A common phrase in use was, 'As Mr. Cooke showed us,' or, 'As Mr. Cooke said;' and then they would quote the words that had fixed themselves so tenaciously in their memories."

Having accepted a " call " from the congregation of Killyleagh, Mr. Cooke resigned his charge at Donegore on the 6th of July, 1818, and on the 8th of September he was installed pastor of his new parish. Killyleagh is situated on the banks of Strangford Lough, in one of the richest and most picturesque districts of county Down. The village is built on the steep sides of an eminence, from whose summit rise the towers of the castle, the ancestral seat of the Hamiltons. It was one of the earliest Scotch settlements in Ulster ; and the parish was under the spiritual care of ministers of the Church of Scotland from the time of the settlement, until the Rev. William Richardson was driven out for nonconformity by Jeremy Taylor. The great body of the gentry, farmers, and yeomen belonged to the Presbyterian Church in Mr. Cooke's time ; and their names—Blackwood, Heron, Montgomery, Campbell, Hay, Stewart, Howie, Ferguson—showed that they held by the faith of their Scottish forefathers.

The lord of the manor, Archibald Hamilton-Rowan, whose life, as rebel or patriot, formed not the least romantic episode in Ireland's history, was professedly a member of Mr. Cooke's flock, though he had unfortunately adopted New Light views on theology. His younger son, Captain Sydney Hamilton-Rowan, was a ruling elder in the Presbyterian Church. He was mainly instrumental in taking Mr. Cooke to Killyleagh, and he became one of his most attached friends and devoted fellow-labourers. It would be impossible to estimate the amount of influence Captain Rowan exerted over the mind and subsequent career of Mr. Cooke. In him Mr. Cooke found, for the first time, that cordial sympathy and encouragement of which he had been so long in search.   He was a man of sound judgment, extensive theological knowledge, refined taste, ardent piety, and, like all his race, undaunted courage.   He was animated by the same love for evangelical truth, the same strong attachment to the Church of Scotland, and the same earnest desire to eradicate from the Presbyterian Church in Ireland a fatal heresy, which so remarkably characterised Mr. Cooke.   He was descended from Archibald, second son of the Rev. Hans Hamilton, minister of Dunlop, Ayrshire ; and was connected with the noble houses of Dufferin, Bangor, and Roden.

Killyleagh had once been the seat of a Presbytery, which was probably the most heterodox in faith, and the most revolutionary in politics, of any connected with the Synod of Ulster.   It was dissolved in the year 1796, and its members were distributed among the Presbyteries of Dromore, Bangor, and Armagh.   Mr. Cooke's immediate predecessor, the Rev. W. D. McEwen, was an Arian ; and during his short ministry he appears to have gathered round him a small party, who were patronised by the lord of the manor.   But the Presbytery of Dromore, under whose ecclesiastical jurisdiction the congregation of Killyleagh was now placed, was a *subscribing* presbytery ; and among its members Mr. Cooke found some prepared to aid him in the work of reform.

It was evident to all thoughtful observers that a change was approaching in the Synod of Ulster.   The numbers of evangelical ministers had of late largely increased.   The people were beginning to value a pure gospel.   " The spirit of inquiry," writes Mr. Cooke, " hath again been roused from the lethargy of ages ; and the spirit of God hath been poured out upon churches that had been lying like the dry bones in the valley of vision, and they have been clothed with flesh, and endowed with life—and they stand upon their feet, an exceeding great army.   The Synod of Ulster has enjoyed a portion of this renovating influence.   The people are beginning to inquire what it is the ministers preach. They are searching their Bibles to see if these things be so. Ministers are beginning to speak out more boldly their religious sentiments. The days of indifference are nearly gone by; and the friends and enemies of evangelical truth are ranging themselves distinctly in the opposing lines of assault and defence."

The New Light party, seeing their cause waning, resolved to attempt its revival. Hitherto their theology had been of a negative character. Their opinions were to be gathered from their silence rather than their statements. In the pulpit they studiously avoided doctrine. They dwelt on the lighter and less critical themes of morality and benevolence. But now inquiry was awakened, and the people were no longer satisfied with a negative theology. The two parties in the Church became more defined, and the people wished to know with certainty wherein they differed. Orthodox ministers preached a crucified and living Saviour. With them the doctrine of the atonement was the fundamental principle of Christianity. The New Light party were called upon to declare their views, and they thought it best that a stranger should inaugurate the new era in their history.

During the spring of 1821, an advertisement appeared in the Belfast newspapers to the following effect :—

"UNITARIAN MISSION.

" The Rev. J. Smithurst, from the neighbourhood of Exeter, being appointed by the ENGLISH UNITARIAN FUND to visit the Province of Ulster, intends shortly to commence his missionary labours by preaching in Belfast, Carrickfergus, Lisburn, Saintfield, Downpatrick, Killyleagh, and adjoining districts. His object will be to advocate the cause of Christian truth without any reference to sect or party."

Mr. Smithurst was not a volunteer apostle. He was invited to Ireland. He was patronised by the Arian Presbytery of

Antrim. One of the teachers in the Belfast Institution introduced him by letters, and by personal influence, to pulpits in Ulster. Writing to an Arian minister in county Down, he said Mr. Smithurst had come as a missionary from England, "to explain our doctrines more fully." In the advertisement it was declared that "he would advocate the cause of Christian truth without any reference to sect or party." Under this fair profession he was smuggled into many of the churches and parishes of the orthodox ministers of the Synod of Ulster. There he assailed the doctrine of the Trinity. Of course an apostle of Arianism must do so. He went further. He insulted Trinitarians. He told them they were like the silversmiths of Diana at Ephesus—they taught the supreme Deity of the Saviour, not because they believed it, but because they lived by it. He made use of the most horrible expressions regarding the doctrine of our Lord's divinity; and he generally concluded his addresses with a few political touches advocating advanced liberal views, which most thoughtful men would call revolutionary. He was at first successful. His free theology and still freer political creed attracted the multitude, especially those who retained or had imbibed the spirit of '98. The graces of his oratory pleased the ear of a few of the higher classes. The New Light party anticipated great results; but they were doomed to disappointment.

There were a few Arians in Killyleagh, patronized by Mr. Archibald Hamilton-Rowan; but Mr. Cooke's pulpit services and Captain Rowan's private labours had well-nigh destroyed their influence as a party. It was thought that a visit from the English apostle would serve to re-establish the declining cause. A house was engaged; Smithurst's visit was announced; friends were summoned from far and near. The hour came, and the meeting was crowded. Among the first to take their places were Mr. Cooke and Captain Rowan. The lecture was brilliant. New Light views, political as well as theological, were expounded and glorified. The orator concluded amid thunders of applause, and the Arians looked round with triumph upon their orthodox brethren. But their triumph was short-lived. Captain Rowan rose and said—" I have listened, sir, with deepest attention to your lecture. I have heard your doctrines with much surprise. They are not the doctrines which our pastor teaches. He is here himself to say so, and to tell you and this meeting that the views you have propounded are opposed to the Word of God." These words, uttered with calm dignity, by a man high in position and universally respected, went through the meeting like an electric shock. Smithurst began to feel that the field was no longer his own. He was a practised controversialist, however, and he declared his readiness and wish, then and there, to discuss each topic with any objector. Mr. Cooke was not to be so taken at a disadvantage. With tact equal to that of his antagonist, he replied :—

" You, sir, have chosen your own time and mode for invading my parish, and stating your views: I shall choose mine for reply. I here declare your doctrines to be false and pernicious. I invite this assembly, and the whole parish of Killyleagh, to my church on next Sunday; you, too, sir, shall be welcome ; and I pledge myself fairly to review, and fully refute, by scriptural arguments, every dogma you have this day propounded. When I have thus removed the evil impression now made on the minds of my people, I shall be ready to meet you in public discussion, here or elsewhere in Ulster."

The effect of these spirited words may be well imagined. They were received by the great bulk of the audience with a ringing cheer. They sped from mouth to mouth, from house to house, throughout the parish and the county. On the Sunday named the Presbyterian Church in Killyleagh was filled in every part, and many, unable to gain admission, clustered round doors and windows. Never had the quiet village witnessed such a scene. From far and near the people came— old men and youths, matrons and maidens, to hear their courageous young pastor defend their insulted faith. Mr. Cooke's discourse was worthy of the occasion. Point after point advanced by Smithurst was placed in the clear light of divine truth, torn to atoms by a relentless logic, and then scattered to the winds by bursts of impassioned eloquence. Having carried the convictions of his hearers, he concluded by a noble appeal. In language of equal power and pathos he depicted the sinner's guilt and helplessness ; the infinite love of God in laying the guilt upon his Son ; the sufferings, death, and resurrection of the divine Saviour ; and the everlasting joy that Saviour secured for His people :—

" These are the doctrines, these the hopes, these the joys, which God in His holy Word places before you. Will you then suffer vain man to rob you of God's noblest gifts ? Will you accept a withering philosophy for the life-giving truths of the Bible ? Forsake not, beloved brethren, the faith of your martyred forefathers. Rest still upon the Rock of Ages—Jesus the Lord—God manifest in the flesh. Then, then only, will you be safe ; for, founded upon Him, you will remain a building of God, firm and steadfast, amid the ruins of the universe."

The appeal was irresistible. The first shock of the Arian struggle had taken place, and the first victory was gained for truth. Arian influence was extinguished in Killyleagh, and Smithurst appeared there no more. In his further progress he tried to ignore Mr. Cooke ; but Mr. Cooke would not be ignored. Hearing that Smithurst had fled, he announced, at the close of his sermon, that he would follow him from village to village, and from town to town, through Ulster and Ireland. He declared that wherever heresy was broached within the bounds of his Church he would meet and expose it. He kept his word. Wherever Smithurst lectured, Cooke followed with a triumphant and withering reply. Every pulpit was opened to him. Thousands crowded to hear him, and listened with rapture to his refutations of error and expositions of truth. Ulster soon became too hot for the emissary of the English Unitarian Fund Association. The New Light party saw that their cause was suffering in his hands. Instead of advancing their doctrines, he only exposed them, in every part of the province he visited, to a crushing refutation. Mr. Cooke's labours were enormous; but his success was complete. Smithurst, defeated and humiliated, fled from Ireland. Ere the brief campaign closed, Cooke was recognised throughout Ulster as the champion of Bible truth. His faithful exposition of the fundamental doctrines of the gospel, and his fervent appeals to the heart and conscience, were the means of infusing new life into the Presbyterian Church, and rousing to spiritual activity a race of men who have proved a blessing to their country and an ornament to Christianity.

The discomfiture of Smithurst encouraged Mr. Cooke to assail another stronghold of Arianism. In the year 1810 the Belfast Academical Institution was founded by royal charter for the purpose of giving a high-class education to the leading youths of Ulster. A collegiate department was subsequently added, arranged on the plan of the Scotch universities, chiefly with the view of supplying home training to candidates for the ministry in the Presbyterian Church. The sanction and aid of the Synod of Ulster was sought by the Board of Managers; and the Synod resolved, in 1814, that "the same respect be paid to the certificates of the Belfast Institution as to the certificates from foreign universities, so soon as adequate professors are appointed to lecture in this Institution on the different branches of science which the Synod points out to the students under its care." Without the patronage and support of the Synod it was well known the college could not exist; for the vast majority of the students would necessarily be Presbyterians and candidates for the ministry. The action of the Synod was perhaps premature. The organisation of the Institution was not yet sufficiently developed, nor was its character sufficiently high, to warrant the Synod in classing it with the Scotch universities, or in giving it the Church's sanction. Had the Synod been less hasty in its decision, the result might have been more satisfactory both to the Institution and to the Presbyterian Church. It was too evident to close observers

that, from the first, New Light or Arian influence prevailed in
the Board of Management. Strong political views, not favourable to constitutional Government, were also held by some
of the leading men connected with it. In consequence of
disloyal sentiments expressed at a political banquet given in
Belfast on the 16th of March, 1816, at which some of the
managers and masters of the Institution were present, the
Government withdrew a grant of £1,500 a year, which had
been made only a short time previously. Yet, notwithstanding
these patent facts, and notwithstanding a somewhat incautious
remonstrance on the part of an influential member of the
legislature, the Synod not only resolved to place the general
certificate of the Institution on an equality with the degree of
Master of Arts from a university, but even appointed a professor
of divinity to lecture in the new college, so as to complete
within its walls the whole collegiate training of the clergy of
the Presbyterian Church. The Board of Management saw it
to be for their interest to propitiate the Synod of Ulster, and
the Synod naturally expected to be largely benefited by a
college growing up in the capital of Irish Presbyterianism.
But there were some members of Synod who felt less
hopeful. They saw how deeply rooted Arianism was in the
Institution. They feared the effect of its teachings upon
Presbyterian students. They endeavoured, by the appointment
of a special synodical committee, by searching examinations,
and by unceasing watchfulness, to guard their young men
from error, and at the same time to secure a high-class
training. The attempt was vain, as every such attempt must
be. False principles, whether in religion or philosophy, when
held by able and earnest teachers, cannot fail, in a greater or
less degree, to permeate the minds of the pupils. No amount
of external watchfulness will prevent the tares from lodging
and germinating in the youthful mind.

Arian influence, instead of waning, increased in the Institution. On a vacancy occurring in the chair of Greek and
Hebrew, an orthodox candidate of high attainments was set

aside, and a professed Arian appointed. The appointment
was rendered all the more obnoxious to the Old Light party
by the fact that the new professor was minister of an Arian
congregation in the immediate vicinity of the Institution; and
that at his ordination, a short time previously, it had been
publicly stated by one of those who officiated that " Trinitarians, whatever they might pretend before the people, did
not and could not believe what they taught of the Trinity."
It was felt that a Hebrew professor could not instruct his
students in the language of the Old Testament without, directly
or indirectly, enunciating his views regarding the Trinity. It
was felt also that, as the Greek New Testament was a class-
book, the Greek professor must, in critically examining its
text, interfere, in one way or another, with the vital doctrines
of Christianity. If honest and conscientious, an Arian would
necessarily teach Arianism, and poison the minds of those who
were being trained for the ministry of the Presbyterian Church.

Some, of whom better things might have been expected, stood
aside, and did not use their legitimate influence in opposition
to the appointment. Dr. Edgar, theological professor for the
Secession Synod, acted an open and manly part, and opposed
the election on behalf of his Church. Mr. Cooke, with characteristic energy, opposed it in the interests of the Synod of
Ulster. He failed; but at the annual meeting of Synod, held
in Newry, in 1822, he called special attention to the appointment, and solemnly warned his brethren and the whole Church
of the danger of permitting a man professing Arian views,
however profound his scholarship, however high his qualifications in other respects, to instruct candidates for the Christian
ministry in the languages of Scripture. He soon found that
the task he had undertaken was both difficult and delicate.
He expected the sympathy and aid of a large body of his
brethren, but, to his amazement, he stood almost alone. The
leaders were against him. The moment he rose and announced
his purpose he was met by a frowning audience. As he proceeded, in clear and forcible language, to detail the evils the

Church had already suffered from Arianism, and the still greater evils pending, murmurs of disapproval ran through the assembly. The very elements seemed to be against the bold speaker. Though it was mid-day, thick darkness gathered round the building, and a terrific thunderstorm burst over the town. It was a trying moment. Mr. Cooke saw, and saw with feelings of grief and shame, that his brethren, whatever their secret belief or open profession, were not yet prepared to shake off the fetters with which they had been so long bound. But strong in the justice of his cause, impelled by deep conscientious conviction, he spoke fearlessly and faithfully :—

"I speak openly before the world, and I declare that the doctrines held and taught by the Arian ministers and professors in Belfast are in direct opposition to the Scriptures. Not creed nor catechism, but the Bible has taught me to approach my Redeemer as 'God manifest in the flesh,' 'God over all, blessed for ever,' and to regard the Holy Spirit, not as an inferior created agent, or a mere attribute. The Bible has taught me that the Father, the Word, and the Holy Ghost are one God; it has taught me that the carnal mind is enmity against God, and must remain so until quickened and renewed by the power of the Eternal Spirit; it has taught me that the Saviour offered a real vicarious sacrifice for sin, that 'He was made sin for us that we might be made the righteousness of God in Him.' Thus I believe, therefore I speak. I cannot, I dare not be silent. Misrepresentation, obloquy, persecution, and if there even be one stroke beyond them all,—yet, through the grace of God our Saviour, I shall meet them all, endure them all, contending earnestly for the faith once delivered to the Saints. I shall not quail before the most powerful adversaries of the truth; nor shall I suffer myself to be drawn aside by the timidity or the interests of its mistaken friends. I do not stand here now, nor have I ever yet stood, as contending for petty doctrinal distinctions. The foundations of our faith are at stake. There are three doctrines peculiar and essential to the Christian system—the Trinity, the vicarious atonement of Christ, and the necessity of the work of the Spirit of God to originate faith and repentance in the heart of man. He that holds these principles, whatever be his name, I call a brother in Christ, and offer him the right hand of fellowship; but, he who denies these, or any of them,

I look upon as fatally in error. In my opposition to the appointment of Arian professors, I seem this day to stand alone. Yet I am
not alone. Men may draw back in fear, but God and truth are with
me. I believe, too, that the hearts of many of my brethren in the
ministry are with me. I know that the great body of the Presbyterian laity are with me. They will never quietly look on while the
enemies of every doctrine they hold sacred are here, as elsewhere,
scaling the walls, and entering the inmost chambers, and occupying
the highest towers of their Zion."

It was vain. His eloquence made no visible impression.
Timid counsels prevailed. He retired from the Synod
with a sad and anxious heart, and returned to his home
at Killyleagh. Never during his long career did he feel so
much discouraged. The result of his effort was, in his
opinion, worse than a defeat. There was an apathy, a faltering timidity, a humiliating cowardice, shown on the occasion
by some of his orthodox brethren, which made him fear that
the regeneration of his Church was hopeless. He almost
resolved to relinquish the struggle in despair. His mind
was so deeply moved, that, waking or sleeping, the Arian
controversy was its one absorbing thought. This was shown
by a singular dream he had the night after his return from
Newry. The dream was at first confused. A battle was
raging. He was in the thickest of the fight. He was alone
and borne down by numbers. Shadowy forms pressed upon
him. His blows, however skilfully aimed and vigorously dealt,
fell harmless. Smithurst, Bruce, and Henry Montgomery were
close upon him; while in the background, cold and scornful,
were the dim forms of orthodox brethren. The scene changed.
The dreamer was in a spacious hall filled by an excited crowd.
He stood upon a platform. The eyes of the assembly were
fixed upon him. Suddenly the devil appeared by his side and
challenged him to a discussion on the leading dogmas of
Arianism. Henry Cooke never refused a challenge. The
discussion commenced. Argument after argument was advanced on both sides, and truth always triumphed. At length

the devil, weary of logic, tried to overwhelm his opponent by bold assertion. " I have more experience than you," he exclaimed ; " I have seen what you never saw; I have heard what you could never hear ; I have been in heaven where you never were ; and I now affirm on indisputable authority— the authority of my own personal knowledge—that Jesus Christ is not God." " And I affirm," said Cooke, in reply, " I affirm, on the infallible testimony of God's own Word, that when the devil speaketh a lie, which this is, he speaketh of his own ; for he is a liar and the father of it." These words were uttered with such strength of voice, and vehemence of action, that not only did the dreamer himself awake, but Mrs. Cooke started up in alarm, believing her husband to be struggling with a midnight robber.

Mr. Cooke's bold course in the Synod at Newry exposed him to the attack of a Belfast journal, which was then, and for years afterwards, the organ of the Arian party, and which was inspired besides by some leading men connected with the Academical Institution. Most of the attacks he bore in silence. Only when public interests were affected did he think it necessary to reply. The subject of the Greek professorship was again introduced to the Synod at the annual meeting in Armagh, in 1823, by a motion to the effect that the Synod should express unqualified approval of the Institution. This was vigorously opposed by Mr. Cooke, who was, on this occasion, joined by his old college friend, Robert Stewart. After two days' debate, it was resolved that the matter should be allowed to drop, and that no notice, public or private, should be taken of the discussion. This agreement was kept in so far as the Synod Records were concerned ; but, as usual, an *ex-parte* account was given in the *Northern Whig*, and Mr. Cooke was loaded with obloquy and reproach. The plan adopted by the Arian party from the first appeared to be, not so much to assail the arguments, as to blacken the character of their opponents.

Although the ministers of the Synod of Ulster showed as yet no wish to grapple with the Arian heresy, the Presbyterian laity manifested an earnest desire to hear pure gospel doctrine. Mr. Cooke's services were eagerly sought for, and willingly rendered. During the years 1822 and 1823 he preached generally two or three times a week, travelling many miles on foot or horseback. Crowded audiences everywhere awaited and welcomed him. He explained and defended the truth; he warned backsliders; he encouraged the weak and wavering; he roused the careless and indifferent. At length, by the wondrous power of his eloquence, he succeeded in infusing a spirit of new life into the laity of the Presbyterian Church. His mind and body were taxed to the utmost. None of his brethren as yet stood by him. They hesitated, they wavered, they questioned his prudence; some denounced him as a rash enthusiast, who would rend the church. The whole New Light party opposed and maligned him. He was harassed by the attacks of open enemies; he was wounded to the heart by the indifference of friends. " Peace, peace," the old Syren cry, was still echoed by the vast body of the Presbyterian clergy. Mr. Cooke would have no peace with error; he would have no compromise with Arianism. Once and again he said, in private and public, to the preachers of peace :—"If you can convince me from Scripture that Trinitarians, Arians, and Socinians, can form a scriptural church, and cordially unite in licensing and ordaining one another, I shall resign my present views, and unite with you in preserving our present Constitution." He felt that purity of faith, firm belief in the fundamental doctrines of the Gospel, was the first requisite in Christ's Church; and he resolved to secure it to the church of his fathers, even though peace should fall a sacrifice in the struggle.

While labouring so successfully in the north of Ireland, Mr. Cooke still endeavoured to promote the mission work which he had been largely instrumental in initiating in the south. At the meeting of Synod, in 1820, a committee was appointed for "promoting the revival and extension of Presbyterianism in the south and west of Ireland." Regular services were established in some of the leading towns, where Presbyterian families resided. At the request of the committee, Mr. Cooke and Mr. Carlile, of Dublin, visited Scotland, "to explain to friends in that country the circumstances of their brethren in the south and west of Ireland, and to solicit their aid in support of missions in those quarters." Their appeal was successful. An influential committee was appointed in Edinburgh, and it was resolved to "make every exertion to raise funds, by congregational collections or otherwise, for providing ordinances of religion for the Presbyterians scattered over the south and west of Ireland, many of whom are from Scotland." The Presbytery of Glasgow, after an eloquent appeal by Mr. Cooke, unanimously agreed "that a collection should be made in the several parishes and chapels," and the proceeds handed over to the Irish Committee, for the purposes of Church extension. Collections were also taken up in all the churches of the Synod of Ulster, and the sum of £513 was raised—a large amount in those days. The Home Mission work of the Irish Presbyterian Church was thus inaugurated ; and the thanks of the Synod were given "to the Rev. Henry Cooke, and others, who, by their diligence, piety, and exemplary conduct, not only contributed to the interests of religion in general, but left a most favourable impression of our Church upon all classes."

Though Mr. Cooke had undertaken such a gigantic work in Ulster, in defence of truth, his heart was so intent on the prosecution of the new mission in the south and west of Ireland, that he visited Scotland again in the beginning of 1824. He preached several times in Edinburgh and Glasgow, advocating the cause of his neglected countrymen with his wonted power and success. How his own mind was cheered by his visit, appears from a letter to Mrs. Cooke :—"We are to have a public meeting here (in Glasgow) on Thursday, in Trades' Hall, where I attended a Juvenile Tract Society Meeting last night. All is life in the way of doing good. I

wish Rowan were with me to witness the excellent spirit the
Lord has shed abroad in the hearts of His people ; and, though
there is much sin, no doubt, he would see more practical piety
than is elsewhere to be found in the same compass, except,
perhaps, he should go to Pitcairn's Island, or Tahiti."

Just before his visit to Scotland, the Congregation of Armagh
became vacant. Armagh was then, as now, one of the most
important charges in the Presbyterian Church. Mr. Cooke
was invited to preach as a candidate. Personally he was a
stranger to the people, but his labours were known. Influenced
by those labours, the great body of the congregation were
anxious to have him as their pastor ; but a few, who had
adopted the New Light theology, were just as anxious to
prevent his settlement among them. Ere the formal invitation
reached him, he received a private letter from the late Mr.
William Kirk, long M.P. for Newry, giving him full information
as to the state of feeling in the congregation. Mr. Kirk had
known him almost from the commencement of his ministerial
career. He had heard his remarkable extemporary addresses
at the Communion in Connor ; he had heard him preach
repeatedly in Donegore ; and one noble sermon, preached on
the first Sunday of 1814, had left an indelible impress on his
memory. Mr. Kirk's thoughtful and highly-cultivated mind
recognised the talents of the young minister, and anticipated
his distinguished career. "You will doubtless be surprised,"
he wrote, "at receiving this communication from a person
whom, perhaps, you can scarcely recollect, at my uncles', the
Messrs. Millar, of Rose Lodge. From what I then knew, and
have since heard of you, I felt it my duty to give you my best
and warmest support here yesterday. It was singular that I
was the only person present who had ever heard you preach
. . . . Be assured I have no motive but a strong desire
to see you unanimously placed here, as, without flattery, I
know no minister in the Synod who, in my mind, is so well
calculated to promote Gospel doctrine and practice among us."

Mr. Cooke does not appear to have courted, or wished for a

removal to Armagh. He consented to preach, however, for he was desirous to follow the line of duty. His text was the Parable of the Ten Virgins. The discourse was characterised by great eloquence, and powerful appeals to the heart and conscience. Towards the close, the preacher touched on the question of the eternity of future punishments, which was peculiarly objectionable to the New Light party. He concluded one thrilling appeal by pronouncing, in tones which touched every heart, the words of our Lord—" And the door was shut." In the hush which followed, a hissing whisper was heard from the lips of the leader of the New Lights :—" Yes, ' the door was shut,' and that shuts you out of Armagh." It was true. The Arians triumphed for the time. Ere many months, however, the congregation called an eloquent and accomplished young orthodox minister, the Rev. P. Shuldham Henry, now President of Queen's College, Belfast.

During his short visit to Armagh Mr. Cooke wrote to Mrs. Cooke—" You will not expect that I can tell you much about Armagh at present. There are a great number of religious people here. One poor woman I visited this day, and she was, I think, the first over-match I ever met in the recollection of passages of Scripture. She was dying in faith and hope, and is going to inherit the promises. Religion appears to have made good progress : many are looking Zionward. I feel myself unworthy of all God has done for me, and all the favour he has given me amongst the people. But if the Lord give grace, there is a time for working even now at the eleventh hour. If I be made humble and holy, the Lord will make me useful. I cannot say whether I wish to stay at Killyleagh or to come here. God's will be done. Stay or come, the only thing that will influence me will be the view of usefulness. Had I not seen the possibility of good here, I should have preached and gone home with a farewell; but from the state of religion I feel induced to wait a little longer for decision."

CHAPTER V.

1824—1825.

Elected Moderator of the Synod of Ulster—Royal Commission on Education—
Memoir on the State of Irish Schools—School-books at the Close of the 18th
Century—Mr. Cooke's Evidence before the Commissioners—Assailed by
Arians and Roman Catholics—Arian Protest to Spring Rice, M.P.—Indigna-
tion of the Heads of the Belfast Institution—Mr. Cooke's Defence—His
Opinions on Catholic Emancipation—Charges against the Belfast Institution
—Exposure of Arian Dogmas—Opposition to Mr. Cooke—Sympathy of
Orthodox Protestants—Presentation of Plate by Congregation of Comber—
Address from Parish of Killyleagh—Letter of Sir Robert Peel—Meeting of
Synod at Coleraine—Mr. Cooke's Sermon—Debate on the Ordination of Mr.
Nelson in Dromore—On Mr. Cooke's Evidence before the Royal Commission
—His Speech and the Result—Resolutions regarding the Belfast Institution
—Connection of the Synod with the Presbytery of Antrim—History of the
Code of Discipline—Thanks of the Synod.

An event occurred in 1824 which brought the Arian controversy to a crisis. Mr. Cooke's fame as a pulpit orator, and as
a champion of evangelical truth was established. The services
he had already rendered to orthodox Presbyterianism were
known and acknowledged throughout Ulster. In spite of the
hostility of the Arians, and the timid counsels of many among
the orthodox, he had now conferred on him the highest honour
his church could bestow, being elected to the Moderator's
chair. It was a critical period. The state of education in
Ireland was beginning to attract the attention of the Legislature. In 1824 a Royal Commission was appointed to " inquire
into the nature and extent of the instruction afforded by the
several institutions established for the purposes of education,
and to report as to the measures which can be adopted for
extending generally to all classes of the people the benefits of
education." Mr. Cooke, expecting to be examined, studied

the question in all its bearings. He instituted searching inquiries, he gleaned information from every available source, and he drew up a valuable Memoir, which was communicated to leading members of the Government interested in the matter.

The Memoir is dated 29th November, 1824, and is prefaced by a private letter addressed to John Leslie Foster, Esq. It is extremely interesting from the graphic sketches it contains of the state of primary education in Ulster at the close of last century, the nature of the school-houses, the character of the teachers, and the singular class-books used. Mr. Cooke gives many details of his own school days, some of which have been embodied in this biography. The class-books he read will probably amuse and astonish the advanced school-master of the present day. " The chief books, when I entered school in 1796, were 'Fenning's Universal,' and 'Manson's Spelling-Book.' Some had the 'Youth's Instructor,' and the 'Lilliputian Magazine.' These were all excellent in their way . . . but when we took a step forward in reading, our books were bad indeed. I read 'The Labours of Herculus,' and ' Destruction of Troy,' 'The Seven Champions of Christendom,' the 'Romance of Parismos and Parismenos,' The 'Chinese Tales,' a book of Transmigration, 'Don Bellionis of Greece,' the friend of Don Quixote. In history I read 'The Irish Rogues and Rapparees,' 'Valentine and Orson,' 'The Adventures of Redmond O'Hanlon,' a noted robber, 'The Life of Bold Captain Freney,' and others of a similar kind."

Mr. Cooke's Memoir helped to open the eyes of the Royal Commissioners to the wants of Ireland in regard to education. It prepared the way for thorough inquiry. It suggested the leading points on which information and reform were needed; and it laid down principles at once sound and suitable for the divided state of parties and religious sects in the country.

The Commissioners spent the greater part of the year 1824 in a personal inspection of Irish schools. They examined upon oath a large number of leading men of all sects and parties supposed to be conversant with the subjects under inquiry. Their report, with the evidence taken, fills a Blue Book of more than a thousand pages. The historical sketches given in it are interesting and valuable. The defects are detailed with clearness and judicial discrimination; but the recommendations of the Commissioners show that they did not fully understand the wants of Ireland, or the character of her people. Mr. Cooke saw much more clearly than the Commissioners the jealousies of Protestant and Catholic. He was ready to make to the latter all reasonable concessions; but he warned the Commissioners and the Government, then and afterwards, that undue concession to the Roman Catholic party, instead of satisfying them, would only incite to farther demands, and in the end tend to overthrow any scheme of united education.

Mr. Cooke was examined by the Royal Commissioners on the 5th and 6th of January, 1825, and again, in the April following, by select committees of both Houses of Parliament, appointed to inquire into the general state of Ireland. Portions of his evidence found their way, but in an imperfect form, into the public press. They created great excitement throughout Ireland. He was particularly examined by the Select Committee of the Lords regarding the Belfast Institution, its Arian tendencies, and its connection with and influence upon the Presbyterian Church. He was closely questioned on the history of Arianism in Ireland, and the extent to which it had spread in the Synod of Ulster. His elaborate replies were particularly obnoxious to the New Light and Roman Catholic parties. His statements were indignantly denied; his opinions were violently assailed, and he became the subject of wide-spread abuse and misrepresentation. A fragment of his evidence appeared in the Belfast *News Letter* of April 20th, and formed the subject of a leading article. "We beg leave," it said, "totally to differ from Mr. Cooke respecting the alleged tendency of the Belfast Institution to disseminate the principles of Arianism through the community. We hold the very contrary to be the fact." Thus the controversy spread. Mr. Cooke was charged with assuming a false position in professing to represent the Synod of Ulster; he was charged with misrepresenting the opinions of the Protestants of Ireland, by saying that there was a growing feeling of hostility among the great mass of them against Catholic emancipation. But the chief ground of complaint was his declaration that he entertained fears that the Belfast Institution "would finally become, as it has already in some degree become, a great seminary of Arianism." A few ministers and elders belonging to the Arian party in Belfast, headed by Henry Montgomery, drew up an indignant protest against Mr. Cooke's alleged calumnies, and forwarded it to Thomas Spring Rice, M.P. They denied the accuracy of his evidence, both in regard to the Belfast Institution, and the sentiments of Presbyterians on the subject of Catholic emancipation. The Board of Managers and Visitors of the Institution affirmed that Mr. Cooke's "representation of the present state and future tendency of the Institution is altogether groundless and imaginary; that it has never been at any time, nor in any degree, a seminary of Arianism." The professors published a strong declaration, that if Mr. Cooke's words were meant to convey the impression that the doctrines of Arianism had been taught by them in their class-rooms, "they contain a gross and scandalous libel, not only unsupported by facts, but in direct and known opposition to them." The students, too, held a meeting and issued a paper similar in form and tenor.

Mr. Cooke's position was now one of very great difficulty. He was beset on every side. He stood alone. Many of his orthodox brethren joined the ranks of his assailants. Doctors Hanna and Edgar, the Presbyterian professors of theology, signed the declaration published by the Faculty. The Press was against him, headed as usual by the *Whig*. The very papers which published the letters of his assailants, and which contained leading articles against him, refused to print his replies. At length, however, the columns of the *News Letter* were opened to him, and through this medium he vindicated his character, and demonstrated the accuracy of his evidence :—

"I have been attacked," he wrote, "by the *Irishman* and *Whig.* I attempted a reply, but the necessary length of the article precluded its insertion in the *Commercial Chronicle.* For a short, and, consequently, insufficient defence the editor of that paper kindly afforded space. But as I judge it absolutely necessary to treat the matter at large, I cast myself on your protection, as a public journalist. I am unarmed ; an enemy has made the most deadly thrusts at me ; lend me but the arms and I shall defend myself.

"To the *Irishman* I offer no reply ; but to the *Whig* and its reverend editor, I owe a word or two. He has his own reasons for his deadly hostility.

"I am accused, in the first place, of imagining that my office as Moderator gives me a representative character, or enables me to speak *ex cathedrâ* of the opinions of the Presbyterian laity. Had my accusers waited to examine, not a part, but the whole of my evidence, they would have found that I gave, before the Committee of the House of Commons, such a description of the nature of my office as will fully acquit me of this charge. . . . I did not attempt to represent the Synod—the writers of the charge did not believe it when they invented it. My evidence will prove their representation to be untrue.

"The second capital charge against me is that of being illiberal and unfriendly to Catholic emancipation. This charge I flatly deny. And to this point I specially request the attention of the public.

"The origin of the charge seems to me to be the following. A portion of my evidence, wherein I detailed what changes I believed to have taken place unfavourable to Catholic emancipation, was in some newspapers culled for insertion to serve special purpose ! The man who would dare to tell that others were unfavourable to Catholic emancipation, was unthinkingly supposed to be also unfavourable. My evidence in favour of Catholic emancipation was kept studiously back. The cry was got up ; and when an additional portion of my evidence, that would have explained the other, was published, I was already condemned, and no man would listen to explanation or defence.

"My evidence is divided into three parts :—1. My general idea of the state of public opinion ; 2. My own opinion; 3. My ideas of any late change.

"On the first part I said, 'I think the opinions are exceedingly various among all classes of the people, both the more and less learned. I think in general among the more informed classes of the Presbyterian body, they entertain less fear about it. Some of them dislike it ; some of them disapprove of it ; some of them do approve and wish for it ; but take the less informed of the Presbyterians altogether, I think they almost entirely disapprove of it.' By less informed I mean possessed of less political knowledge. Now I do ask any honest juror who ever sat in a court of justice, is not this true testimony ? . . . . I say it without boasting, but when I say it those who know my habits will believe me, there is not a minister, there is not a man in Ulster, who has better means of knowing the state of mind of the common people among orthodox Presbyterians than I have ; I am an humble individual, but I possess some of their confidence. I have preached in more of their congregations in Derry, Antrim and Down than any other member of the Synod ; and, therefore, when I stated this opinion to the House of Lords I had good grounds for believing myself correct. Nor could the assertion of any possible number of Arian, or Socinian ministers, or elders, ever shake or invalidate my testimony. They know as much of the opinions of the people of Hindustan as they do of the opinions of Old Light Presbyterians or orthodox Churchmen.

"As to my own opinions, I am aware they are of little weight on any side ; yet let me get the praise or blame they deserve. I am questioned :—'Do you think the admission of Catholics to equal rights would diminish or increase certain animosities ? I think in the north it would diminish them. By the admission of the Catholics to the honours of the State their chief source of prejudice and alienation would be done away. The admission of Catholics to equal privileges would, in the south of Ireland, be productive of great good.' Are these the answers, my Catholic countrymen, of the man who is represented as your enemy ? You see it is a foul slander they have attempted to cast upon me.

"I now come to the third part of my evidence, in which I state that 'I think there has lately been an increase of feeling amongst Protestants very much against Catholic emancipation.'"

He goes on to give clear proofs of the truth of this assertion

from facts well known in Belfast and over Ulster. He then
continues—

"On coming a second time before their Lordships, I felt it necessary more minutely to explain what I meant by saying that many
Protestants were opposed to an extension of equal rights to Catholics.
I observed that if the phrase 'equal rights' were taken to mean
equal rights to personal protection, enjoyment of property, profession
of religious opinion, and practice of religious worship, I never knew
any Protestant who would object in that sense. But, if by equal
rights were meant admission to all offices of the State, it was in that
sense alone that I believed many Protestants would be found to object.
I stated that to certain concessions and advancements to the Catholics, in places of honour and emolument, I believed the most considerate part of the Protestants would not much object; and that
with certain limitations of office, to operate as securities, I believed for
certain reasons stated, the matter might be settled without any very
serious obstacles, conceiving, as I still do, that the chief objections
arise from the idea of unlimited concession. I was then questioned
as to what offices did I suppose that, on these grounds, Catholics
might be admitted with a tolerably general approbation of Protestants?
I mentioned Parliament, the Bench, and the Sheriffalty. . . . I
was further questioned, What offices I conceived should be considered
exclusively Protestant? I judged it unnecessary to mention the
Throne, but specified those of the Lord Chancellor, Lord Lieutenant,
and some of the Chief Secretaryships connected with the executive
departments of the Irish and British Governments; also the office of
Commander-in-Chief, though I believed that, as the law at present
stands, Catholics might be eligible to that high office. My reasons
for these opinions I need not obtrude upon the public. I lament,
that in my own defence I have been compelled to say so much; yet
I am not afraid to avow my sentiments. I may be perhaps as liberal
as those who call me otherwise; but if any man says that the Throne
and the other exalted offices of the Executive are to be thrown open
by one single act of legislation, and that there is to be no barrier to
preserve an essential Protestantism in the State; then, if to oppose
this opinion and proceeding in every form and shape be illiberal, I
rejoice in the epithet; I glory in the accusation. I was born the
subject of a Protestant Government, the original liberty of which
my Presbyterian forefathers chiefly contributed to establish and
maintain. *Esto perpetua* is the fervent prayer which I breathe over

it ; nor shall word or act of mine ever tend to interrupt its fulfilment.   Yet, as I love that constitution, and as I cherish its liberty, and as I would speak and act for its defence, so would I wish to extend its every blessing to all within the pale of its power, so far as I could be persuaded that the extension was consistent with the integrity and permanence of its structure."

These noble sentiments, embraced in boyhood and confirmed by experience, constituted the foundation of Mr. Cooke's political creed, and they were maintained, unchanged and unimpaired, to the last moment of his long life.   His defence was felt to be triumphant.   His adversaries were silenced, in so far as their charges against his political consistency and accuracy of statement were concerned.   Something, however, of the animus that prevailed against him in certain quarters may be gathered from the fact, that the copy of the *Belfast News Letter* which contained his defence was torn from the file preserved in the Commercial News-room; and, it was only on his calling attention to this act of mean and dishonourable spite, that another copy was purchased.

Dismissing the political, Mr. Cooke turned to the religious phase of the controversy.   He felt this to be far more important than the other.   He knew, and all thoughtful observers knew, that his exposure of Arianism was the chief source of the hostility to which he had been subjected.   He therefore reprinted his defence in a pamphlet for circulation through the kingdom, especially among Irish Presbyterians, and members of Parliament.   He states that the questions asked regarding the Belfast Institution were totally unexpected by him ; they were asked, not by enemies of the Institution, but by warm friends, and for the purpose of eliciting information favourable to its interests.   Yet, though taken by surprise, he does not, on a close scrutiny, retract, alter, or modify one iota of his evidence ; on the contrary he says :—

" There is no event in my life for which I more sincerely bless God than that I was permitted to bear testimony against Arianism before the most august tribunal of the Universe."

His great charge against the Institution was that it tended, as then constituted, to foster Arianism. There was, however, another :—

"I have declared, but only when pressed for any other reasons of objection, that I had some fears from a few political characters (whom I am happy to have been able justly to describe as nearly sunk into nonentity) endeavouring to give a political bias to the rising generation of our ministers."

Belfast was one of the centres of the rebellion of 1798. Some of the leading spirits among the United Irishmen belonged to the New Light party of Presbyterians. A few of them still lived, and embraced every opportunity of propagating their principles. They fraternised with Repealers ; they advocated extreme views on Catholic emancipation : and they otherwise aided the schemes of O'Connell. Their parade of disloyalty had brought the Institution into trouble in 1816 ; and Mr. Cooke naturally feared the effects of their influence on the minds of young and inexperienced students.

But Arianism was the evil against which Mr. Cooke showed determined hostility.—

"I have declared that I consider the Institution has become in some degree a seminary of Arianism. Had I said Arians, which was literally my meaning, no man could have quibbled about my correctness. However, lest my meaning should be mistaken, I explained before the Commons that 'I did not intend to convey the idea that Arianism had ever been directly taught by any professor in the Institution, but acknowledged that I had not a mind sufficiently acute to discover how an Arian professor, occupying a collegiate chair five or six days in the week, and afterwards on Sunday, in his pulpit, in the hearing of such of his students as, attracted by his professorial influence, might choose to attend, preaching Arianism defensively and offensively, could be supposed not to exercise an undue and dangerous influence over the minds of students committed to his care."

He felt that the interests of his church and the truth of God were at stake. His resolution was therefore taken—

"Against that poison have I spoken and acted, and will speak and act, while, either from the Synod or the Government, there is a hope of remedy."

That no doubt might exist as to the character of the doctrines held by the Arian professors in the Institution, Mr. Cooke stated them :—

" The doctrines of Arianism, in opposition to the Articles of the Churches of Scotland and England, and, as I believe, in opposition to the Sacred Scriptures, degrade the Word that ' was with God, and was God, without whom was not anything made that was made,' into a mere created being, whom the Scriptures, they tell us, seem to warrant us in supposing, at least, one of those superior spirits, who, in the course of numberless ages that must have elapsed since the Deity first exerted His creative power, have been rising to superior degrees of divinity and excellence. That, both in the Old and New Testaments, the usual meaning of the Holy Spirit is merely the Divine influence ; and that, when not so taken, the Holy Spirit is inferior to Christ ; a separate Intelligence in subservience to Christ ; that there is not the slightest ground for identifying the Holy Spirit with the Supreme God ; and that no person professes to believe in His divinity, or is required to do so in Scripture.

" The doctrine of the fall of man, as taught in the Catechisms and Confession of the Westminster Assembly, and in the corresponding doctrines of the Thirty-nine Articles, is described as calculated to counteract the affectionate invitation of their gracious Lord ; to produce feelings of horror and disgust in parents ; distrust, aversion, and gloomy horror between husbands and wives ; anguish and despair at the hour of death ; that it has no foundation in the history of Moses, or the reasonings of Paul; is inconsistent with the moral character of God ; is directly opposed to the doctrines of Christ ; encourages profligacy, infidelity, and hardness of heart.

" That Christ was neither priest nor victim literally ; that there was in the death of Christ neither sacrifice, ransom, imputation of sin, nor vicarious punishment; that all such expressions are merely figurative.

" That while the sinner is never to be restored to favour or happiness, but must spend his whole existence in misery, a misery protracted to an incalculable length, he is finally to terminate his sufferings by annihilation.

" Such is a brief, and, as I believe, faithful picture of Arianism in

Belfast, extracted from a modern work of an eminent Arian divine.
I speak openly before the world, and declare, I consider these doctrines as in direct opposition to the Scriptures, and the last of them
far surpassing most of the vagaries of infidelity."

It has been shown that the chief object in establishing the
collegiate department of the Belfast Institution was to provide
a home training for candidates for the ministry in the Presbyterian church. The great body of the students who attended
it were Presbyterians. Had not this been the case Mr. Cooke's
interference would have been unjustifiable. It might even
have been regarded as persecution. But he was bound to watch
with careful and jealous eye over the training of the students of
his church. It was his duty to see that, in so far as he could
prevent it, they received no wrong impressions, that they were
imbued with no false principles. The Presbyterian church had
already suffered much in this respect. Ministers trained under
heretical professors in Scotland and Holland, had introduced
deadly errors which were now distracting her, and which
threatened eventually to rend her asunder. To secure a home
education, and to keep their students under their own guardian-
ship, the Synod of Ulster approved of, and aided Belfast College.
Without the aid of the Synod it could not have existed. Its
projectors acknowledged this, and Mr. Cooke stated the point
clearly in his evidence.—

"To meet the views and wishes of the great majority of the Presbyterian churches, the original professors of the Belfast Institution
were all of the orthodox creed. I offer in evidence before the Select
Committee of the Lords and Commons, or before His Majesty's Commissioners of Education Inquiry, that one of the arguments employed
by the Managers and Visitors to induce the Deputies of the General
Synod of Ulster to send their students to the Institution was, the
orthodoxy of all the Professors with whom their students would come
into contact. They forgot this arrangement when the point was
gained. I offer in evidence that most of the changes that have since
taken place have been in favour of Arians—of men professedly
Arians—some of them teaching it in their pulpits, in the very

vicinity of the Institution, or propagating it diligently from the press. I was among the earliest friends of the Belfast Institution ; I remained so without a shadow of change till 1821."

In that year a change took place in the professorial staff. Mr. Bruce, an Arian minister, was elected to the chair of Greek and Hebrew. His election, as has been seen, roused Mr. Cooke's opposition. The managers of the Institution did not then renounce connection with the Synod. They submitted to it annual reports ; they sent to it deputations ; they admitted the Moderator to sit *ex officio* among them ; in applying to the Government for aid, connection with the Synod was their main plea. Mr. Cooke, therefore, says :—

"Look to the petition presented to Parliament last year, and is not the great motive pressed upon Government by the petitioning proprietors, the education of the Presbyterian ministry ? It is twice pressed in the body of the petition, and by three Members of Parliament who gave it their support. Sir John Newport in particular affirms that the Institution was founded for educating the Presbyterian clergy."

Mr. Cooke was further persuaded that Arian influence had been used to put Mr. Bruce in the chair. He had evidence of the fact :—

"Previously to the election of Mr. Bruce I received a letter from one of the managers of the Belfast Institution—a man as little fearful of stating his opinions, and a man as capable of supporting them, as any individual connected with its concerns. In this letter he plainly and decidedly states that, in the opinion of Dr. Hanna, Professor Thompson, and others, not Mr. Bruce, but another was, without all comparison, the best qualified for the chair. He points out to me the influence exerted to secure Mr. Bruce's election, and warns me of the danger of placing a person of Arian sentiments in the Greek and Hebrew chairs. He further informs me that Mr. Bruce is notorious for attacking such doctrines as the imputed righteousness of Christ, and the atonement made by Him, as the grounds of a sinner's justification in the sight of God ; denying the doctrine of the Trinity as absurd, and ' only fit for fools to believe or knaves to teach.'

" The consequence of Mr. Bruce's election has been, in my mind, to put the election to the professorships of the Institution nearly into new hands. The accession of Mr. Bruce's friends introduced an additional and powerful body, either of professed Arian subscribers, or of persons who view Arianism with no unfavourable eye —persons who, from their residence and influence in the neighbourhood of Belfast, will, if left uncontrolled, continue to command majorities at every ensuing election."

Mr. Cooke held that it was not enough to have orthodox professors in the chairs of theology. He believed that moral philosophy, Hebrew, and New Testament Greek were so closely allied to religion, that they could not be critically treated without discussing the fundamental truths of Christianity. He gave illustrative proofs from the actual teaching of the recently appointed professor of Hebrew, who, as well as Mr. Bruce, was known to be an Arian.

This was not all. The managers of the Institution had broken faith with the Synod of Ulster. At a meeting of Synod held in Moneymore, in the year 1824, deputies from the Institution were commissioned to obtain from the Synod an unqualified approbation of the collegiate department, as a place of training for the Presbyterian clergy, without which, they were instructed to say, no grant could be obtained from the Government. Several conferences were held without effect. Mr. Cooke narrates the final result :—

" The deputies were about setting out for Belfast, without even appearing before the Synod, when the following plan occurred to me, which I hoped might save the Institution from being overwhelmed by the Arian deluge, and at the same time gain to it, through the Synod's recommendation, the countenance and support of Government. This plan was to obtain, in all cases of election of Professors, an efficient representation of the Synod of Ulster, by having the names and certificates of candidates submitted to the Synod's fixed committee, whose opinion the Moderator should communicate to the electors, and by whose direction he should vote as a member of the

electing body. I did conceive that by this means an effectual barrier would be opposed to the future admission of Arian candidates.
I did conceive that this overture, once formally recognised by the
Court of Proprietors, the Synod might repose in the secure possession
of an efficient *veto*. On privately suggesting my intended overture,
the two deputies expressed their entire acquiescence, and promised to
use their influence to have it accepted and carried into effect. My
overture was unanimously accepted by the Synod. Here I rested in
decided contentment as to the future, fully relying on the promise
and influence of the deputies, and looking for the recognition of the
overture at the next ensuing meeting of proprietors.

" What was my astonishment to find, at this next ensuing meeting,
that the overture was not only not recognised, but its propriety was
even questioned by various gentlemen, as an attempt of the Synod
to acquire an increased influence over the Institution? The neglect,
the rejection of this overture, leaves the Synod and the Institution
exactly as they stood before the overture passed the Synod. The
door stands as wide as ever for Arian Professors. I must speak once
for all. If the proprietors do not concede to the Synod such a recognised right of representing their opinions, as will in future exclude
candidates who may be unacceptable to the Synod on account of
religion, I shall pursue the measure of opposition with unabated
zeal, and hope to receive the cordial support of a large majority of
my brethren.

" But why, it will be said, should the Synod of Ulster seek an influence over the Belfast Institution, seeing they never possessed any
over the Scottish Universities? True, the Synod had no power over
the Scottish Universities; but the Church of Scotland, of which the
Synod was an original branch, and in which her ministers felt confidence, possessed and exercised a salutary influence and corrective
power. But now the Synod of Ulster have, in the majority of the
managers and visitors of the Belfast Institution, no such guardians
of religious education as they had in Scotland; nay, instead of having men who would keep or turn Arians out, they have those who
knowingly put them into the office of Professors. The Synod,
therefore, ought to obtain such an influence as will enable them to
prevent the election of Arian Professors for the future; or, if this be
denied by the proprietors of the Institution, the Synod should return
to the Scottish Universities."

Mr. Cooke's eloquent and powerful defence was effective.

Enemies quailed before it; and friends, hitherto lukewarm, felt that they must rouse themselves for a struggle. Numbers of replies were attempted. The newspapers were filled with them. Only a few, however, were thought worthy of special notice. Among these were letters from Professors Bruce, Hincks, and Thompson. Mr. Cooke dealt with them in a style which showed the marvellous resources of his mind and acuteness of his logical faculty. Assertions and arguments were conclusively met. His memory was so tenacious of even the minutest details of events and conversations; his judgment was so clear and discriminating; his wit was so playful, and his satire so keen, that, while he carried conviction to the minds of all impartial readers, he made his opponents subjects of merriment or ridicule.

The agitation was not confined to Ulster. The political element, which was mixed up with the religious in his evidence, stirred the resentment of the Roman Catholics and all who sympathised with them. Mr. Cooke's evidence was felt to be damaging to their aspirations. A monster meeting was held in Dublin; and there, after speeches, characterized by the usual Celtic force of expression, Mr. Cooke's evidence was condemned as "false and unfounded."

Amid all this storm Mr. Cooke stood alone. Not a man among his brethren in the ministry ventured to aid him. He was fighting the battle of his church and of his country. He was contending against a deadly heresy on the one hand, and a powerful and dangerous political movement on the other; and yet he was forced to repeat what he had said in the Synod at Newry:—"I seem to stand alone." This painful and melancholy fact was noticed with joy by his opponents; and one of them, under the mask of "A Friend in Need," wrote a letter filled with cutting irony and personal invective. Irony was a dangerous weapon to employ against Mr. Cooke. He was himself master of it. It roused him to retaliate. He tore aside the mask under which his opponent tried to conceal his identity, and he exhibited the writer in no very favourable aspect to the gaze of the people of Ulster. The author of the letter proved " a friend in need " after all ; for he was the means of calling forth from the Presbyterians of Ireland, and from thousands of Episcopalians, not in Ireland merely but in England, a response which none had anticipated. Mr. Cooke had said, even when he seemed most alone, " the hearts of many of my brethren in the ministry are with me ; and the great body of orthodox Presbyterians are with me." This was now proved. Letters and resolutions of confidence, sympathy, and congratulation, from ministers, congregations, and Presbyteries, in all parts of the church, began to appear in the newspapers. The *Belfast News-Letter* of June 7, 1824, says : " We are duly authorized to publish the following advertisement respecting the testimony of the Rev. Henry Cooke before the Committee of the House of Lords, &c. The statement it contains is numerously signed by Protestants of all denominations, some of them in the bounds of the congregations of Ballymoney, others in Clough, Broughshane, Bucknaw, Ballymena, and Connor. Amongst them are persons of the first respectability. We are farther empowered to state that ten times the number could have been easily obtained, if the least effort had been made to procure their signatures."

The document says that Mr. Cooke's evidence was " talented, manly, and candid." It was signed by nearly three hundred persons, eight of them clergymen. The *News-Letter* of June 17th contains a series of resolutions to the same effect, signed by the Archdeacon of Raphoe, and nine other clergymen of the Established and Presbyterian Churches—most of the latter signing on behalf of their congregations. Others resolved to tender to Mr. Cooke more substantial tokens of confidence and respect. At an influential meeting held on the 19th of June, the following resolution was adopted :—

" We the undersigned, elders and parishioners of the congregation of Comber, with the view of testifying our approbation of the Rev. Henry Cooke's evidence before the Lords' Committee ; and in order to give a lasting memorial of the high sense we entertain of his late manly and able defence of the principles of Christianity, do agree to pay the several sums annexed to our names, to purchase a piece of plate to be presented to him ; and we farther state that we consider him well qualified to give an opinion concerning the Presbyterian body."

In due time a massive and elegant silver vase was purchased and presented.   It bears the following inscription :—

" Presented to the Rev. Henry Cooke, Moderator of the General Synod of Ulster, by a number of Presbyterians of the congregation of Comber, as a testimony of their respect for the knowledge, piety, and zeal with which he gave his testimony before the Committees of Parliament, and with which he defended it afterwards against the numerous and reiterated attacks that were made upon it."

Mr. Cooke's own congregation now also broke silence :—

" We, the session and congregation of Killyleagh, have refrained hitherto from interfering on the subject of your evidence before the Committee of the Lords.   We so refrained, inasmuch as we were in-cluded and represented in a public resolution of the Presbytery of Dromore, in support of your evidence, and also from the conviction that when you were personally known, your public and private cha-racter would raise you above contradiction.   But we do now feel ourselves imperatively called upon to come forward, not only in conse-quence of various statements which have from time to time appeared in some of the public journals, but more especially from the unwar-rantable attack made on you, as the Moderator of the Synod of Ulster, at a late aggregate meeting of the Roman Catholics, held in the city of Dublin, on which occasion a resolution was passed, condemning your evidence as ' false and unfounded.'   In opposition to said resolution, we feel ourselves called upon thus publicly to declare our conviction that in your evidence you gave a correct estimate of the political feelings of the Presbyterians of the North of Ireland. . . . . We gladly embrace this opportunity of testifying the high regard we bear you in your private character, and the value in which we hold your labours as our minister.   As a congregation, we have greatly increased under your ministry, owing, under the blessing of God, to your indefatigable labours in preaching, catechising, and exhorting throughout the parish."

This important document bears the signature, as Chairman, of James Heron, a member of one of the oldest and most respectable families in County Down—a family which transplanted to the soil of Ulster the enterprise and the faith of their Scottish forefathers.

But perhaps the most remarkable of all the testimonies borne to the importance and the faithfulness of Mr. Cooke's evidence, was that of the late Sir Robert Peel, at whose instigation the Royal Commission on Education, and the Committees of the Lords and Commons, were appointed. Sir Robert had given great attention to the state of Ireland. When Chief Secretary he had the fullest opportunity of obtaining authentic information, and no point escaped his watchful eye and inquiring mind. He was the last of our statesmen who seemed really to understand the condition of Ireland, and honestly to aim at its reform. Dr. Cooke long enjoyed the honour of his friendship, and their correspondence shows that his counsel was sought on all those great measures which Sir Robert Peel inaugurated for the benefit of this country. In 1825, Sir Robert writes, after discussing other matters of public importance :—" I cannot conclude this letter without assuring you that, although I read the observations which were made in Ireland upon the evidence which you had given before the Committees of Parliament, those observations did not weaken in the slightest degree, my confidence in the correctness of your statements, or in your high moral and professional character."

The annual meeting of Synod was now approaching. Mr. Cooke could scarcely look forward to it without some feelings of apprehension. Filling the Moderator's chair he was, to some extent, the representative of the Presbyterian Church. The honour of the Synod was involved in the nature of his public and official acts, during the year. He knew that the Arian party was still strong in influence. He knew that the majority of the Old Light party were still lukewarm. Little aid or sympathy could be expected from them. If threats could frighten him they were profusely employed. Dr. Bruce of Belfast, who

had shown himself such a true " Friend in need," and who had
got his reward, wrote on the 18th June with characteristic
irony :—" I sincerely congratulate our friend on his deliverance,
and hope that he will use the same caution and address at
Coleraine, where a more formidable trial awaits him.   There,
like Paul at Ephesus, he will have to fight with wild beasts.
If he come off unhurt I shall hail him a second Daniel and a
second Paul."   He did come off unhurt, and he attained besides
a higher place in the affections of all true Protestants than he
ever held before.

The Synod met in Coleraine on Tuesday, June 28th, 1825.
Mr. Cooke's opening sermon was a sign of the times.   It
pointed to dangers great and imminent which threatened the
very existence of the church.   It roused the members of the
Synod to a sense of their duty.   It summoned the Presbyterians of Ireland, as with trumpet note, to contend earnestly
for the faith once delivered to the Saints.   "Never before,
within the memory of man," says one who heard it, "had words
of such wondrous power and thrilling eloquence been heard
from Moderator's lips."   The text was Rev. iii. 1 and 2, " Thou
hast a name that thou livest, and art dead.   Be watchful, and
strengthen the things which remain, that are ready to die."

" The most important discovery in the Word of God," proceeds the
preacher, " is that of redemption by the Lord Jesus Christ from sin
and death and misery.   One of the most vital doctrines must therefore be what relates to the person and work of the Redeemer."

Then, after briefly sketching the views held by the various
sects of professing Christians on this great dogma, he concludes :—

" The power of a creature, however exalted, can never give life to
the church.   There is in the awakened conscience of the sinner a
fear that can find no repose but in the bosom of the Eternal, and
can put no confidence in any redemption but that which is effected
by the arm of Omnipotence.   The first movement of the life of hope

in the penitent sinner, and, consequently, of the life of holiness in the church, originates from receiving Christ as 'God manifest in the flesh.' "

With equal clearness he developes the teaching of Scripture regarding the person and work of the Holy Spirit, showing that the entire efficacy of religion upon the soul is due to Him. Then he adds : —

" These are the doctrines by whose mighty energies the Church of God arises to life and glory.   These are the doctrines that gave life to the labours of Paul, and of Peter, and of John, and the noble army of martyrs and confessors.   These are the principles, obscured during a long night of mental darkness, or entombed through ages of spiritual death, which again sprang to life in the morning of the Reformation, and propelled the life-pulse of their divinity through the renovated churches.   These are the living doctrines which warmed the hearts, and guided the pens, and gave eloquence to the tongues of Luther and Calvin, and Zwinglius, and Melanchthon, and Knox. These are the doctrines which, in more modern times, stirred within the souls of Wesley and Whitfield, when they burst irresistibly over those barriers of formality within which a cold, and lifeless, and almost heathenish theology had entrenched herself.   These are the doctrines by which they stirred up the life of God in the cold hearts of multitudes sleeping in sin and the shadow of death.   These are the doctrines which sent an Elliot, a Brainard, and a Schwartz, and a Vanderkemp, and a Martyn to the Indian, the Hottentot, the Hindoo, and the Persian.   These are the doctrines which wafted life around the globe, and made the scattered islands to blossom as the garden of God.   These are the doctrines by which the church shall live, unchanged by time, and shall hail the Redeemer in her hymns, and her sermons, and her prayers, when He shall come the second time without sin to salvation.   .   .   .   .

" It is a favourite object with those called philosophical Christians, to discard all importance from the belief of the truth, and to attach everything valuable to moral conduct.   And, indeed, could it be proved that genuine morality, having equally the love of God and man for its motive and its object, could exist without the belief of the truth, then might it be granted that the doctrines we believe are of little importance.   But so long as practice must arise from principle, the value of our outward conduct must be estimated by the inward principles from which it springs. The fact is, that whenever men begin to extol morality, and depreciate doctrinal truth, they are generally found to be equally strangers to both. They have a name to live in some partial and conventional virtues—virtues founded in pride and self-love, and which therefore are the parents of the most revolting crimes. Of this fact we have a remarkable instance in the case of the Pharisees. They prided themselves upon the unimpeachable correctness of their outward morality ; yet Our Saviour tells them : ' I know you that ye have not the love of God in you.' And the fruit of their morality was awfully exhibited in their persecution and crucifixion of the Lord of Life and Glory. The life of the church, produced by the Spirit of God, is truth in the understanding, the love of God in the heart, humility because of our unworthiness, watchfulness unto prayer, and holiness in all our conversation."

While dealing thus with fundamental doctrines, he did not overlook the practical, in its especial application to the state of his own church. Among " the things that remain " to it, he noticed a Gospel ministry, candidates for the ministry, ruling elders, ordinances, prayer, and the Word of God. Upon the last he said :—

" The Scriptures remain to us. In the days of Our Saviour the Scriptures were a book of examination, and an authority for appeal. In the course of years their authority was superseded and their light withheld. At the Reformation the Bible appeared as a prisoner unshackled from the thraldom of his dungeon. Its light issued forth from the gloom and damp of the cloister and the cell. It illumined palaces, it blazed in churches, it cheered the cottage of the labourer, and the workhouse of the artizan. It shone before the world a new sun in the heavens ; and before the radiance of its beams there fled every creature of night, and everything that loveth or maketh a lie."

He next referred to those things on which the church required to exercise new watchfulness ; specifying the training of ministers, the employment of licentiates to assist in the working of large congregations, and the establishment of missions at home and abroad. His remarks on the last point show how

broad and clear were his views regarding the church's duty :
" The plan I should suggest is that of a society for sending
some of our probationers to America, to preach the Gospel to
their Presbyterian brethren from Ireland, or from Scotland.
In America, it is well known, the number of congregations far
exceeds that of the candidates ; with us, the number of candidates far exceeds that of our congregations. . . . Since
then we know that too many congregations of Presbyterians
in the British American settlements are in want of ministers,
why not combine ourselves into a society to send out young
ministers of talent and piety, to furnish them with books, where
necessary for ministerial study, and to allow them a small
annuity till settled in congregations ? " Thus did his clear
foresight sketch, nearly a quarter of a century beforehand, that
plan which has since been adopted by the Presbyterian churches
of Ireland and Scotland, and which has been attended with
such signal blessings in the colonies of the British empire.

Another point he touched on with equal power and appropriateness :—

" Would you strengthen the things that remain, unsecularise
your clergy? The genuine description of a minister is to be found
in Acts vi. 4, where the Apostles announce :—' But we will give ourselves continually to prayer, and to the ministry of the Word.' Is it
not, on the contrary, a melancholy thing to see the description reversed,
and, ' We will give ourselves to worldly occupation,' appear to be substituted in its room ? Is it not a melancholy thing to see a youth
spend long years . . . in study. . . . to see him licensed,
elected, ordained ;—if after all this waste of time, accumulation of
learning, solemnity of dedication, the whole be found to terminate
only in forming the most intelligent farmer, or the most laborious
schoolmaster in the parish? Verily it were enough to make angels
weep to see such time, such acquirements, and such solemnities, come
to this termination."

The duties of Presbyteries were not overlooked ; and here,
too, Mr. Cooke indicated a line of action which has since been

adopted, and which has done much to infuse new life into the
Presbyterian church.

" Revive the primitive discipline of Visitation Presbyteries. A
revival of religion may fairly be expected when Presbyteries divest
themselves of the character of mere routine meetings, attending
to literary examinations, or the secularities of the church, and make
the business of vital religion the chief object of their inquiry, their
solicitude, and their discipline. For the effecting of this happy
revival, let the Church Courts turn their serious attention to the
religious statistics of their congregations. . . . Let Presbyteries
ascertain the number of families in each congregation, the number
of Bibles in each family; the state of family religion as evidenced by
family prayer; the number of communicants in each congregation;
the state of attendance upon catechisings. Thus will they be made
acquainted with the outward facts in which spiritual religion is
involved, and be enabled to apply remedies to disease, to minister
strength to the feeble, to stimulate the sluggish, and give additional
life to the exertions of the most active."

The concluding paragraphs were specially appropriate to the
body he addressed. They are scarcely less appropriate to the
state of a large section of the Protestant churches in these
lands at the present day.

" In all the pages of historic record we find the life of the church
endangered by two diseases. The first of these is, Conformity in church
rulers to the spirit and pursuits of the world. When the clergy of
a church become so conformed to the world, that in secularised
employment, frivolous amusements, epicurean indulgence, and idle
conversation, they so assimilate with the general picture of society,
that the eye of the most experienced searches in vain for the distinctive features of the primitive ministerial character ; or when
they are only distinguished from the crowd of busy men, by the
weekly routine of their allotted employment ; and when, with
intensity of application, they are bound down to the profitable but
perishable secularities of time, disregarding the imperishable riches
of their people's eternity: then is the time when their fellow-
labourers, who have not yet been fascinated by the spirit of the
world, should speak aloud in their ears, and awake them from their

fatal lethargy, and raise them from their earthly pursuits, and compel them to the reproduction of the talent which they have hid in the earth, that their souls may be saved in the day when their Lord cometh.

"The second disease that threatens the life of the church is a spirit of indifferentism about religious truth. The doctrines of the Gospel are of vital operation, and of paramount importance. To be indifferent about them is the first symptom of an infection which, if not remedied, must terminate in death. While Christians exercise charity towards the prejudices or faults of one another, it by no means follows that, in the exercise of this charity, they are to sacrifice the truth to the errors of a false philosophy or a spurious Gospel. The great basis on which this indifferentism is founded is the plausible and imposing proposition, 'that if we be *sincere* in our profession, it is no matter what we believe.' This dream about sincerity is a sad delusion. It reduces to one common level the religion of Jews, the Saviour of sinners, of Mahomet the Impostor, of the Brahmins of India, the Sophis of Persia, and the Cannibals of the South Seas. They are all sincere; therefore, all their religions are alike. It supersedes the necessity of searching the Scriptures for the mind of the Lord, or of praying for the light and guidance of His Spirit. It puts the sinner's sincerity in place of the atonement of Christ, and in place of the work of the Holy Spirit in purifying the heart. The Word of God tells us, with all possible plainness, 'except ye be converted,' 'except a man be born of water and of the Spirit,' 'ye cannot enter into the Kingdom of God.' But this specious indifferentism tells us at once, ' Mind none of these declarations ; for if a man be sincere, there is no doubt he will be saved.' God forbid I should undervalue real sincerity. It is an essential principle of vital Godliness. It was the principle of the disciples, when they left all to follow Christ; it was the principle of Paul, when he said, ' Lord, what wouldst Thou have me to do ? ' But the pretended sincerity against which I speak is the sincerity which begins in carelessness about religious opinions or practice, and then wishes to beguile others to a similar indifference. I speak of those men who, too much prejudiced to inquire, and too obstinate to be convinced of the truth as it is in Jesus, yet seek, under the plea of sincerity, a shelter for their voluntary errors. The sincerity of the Christian makes him a candid inquirer, and a humble receiver of the truth. His test of truth is not his own sincerity, but an appeal to the Scriptures, the standard of truth. His test of conduct is, not the declared sincerity of his

convictions of duty, but conformity to the will of God, with the
fruits of the Spirit in knowledge, righteousness, and true holiness.
This conformity is true evidence of the life of God in the soul, or in
the church; all other sincerity is pretended, and merely proves the
mental disease of those by whom it is pleaded in defence of their
aberrations."

The sermon made a profound impression. It prepared the way
for the discussion of those great questions which were to come
before the Synod. The *Belfast News-Letter* says :—

" When speaking of Luther, Calvin, and Zwinglius he expatiated
with great animation on the zeal, perseverance, energy, and effect
with which they inculcated the truths of the Gospel; and, in a strain
of eloquence seldom surpassed, he seemed to electrify the audience,
and carry them along with him in all his arguments and deductions.
We cannot attempt to give any detail at present of this powerful
discourse, which was listened to with the most profound silence. It
occupied two hours in delivery. Every corner of the meeting-house
was crowded to excess, and the outside of the doors and windows
was perfectly besieged by multitudes of people that could not gain
admission."

Among the first points discussed in the Synod was the ordination of Mr. Nelson, a licentiate of the Arian Presbytery of
Antrim, over the congregation of Dromore. It appeared that
Mr. Cooke had warned the Presbytery of Armagh, under whose
jurisdiction Dromore was placed, not to ordain Mr. Nelson, on
the ground that he had not completed a full college curriculum,
and that the Presbytery of Antrim was not in communion with
the Synod of Ulster. The warning was neglected. Mr. Nelson
was ordained, and the conduct of the Presbytery of Armagh
came under review. The debate was long and animated. Mr.
Cooke in a speech of great power, exposed the heretical doctrines held by the Presbytery of Antrim, especially as exhibited
in a volume of sermons recently published by Dr. Bruce, of
Belfast. He concluded in these solemn words :—

" Sooner shall I permit this right hand to be severed from my body than sign an act confirming the introduction of any man into the Synod who might infect it with Arian principles.   It has now come to this : we must put down Arianism, or Arianism will put us down."

These words were received with thunders of applause by the crowded assembly.   Notwithstanding the eloquent appeals of Messrs. Porter and Montgomery, a motion was carried to the effect that the conduct of the Presbytery of Armagh was highly reprehensible, and that the advice given to it by Mr. Cooke had been "well intended, judicious, and salutary."   After all, this was but a half-measure.   It showed the distracted state of feeling in the Synod.   The result, so far as Dromore was concerned, was calamitous; for that congregation was lost to orthodox Presbyterianism.

The next important subject of debate was Mr. Cooke's evidence before the committee of Parliament.   The excitement was now intense.   The House was crowded.   All felt that on the result of this debate depended the reign of Arianism in the Synod.   If Mr. Cooke's evidence should be condemned, as had been threatened and predicted, the New Light party would obtain a signal triumph.   If the evidence should be approved, the fall of Arian power was certain.

The debate was opened by Mr. Morell, of Ballibay, who moved—

"That the Synod, entertaining the highest respect for the character of their late Moderator, the Rev. Henry Cooke, do deprecate the unwarrantable attacks which have been made upon him regarding his evidence before the House of Lords."

The motion was strongly opposed by Mr. Montgomery.   Mr. Stewart, of Broughshane, followed.   He said their Moderator had been vilified and abused.   Some portions of the press, influenced by political feeling, had even denounced the Synod for electing such a man to an office so important.   At a meeting of Roman Catholics in the city of Dublin, where seven thousand people were said to have been present, Mr. Cooke's evidence was characterised as "false and unfounded;" and these words were embodied in a resolution thanking the Presbyterians of the north, who had come forward manfully to refute the testimony.

"This certainly required," he said, "the interference of the Synod. Their own character and respectability were involved, when their first public officer, whom they had clothed with the highest dignity, honour, and authority the Presbyterian Church could confer, was thus scandalously treated and maligned."

An amendment was proposed by Mr. Finlay, of Dundonald, to the following effect :—

"That, without giving any decision with regard to the testimony given by Mr. Cooke, various parts of it being matter of opinion on which wise and good men have differed, and on which we leave it to the world to judge, we feel ourselves called on to declare that we have the utmost confidence in his integrity, are convinced that he possesses an extensive knowledge of public opinion, and are firmly persuaded that he gave his testimony strictly according to the dictates of his conscience."

In supporting it Mr. Hay, of Derry, said that Mr. Cooke had been most grossly assailed; that the attacks had been only disgraceful to those who made them ; but that he could repose with confidence on the reputation he had gained in the Synod and the world, and the envenomed shafts aimed against him would fall innocuous to the ground. He thought the amendment proposed would satisfy Mr. Cooke, and should be adopted unanimously by the House.

Mr. Cooke at length rose to address the House. There was a momentary burst of applause, followed by a death-like stillness. All felt that a crisis had come. The power of Arianism in the Synod largely hung on the speech he was about to make. In language calm, clear, and temperate, he detailed the main points of his evidence. He stated and refuted *seriatim* the objections brought against it. As proofs of its accuracy, he appealed to the numerous addresses of thanks and congratulation sent to him from all parts of Ulster. Then, referring to the personal attacks of which he had been made the subject—attacks upon his character and truthfulness—he became more and more animated, until he finally burst forth in a strain of impassioned eloquence that electrified the assembly :—

"I have been loaded with obloquy. I have been charged with publicly degrading the high office to which you elected me. I have been threatened with the censure of the Synod. Yet I stand before you fearless, for I am conscious of rendering back my office clean and unsullied; and I know I can rely on the impartiality, the wisdom, and the justice of my fathers and brethren. I now stand in my native county; I stand in the Church in which I first preached the gospel; I stand in the midst of those reverend presbyters who first received me into the ministry; I stand in the presence of that august Synod which lately honoured me with the highest office in its gift; and here I this day fearlessly and scornfully repudiate the foul imputation cast upon me by the seven thousand Catholics of Dublin. I appeal to you, fathers and brethren, with whose censure I have been threatened, whether that evidence was 'false and unfounded.' I appeal to all around me—aye, even to those galleries, crowded with the free men of my native county, to whom I was told I dare not look lest a burst of indignation would overwhelm me—to you, to all, I confidently appeal for a unanimous and cordial verdict of acquittal."

A burst of enthusiastic applause followed these words. It was taken up again and again by the entire audience ; and it was re-echoed by the crowds assembled outside. The amendment was carried, almost without a dissentient voice. The first fatal blow was thus given to Arianism in the Synod of Ulster.

At a subsequent session a letter was read from the Board of Managers of the Belfast Institution, expressing their anxiety to do everything in their power to meet the wishes of the Synod, so as, if possible, to arrive at a satisfactory and permanent arrangement. Mr. Cooke thereupon moved a series of resolutions. He said his object was to secure peace, while preserving the faith of the Church. Public confidence had been shaken in the Institution ; he wished to re-establish it. The confidence of the Synod had been shaken ; he wished to place it on such a steadfast basis as would lead to a restoration of the Government grant. He had in his private negotiations met with a corresponding desire for conciliation, and he had freely yielded everything short of a compromise of principle. The resolutions he moved were adopted by the Synod, and had an important bearing on the subsequent history of the Institution. They were the means of preserving the connection between it and the Synod, and thus securing the attendance of students ; they were the means, too, of recovering the Government grant of 1,500l. a year. Unfortunately the managers of the Institution only adopted them in part, and did not even carry out in good faith the compromise which they themselves sketched. This led eventually to difficulties which ruined the collegiate department. The resolutions were as follows :—

" That so soon as the Moderator of this Synod shall learn that a Professor is to be chosen in the Institution, he shall advise the several presbyteries, and each presbytery shall appoint a minister and elder to meet the Moderator in Belfast ; and, after examining testimonials, give their opinion respecting the qualifications of the candidates ; which opinion the Moderator shall communicate to the electors, specifying the candidates whom they consider eligible.

" This Synod direct their committee that, in all cases of the election of Professors, they recommend to the electors none but persons of orthodox sentiments ; and do expect and trust that the managers of the Institution shall, in all cases of election, hold in view the opinion of the Synod, respecting the necessity of electing such persons to Professorships connected with the students of this Church."

Another important resolution was moved by Mr. Cooke. During his controversy with the Arians and the Institution it had been frequently affirmed by his opponents that the Presbytery of Antrim formed a part of, or was recognised ecclesiastically by, the Synod of Ulster. The Presbytery of Antrim was notoriously Arian ; some of its members were currently re-

ported to hold Socinian views.   It was true that in some
matters of finance, including the Widows' Fund, the two bodies
acted in concert ; but in all other respects they were distinct.
Mr. Cooke had affirmed this fact ; others had called it in question.   To set the point at rest, the following resolution was
put to the House, and carried with only one dissentient voice :—
" That, in the year 1726, the Presbytery of Antrim were separated from the General Synod of Ulster, and have not since
that period held any ecclesiastical connection with the Synod
in matters of doctrine, discipline, or jurisdiction."

At the meeting in 1825, the first Code of Laws framed by the
Synod of Ulster was formally sanctioned.   It had been projected so far back as the beginning of the century.   In 1810, a
small committee was appointed to prepare it.   They gave in a
report in 1815, when a fragmentary draft Code was printed.
The work was recommitted to them, but it proceeded slowly.
In 1819, Mr. Cooke was added to the committee, and from that
time the chief labour devolved upon him.   He was eminently
qualified for the task.   He had an acute logical mind ; he had
extensive legal knowledge ; he was intimately acquainted with
the history of the Church, and with the forms of procedure
sanctioned by long practice in its courts.   In 1821, a draft
copy was presented to the Synod and ordered to be printed,
and a proof supplied to each member for revision.   New difficulties arose, especially in regard to the law of subscription,
which the Church wished henceforth to enjoin on all its office-
bearers.   In 1824, Mr. Cooke, apparently worn out by years
of strife, reluctantly consented to a compromise, which left it
in the power of each presbytery to appoint such formula of
subscription as it might deem right.   The Code, as thus
amended, was adopted, and ordered to be published under the
care of Mr. Cooke and five others.   This editorial committee
again deemed it necessary to make certain alterations and additions, which were submitted to the Synod in 1825, and finally
approved of.   The Synod knew the great amount of time and
labour Mr. Cooke had expended on the Code, and the rare

talent he had displayed in the work ; the following resolution
was, therefore, passed by acclamation :—

"That the warm thanks of the Synod be returned to the committee, particularly to Mr. Cooke, for the zeal, diligence, and ability
evinced by them in the discharge of their laborious duty."

The importance of this work on "The Constitution and
Discipline of the Presbyterian Church" cannot be over-esti-
mated. The Church had now an authoritative directory for
the due celebration of ordinances and the performance of
ministerial duties. Hitherto a certain degree of laxity had
prevailed, especially in relation to the training of candidates
for the ministry, and to licence and ordination. Some presbyteries required unqualified subscription to the Westminster
Standards ; others did not. Students and licentiates of
doubtful orthodoxy were thus enabled to gain admission into
the Church ; and men holding Arian views were occasionally
ordained to the ministry and eldership. Under the new Code
the spread of heresy became almost impossible. The Code, it
is true, was not perfect. It provided that "Presbyteries, before they license candidates to preach the gospel, shall ascertain the soundness of their faith, either by requiring subscription to the Westminster Confession of Faith, or by such
examinations as they shall consider best adapted to this purpose." The principle was laid down that all candidates should
be sound in the faith ; and presbyteries were required to test
their soundness. This did not go the whole length of unqualified subscription, but it was a great step in advance, and it prepared the way for a still greater. Even though a presbytery,
through Arian influence, should decline to require absolute
subscription, any orthodox member had it in his power, under
the new Code, to institute a searching investigation into the
doctrinal views of each candidate. The Arian party were
satisfied with the enactment, or at least professed to be so,
accepting it as a compromise. Mr. Cooke, with clearer perception, saw how it would gradually purge the Church, especi-

ally under the now awakened zeal and watchfulness of the
orthodox party. He had, himself, proclaimed open war with
Arianism. He had publicly declared his intention to put it
down. Here he had prepared, with the formal sanction of
Arians themselves, an instrument which, in skilful hands, would
accomplish his purpose. Had his labours now ceased, he
would have been entitled to the lasting gratitude of his Church,
and to the honoured name of Reformer.

Even his enemies were forced to acknowledge the enthusiasm
with which he laboured, and the results to which his labours
must eventually lead. A writer in the *Christian Moderator*,
the organ of the Arian party, reviewing Mr. Cooke's sermon
and the proceedings of the Synod at Coleraine, says :—" Let
the consequences of the present excited state of feeling in the
Synod of Ulster be what they may, let them be adverse, or let
them be prosperous, the principal part of the blame or the
praise, the merit or the demerit, will rest on the head of the
Rev. Henry Cooke. He is the man who sounded the earliest
note of alarm. He it is who blew the first, the loudest, and
the longest blast—a blast with which the walls of our Church
still continue to reverberate. So great is his ardour, that he
roams, like Peter the Hermit, from one place to another,
preaching a crusade against Arianism." It was true : Mr.
Cooke did preach a crusade against Arianism. And he never
desisted until the forces he gathered round him, and inspired
with his own ardour, achieved the freedom and the purity of
his Church.

CHAPTER VI.

1825—1828.

Opposition to Mr. Cooke's Political and Ecclesiastical Principles—Determination to eradicate Arianism from the Synod of Ulster—Presentation of Plate by People of Belfast—Dangerous Illness—Deep religious Impressions—Meets M. Malan, of Geneva—Visit to Lord Mount-Cashell—Letters to Mrs. Cooke —Views on Personal Religion—Correspondence with Mr. Stewart, Mr. Kydd, and others—Meeting of Synod in Strabane—Resolution requiring Declaration of Belief in the Trinity—Speeches of Messrs. Montgomery, Stewart, and Cooke—Encounter with Rev. H. Brooke—Letters of Lord Mount-Cashell— Controversy with Archibald Hamilton Rowan—Scene in Killyleagh Church —Ministry in Killyleagh—Letter to a young Clergyman.

Mr. Cooke had for so far triumphed over all opposition. Alone and unaided he had defeated, if not silenced, a host of noisy, inveterate, and in some cases unscrupulous assailants. His strong political principles, formed, as has been seen, in early youth, combined with theological opinions still stronger, made him obnoxious to a large majority of the people of Ireland. His opposition to the revolutionary views and dangerous agitation of O'Connell was scarcely less determined than his opposition to Arianism. He was a true son of the Church of Scotland, firm in his allegiance to Throne and Constitution, as well as to the doctrines and ecclesiastical polity developed by Knox. His principles had now become known throughout Ireland. His ability to defend and promote them was admitted. It was felt that he was destined to be a leader, and that his rule, unless checked, must result in the overthrow of Arianism in the Synod, and the consolidation of constitutional principles in Ulster. Hence the origin of all the opposition he encountered, and of all the obloquy heaped upon him. With the New Light party it was a struggle for

life. They had hitherto ruled in the Synod. Though their
doctrines had not gained ground among the people, their
influence in the church courts had increased to such an
extent that the very foundations of the faith were shaken, and
the safeguards of orthodoxy all but destroyed. Timid men
trembled before the frown of Porter, the eloquence of Montgomery, and the polished satire of Bruce. Some of the ablest
among the orthodox party were content with peace at any
price. Others were not yet educated up to the necessity of
unqualified subscription, or entire separation from Arianism ;
others were lazily indifferent both as to the present state and
future prospects of their Church. Mr. Cooke saw all this ; and
he was the first who resolved on thorough reform. He knew
how severe would be the conflict, and he had made preparation for it. He stood alone ; yet with characteristic courage
he persevered. He made no secret of his object. He announced it publicly in the Synod at Coleraine :—" We must
put down Arianism, or Arianism will put us down."

In the Synod, among his brethren of the ministry, Mr.
Cooke found none who thoroughly sympathised with him.
But the great body of the Presbyterian laity were on his side.
He was already the most popular man in Ulster. When
assailed by the Arians of the north, and denounced by the
Roman Catholics of Dublin and the south, votes of confidence
and addresses of congratulation were forwarded to him by
presbyteries and congregations. In Belfast he was a special
favourite. He was the adopted leader of a rising party. His
friends there resolved to give him a substantial token of their
esteem. Accordingly, after the close of his eventful year of
office, they presented him with a service of plate, inscribed as
follows :—

" A number of the inhabitants of Belfast, impressed with a deep
sense of the sterling worth and talents of the Rev. Henry Cooke, A.M.,
Presbyterian Minister of Killyleagh, late Moderator of the General
Synod of Ulster, present to him a service of plate, as a testimonial
of the high estimate in which they justly hold his character as a

scholar and a philanthropist, a useful, zealous, and indefatigable
preacher of the gospel, and a firm supporter of orthodox principles.
1826."

But the strain upon body and mind during his Moderator-
ship had been too much for him.   His health gradually gave
way.   His strong will struggled long against the disease which
was preying upon his constitution.   He still responded to the
frequent calls for charity sermons and platform addresses.   At
length his strength failed ; he could work no more, and for a
time life was despaired of.   There is a precious record of this
period, which proves how real a comforter the Bible becomes
in the darkest hours of human suffering.   Writing to a friend,
when recovery seemed all but hopeless, and when death and
eternity were before him, Mr. Cooke says :—" I have never
fully realised the preciousness of my Saviour's words, and the
joy inspired by His promises, until now.   My body is weak ;
but I feel Him by me, in me, whispering sweetly, ' I will never
leave thee;' ' My strength is sufficient for thee.'   I am in pain,
but He soothes my pain with the comforting words—' The
sufferings of this present time are not worthy to be compared
with the glory which shall be revealed in us.'   I look on my
wife and my little children, and my heart almost fails; again
my Saviour comes with the blessed assurance, ' A Father of
the fatherless, and a Judge of the widows, is God.'   I see the
dangers of my poor Church, and I tremble for her future ; still
Jesus reminds me of His promises, ' Fear not, little flock ; '
' All power is given to me in heaven and in earth. . . . And
lo, I am with you alway, even unto the end of the world.'
The horror of death flashes for a moment before my mind,
I tremble ; but then I hear, and in faith I can re-echo,
the triumphant exclamation, ' O death, where is thy sting ?   O
grave, where is thy victory ? . . . Thanks be unto God which
giveth us the victory through our Lord Jesus Christ.'   Whatever be the issue, it is in the hands, and I am in the hands, of
my loving heavenly Father ; and I can say with the Psalmist,

' It is good for me that I have been afflicted, that I might learn Thy statutes.' "

In July, 1826, he went to Dublin to obtain medical advice ; and he found a home in the house of his friend, Dr. M'Dowel. Under the good hand of God his illness proved a blessing, not to himself merely, but to others. The stormy scenes in which he had taken part during four years had absorbed nearly all his time, and had largely drawn away his thoughts from the higher concerns of personal religion. Now that physical weakness had removed him from the strife of political and religious controversy, he had time for reflection. His letters show how deep and solemn his reflections were. In Dublin he met, for the first time, M. Malan, of Geneva. They were kindred spirits ; and they took sweet counsel together. He wrote to Mrs. Cooke, on August 2nd, " I am not better, but could not expect to be so in so short a time. My appetite is pretty good, and, thank God, my spirits are excellent. I have been much pleased, and I hope blessed, by my intercourse with M. Malan. I long to be home with you, to explain to you his plain, simple, and delightful views of the Gospel of our Saviour. I believe my light, comfort, hope, and heart are all improved by my intercourse with him. I long to see you enjoy the same happy assurance in the Lord." On the 4th he again writes— " I am going this evening to Lord Mount-Cashell's, and intend staying there for a fortnight, and hope to return to you in better health. But as to my poor body, let the Lord do as He will. He has saved my soul from doubt, darkness, fear, and the power of sin. I am my Saviour's now. I shall be with Him through eternity. Oh ! how I do long to see and hear you speak the same words of joy which in true faith I am now enabled, by the grace of God my Saviour, to address to you. Read 1 John v. 1, and see if you believe it all. If you really believe that Jesus is the Christ, then are you ' born of God.' But you will say, I have a weak, sinful heart, and cannot believe I am born of God till I feel my heart better. Nay, nay, the simple question is, Do you believe the testimony of

God, who says that 'Whosoever believeth that Jesus is the
Christ is born of God'? If so, then you will see that, being a
child of God, you can pray for grace; you can pray against
sin; you can conquer all the enemies of your heart through
Christ strengthening you. Pray for me that my faith fail not,
as I pray for you that God may keep you and my little ones
in peace. Read also Rom. v. 1. Have you peace with God?
Then you cannot be troubled nor in fear. For, 'if God be for
us, who can be against us?' May God keep you in faith, love,
and peace!"

Lord Mount-Cashell, hearing of Mr. Cooke's illness, and
knowing the harassing controversies and labours into which he
was necessarily thrown in Ulster, took him away to the south.
There, in the quiet mansion, and amid the beautiful scenery of
Moore Park, he found that repose which, under God, was instrumental in restoring health. There he found something still
better than rest of body. He found a family deeply imbued
with the principles of a living Christianity, and striving to
diffuse them among an ignorant and superstitious populace.
The visit was mutually profitable. The piety of Lord and
Lady Mount-Cashell was refreshing to the weary spirit of Mr.
Cooke; while his theological and historical knowledge proved
invaluable to them. A few days after his arrival a meeting of
the Bible Society was held at Kilworth, a village close to the
park. It was largely attended by Roman Catholics; and Mr.
Cooke delivered an eloquent and touching address. Of course
opposition was raised. The Society was denounced by the
priests. Subscriptions were not only refused, but attempts
were made to show that the refusal was justified by the laws of
the Church. This called forth an able letter from Lord Mount-
Cashell. It was written during Mr. Cooke's visit, and appears
to bear, in more than one passage, the impress of his hand.
It had a wide circulation, and made a deep impression on the
minds of those for whom it was chiefly intended.

Mr. Cooke's letters to his wife while at Moore Park continued to breathe the same spirit of earnest piety and confidence

in Christ.   In regard to personal experience in religion Mr.
Cooke was never demonstrative.   He shrunk with a keen sen-
sitiveness from everything which might bear the semblance of
ostentation, whether in act or word.   His temper was naturally
cheerful ; his wit was ready and brilliant ; his range of
knowledge was immense ; and his conversational powers were
unsurpassed.   He was the very life of the society in which he
moved.   He never intruded his religious views at inopportune
moments ; but he has often, by a well-turned remark or a
short incisive argument, silenced a scoffer, and put to shame a
flippant gainsayer.   It was only in the privacy of his own
family circle, or in the society of some old and attached friend,
that he gave full expression to his religious convictions.   Even
then he spoke with reserve.   There was nothing of cant,
nothing of enthusiasm, nothing of ostentation.   Every word
was suggestive of humility and childlike faith.   The same
characteristics pervade his correspondence.   To Mrs. Cooke,
and some members of his family, he may reveal the workings
of his heart ; but to an ordinary correspondent, never.   In his
view, religious feelings were too sacred to be thrown broadcast
over the world.   He would never unnecessarily venture on a
remark that might provoke a sneer from the scoffer, or a smile
from the thoughtless.   In this respect he never either wrote or
acted from a desire for publicity.   He must know and feel that
the world was excluded ; that heart was communing with heart
for mutual profit, in the presence of a heart-searching God,
ere he would utter a word, or write a line, such as we see in
these letters.

" Moore Park, 12th August, 1826.

" I am not yet better than when I left you, so far as this
poor body is concerned ; but, so far as my soul is concerned, I
am infinitely more healthful than I have been for months or
years.   The good Lord has with more light shined into my
darkened heart, and called me into the marvellous liberty of
the sons of God.   In spite of my sins, my fears, and all

Satan's temptations, I remain and rest upon God's record of
His Son. I take His salvation as a gift. It is finished. I am
justified, and that freely, by His grace, and I have peace with
God. I have not seen my Saviour; but I do love Him,
and rejoice in Him with joy unspeakable and full of glory,
receiving the end of my faith, the salvation of my soul.
All that I desire for you and my dear children is, that we
may be partakers together of grace here and of glory hereafter.

" So far as the world can make any one happy, I am happy
here. This is a superb place. The planting and the grounds
are magnificent. The demesne is very extensive—finely
wooded with giant trees, as well as young plantations. The
walks are endless, with seats at every winding and in many a
sweet recess. A noble stream flows through it; and there is a
spring in a romantic spot, which might have been the prototype
of the Fountain of the Spirit, in the ' Bride of Lammermoor.'
There is a grand old ruin, once the residence of the White
Knights—Lord Mount-Cashell's ancestors, who lived as bold
feudal chiefs, and held by the sword what they won by the
sword.

" Lord and Lady Mount-Cashell are in the highest degree
kind and amiable. They seem to think me, in my present delicate health, as intended not to touch the ground with my
feet. They will not permit me to move without a carriage, so
that I almost begin to realise the fancy I have often mentioned
to Rowan, that I had but one symptom of nobility about me,
and that was my love of a carriage as the only bearable mode
of conveyance. In the family there are three young ladies, of
the name of ——, one handsome, all amiable, especially as
partakers of God's grace and heirs of His kingdom. I have
seldom met their equals. Such gentleness; such simplicity;
such love of Christ; such teachable spirits; such unfeigned
humility; such zeal to do good; such cheerfulness! They are
to me as sisters in Christ, and are as careful of my poor health
as if they depended upon me for existence. Tell Rowan how

I enjoy this society. We have ease without familiarity; we have elegance without forgetting our Saviour.

" On Thursday, we had a meeting of the Bible Society in Fermoy. We had Mr. Pope. He is a delightful man. He is a Goliath trusting in the God of Israel. I spoke on the occasion. I was nearly thrown out at first by observing that, when introduced to the meeting, every eye was turned on me with such attention as almost overwhelmed me. This might once have made me vain; now it makes me pray for humility. May God enable me to dedicate the talents He has given me to His glory, and to know nothing but Jesus and Him crucified. It is vain to suppose myself ignorant that God has given me a portion of eloquence; but I should rather be dumb for ever than be proud of His gifts. I shall, by His grace, employ the gift in His service, if it please Him to continue the power to employ it. . . . . . My poor body may never be strong enough again; but I am not without hope. God, indeed, has no need of me; but there is work for some one in Ulster. 'Lord,' I say, 'if it be Thy will, send me. If not, take me to Thyself, or use me as a mere hewer of wood and drawer of water, if so be that thus I may honour and win Christ.' 'If so be,' I say not in doubt of God's promise, but in hope of His employment. Oh! how I long for the honour of bringing souls to the Lord. I never rightly or fully knew the Lord before. I had heard of Him with the hearing of the ear, but now mine eye seeth Him; wherefore I abhor myself, but adore and love Him."

" MOORE PARK, 14th *August*, 1826.

" I am inclined in unbelief to say, I hope my heart is changed; but God's record tells me I know it. Like Abraham, who in hope believed against hope, so I, in faith of God's promise, will believe even against the fears and faltering evidence of my own heart. Now faith is the victory that overcometh the world; so in Christ's strength I will fight for the victory, not as one who beateth the air, but as one who relies upon God, and therefore must succeed. . . . . May Father, Son, and Holy Spirit make me meet for the inheritance of the saints in light, and give me you and my children companions of my journey Zionward !

" Among the many beauties of this place is the river, which runs in a deep valley, with holms of rich turf along its borders ; and beyond these rise high, steep, and rugged banks of limestone, planted with noble trees, and having walks running along them in all directions, wherever a path can be found or cut. Here I have been wandering this morning, thinking of you, praying for you, hoping God would restore me to you in better health. Poorly as I have been, I could not remain longer silent ; so yesterday I preached in Kilworth and Fermoy—in the latter to an audience of three or four hundred people. Oh! that the Lord would strengthen me to testify the grace of the gospel, and to preach a finished salvation for sinners — present, not future — enjoyed, not hoped for ! To me, to live is Christ ; to die is gain. I shall join my Lord. Oh! my good Lord, give me my dear wife and children, and many other souls, as my crown of rejoicing in that day !

"I take it that among God's greatest blessings to me has been my present journey. It was one in which you were earnest for my health's sake ; and it has brought a spiritual blessing of light, and life, and love in Christ. First, I spent so many happy days in the midst of that heavenly family at Mount Panther ; then at Lord Roden's, where every word was purity and peace ; then with that man of God, Malan ; then I was brought to this seat of meditation, where I have sweet intercourse with kindred spirits, and where everything is done for me that Christian kindness could devise, or Christian hospitality proffer. In the midst of it all, too, I have still as much opportunity of teaching, of exercising my office, as keeps my mind in constant exercise. In all this you must see, as I see, the wonderful mercy of God. In soul and body He is preparing me to return to my duties and difficulties."

" After much anxiety, I have at last received your letter. I trust in God my little ones are all better. I am not myself much better; but still mending. I am going to-morrow to meet Captain Gordon and Mr. Pope at Donneraile, at a meeting of the Hibernian School Society, and I am pressed to go to Cork to a meeting of the Church Missionary Society; and, thanks be to God, I am earnestly desired to be present at Fermoy again, although I had bade them farewell. Oh! there is a power and a demonstration in the doctrine of a full and finished salvation that I never felt in all its force before. It has opened my heart, and loosened my tongue in private also, so that yesterday I believe I spoke of it not less than five or six hours, reasoning out of the Scriptures—convincing some and shaking others. It is the first doctrine I ever saw draw tears in private from the listener. My heart is full of it. The Lord keep me steadfast and immovable, that I may abound in the work of the Lord. Surely, by means of it, the good Lord has freed me from many temptations, and given me a permanent feeling of purity and peace I never knew before; and an earnest spirit of prayer against sin; and a confidence in His mercy and love; and a love of my Saviour, and a love of His people, that were all at one time almost strangers to my heart. Oh! that I might praise Him as I ought! Unseen, I love Him—unseen, I rejoice in Him. He loved me from everlasting, and no one is able to pluck me out of His Father's hand. I seek all things from Him in prayer, nothing doubting that what I ask, agreeable to His will, He will assuredly bestow."

" I shall leave this happy place to-morrow. But you are not to expect me before next week, as I go by Donaghadee to open the new church. . . . . After this you may expect me to stay at home without moving. The Lord knoweth whether I shall ever be able to move much. I am not im-

proving; but I am not worse. Thank God, to me to live is
Christ—to die is gain. May the good Lord bless you and all
our little ones! My soul is in constant happiness; I rejoice
in my Saviour. I know whom I have trusted, and am persuaded that He is able to keep what I have committed to Him
against that day."

Mr. Cooke's residence at Moore Park was pleasant and
profitable, not to himself alone, but to his kind hosts, and
others who had then the privilege of enjoying their hospitality.
It was profitable to large numbers who heard his eloquent
sermons and speeches in and around Kilworth and Fermoy.
This is shown by the following extract from a letter of Lord
Mount-Cashell, dated 30th January, 1827:—" The impression
you made here on the public mind is still talked of. You have
shaken the foundations of bigotry and superstition in many
hearts, and if you could have remained a little longer, I think
great and lasting effects would have followed. No doubt where-
ever you preach the same thing has occurred. But I can judge
best by what falls under my own eye, and I wish most earnestly
you may be able to come and pay us a visit this next summer,
about the time of the anniversary of our Bible meetings in
Fermoy. I shall say nothing about the pleasure we shall feel
to see you again, for I cannot express it in the way I could
wish. But in my invitation I go upon stronger grounds. I
beg of you to come for the welfare of perhaps eventually thousands, and I know the love of God will constrain you, if your
bodily health will permit it. I am happy to tell you, that long
before I had the pleasure of hearing from you I had established
morning and evening prayers in this house. All my servants,
whether Protestants or Romanists, attend. In the morning I
read to them a chapter out of the Old and New Testaments,
and explain some of the most striking passages. This has
done much good, and has evidently made an impression on the
minds of many Roman Catholic hearers. The priest is, of
course, displeased, and has denied them the sacrament; but

they remain steady. There is at this moment, I think, a far greater spirit of inquiry than last year. . . . Lady Mount-Cashell desires her sincere regards to you. She hopes most earnestly to hear of your being restored to good health. May I beseech of you not to overwork yourself. Your life is precious to Ireland ; and the good you may effect at this present moment will never compensate for the loss of that you would be able to effect if once more you could regain strength and vigour of body."

The letters of Lady Mount-Cashell to Mr. Cooke are still more expressive of deep thankfulness for the good he effected, and the ardent spiritual feelings which he was able to inspire in the hearts of all with whom he associated. These letters are so tender, so touching, so full of grateful mementos of Mr. Cooke's wise counsels and instructions, that it is with reluctance I withhold them.

Mr. Stewart, of Broughshane, visited Moore Park in the November following. He, too, heard much of Mr. Cooke's labours there, and of the wonderful impressions he made upon all classes. He thus writes to his old college friend :—" The Great Master of the labourers has given you a blessed success here as elsewhere. You have mightily smoothed my way." Mr. Stewart was afraid, however, from what he heard from Lord Mount-Cashell and others, that Dr. Malan's intercourse with Mr. Cooke had produced a dangerous change in some of his religious principles. He feared that while his heart had been impressed by the earnest Frenchman, his views regarding faith, and its evidences and fruits, had been seriously changed. Mr. Stewart wrote to Mr. Cooke for full information, stating his fears with all the plainness of friendship. In reply, Mr. Cooke detailed his own views and those of Dr. Malan. Mr. Stewart's answer to this letter was characteristic. He wrote from Moore Park, and is, as usual, clear, logical, and exhaustive in his treatment of the points raised. He agrees with Mr. Cooke in all essential doctrines ; he gives him full credit for unvarying and untainted orthodoxy. Yet still he is

not entirely satisfied. The zeal and enthusiasm of his early
friend are to him inexplicable. He cannot account for them;
and though he can detect no flaw in doctrine, he still believes
that so much enthusiasm scarcely accords with the staid
sobriety of sound Calvinistic theology.

Mr. Cooke's health remained delicate during the autumn of
1826. His recovery was very slow; and though he continued
to discharge many public duties, to animate the little party of
orthodox men which he had succeeded in organising, his best
friends feared that his labours were nearly ended. In December
he began to revive ; but the unceasing hostility to which he was
exposed retarded his recovery. His eloquent advocacy of the
Bible Society had brought him into conflict with the Roman
Catholic clergy; his political principles had excited the enmity
of the Roman Catholic laity ; and his triumphant defence of
orthodox truth had exposed him to assaults from every weapon
which Arianism could wield. The following extract of a letter
from the Rev. Mr. Kydd, minister of Boveva, will show something of the character of that opposition against which he had
to battle. After referring to the exertions made by members
of the Episcopal Church against Popery and infidelity, he
says :—" Are we asleep ? Or are we cast aside as unfit or
unworthy to be employed by the Master ? One or other of
these seems to be the case. We are formal, prayerless, lifeless—with scarcely even a name to live ; whilst on the Church
of England there has evidently been poured out a spirit of
grace and supplication. The dry bones in her have been
breathed upon, and we see the effect of the Spirit's power.
We have amongst us a number of Arians and Socinians, sufficient not only to paralyse our exertions, but to bring down
upon us God's wrath. ' If any man,' says the Apostle, ' love
not the Lord Jesus, let him be anathema.' Look at Bruce's
Sermons. Yet a Covenanter has to answer them. Look at
the periodical called ' The Christian Moderator,' encouraged,
supported, and written for by Porter, a minister of our own
synod. A more wicked production does not issue from the

press. With Bruce we have nothing to do, but with Porter we have. He is a writer for 'The Christian Moderator,' of which his own son is acknowledged editor. In it he has published more abuse of the Synod of Ulster than all its other enemies put together. He charges them, a few Arians excepted, with being ignorant, illiterate fools, devoid of common sense, and, to use his own elegant language, 'brainless skulls.' I mention these things that you may think them over, and see if this man ought longer to hold the situation of Clerk to the Synod of Ulster. Write to me soon. Union is strength. And when we find so many combining against the Lord and His Anointed, it does become the true friends of Jesus to unite for their defence."

The annual meeting of the Synod in 1827 was looked forward to with intense interest and anxiety. Both parties mustered their forces, and prepared for a struggle. The Reports of the Parliamentary Committees were now before the public, and the revelations they contained regarding Arianism attracted the attention of the whole Presbyterian Church. It had been long known that Arianism existed in the Synod; but hitherto it had generally been exhibited in a negative aspect. Its advocates were known as Non-subscribers. They refused to sign any confession, or to acknowledge their belief in any doctrine. They refused to answer any question regarding their faith, whether put by individuals or Church Courts. Now, before a Committee of Parliament, the Rev. William Porter, Clerk of Synod, avowed himself an Arian. He affirmed that there were " more real Arians than professed ones " in the Synod. He stated that Arianism was gaining ground " among the thinking few." Such statements could not be passed over in silence. When Dr. Bruce wrote, in the Preface to his volume of " Sermons," that the principles advocated in them were making extensive, though silent, progress in the Synod of Ulster, that body, at its meeting in 1824, gave a public and authoritative contradiction to the assertion. Dr. Bruce was a member of the Presbytery of Antrim, and the

Synod had no jurisdiction over him. Mr. Porter was a minister of its own; he held the responsible office of Clerk. His bold avowal, therefore, seemed to challenge investigation. Mr. Cooke felt that it was a public defiance of his famous manifesto, which had become the watchword of the Old Light party :—" We must put Arianism down, or Arianism will put us down."

The Synod met at Strabane. The Rev. J. Seaton Reid, afterwards Professor of Church History in the University of Glasgow, was elected moderator. As soon as the meeting was constituted, Mr. Magill, of Antrim, moved,—

"That the Rev. William Porter, having publicly avowed himself to be an Arian, be no longer continued clerk."

The debate which followed was long and stormy. The motion was not approved of by all the Old Light party. It gave an advantage to the Arians of which they were not slow to avail themselves. It was admitted that Mr. Porter had discharged with fidelity the duties of his office. There was nothing in that office, it was urged, specially requiring orthodoxy of faith. If a man were fit to be a minister of the body, there was nothing, so far as creed was concerned, to unfit him for the clerkship. An amendment was, therefore, proposed to the effect that,—

" Although this Synod highly disapproves of Arianism, yet Mr. Porter having always discharged his duties of clerk with ability and fidelity, that he be continued in his office."

Neither motion nor amendment satisfied Mr. Cooke. He would have no half measures. He desired thorough reform. He declared the time had come for separation. He, therefore, proposed that both motion and amendment be withdrawn, and that a resolution be framed for the separation of Orthodox and Arians. The proposal was rejected; and a new amendment, drafted by Mr. Stewart, of Broughshane, was carried. It declared,—

" That the Synod had heard Mr. Porter's avowal of Arianism with the deepest regret, that it expressed its high disapprobation; yet, as the removal of the clerk from office on this account might be construed into persecution for the sake of opinion, they do not consider it expedient to remove him."

A protest was immediately entered by Mr. Cooke, mainly on the grounds that it was inconsistent with the constitution and injurious to the religious interests of the church, that Arians should be either members or officers of its courts ; and that Mr. Porter's character as an Arian, being now matter of notoriety and record, his continuance in office as clerk was deeply injurious to the religious character of the body.   The protest was signed by forty-one ministers and fourteen elders—about one-third of the members present.

Mr. Cooke was not satisfied.   He resolved upon a more decisive step ; and Mr. Porter's evidence gave him fitting opportunity.   He had sworn that the Synod of Ulster contained " more real Arians than professed ones."   Mr. Cooke saw the advantage the statement gave him.   The character of the Synod was involved.   The honesty—the truthfulness of every member was indirectly questioned.   Orthodox men would not hesitate to state their opinions, and thus free themselves from a foul charge.   He, therefore, moved as follows :—

" Whereas some members of the Synod have made open profession of Arian sentiments ; and whereas Mr. Porter, in his evidence before the Commissioners of Education Inquiry, has declared that, ' in his opinion, there are more real than professed Arians in this body ;' and whereas Mr. Cooke, in his evidence before the said Commissioners, has declared his opinion, ' that there are, to the best of his knowledge, thirty-five Arians amongst us, and that very few of them would be willing to acknowledge it ;' and whereas Dr. Hanna, on a similar examination, has declared his opinion, ' that he presumes there are Arians amongst us,' we do hold it absolutely incumbent on us, for the purpose of affording a public testimony to the truth, as well as of vindicating our religious character as individuals, to declare that we do most firmly hold and believe the doctrine concerning the nature of God, contained in these words of the Westminster Shorter Catechism, namely, ' That there are three persons in the Godhead, the Father, the Son, and the Holy Ghost and these three are one God, the same in substance, equal in power and glory ; ' and that we do affix our signatures to this declaration in the minutes of Synod ; and that the Moderator be instructed to issue a circular letter to the absent members of the Synod, in order to afford them an opportunity of forwarding to him their signatures of concurrence, before the printing of the minutes."

A debate followed, which for power, eloquence, and intensity of excitement, had never been equalled in the body. The leading men on both sides put forth their strength. The syren song of peace, which had so long served to calm the troubled waters of controversy, was heard no more. Each speaker felt that truth and religious consistency must be vindicated at whatever cost. The debate began on Thursday and continued during Friday and Saturday. Various amendments were moved and negatived. On Saturday, after some consultation among the Orthodox party, and to overcome a point of order which had been raised, it was agreed that the latter part of the original motion should be modified as follows :—

" That the members now absent be, and are hereby, directed to attend the next meeting of Synod, to express their belief concerning the foregoing doctrine ; and that such of them as do not attend shall send to said meeting an explicit declaration of their sentiments on this important point, which declaration shall be addressed to the clerk."

The only change, therefore, was a verbal declaration instead of a written one. The one was as effective as the other so far as Mr. Cooke's object was concerned.

On Saturday, after the modification of Mr. Cooke's motion, the Rev. Henry Montgomery rose to address the house. His appearance was hailed by his friends as the signal of victory. His oratorical powers were well known, and had already, on more than one occasion, swayed the Synod. He now surpassed all former efforts. His declamations and appeals electrified the assembly. The folly of man-made creeds, and the blessings of unity and peace, were his themes. The house was crowded to excess. Every hearer hung enchanted on the lips of the orator. When he concluded he was greeted with thunders of applause. The excitement was so intense—the visible effect produced so great, that many Orthodox men began to despair. Mr. Stewart, of Broughshane, with much difficulty obtained a hearing. His speech was calm, cold, and as usual brief. But every sentence told. Like a mental anatomist he dissected the oration of his brilliant antagonist. He laid bare every sophism. He stripped each fallacy of its gorgeous clothing, and exhibited it in its naked deformity. He demonstrated to every thinking man that, in so far as argument was concerned, the speech of Mr. Montgomery was only a splendid failure.

The debate was closed by Mr. Cooke, who, as mover of the original resolution, had the right of reply. He reviewed briefly the leading arguments of his opponents, and then turned to Mr. Montgomery. The few shreds of that oration which Mr. Stewart had left untouched he tore to atoms. With masterly reasoning he demonstrated the use and necessity of creeds, illustrating his point from the history of his own church. He showed that he and his party were neither opposed to the right of private judgment, nor to the principles of civil and religious liberty !

" Opposed to liberty ! " he exclaimed ; " it is a calumny. We are the determined friends of the British Constitution. We were so in days past, when some of those who now oppose us set up the standard of rebellion. To our Puritan forefathers even the infidel Hume has acknowledged that our country stands indebted for every principle of her freedom. We are the lineal inheritors both of their religious creeds and their political principles. Our present effort is not an effort to enslave other men to our opinions, but to free ourselves from the shackles and thraldom of Arianism."

Towards the close he alluded in terms of cutting irony and stirring eloquence to Mr. Montgomery's plea of peace :

" Peace ! " he said ; "peace ! without purity of faith, which is its fundamental principle. Peace ! amid the opposing elements of

theological dogmas. Peace ! where the very Giver of peace is dis-
honoured and degraded by the men who clamour for it. There can
be no peace apart from purity and truth. The words of the Apostle
are whispered in our ears in accents so tender, and of such deep
pathos, that we are appalled by them—' Keep the unity of the Spirit
in the bond of peace.' But pathos cannot palliate error. It is a
false interpretation, and a false application of the Apostle's words.
The context which shows their true bearing and meaning, was forgotten—' There is one body and one spirit, even as ye are called in
one hope of your calling ! one Lord, one faith.' The unity of the
spirit, then, is a unity of faith. Have we this ? Do Trinitarians
and Arians hold one Lord and one faith ? The Spirit is a spirit of
truth. He is truth. Can he reign—can peace reign, where truth
and error co-exist ? Peace here, under existing circumstances, is a
delusive cry. It is a syren song luring to destruction. Hearken to
it, be lured by it, and your influence is lost, your religious character
is lost, your Church is lost."

Truth was triumphant. Mr. Cooke's searching logic and
manly eloquence, were irresistible. The appeals, warnings,
threats of the Arians were in vain. Orthodox men, who had
before held back, through fear or desire for peace, now came
boldly forward and declared their views. It was ruled that the
question should be put to the house—" Believe the doctrine
or not." Each member was directed to stand up when giving
his vote. It was a solemn moment—one of the most solemn
perhaps in the history of the Presbyterian Church in Ireland.
" Before the sense of the house was taken four ministers obtained leave to withdraw. The roll was then called. One
hundred and seventeen ministers and eighteen elders voted
' believe ; ' two ministers voted ' not ; ' and eight ministers declined voting." A feeble protest was tabled, and eventually
signed by ten ministers and five elders ; but it was felt that
Arian influence was at an end in the Synod ; and that the only
honourable course open to the defeated party was a speedy
withdrawal from the body. This was just what Mr. Cooke
wanted. He feared that the extreme measure of a motion for
their expulsion might fail, or might be carried by such a

narrow majority as to endanger the stability of the Church. It was, therefore, a wiser policy to pass a law so clear and stringent that it would make a voluntary withdrawal of the Arians a matter of necessity.

Mr. Cooke's skill as a leader, and his tact and temper as a public debater were more severely tested at this meeting than they had ever been before. It was not merely the arguments and special pleadings of the speakers in open Court he had to withstand ; but, in addition, the leaders of the opposing party assailed him, during the intervals of debate, with jibes and sarcastic pleasantries, and specious sophistries, calculated to distract his attention and wear out his temper. With imperturbable coolness, and, when occasion required it, smart repartee, he overcame all. The Rev. Hugh Brooke, a man famed for the keenness of his irony, and the brilliancy of his wit, came especially forward. He was not a professed Arian ; but he was known to sympathise with the party, and his talents were often used by the Arian leaders. Mr. Montgomery's argument of the human origin and consequent imperfection of creeds, was Brooke's text. He plied Mr. Cooke with it under every form. He placed subscription before him, and those who stood round him, in every absurd light which ingenuity could devise, or humour suggest. For a time Mr. Cooke bore with him in silence. He listened with the utmost gravity to every new sally of wit and sarcasm. Feeling that matters were going too far, and that Brooke's remarks were beginning to produce an effect upon some, Mr. Stewart said to Cooke, " Do you not hear Brooke ? "   " Yes," he replied, " I list the murmurs of the babbling *brook*." A roar of laughter followed this sally, which irritated poor Brooke. " The repartee is good," he said ; " I admit it ; but Mr. Montgomery's logic is better. The Bible is the work of God. By framing a creed you are, therefore, presumptuously attempting to improve a work of God. How do you reply to that, sir ? Can you improve a work of God ? "   " My reply is easy," said

Cooke, "and it is self-evident. You are a work of God; and
even your best friends will admit that you are capable of
considerable improvement." Cooke's repartees were as effective in private as his brilliant speeches were in public.

The news of the Synod's decision quickly spread over Ulster
and Ireland. The great body of the Presbyterian people
rejoiced, and all Evangelical Protestants rejoiced with them.
Letters of congratulation poured in upon Mr. Cooke, hailing
him as the successful leader in a victory for truth. Among
others is one from Lord Mount-Cashell, who, after referring
to recent struggles, and expressing regret at the still delicate
state of Mr. Cooke's health, says, "I trust now neither of
these causes will prevent your acceding to the request I am
about to make. It is to beg of you to favour us with your
company at Moore Park as soon as convenient. You know
the quiet retired life we lead here, and the change of air
I doubt not will be of service to you. I must also mention
what will, I think, tempt you to come speedily, and that is our
Bible Society Meetings, I am told, will be held about the
beginning of the month of August. The effect your great
talents produced on a former occasion, and the respect and
esteem the Roman Catholics feel for you here, would enable
you to do incalculable good. Since you left us we have been
indefatigably preparing the way, and a few more powerful
shocks will shake the strongholds to their foundations. You
cannot conceive what a change has taken place in so short a
time. Every day curiosity and a spirit of inquiry increases.
The priest is visibly losing his influence, and even the very
lowest orders begin to think for themselves."

Lord Mount-Cashell was deeply interested in the spread of
Evangelical truth. He lamented the existence of Arianism in
the Presbyterian Church; and he was one of the few who
entirely sympathised with Mr. Cooke in his struggles, and in his
efforts to effect a separation between the Arians and Orthodox
in the Synod of Ulster. "I strongly recommended him to
bring about a separation," Lord Mount-Cashell writes to me;

" this he afterwards effected; and I have always thought that the course he adopted was in a great degree prompted by my advice."

Mr. Cooke's difficulties were not at an end. His partial triumph in the Synod appeared to make his enemies all the more determined in their opposition. The strong political feelings of Mr. Archibald Hamilton Rowan, of Killyleagh, have already been mentioned. He had been implicated in the rebellion of '98. He had been driven into exile; but his sufferings did not change his views. Though a very old man, though long an absentee from Killyleagh, though his son was one of Mr. Cooke's staunchest friends, yet his influence was considerable, and he resolved to exert it in favour of his political friends and old allies, the Arians. On the 20th of August, 1827, he sent to Mr. Cooke the following printed document :—

" NOTICE.

" The late discussion in the Synod of Ulster seeming to have a tendency to divide the Presbyterian interest, to restrict its liberty, and compromise its independence, it is desirable to ascertain whether such proceedings meet with the unanimous concurrence of the body of Presbyterians.

" I do therefore request a meeting of the Presbyterian inhabitants of Killyleagh, to take this subject into their consideration, at ——, on the ——.

" ARCHIBALD HAMILTON ROWAN."

It was accompanied by the following letter :—

" LEINSTER STREET, 20th August, 1827.

" SIR—The contrariety of our political opinions would not alone have caused the proceeding which the enclosed notice announces, so much do I deprecate any disunion among dissenters. But your conduct at the Ulster Synod proves to me that the same spirit of intolerance prevails in your religious conduct.

" This appears to me so discrepant from what I supposed to
have been the precepts and principles of the body of citizens
whom I have joined in religious worship, that I think this
appeal becomes a duty which I reluctantly adopt.

" I am your very obedient servant,

" ARCHIBALD HAMILTON ROWAN."

Immediately after writing the above, Mr. Rowan proceeded
to Killyleagh. Finding that the notice had not been made
public, he again wrote :

" Mr. Hamilton Rowan's respects wait upon Mr. Cooke
with a request that he would insert the time and place of
meeting in the enclosed notice that may suit his convenience ;
which he requests may be as early as proper, on account of his
frail state of health—perhaps on Monday next.

" KILLYLEAGH, Thursday morning, 6 a.m."

Mr. Cooke replied :—

" KILLYLEAGH, 24th August, 1827.

" SIR,—I beg to acknowledge the receipt of your first letter
upon Tuesday, and your second this morning, containing a
request that I should insert the time and place of a public
meeting of the Presbyterians of this parish. To comply with
any request from you would give me great pleasure, whenever
I could do so consistently with my sense of duty. Permit me,
then, respectfully to state the reasons why I decline, for the
present, to call any meeting of the parish for the purposes
stated in your notice.

" 1st. I do not consider myself authorized to call any extraordinary meeting of the parish without previous consultation
with the Session and Committee.

" 2nd. Because of the foul injustice with which the majority
of the Synod of Ulster have been treated by the Editor or
reporter of the ' Northern Whig.' He has put sentiments in
our mouths we never conceived nor uttered ; he has omitted
our most cogent arguments and statements, while he has

amended or enlarged those of our opponents ; he has misrepresented our arguments by omissions and transpositions ; and, to crown his delinquencies, he has broken his voluntary pledge to publish my reply to Mr. Montgomery, and has sent his speech into the world as 'unanswered and unanswerable.' I did reply to Mr. Montgomery ; and, in the opinion of the Synod, did so triumphantly. If I left a word unrefuted, it fell into the hands of Mr. Stewart of Broughshane, from whom an opponent in argument never escaped ; but the veracious 'Whig' has consigned both our speeches to oblivion—and mine in violation of his express and voluntary promise. Now, Sir, for this reason, had I no other, I decline all public meetings, except it be your purpose to follow the rule *Audi alteram partem.*

" 3rd. Should you, as I think from your knowledge of the principles of justice you must, conclude *audire alteram partem,* before you make any proposal to a point on the subject of which the public have never heard or read in discussion :— I then beg to suggest to your consideration the following plan, as what appears to me necessary to the purposes of justice, and best calculated to answer the important ends you have in view.

" I beg to propose that you choose one or more ministers of the Synod of Ulster, who hold your views, to discuss the matter publicly. The subject is twofold—First, it involves the question of truth or falsehood in Arianism and Humanitarianism. Second, it involves the point of ecclesiastical union between those parties, and believers in the Deity and Atonement of Christ. Now I am ready by myself, or with any stipulated number of friends to discuss these points, with an equal number of opponents, at any time or place.

" Should you feel inclined to accept of my proposal, I shall nominate a friend to meet any friend of yours, in order to settle persons, time, and place for the discussion.

" Should you decline my proposal, the regular plan of procedure is to call the Session and Committee to consult upon the propriety of a parish meeting, and as chairman of the Session I am ready to summon them according to Synodical law; and I daresay the Chairman of the Committee will be equally willing to comply with any request for that purpose. I am, Sir,

" Your obedient Servant,

" H. COOKE."

" Archibald Hamilton Rowan, Esq."

" Half-past 12, Thursday.

" Sir—I have received your answer to my request that you would name the time and place of meeting of the Presbyterians resident in Killyleagh.

" This meeting I think necessary to clear your character, from your complaint of the insertions in the public papers, as well as the parish over which you preside; and is, I think, in coincidence with your appeal to—*audi alteram partem.*

" All I wish is to establish the independence, and avoid the disunion of the Presbyterian interest.

" In the enclosed two resolutions I have explained my sole object, and your assent to them will preclude the necessity of any meeting.

" Not being acquainted with the mode of calling Presbyterian congregations to assemble, if you do not approve of them, you will oblige me by signing a notice for a meeting of the Committee to-morrow, as the state of my health requires my early return to Dublin.

" Yours, respectfully,

" A. H. ROWAN."

The resolutions enclosed were as follows :—

" Resolved, that, considering the Presbyterian Church to be established on the indefeasible rights of private judgment as declared in the Word of God, and recognised by the laws of our country, we do not conceive the honest exercise of that right to form any ground for division among the members of that Church."

" Resolved, that, highly prizing our religious liberty, we deprecate the adoption of any measure in the Synod of Ulster by which that liberty might be infringed or curtailed. "

Mr. Cooke's reply is lost; but the following are the resolutions which he proposed to be submitted to, and adopted by the congregation, instead of the two forwarded by Mr. Rowan:

" 1. That, viewing man as possessed of understanding, and thereby capable of judging between right and wrong, and considering that, as he has derived these powers from God, and not from man, to God and not to man he must be accountable for the use or abuse of them ; we conceive, therefore, that, by the constitution of nature, no man possesses a right of restraining another in the exercise of his mental powers.

" 2. That, considering the Presbyterian and all other Scripture Churches to be established upon the indefeasible right of private judgment, as declared in the Word of God (John v. 39 ; 1 Cor. x. 15), we do not conceive that any Christian, or assembly of Christians, should attempt to prevent any individual, or individuals, from the free and unshackled exercise of that privilege which God has revealed, recognised, and established in His Holy Word.

" 3. That as God has bestowed upon us an understanding, and made us accountable to Him alone for its exercise, so whatever light He has vouchsafed for his guidance, man is, in conscience and duty, bound to follow ; and whatever limits of right or wrong in judgment and practice God has been pleased to prescribe, within these limits man is bound to confine himself.

" 4. That, agreeably to the foregoing principles, man, in the exercise of his private judgment, is to be guided and limited, in doctrine and practice, by the Word of God ; and that this principle is founded upon Divine injunction (Is. viii. 20), Apostolical practice (Acts xvii. 11), and prophetic denunciation (Rev. xxii. 19).

" 5. That while we thus deny to any the right of coercing man in judgment and conscience, we yet hold it to be a necessary result of the indefeasible rights of nature, that every human being, acting as a voluntary agent, and every human society constituted upon voluntary principles, be free to choose their own companions, or to withdraw from companions who have become disagreeable to their best feelings, who are opposed to their views of duty, or who are acting in opposition to their best interests, or the interests of their superiors or employers.

"6. That we conceive the Presbyterian, and all other Scriptural Churches, irrespective of the temporalities of any of the members, to be, as Churches, purely voluntary associations ; and that, therefore, upon the common principles of nature, even if the Scriptures were totally silent in the matter, the members of these Churches are free to choose their several associates, or to withdraw from those who may have become disagreeable to their best feelings, or who are acting in opposition to their views of duty ; who are acting in opposition to their best interests—viz., the edification of the body of Christ, or to the best interests of the Redeemer, from whom alone ministers derive their commission, and the members of the Churches their faith of salvation, and their hope of glory.

"7. That while the principles of natural right confirm the preceding resolution, we are further authorised by the Divine Word to exercise a strict scrutiny into the doctrine and character of those whom we recognise as ministers of the gospel (1 John iv. 1—11), or receive as members of the Church (Rom. xvi. 17) ; to judge them by the Word of God (1 Cor. v. 12), and to separate from them when their disorder appears incurable (1 Cor. v. 13 ; 2 Thess. iii. 16 ; Titus iii. 10).

"8. That, highly esteeming the labours of the Rev. Fathers of the General Synod of Ulster, of which Synod we as a congregation form a constituent part, and highly prizing our religious liberties as members of the Presbyterian Church, we trust that no measure will ever be adopted by that reverend body calculated to infringe, impair, or curtail the real liberty from the bondage and curse of the law wherewith Christ hath made us free ; or the privilege of reading, and studying, and judging of the Scriptures ; or the apostolical practice of choosing our church rulers and teachers ; or any other of those blessed rights agreeable to the Word of God, for which so many of our forefathers shed their blood, when pursued on the mountains or dragged to the scaffold ; but that we rejoice in all the proceedings of that reverend body by which purity in doctrine, faithfulness in discipline, devotion in worship, and holiness in practice, may be fostered, extended, and confirmed."

To this Mr. Rowan replied :—

"KILLYLEAGH, 24th August, 1827.

" Sir,—I have received and read your letter, and the eight resolutions you sent me, with all the attention I am capable of, and I thank you for the candid information of the line of conduct you mean to pursue, by proposing them instead of the two I submitted to you, in the event of a public meeting.

" The two first of yours I willingly assent to. They were more full, and perhaps convey my meaning in more suitable language, than those I sent you; but the other six I really do not understand, neither am I capable of entering into a discussion of the opinions which are held by each party. My sole object is to ascertain whether the honest exercise of private judgment on the Christian system belongs to Presbyterians.

" Formerly belonging to the Church of England, the supposition that it was, induced me to join their communion on my arrival in Ireland. In England it is true that some ancient doctrines of the Established Church are disavowed even by Churchmen, without incurring censure; but all Dissenters are obliged to be relieved each session from the penalties they have incurred by their contumacy. Then they are protected by law. This was my inducement to refer to the law of the land in my resolution; but as you say it is irrelevant, I have no objection to expunge it; and if these resolutions alone meet your concurrence, the public meeting seems unnecessary. Otherwise I shall forward your notice as you direct to Mr. Heron.

" As to the six remaining resolutions, they appear to me to be corollaries which I cannot subscribe to, and leave the decision on them to more learned persons than myself, or possibly most of those you would address; while I attach to what I thought was the essence and fundamental principle of Presbyterianism—the honest exercise of private judgment.

" I agree with you in your definition of voluntary associations, and that every society has a right to form rules and regulations for the admission of its members; but, as you refer to my principles of justice, I must ask you—If after those rules had been long discussed, they have been suspended, and in effect abandoned, for nearly a century, and members known to hold various opinions have been admitted in the meantime;

is it just, or even Christian, to turn upon them on an accidental
majority ?   I therefore inserted the deprecation addressed to
the Synod of Ulster, not to adopt any measure in Synod
which may tend to infringe the liberty hitherto enjoyed by its
members.   But if the rejection of the words 'in the Synod of
Ulster' will satisfy you, I consent to that also.

" I observe in your open note to Mr. Heron an allusion to a
supposed attack on your character, which I assure you never
entered the mind of your sincere

" And respectfully obedient Servant,

" ARCHIBALD HAMILTON ROWAN."

" Rev. H. Cooke."

" 24th August, 1827.

" SIR,—I have the honour to acknowledge your favour of
this date, and shall reply to its principal points.   You admit
you do not understand my six corollaries to my two principal
resolutions :—then I beg you to consider that, if a gentleman
of your education, habitual study, and large acquaintance with
the world, profess ignorance of the matter, and if the matter
be in itself important, as your anxiety and that of the public
clearly evince, let the public discussion formerly proposed be
adopted, so that a better judgment may be formed of the arguments on all sides ; and this indeed is the plan which I shall
submit to the session and committee for their sanction.

" The honest exercise of private judgment is not peculiar to
Presbyterians—it is the birthright of man, the recovered right
of Protestantism, wrested from superstition and tyranny.   A
Presbyterian is a Protestant, and therefore it is his inalienable
inheritance.   But the essence of Presbyterianism is parity of
rank in the ministry, as the essence of Prelacy is superiority
and subordination.

" I cannot in any degree rest satisfied with the two first
resolutions in my series.   I feel it necessary to state, that in
the public meeting of the parish I shall probably add one or
two more.

" Your idea that a century of inattention to rules and fundamental principles precludes any reformation, is surely not in unison with your religious or political creed. It would extinguish the light of the blessed Reformation, and condemn the heroes of the glorious Revolution. All these rose up against evils in Church and State sanctioned by use and wont, and venerable in their antiquity. Just so in the Synod of Ulster. If an abuse has been original, let it be reformed. If an abuse have crept in, let it be reformed. Whatever is wrong, let it be reformed. We must then come to general principles of right and wrong as revealed in Scripture. That is our Magna Charta by which we must be judged. However, in the discussion I shall even show you that no such principle as you assume—that of a century of neglect of original laws—is to be applied to the Synod of Ulster. Her members have always been engaged in reformation; and observance of original law has been her normal state.

" Your denial of any reference to my character in the discussion, as I had intimated in my note to Mr. Heron, I waive for the present, and reserve for the meeting; but will then show from two of your letters, and from other sources. But, if you say so, I am ready to admit that I may have been too sensitive, and shall consign that part of the subject to oblivion.

" And now, sir, again permit me to express my regret at any collision of opinion between us. You are my senior in age and experience; and I receive your observations with the respect to which they are entitled. From yourself and many members of your family I have received many favours. To Captain Hamilton, under Providence, I believe I am indebted for my removal to Killyleagh; and sorry should I be to meet in public discussion his respected and beloved father.

" In conclusion let me say, I have been dragged more than once into discussions I should rather have avoided; I would have avoided them if truth could have permitted me to be silent. Discussions are apt to beget strife. I would to God

that instead of any discussion with you about the world that
passeth away I might rather direct your eyes to Jesus Christ,
' the Lamb of God which taketh away the sins of the world.'
You are near the end of your journey. So am I. Young in
years, I am old in constitution. We are both, as others, beset
with many infirmities. I have many sins to wash away.
Blessed be God! He has called me out of the kingdom of
darkness and translated me into the kingdom of His dear Son;
and my earnest prayer is, that the Lord may so call you to His
love, His kingdom, and His glory, that we may there meet in
peace.

" I remain, respectfully,

" Your obedient Servant,

" H. COOKE."

" Archibald Hamilton Rowan, Esq."

" KILLYLEAGH, 25th August, 1827.

" SIR,—I have received your determination not to permit
the question I have wished to be decided by the Presbyterians
of Killyleagh unencumbered by discussions which, I think, are
irrelevant:—viz., Whether the essence of Presbyterianism is
contained in the two resolutions I sent you; or, as you say, it
consists only in the mere parity of rank in the ministry, as the
essence of Prelacy is superiority and subordination.

" I must, therefore, decline your assistance, and take other
means of collecting the public voice.

" I am, yours respectfully,

" ARCHIBALD HAMILTON ROWAN."

" The Rev. H. Cooke."

Mr. Rowan was acting under the advice and direction of the
Arian leaders in the Synod, whose object was to weaken Mr.
Cooke's influence in Killyleagh. They had another object—to
neutralise the exertions of Captain Rowan, Mr. Cooke's indefatigable and accomplished elder. It was in vain. Mr. Cooke's
influence was paramount in Killyleagh. It could not be shaken

even by the aged and venerable lord of the soil, whose eventful career was not calculated to secure the confidence of the loyal men of Down. The character and labours of Captain Rowan, too, had already gained for him a high place in the hearts of all Presbyterians, so that, though only a younger son, his influence in the parish far exceeded that of his father.

Unfortunately Mr. Rowan did not desist. His over-zealous advisers urged him to a course which resulted in a humiliating defeat. On the Sunday following the date of his last letter, he attended divine service in the Presbyterian Church. It was, as usual, crowded. Immediately on the benediction being pronounced, he rose in his pew and requested the people to remain for a few minutes, as he had some important resolutions to submit to them. The resolutions, he was confident, would meet their entire approval, as free Presbyterians ; but it was necessary, on account of recent events, that they should be formally adopted by the congregation. Mr. Cooke was taken by surprise. He did not anticipate a step so bold. But he was equal to the occasion. He at once left the pulpit, took his stand on the top of the stairs in full view of the people, and addressed to them a few calm but determined words :—

" You have not come here for the purpose of hearing resolutions. Even were they regularly submitted to you, possibly most of those present would not, without long explanations, understand their meaning or bearing. You have assembled for the worship of God. To force upon you other matters without due notice is unprecedented and illegal. If resolutions are to be submitted to this congregation, let their purport be made known ; let a week-day be appointed, and then let them be fully and fairly considered. I now counsel you to return to your homes, and to close the Lord's-day in the spirit.of those solemn exercises in which we have been engaged."

With even more than customary quickness the congregation dispersed. Not a man remained. The minister followed the people ; and the last object he saw as he crossed the threshold was the venerable form of Mr. Rowan, standing erect in his pew, with the resolutions, still unread, in his hand.

During the following week a printed paper was extensively circulated in the parish of Killyleagh. It bears the impress of the *Northern Whig* office, Belfast. The *Whig* was the organ of the Arian party, and it is easy to conjecture under what counsel Mr. Rowan had all along acted. The paper contained the two resolutions submitted to Mr. Cooke, with the following letter :—

" Sirs,—On reading the minutes of the last Synod, I found a resolution entertained, which made me doubt whether I was a Presbyterian.

" It proposed limits to private judgment, honestly exercised according to the Word of God, in the case of *William Porter*.

" Having occasion to visit Killyleagh, I reduced the essence, as I thought, of Presbyterianism to the two preceding resolutions, which I was prevented from reading to the congregation on Sunday, and now submit them to your consideration.

" I may be asked, why did I not accept of Mr. Cooke's offer to appoint a week-day for discussion on the subject ? My answer is threefold :—

" 1st. I thought those resolutions were undeniable axioms.

" 2nd. That discussions tend generally to disunion.

" 3rd. That it would trench too much on the occupations of the season, and would be ill attended.

" Archibald Hamilton Rowan."

The Reverend William Campbell, of Islandmagee, the kind friend who furnished the details of the foregoing scene, of which he was a witness, has added the following reminiscences of Mr. Cooke's ministerial life and labours in Killyleagh :—" I knew Dr. Cooke well, and while life holds on I shall gratefully remember his kindness to me when a school-boy, a student, and afterwards a minister. He was to me a friend and a father. He superintended my studies when at school. During my whole college course his attention, advice, and instructions were unremitting. When a student of divinity he prescribed my course of reading, corrected my written exercises, and placed before me in clear light portions of the Word of God that were previously obscure. When near the close of my college course, he often asked me to accompany him in his ministerial visitation. I did so cheerfully. It was a high privilege. It was impossible to be in his society and not be instructed and edified. He was at all times humble, communicative, and dignified. When in the cottages of the poor, the inmates at once found that they had in him a true friend. He condescended to men of low estate. How faithfully and affectionately did he warn the impenitent, and instruct the ignorant! His prayers at the bedsides of the afflicted and dying had a special unction. In all his ministrations, in private as well as in public, he set forth Christ as the alone life of the soul—the sure foundation—the hope of glory.

"To know Dr. Cooke he must be known in private. To know him as 'a prince among men' in public was only to half know him. In private he shone pre-eminently. The law of truth, kindness, and generous feeling was written in his heart. There was an entire absence of evil surmisings. He could not speak bitterly or reproachfully even of an enemy. Of most great men it can be said they have intellect, judgment, and energy of character. These qualities characterized Dr. Cooke in manner and degree such as fall to the lot of few. But in addition to these he was gifted with a heart—largeness of heart—a heart feeling, kind, tender, compassionate; a heart that ever throbbed responsive to the cry for sympathy; and, no doubt, while 'the heart of the wise teacheth his mouth,' it is also mighty in influencing and directing his actions."

What deep interest Mr. Cooke felt in young ministers—how he advised, instructed, and cautioned them, may to some extent be seen from the following letter, which is but a type of

many. It was addressed to Mr. Campbell, shortly after his
settlement in Islandmagee.

"KILLYLEAGH, 8th *February*, 1829.

"MY DEAR FRIEND,—I never thought that in going to Islandmagee you were going to repose upon a bed of roses; and I am
sure God can keep it from being one of thorns. I feel happy
at receiving a letter from you, especially one that proves you
are doing some work for your Master. Christ is a good
Master; and blessed are all they that serve Him. 'If any
man serve Him, him will the Father honour.'

"As to the 'wakes,' they are utterly to be discouraged; yet
the work must be done gently, and prudently, and scripturally.
As to your going and staying till twelve at night, it is such a
thing as I would not do, nor advise you to do. Yet still if
you find that your neighbouring ministers—I mean your co-
islanders—do it, you must in some degree conform to the old
practice, till you can substitute a better. You know my plan.
I generally refuse to go to houses of the dead, if 'spirits' are
given to the people. If I go to such houses, I taste not of
their dainties. If any consent to give no 'spirits,' I preach or
lecture. Then I usually take the corpse into the meeting-
house, read a chapter, comment, sing, and pray. I do not recollect whether in Islandmagee there be a burying-ground at the
meeting-house; but if there be not, and yet there be sufficient
ground, I advise you to get one as soon as possible. There
are many reasons for this. By Act of Parliament you cannot
speak in a grave-yard at the church without the permission of
the incumbent. This is a little irksome. Then I like to have
the dead sleeping around me where I preach. They are a
kind of witnesses for us. They attach the people to the house
around which are their fathers' graves. Anything of this kind
you will propose gently, and, I trust, effect in time. Introduce
no violent departure from old custom, except where it is
sinful; but introduce improvement gently and rationally, and
God will bless your labours. Substitute for the late hours at

wakes something better so soon as you can ; but even that do with caution, lest your good be evil spoken of.

" Your text (Phil. iii. 9) is a very important one. I am in doubt about the correctness of the translation of the last clause 'by faith.' You know I keep no commentary, except grammar and lexicon. These do not seem to warrant ἐπὶ τῇ πίστει to be translated 'by faith ; ' but '*to* (or on) the faith,' viz., of the believer. I recommend your attention to this, as it seems to me to elucidate, in some degree, the import of the text. The text contains three things—1. The believer's desire, 'to be found in Him,' as a branch, John xv. ; as a member, Eph. v. 30. 2. What the believer does not desire, ' to have his own righteousness, which is of law,' not *the* law, as you will see in the original. 3. What he wishes to have on,—' The righteousness of God,' &c. The believer's righteousness is God's own righteousness —that of God manifested in the flesh ; and it is added, or given to, or imputed, if you will, to our faith in Christ. This is a vastly important point, and will require delicate and honest handling. After glancing at all, I should prefer handling the first—a believer's union with Christ. The subject is well treated in ' Dickenson's Letters.' But you have heard me so often on the subject I think you know it thoroughly. He is the Head ; we are the members. He is Head over all things to the church, Eph. i. 22 ; we are members by the common spirit of life, 1 Cor. xii. 4, 11, 13, 20, 27 . . . . Many other things I could suggest, did space permit. Be much in prayer. May the Lord bless you.

" Yours faithfully,

" H. Cooke."

CHAPTER VII.

1828.

Synod of Munster on Mr. Cooke's Evidence—Mr. Cooke's Reply, and Controversy with Mr. Armstrong—Dr. Chalmers' Visit to Belfast—Views on the Arian Struggle—Mr. Cooke's Views—Letters of Messrs. Steele and Kydd—Messrs. Cassidy and Paul on the Arian Controversy—Mr. Cooke's Letter to the Ministers and Members of the Synod of Ulster on the approaching Conflict—Meeting of Synod in Cookstown—Mr. Morell's Motion for Committee of Inquiry—Mr. Cooke's Tribute to the Memory of Rev. John Thompson—Members of Synod declare Belief in the Trinity—Resolutions of Mr. Carlile—Amended Resolutions of Mr. Cooke—Speeches of Messrs. Montgomery and Stewart—Mr. Cooke's Notice of Motion for Reform—Speech containing Illustration from Aladdin's Lamp—Memorials for the Expulsion of Arianism—Controversy between Messrs. Carlile and Paul—Meeting of Arians in Belfast, 16th October, 1828—Letter of Messrs. Cooke, Stewart, and Henry—Encounter of Montgomery and Cooke—The Arian REMONSTRANCE: Review of, by a Minister of the Synod of Ulster.

DURING the controversy with Mr. Rowan, Mr. Cooke was involved in one of a much more serious nature. His evidence before the Parliamentary Committees had roused the enmity of the Synod of Munster. That reverend body, after two years of solemn deliberation, accompanied with no small amount of internal bickering, agreed upon an ecclesiastical critique of that part of the evidence which related to them. Mr. Cooke had been asked how he accounted for the remarkable decline in the number of congregations in the Synod of Munster. He replied, "I must chiefly attribute it to the growth of Arianism and Socinianism in that Synod, and the unacceptableness of those doctrines to the people." He farther stated in answer to questions :—" I have heard it said, I do not know how good the authority may be, that some of the ministers there have no great objection to the old congregations dying away, that they might have an increase of annuity, by dividing the lapsed *regium donum* among themselves." He affirmed that modern Arianism denies the integrity and divine authority of Scripture; that for this reason the ministers of the Synod of Munster would not subscribe the Westminster Confession, or any prescribed form of creed, and that they had no ecclesiastical connection with the Synod of Ulster.

The Synod of Munster published a lengthened review of Mr. Cooke's evidence :—" We avail ourselves of the earliest opportunity, after the examination of Mr. Cooke before the Committee of Parliament, to take into consideration the statement respecting our body therein contained." The document goes on to consider point after point, charging Mr. Cooke with gross errors, calumnious insinuations, conduct " utterly unworthy of a man who has any pretension to Christian candour," and " wilful and deliberate misrepresentation." Their observations upon doctrinal points were ingenious, if not logical. They profess to deny the truth of Mr. Cooke's statements, while in reality they admit all he said.

This document was forwarded to Mr. Cooke, accompanied by a letter from the Rev. J. Armstrong, clerk of Synod :—

" I send herewith a copy of the ' Observations of the Synod of Munster,' on that part of your testimony before the Committee of Parliament which relates to them. These remarks have been finally agreed upon only within last month. They would have been prepared and transmitted to you at a much earlier period, but for some difference of opinion among my brethren, with respect to the fittest method of showing their sense of the manner in which they have been represented in your evidence. . . .

" From my own experience of your private character, I am justified in inferring that bigotry is no part of your disposition. I am persuaded that this unchristian temper has been engrafted on your character by some external influence, or the operation of some sinister motive. I cannot, indeed, agree with those who ascribe your recent exhibitions of this temper to the low ambition of being the head of a party ; neither can I concur with those who ascribe them to what is much worse, the rancour of personal animosity. But, as such a fruit cannot grow upon a sound branch, I may be permitted to take the liberty of imploring you, my once highly esteemed friend, as you value your everlasting welfare, to try and examine your own heart, in the presence of that God before whom no subterfuge or disguise can conceal the naked truth. . . . To errors of judgment we are all liable ; and it would relieve my mind of most painful surmises, if I could attribute your erroneous assertions to mistakes of this kind. In our vindication you will see that we have confined ourselves to a simple statement of facts, and have studiously avoided all asperity of language. . . . That offences have come in is but too manifest. Our Saviour hath declared that it must needs be so : but He has also added the alarming denunciation ' Woe to that man by whom the offence cometh.'

" I beg you will not consider any expression in this letter as indicating the smallest degree of personal hostility. I assure you, you have my warmest wishes for your welfare ; and my fervent prayers that the Father of Lights may illuminate your heart and mind, rectify your errors, and lead you to true repentance and amendment."

This was an extraordinary letter. It was even more severe than the document which accompanied it. The charges it contained were so grave that Mr. Cooke could not permit them to pass unnoticed. His character was at stake, and he resolved to vindicate it. To prevent the possibility of error, and to fortify the observations he had made during repeated visits to the south of Ireland, he wrote for information to Mr. Horner, of Dublin ; Mr. Morgan, then of Lisburn, formerly of Carlow ; Mr. Magill, of Antrim ; Mr. Stewart, of Broughshane, and several others both in the north and south, who were intimately and personally acquainted with the history, the existing state, and the doctrinal views of the Synod of Munster. The replies were most satisfactory. They corroborated in every particular Mr. Cooke's evidence. They did more—they revealed important facts, of which he made full use in his replies to the Synod and its clerk ; and they assured him of the cordial sympathy of the men who, by self-denying labours, had shown their desire for the spread of a pure gospel in the south of Ireland.

Mr. Cooke's reply to the Synod of Munster is dated 5th September, 1827. It appeared in the *Belfast Guardian* of the 11th, and was afterwards published in a separate form. With great clearness he met the arguments and assertions, and with cutting irony exposed every sophistry :—

"In your first paragraph you say 'you avail yourselves of the earliest opportunity after the report of my examination, to take this subject into your consideration.' Do you really expect the world to believe you ? ' *The earliest opportunity !* ' . . . Let the public hear and judge. The first Report of the Commission of Education was published 3rd June, 1825; that before the Committee of the Lords in March, 1825. The precise date of the Report of my evidence before the Committee of the Commons I do not know, but I am fully convinced it was anterior to June, 1825, as I understood copies of it were at the Synod of Ulster, held at Coleraine, in June, 1825.

"At that Synod the Rev. Mr. Horner applied to me in the name of Mr. Armstrong, informing me that he (Mr. Armstrong) had taken offence at some of my statements respecting the Synod of Munster ; and requesting me to write such an explanatory or apologetic letter as might satisfy the Synod of Munster. My reply was, ' My state-ments were true, and required neither explanation nor apology.'

"The next meeting of the Synod of Ulster was in Ballymena, June, 1826, and here again Mr. Horner repeated his application. I told him ' The Commissioners of Education were the proper court for Mr. Armstrong, and it was still open to him.'

"Will that part of the world who know little of the Synod of Munster believe, that after my examination, and after the message of Mr. Horner, the Synod of Munster met in 1825, but published nothing ? After the second message, in 1826, they met and published nothing ; and till August, 1827, they published nothing. . . . Full well did the Synod of Munster know that, had they come forward sooner with their 'Observations on Mr. Cooke's evidence,' the Commissioners would, in justice, have 'observed' them ; and the Rev. Messrs. Hutton and Armstrong knew that a little catechis-ing by the Commissioners might a tale unfold, that would be better locked up in the secrets of their own breasts ; therefore, they waited most prudently till the danger of an examination was over.

"Before I proceed to consider the several paragraphs of the Observations, let me say a word or two of the Synod of Munster. In
Ulster the word Synod sounds somewhat formidable and important.
. . . The Synod of Munster consisted once of about fifty congregations; the Synod of Munster consists now of eight or nine congregations, and eleven or twelve ministers."

Mr. Cooke then gives detailed proof of his statement that
Arianism and Socinianism were the chief causes of the decay
of the Synod; he proves, too, that the other parts of his
evidence were equally accurate. In closing, he says:—

"You have thrown out against me grievous insinuations and
heavy charges. I have seen the time I would have been angry at
such unfounded and deliberate misrepresentations. Thank God ! I
can forgive you for them all. . . . It has so occurred, in the
providence of God, that a few members of the Synod of Ulster, of
whom I am one, have taken an earnest share in the public cause of
evangelical truth, in opposition to Arianism and Socinianism. Your
plan, therefore, was cunningly chosen. Could you weary out, terrify,
or ruin any individual of this body, you counted on an easier conquest of the rest. You have wisely chosen me as the weakest. But
I have a strength you did not count upon. I am strong in knowing
my own weakness. You, and such as you, have taught me to come
more earnestly to the Throne of Grace, for grace to help me in time
of need ; and this grace has supported me in a harder battle, and
with more powerful enemies. My mind has for several years been
deeply occupied with the state of the Presbyterian churches ; and I
have been, however feebly, labouring for the reformation of the body
to which I belong. One of your veracious assistants, the editor of
London *Morning Chronicle,* has accused me, I hear, of having myself
been an Arian, and of having deserted Arianism from motives of
interest. May God forgive him ! I have seen the time when even
a tincture of Arianism would have advanced all my temporal
interests ; but, thank God, I have ever held the faith once delivered
to the saints, and I trust, in His grace, He will confirm me to the
end. . . . The union of kindness may subsist between men of
any religious denominations, between the Christian, the Jew, the
Mahomedan, and the Heathen. But the union of church fellowship
can never be established between the believer in Jesus, the reviler of
Jesus, and those who deny Him or know Him not. No more do I

believe can genuine fellowship be established between him who
adores Jesus Christ the Lord, as God manifest in the flesh ; and
him who merely respects Him as a created being, of however high an
order; and him who acknowledges Jesus to have been a mere fallible
man like himself.

"Gentlemen, you wish to be called Presbyterians. Oh ! that you
were like the Hamiltons, the Knoxes, the Welshes, of the olden time;
or the Erskines, the Moncrieffs, or the Wilsons, those genuine Presbyterians of more modern days ! My soul would rejoice over you as
my brethren in the Lord. I should wear you in my heart of hearts.
But, alas ! you form a part of a degenerate Presbyterian church ;
part of which has fallen from its original purity into the depths of
Arianism, or Socinianism. You are the admirers of Taylor, and
Price, and Priestley, and Ramohun Roy ; therefore do I disavow connexion with you. That God may direct you to see the light and flee
from error, is the earnest prayer of		" H. COOKE."

Mr. Armstrong replied, and something of the style of the
reply may be gathered from the following extract from Mr.
Cooke's answer :—

" You intimate that I am 'a fanatical enthusiast—rather hypo-
crite.' You accuse me of holding 'the gloomy unscriptural system
of Calvin.' You say this system has 'a direct tendency to disgust.'
You say it is, and I am 'narrow, bigoted, and exclusive.' You
accuse me of 'blind and misguided zeal.' You apply to me the
record of Judas who betrayed his Master. You pronounce over me
that awful woe reserved for the man by whom the offence cometh ;
and you have pronounced me to be 'infected with the contagion of
fanaticism.' "

Mr. Cooke's answer is in two parts, one dated Sept. 25th,
the other Dec. 7th. Both refer chiefly to points which have
no interest now. They have passed away, and they had
better be buried in oblivion. Some of his remarks, however,
throw light upon that great struggle in which he was then
engaged :—

" Before I proceed to reply to your letter I must address a few
preparatory observations to the Christian public. I have now, for a

period of upwards of two years, been the subject of a series of public attacks in newspapers and magazines. In running over, from memory, a list of the writers who have professedly assailed me during that period, I can enumerate twenty-one, of whom eight were editors of newspapers, or of magazines ; seven wrote each against me but once ; the others, some twice, thrice, &c., whilst a few have continued an incessant and apparently interminable warfare. During the same period I have been attacked by eight public bodies, sometimes in a manner the most violent and personal. I could enumerate petty assaults at will ; but enough has been said on this subject. This enumeration I have given, not from any perverse vanity of reviewing the multitude of enemies, but to plead my excuse for appearing so often before the public, and to bespeak, not their compassion, but their candour and patience, while I again appear before them in the work of self-defence. . . .

"I have yet another reason for bespeaking the candour and patience of the Christian public ; for, though they may have been 'tormented by the concerns of little men,' yet, after all, there have been, and there are, some of these concerns, in which, apart from the individuals engaged in this discussion, the public themselves are most deeply interested. Let the public totally disregard the personal interests, and even, for a little, the personal characters of Mr. Armstrong and Mr. Cooke ; and let them reflect, that, independently of these interests and these characters, their eternity, as individuals, is intimately concerned with the issue of these discussions. There hath not been, since the days of the blessed Reformation, so mighty a conflict between light and darkness, as that which is now going forward both in Christian and heathen lands. The spirit of inquiry hath again been roused from the lethargy of ages ; and the Spirit of God hath been poured out upon churches that have been lying like the dry bones in the Valley of Vision ; and they have been clothed with flesh and endowed with life, and they stand upon their feet an exceeding great army. The Synod of Ulster has enjoyed a portion of this renovating influence. The people are beginning to inquire what it is their ministers preach. They are searching their Bible to see if these things be so. Ministers are beginning to speak out more explicitly their religious sentiments. The days of indifference are nearly gone by ; and the friends and enemies of evangelical truth are ranging themselves distinctly in opposite lines of assault and defence."

Mr. Armstrong's sneer at Calvinism and its effects, called forth the following just and eloquent rebuke :—

"You tell the Christian world that the direct tendency of Calvinism, whose doctrines you suppose me to preach, is 'to disgust well-informed and enlightened Presbyterians, and to drive them off from their places of worship ;' and you add, 'You yourself (Mr. Cooke) could give some remarkable instances, and you require no information from me on the subject.' Oh, ye people of Scotland, will not this open your eyes to the religious state of Ireland! Oh, ye Thomsons, and ye Chalmerses, and ye Gordons, and ye Greys, and ye Wardlaws, and ye Browns, how do you disgust the well-informed and enlightened parts of your audiences ; and how they must flee off from you, as if both parties were full charged with the opposing electricities! How I do deplore your silent churches, and your vacant pews! Do, do come over to us for a little, and learn, either from the 'sage of the north,' or 'the young man of the south,' or the luminaries of the capital in the centre, how you may cease to disgust and drive away your congregations. And you, ye people of classical Edinburgh, shame upon your tastes! Did not the world once think you well informed, and enlightened Presbyterians? I have seen the Sabbath tide of your population ebb and flow twice a-day in your streets ; and when the ebb and flow was over, your multitudes were absorbed into your capacious churches, and ye looked as a city of the dead, for scarce one unhallowed foot awoke an echo. And I have seen you in your congregated masses, hang in mute and edified delight upon the words of these 'disgusting Calvinists ;' and there seemed to be between you a magnetism of the mind that attracted you into a unity of intellect and affection, while it marshalled you in the way of the pole-star of salvation, through the darkness and the dreariness of a world that lyeth in wickedness.

"And thou Glasgow, too, dear to all my classical remembrances, city of the untiring spirit of commerce, yet of mental energies and of mental refinements ; city pronounced by no mean judge, 'the most religious in the world,' when wilt thou escape from the childhood of Calvinism, and grow up into the manhood of Arian intelligence and refinement? You thought yourselves well-informed and enlightened Presbyterians ; but the clerk of the Synod of Munster tells you, that if you were so you would be disgusted with your ministers. . . . Oh, had you but a rushlight from the Synod of Munster, there is no calculating to what proficiency such an intellectual people might yet be advanced !"

It had been insinuated that Mr. Cooke's evangelical views
had disgusted and driven away his people. In reply, he
says :—

" It should give you pleasure to be informed that the congregation
of Killyleagh have rebuilt their meeting-house in a style which,
though plain, like Presbyterians, would yet not disgrace the metropolis. We have not a sitting unoccupied. It would delight your
eyes to see the crowded pews on the Sabbath. And if calculation
pleased you, it might be worth while to tell that the congregation of
Killyleagh is at present paying a stipend double that of any country
congregation in Ireland. And all this they have done, and are
doing, without having solicited a penny from the public. . . . .
You are a Synod. Now I offer, upon any ordinary Sabbath, to produce as many hearers in the congregation of Killyleagh as you can
produce on the same day in the whole Synod of Munster."

Dr. Chalmers visited Ireland during the heat of the Arian
controversy. His fame had long preceded him. On the 23rd
of September, 1827, he opened the new Presbyterian church
of Fisherwick Place, Belfast ; and, on the following day, that
of the Rev. William Craig, of Dromara. His discourses made
a profound impression ; and his praise was sounded throughout Ulster. His opinion and advice were eagerly sought as
to the policy which ought to be pursued in regard to Arianism.
It was reported to be in opposition to that of Mr. Cooke.
This was a noble opportunity for Mr. Armstrong. He took
immediate advantage of it, and published abroad that the most
celebrated of living Presbyterian divines disapproved of the
proceedings of the Orthodox members of the Synod of Ulster.
Mr. Cooke replied, and put the matter in its true light ; he
showed at the same time that even the prestige of a great
name could not turn him from what he believed to be the
straight path of duty :—

" When Dr. Chalmers did come to Ireland, I had the pleasure of
listening to his unrivalled eloquence ; and never could I have
wished for anything more sincerely than that you had enjoyed the
same advantage. He would have reminded you of a principle which, I

fear, you have yet to learn—that ' the wrath of man worketh not the righteousness of God.' I enjoyed not merely the pleasure of hearing Dr. Chalmers, but the honour of his acquaintance. . . . Before our distinguished visitor left our shores, he was pleased to express a wish to see me in Scotland, and in the meantime invited me to correspond with him on the state of the Presbyterian Church in Ireland—an invitation of which I certainly intend to avail myself. And here, sir, I seize the opportunity of correcting a report, which more than once 1 have heard, alleging that Dr. Chalmers disapproved of the proceedings of the orthodox members of the Synod of Ulster at Strabane, and advised that all things should continue in their present form. This account of the Doctor's alleged opinion I heard so often, and so confidently repeated, that I felt myself called upon to obtain from Dr. Chalmers himself the statement of his sentiments upon the subject. I can, then, confidently state that Dr. Chalmers did not disapprove of the conduct of the Orthodox members of the Synod. That, with the modesty which is the constant characteristic of a great mind, he acknowledged he knew so little of the state of our Church, that he did not feel qualified to offer a decided advice or opinion ; but that, so far as he was able to do so, he considered that to allow the present Arianism of the Synod to die its natural death, and to take care that by requiring a decided subscription, as well as by examination of candidates, we should permit no more Arians to become members of the body.

" Now I do bow with sincere deference to the opinion of a man so justly entitled to my respect ; yet I confess I cannot adopt his sentiments. My reasons will in due time be before the public, free from the misstatements and additions with which they have hitherto been accompanied and deformed. In the meantime I may be permitted to say, that my only object is the doctrinal and practical purification of the Synod of Ulster, and the following is the plan on which I believe it attainable :—

" 1. I disavow all idea of interfering with the private judgment of ministers or people.

" 2. I disavow ever having entertained the most distant notion of suspension, silencing, or excommunication.

" 3. I take, as I declared in the Synod, the case of Abraham and Lot for my example. We cannot agree—we teach different gospels. Let us, then, quietly divide.

" But while I deem my own plan of present division the best, I feel perfectly open to the reasonings of Orthodox brethren, who are

for the plan of future exclusion of Arianism. And should I find
them disposed to carry it efficiently, and not nominally, into execution, I know it to be merely a more roundabout way of attaining the
very object I have in view. It will produce division by mining at
night ; my plan is to scale the walls in the face of day."

Mr. Cooke was right. The straightforward, honourable,
and Scriptural course was separation. And the subsequent
history of the Church has shown how largely separation promoted the interests of Christian truth in Ireland.

During the winter of 1827-28, Mr. Cooke's labours continued. His efforts to organize and inspire the Orthodox
party were unremitting. It was no easy task. Many, who
were orthodox in faith, dreaded the effects of pushing matters
to extremity. Many cared little for vital religion. A heartless
formalism had long paralysed a large section of the Protestant
churches of Ireland. As yet it was only partly removed.
Mr. Cooke's sermons and speeches contributed largely to
promote a revival. He was looked upon not merely as the
champion of orthodoxy, but as the advocate of new life in the
Church. An anonymous admirer thus writes. The letter is
one of many ; and the sentiments it expressed were re-echoed
over Ulster :—" That the Rev. Henry Cooke has many foes in
Belfast he is well aware ; that he has many and warm friends
I can testify. To the latter the very sight of him is transport
—transport most disinterested, proceeding only from a love to
him because of his love to immortal souls. In proof, I insert
the following, received this evening from a lady of distinction :
' I had last Tuesday the pleasure of being present at a meeting
of the Society for the Propagation of the Gospel. I had there
opportunity of hearing and admiring the eloquence of many
distinguished ministers. But I could not divest myself of the
feeling that the speeches were more adapted to display their
own talents than the inestimable riches of Christ. There was
one exception. It was that of our favourite preacher, the Rev.
Henry Cooke. The effects produced on my mind by his
speech were altogether different from those produced by the

others. To promote the glory of our Blessed Saviour appeared
to be his one object. While his splendid talents and burning
eloquence entranced all hearers, the truths embodied went
straight to the heart. They came with double force from one
who appears to have learnt his religion at the feet of Jesus.' "

Not in Belfast only, but in the most distant parts of
Ireland, was Mr. Cooke's influence felt. The Rev. Dr. Steele
of Stranorlar, County Donegal, referring to an effort to
establish a branch of the Bible Society, thus writes to him :—
" It appears to me that nothing valuable can be done in this
cold quarter except an able deputation visit us. I am decidedly of opinion that you are the very person who should
first make the noble attempt. Do not charge me with flattery
when I say that the gale of popularity blows so strongly in
your favour that you could command almost anything here ;
and nothing but popularity of the best stamp will attract the
goodwill of the aristocracy around us." Mr. Kydd of Dungiven, after mentioning the efforts of the Rev. Mr. Porter to
propagate his Arian dogmas in and around Newtown-Limavady,
urgently requests a visit from Mr. Cooke :—

" I feel persuaded that your lending your aid in this quarter, and
in this cause, would, under the blessing of God, be attended with
good effect. . . . . I find there are great fears of a division at
next meeting of Synod. I think if we cannot get rid of the Arians
at next meeting we must leave them. The moderate men, as they so
silkenly call themselves . . . . may get their choice, either to
unite with the Arians, and keep with them a Dead Sea peace, or give
them up, and abide with those who, through good report and bad
report, are willing to bear their testimony to the name of Jesus."

The Synod of 1828 approached. It was looked forward to
with intense interest. Each party was preparing for a determined and final struggle. The New Light faith was now no
longer a mere negation. It had of late become positive and aggressive, and, therefore, all the more obnoxious to the vast body
of the people. Some leading ministers of other Churches had
found it necessary to enter the list against Mr. Montgomery in

defence of Evangelical truth. Among the most prominent
were the Rev. Mark Cassidy, Rector of Newtownards, who
published a spirited tract exposing the doctrines of Arianism ;
and the Rev. John Paul, Covenanting Minister of Carrickfergus, whose Defence of Creeds, in reply to Montgomery's
speeches, is exceedingly able and acute. As a piece of sound
argument, and Scriptural exegesis, it is unsurpassed.

A week before the meeting of Synod, a letter was published
in the newspapers, addressed "To the Ministers, Ruling
Elders, and Congregations of the General Synod of Ulster."
It was signed by H. Cooke, John Johnston of Tullylish,
W. Craig of Dromara, and W. D. Stewart of Downpatrick.

" Our sole object," they say, " is to excite the public attention of
the Church. . . . . We wish not to pre-occupy, but merely to
prepare, the minds of our brethren for the important discussions in
which they are about to be engaged.

" We believe it will be admitted that the first object of a Church
should be the character and qualifications of the ministry. The
qualifications we believe to consist in a knowledge of the truth, with
aptness to teach ; and the character, in the personal conversion of
every individual upon whom the office is conferred. A learned
ministry, we believe to be highly desirable ; a converted ministry we
believe to be absolutely necessary."

They therefore recommended the Synod to adopt a new
plan—to commence the religious training and examination of
candidates for the ministry in boyhood ; to continue it during
the whole course of study ; to adopt all necessary means to
ascertain the soundness of their faith, the sanctification of
their souls, and the purity of their lives.

They then proceed to another part of this noble purpose:—

" But, whilst we feel deeply anxious for a reform in the examinations of candidates for the ministry, we cannot overlook the vital
importance of a reform in the examination and introduction of ruling
elders. That reform is necessary, we need not argue. Are there not
ruling elders in the Church who have no prayer in their families,
who do not visit, who do not pray with the sick ? Now a Church

whose office-bearers are so unqualified cannot prosper. Reform the ministry as we may, while the ruling-eldership is unreformed the work is imperfect. The ruling elder, by his vote, equals the minister in the Church Court. He should, therefore, be his equal in those purely religious qualifications required by his office. It will be requisite, then, that the Synod provide for a due and efficient examination into the doctrinal sentiments and personal religion of the men who are to be admitted to so important a share in the government of the Church. Nor do we believe it possible that any considerable religious reform can take place in the ministry or people of the Synod of Ulster, except an equal attention be paid to the ruling-eldership. We delight to contemplate the plain yet lovely form of Presbyterianism as it arose from the hands of the Apostles of our Lord. We delight to contemplate it as it again emerged, disencumbered of the inventions of ages, when the morning of the Reformation dawned upon the mountains of Geneva. We delight to view it as it stood forth, pure, and energetic, and apostolical, from the hands of our Scottish forefathers ; and to their primitive and apostolical models we would seek again to restore it, by removing what has been superadded, correcting what has been done in error, and reforming, by the blessing of heaven, whatever is found contrary to the purity of the gospel in doctrine or in discipline."

This letter went to the root of the whole matter. A thorough reform was advocated. It was clear that nothing short of that would satisfy the writers, and the party they represented. Mr. Cooke was the acknowledged leader of the party. He was candid, bold, and determined. He knew his power, and he resolved to exercise it. He would no longer listen to timid counsels. Half-measures he considered little better than participation in error. Entire separation from Arians and Arianism was what he desired, and was determined, at all hazards, to effect.

The Synod met at Cookstown on Tuesday, the 24th of June, 1828. The Rev. Patrick White, a man of sterling orthodoxy, and a member of a large family long distinguished for attachment to the good old Standards of Presbyterianism, was elected moderator. The attendance of ministers and elders was larger than at any former period of the Church's history, and the house was crowded with an eager and excited audience. All knew what was coming.

As soon as the Synod opened the debate began. The question of the clerkship was still pending. Mr. Porter had publicly declared himself an Arian. His declaration was published to the world in an official document. A large section of the Synod therefore thought he should not be permitted to hold such an important office. Others, however, considered that, when a question of such vital moment as the division of the Synod would come before them, it would be impolitic to create embarrassment with a matter to a large extent personal and subordinate. Mr. Morell, of Ballibay, proposed that a committee " be now appointed to take into consideration the state of this body, and report what course it should pursue to remedy the evils which now prevail amongst us." The motion was seconded by Mr. Horner, of Dublin. It was strenuously opposed by the whole strength of the Arian party, and by many of the Orthodox, including even Mr. Stewart, of Broughshane. Mr. Cooke argued in its favour, and maintained that if the committee were appointed it should consist wholly of Orthodox men.

" Not that I fear the reasonings or the votes of the Arians, but I know their opinions already, while I do not know those of the Orthodox. Arians wish to stay in the Synod, and, like the Greeks in the Trojan War, to burn down the city. . . . If the Synod appoint a committee of Arians and Athanasians, the Presbyterian public will have no confidence in them. I would not prevent them from arguing before the committee ; but I would prevent them from voting. Their object is to Arianize the Synod, to make us, not ' a thinking few,' but a thinking multitude."

After a long debate the motion was formally withdrawn, but the leaders of the Orthodox party met, and prepared a series of resolutions, which were submitted to the house at a subsequent session.

On the following day there was a lull in the storm, during which Mr. Cooke paid the following eloquent tribute to the memory of the Rev. John Thompson, of Carnmoney, who had died on the 22nd of March.

" He was emphatically the father of the Synod ; and throughout a long life of usefulness he fully sustained the high character of a Presbyterian minister. He was, in every sense of the term, a model of what a clergyman ought to be. Venerable for his age, and dis- tinguished for charity ; while he showed himself an unshaken asserter of orthodox principles. His opinion was regarded with parental deference, and his correct views constituted a kind of Synodical dictionary, to which a final appeal was universally made. Though his integrity was unbending, he possessed that urbanity of disposition which rendered him adverse to measures of severity wherever amendment was within the limits of hope. In the world his conversation was such as to embellish the ministerial character, and to shed a lustre over the name of Presbyterianism. The Synod of Ulster occupied a principal share of his attention till his last hour, and even at that critical moment, when usually the brightest intel- lects undergo a temporary obscuration, his mighty mind did not forsake him. He exhibited the character of a dying Christian. His experience was that of a man who could say, ' I have fought the good fight, I have finished my course, and henceforth there is laid up for me a crown of glory.' Long will it be before the Synod of Ulster numbers among its members one so variously distinguished. Rich in Christian experience, ripe in the full fruition of a Saviour's love, he set, like a summer's sun, with all his glories around him."

On Thursday, the 26th, such ministers and elders as had not been present at the previous annual meeting, were required publicly to express their belief in the doctrine of the Trinity. Thirty-eight ministers and fifty-nine elders answered " be- lieve," four ministers and fourteen elders, " not ; " three minis- ters and two elders declined to answer ; one minister withdrew ; and two elders protested against the whole procedure. The course adopted was unquestionably strict ; some may call it harsh ; but few will venture to affirm that, under the extra- ordinary circumstances of the Church, it was not necessary. It served the purpose for which it was intended ; it drew a clear line of demarcation between Arians and Orthodox.

On Friday the great debate began. It was opened by Mr. Morell, who read a series of resolutions agreed to in committee. They were not satisfactory. They were orthodox in tone and tendency; but they were so expressed as to be useless in practice. Mr. Carlile, of Dublin, moved their adoption. His speech, like the resolutions, was a poor attempt at a compromise between truth and error.

"I am placed between so many conflicting elements," he said, "that I am scarcely able to see my way. I have not my own individual views to consult on this occasion, and I cannot bring forward that which I would in all respects approve. . . . The proposed resolutions go no farther than an appeal to the innate power of truth, and there they leave the matter. They do not affix a stigma on any particular party; but acknowledge generally that there are evils in the Synod arising from past laxity. Though Arians may suppose that they are particularly referred to, yet, for myself, I do not particularly refer to them."

In reference to creeds he argued :—" The Christian Church is bound to set forward the sacred Scriptures as the only book that contains rules of faith. It is said we must have some definition of what the Scriptures mean, I do not think so. . . . . Instead of setting up logical men to make a creed, or code of laws, out of Scripture, the Scripture itself should be our creed."

Mr. Cooke followed. He objected altogether to Mr. Carlile's temporising policy; and he severely criticised his plausible arguments. " The proposed resolutions are too vague. They amount in reality to nothing; and that is the reason why Mr. Carlile supports them. They are so expressed that every man can take his own meaning out of them." Mr. Cooke, therefore, proposed an amended series, which provided that every candidate for the ministry, previous to entering a theological class, should be enjoined to present himself at the annual meeting of Synod, to be examined by a select committee respecting his personal religion, his knowledge of Scripture, especially his views on the doctrines of the Trinity, original sin, justification by faith, and regeneration; and that no man should in future receive licence or ordination unless he professed faith in the above doctrines; and farther, that if any thus licensed and ordained should be afterwards found not to preach those doctrines, or should avow any principles opposed to them, he should not be continued in the Church; and farther, should any person be licensed or ordained in opposition to these regulations, such licence or ordination should not be deemed valid.

The debate continued during the whole of Friday and Saturday. Towards its close Mr. Montgomery rose to address the house. He spoke for two hours. As a display of brilliant oratory, sparkling wit, touching pathos, and powerful declamation, his speech had never been surpassed in the Synod. It held the audience spell-bound. His friends then, and afterwards, pronounced it unanswerable. Mr. Stewart, of Broughshane, rose to reply. The contrast was striking. In personal appearance, manner, and style, the two men were as unlike as men could be. Mr. Montgomery's presence was commanding, his manner graceful, his style chaste and classic, his voice singularly sweet. Mr. Stewart made no pretension to elegance or high culture in person, address, tone or style. But in argument he was as far superior to his antagonist as he was inferior in the graces of oratory.* He had the skill of an intellectual anatomist. He detected every lurking sophism. He stripped every fallacy of its beautiful clothing. Cold and keen as polished steel, his incisive logic laid bare the fundamental rottenness of his opponent's oration. He showed that its principles were false, and its practical results a delusion. Mr. Stewart's speech was irresistible. It convinced every thoughtful mind in the assembly. Mr. Cooke was so entirely satisfied with it that he waived his own right of reply. The resolutions were put to the house and carried by a majority of eighty-two, in the largest meeting of Synod ever known in Ulster.

The Arians protested, and placed on record a series of

" reasons," which, certainly, are as defective in logic as they
are in theology. The protest was signed by twenty-one ministers and eighteen elders, some of whom describe themselves as
" believers in the doctrine of the Trinity." One of the
" reasons " will remind the student of Mohammedan history
of Omar's famous argument for the destruction of the Alex-
andrine library. " If any creed, or test of religious belief
contain nothing but what is to be found in the Bible, it is
superfluous ; and if it contain anything contrary to the Bible
it is pernicious, calculated to mislead the understanding, to
prevent the progress of truth, and to perpetuate error." The
protest was vain. It could not stop, or even delay, the determined action of Mr. Cooke. A committee was appointed " to
examine candidates for the ministry in the Church previous to
their entering a theological class ; candidates who have finished
their theological course and Presbyterial trials, and probationers previous to their ordination." Arians were excluded
from the committee.

The orthodoxy of the Presbyterian clergy was thus secured,
as far, at least, as human agency could secure it. No Arian
could thenceforth honestly enter a theological class, obtain
licence, or proceed to ordination. The plan has ever since
been followed by the Presbyterian Church in Ireland, and
has given entire satisfaction. But evils still remained untouched by this law. More than thirty professed Arians sat in
the Synod. Their influence was great. They might largely
leaven the minds of the Presbyterian people, under the sanction of ecclesiastical authority. They were not inclined to
remain passive spectators of the new legislation. All that
eloquence and energy could effect, would be effected, to stop or
thwart it. Mr. Cooke foresaw this, and resolved to counteract
the evil. He believed there could be neither peace nor prosperity in the Church so long as Arianism found a resting place
within its pale. He, therefore, gave notice that, " He intended
to move at next meeting for a consideration of the state of this
Synod, with a view to reform existing evils."

His speech on giving notice of motion was a magnificent specimen of forensic eloquence. It exists in a perfect form, being one of the very few which he himself revised for separate publication. His object in it was partly to defend his past line of action against the misrepresentations and calumnies of a host of assailants; and partly to explain and enforce the duty of the Church in regard to her acknowledged Standards :—

"On reading the reports of the Synod of last year, at Strabane, I was not a little surprised with the picture there drawn of my opinions and proposals. In these reports I am represented as proposing that there should be some kind of committee whose business would be to visit and pray with all Arian ministers; and if this were unavailing for their conversion, to suspend, or, perhaps, finally to degrade them. This plan was called fanatical, and I was, consequently, honoured with the name of fanatic. My opponents exulted, my friends were surprised at the folly, as they called it, of such an absurd proposal; and I do assure you, sir, I had no friend more surprised than I was myself, when I found such a proposal ascribed to my invention. I speak, sir, under the correction of this house, when I say that the man who has given me as the author of the plan has, to use the gentlest language, been guilty of misrepresentation. I never made such a proposal to this house, yet it has run the circuit of some Irish newspapers, has been blazoned in some English and Scottish Socinian magazines; and, if I recollect well, has been honoured with Italics, in order to arrest the attention of readers by its folly or absurdity.

"The plain fact, sir, is, that some such proposal was made in this house, but it was not made by me. It was made by one of the most talented and eloquent opponents of my views of Church fellowship. Whatever merit or demerit—whatever praise or blame belong to it, they are not mine—they are the sole, original, and undivided property of Dr. Wright, to whom I now thus publicly restore the entire and undisturbed possession.

"Before I come to the subject immediately claiming our attention, I feel bound to advert to another mistake. I had said in my evidence before the Commissioners of Education, that I considered there were thirty-five Arians in the Synod. But when the report of the Synod of Strabane gave the appearance merely of ten, I was instantly set down as ignorant of the true state of the Synod, and guilty of a voluntary exaggeration of the number of its Arian members. Various were the accusations I had to sustain under this head. First I was accused of speaking as if possessed of a ' discerning of spirits,' when I called men Arian who had never avowed their opinions. You will, therefore, bear with me when I set myself right with the Synod upon this subject. I pretend to no such extraordinary gift of discerning men's secret opinions ; but I judge on the ordinary principles of the reason and revelation which God has bestowed upon me. . . . I plainly stated to the Commissioners the principles upon which I judged of the number of Arians in the Synod. The first principle I stated to be *open declaration*. The second, *defect in their declaration of sentiments*. There are a few members of this Synod who have always avowed their Arian sentiments. I knew them because they wore no cloak. There are others who have never openly avowed Arian doctrines : I knew them, not by what they avowed, but by what they did not avow. The doctrine of the Supreme Deity of the Word forms such a noble and unshaken corner-stone for the temple of God, that he who holds it, as the foundation of his faith and hope, cannot conceal from the world the glories of his confidence. He who holds the Saviour to be ' God manifest in the flesh,' who feels the full acceptation of His ' coming into the world to save sinners,' he who acknowledges His dignity as ' the mighty God,' yet confides in His atonement as ' the Prince of Peace,'—he, I say, who thus believes and thus feels, cannot be silent. The uncontrollable thought takes full possession of his soul, and ' out of the abundance of the heart the mouth must speak.' When I, therefore, find a minister who preaches not, or who speaks not, of this doctrine, I believe, I know he holds it not ; for to believe, and yet be silent are totally incompatible. Upon these principles I formed my judgment, and the result of this year's inquiry has fully established the correctness of my estimate. The number of those who have openly avowed Arianism, or something akin to it, or who have, for the reasons they have stated, refused, or declined to answer, now amounts to thirty-two. There are of the thirty-five to whom I alluded, some who have not been yet present, and who, from age, cannot be present ; and when all shall thus be added, I am sorry to say, that so far from being incorrect in overrating the Arians of this body, I have underrated them by three or four. The number of Arian members in this Synod I would now say amounts, most probably, to thirty-nine. Should any of the members, whom I have thus classified, deny the correctness of my opinions, they are at liberty to do so ; and I shall rejoice in their denial."

Referring to the alleged hardship of calling upon members of Synod to declare their religious belief, he said :—

"I cannot see how any man could hesitate to answer to the truth of all he knows about religion. Whatever opinions I hold in religion, I glory in proclaiming them. The declaration may entitle me to the honourable sobriquet of enthusiast, or fanatic, or bigot, or what you will, but will never deter me from giving to every man that asketh, an account of the hope that is in me ; or of plainly stating how far, in my opinion, error has made breaches in the walls of our Zion. If any man entrust me with a secret, I shall endeavour faithfully to keep it ; but my opinions in religion, or my opinions of the religious sentiments of others, I shall never consider as a secret, but shall at all times, openly declare them to every one who has a right or an interest in ascertaining their nature. . . .

"Against the whole past proceedings of the Synod, and against the object contemplated in my notice of a future motion, three broad grounds of objection are exhibited :—

"The first of these represents the proceedings of the Synod as opposed to 'the right of private judgment.' Whether our proceedings be, or be not, opposed to the right of private judgment, I shall not take upon me to determine ; as I must confess myself, up till this hour, ignorant of what the right of private judgment, as used by the objectors, can possibly mean. This is a startling confession of ignorance in the midst of 'the march of mind,' and in the full blaze of 'the lights of the nineteenth century.' But the fault is not mine. No member of Synod has condescended to explain what he means by 'the right of private judgment.' Does it mean that every man has a right to think as he pleases, as the lights of the late French, and of some modern schools of philosophy, seem to intimate ? Then, at once, I totally deny its authority. Let me look at thee, thou Idol called 'Right of private judgment !' I am told that if I deny to worship thee, I shall be branded as a rebel to thy high and legitimate powers. It may be so ; yet I will not tremble before the philosophical idol men have conjured into existence, nor bow before the image they are pleased to set up. If by right of private judgment we are to understand a right to think as we please, then what we have a right to think it never can be wrong to think. We cease then to be accountable for our opinions ; indeed accountability becomes impossible ; for where there can be no wrong, the ordinary idea of accountability disappears. Then, as our actions arise from our opinions, where opinions cannot be wrong, actions cannot be wrong. Thus virtue and vice are confounded for ever, and the distinctions between moral right and wrong disappear from the universe.

" But have we not been told a thousand times that the Protestant religion is built upon 'the right of private judgment.' God forbid it were ever built upon any such flimsy foundation. The Protestant religion is built upon the command, upon the Word of God ; upon prophets and apostles, Jesus Christ himself being the chief corner stone. There it rests unshaken upon the Rock of Ages, and the gates of hell shall not prevail against it.

" I know it has been the practice of many called philosophers, and of not a few called Divines, to fix upon human principles, when they should have ascended to divine principles. Hence the modern doctrine concerning right of private judgment. When I therefore deny all allegiance to this phantom king, I am bound to point out to this Assembly what principles I consider to be entitled to the legitimate sovereignty. These seem to me to be the following :—

" 1. It is the duty of every man to search the Scriptures. John v. 39.

" 2. It is the duty of every man to be fully persuaded in his own mind. Rom. xiv. 5.

" 3. It is the duty of every man to receive the dictates and guidance of Scripture, as the revealed will of heaven. 2 Tim. iii. 16.

" 4. As public bodies are composed of individuals, they, as public bodies, are subject to the same laws as individuals. Consequently, it is the duty of public bodies to search the mind of God in the Scriptures, to be fully persuaded in their own minds, and, in all their decisions, to be guided solely by the authority of what God has revealed. Now, if these four principles include what is meant by the right of private judgment, let me just entreat our opponents to reduce their phraseology to some more intelligible, some more definite, some more scriptural standard. And let me assure them, that, if these principles include their private judgment, we will be the last to recede from one iota of them. Let them convince us of departing from one of these principles, and we will thank them for the correction ; but, till they bring this conviction, which I am persuaded they will not even attempt, we will say with Luther, when accused before the Diet—' Here we take our stand ; we pursue no other course : and God be our help.'

" Another ground of accusation taken against us is, that we are unfriendly to liberty. This ground is untenable, for we are the determined friends of the civil constitution of the empire. To our Puritan forefathers, historians admit that Britain stands indebted for every principle of her freedom. . . .

" Having now, sir, cleared away the rubbish with which, during a period of twelve months, misrepresentation has been permitted to disfigure the subject ; and having now beaten in the advanced guards of our opponents, we come to take our ground, and establish our defences. Scripture is adduced against us ; we shall prove that we stand on it. Reason is brought against us ; we shall fearlessly appeal to its decisions. Custom is brought against us ; we shall appeal to honesty. The nature of our views has been misunderstood or misrepresented ; we shall endeavour to explain and vindicate our proceedings.

" We take, then, as our first position, that it is the duty of every Christian and of every Church, to try the doctrine of those who preach. 'Beloved, believe not every spirit, but try the spirits whether they be of God.' 'Now, I beseech you, brethren, mark them which cause divisions and offences contrary to the doctrine which ye have heard, and avoid them.' 'Whosoever transgresseth, and abideth not in the doctrine of Christ, hath not God. He that abideth in the doctrine of Christ, he hath both the Father and the Son. If there come any unto you, and bring not this doctrine, receive him not into your house, neither bid him God speed.' ' I know thy works, and thy labour, and thy patience ; and thou hast *tried them which say they are apostles*, and are not.' . . . .

" We take, as a second position, that the primitive scriptural method of ' trying the spirits ' was by plain questions on the fundamental doctrines of the gospel. Our Saviour sets the example. ' Whom do men say that I, the Son of Man, am ? . . . . But whom say ye that I am ?' . . . . . ' What think ye of Christ' ? ' Whose Son is He ?' When they answer, even in Scripture language, ' He is the Son of David,' Our Saviour puts an additional question, to ascertain in what sense He was called the Son of David. ' If David then called him Lord, how is he David's son ? And no man was able to answer him a word.' . . . .

" We take, as a third position, that it is the duty of every preacher of the gospel to give to every Church of which he is a member an account of the doctrines which he preaches. ' And I went up by revelation, and communicated unto them that gospel which I preach among the Gentiles ; but privately to them which were of reputation,

lest by any means I should run, or had run, in vain.' Here the
Apostle Paul hesitated not to give the Church a retrospective view
of the gospel he had been preaching ; and that not even to the
Churches among which he had been preaching, but to the Church
at Jerusalem, where he had not been since his conversion. It will
require no argument to prove that what Paul did, we, as successors
of the apostles, are bound, after his example, to do.

"Our fourth proposition is, that error in any of the fundamental
doctrines of the gospel is destructive to the Churches. 'And their
word will eat as doth a canker, of whom is Hymenæus and Philetus;
who concerning the truth have erred, saying that the resurrection is
past already ; and overthrow the faith of some.' I now put it
home to my orthodox brethren, for to them I especially address myself, and I call upon them to answer—if an error respecting the
resurrection 'eateth as a canker' and 'overthroweth the faith of
some,' what must be the effect of an error respecting the Lord Jesus
Christ himself ?

"Again, we consider it the duty of the teachers and rulers of
Churches to refuse their authority to the preaching of doctrines which
in their consciences they believe to be erroneous, and subversive of
the faith. 'I besought thee to abide at Ephesus, that thou mightest
charge some that they teach no other doctrine.' I do beseech my
orthodox brethren to pause over this text, and apply it as the measure
of their own conduct. Do they believe that Arianism is the doctrine
of the gospel ? Do they believe that it is subversive of the gospel ?
Yet do they not, year after year, give their public licence to Arians
to preach the gospel ? Do they not, year after year, ordain them to
minister in the gospel ? And have they ever made an attempt to
tell them that the Supreme Deity of Christ is the foundation of the
gospel ? And have they ever attempted to charge them that they
preach no other doctrine ? Our fathers in the ministry, by the
manner in which they have conducted this Church, have been instrumental, I grieve to say it, in laying a snare for the feet of us, their
sons. We have, accordingly, been entangled in it, and are so to this
hour ; and I do beseech my brethren, for the sake of consistency—
for the sake of Scripture truth, to ponder the paths of their feet, and
make an earnest, an humble, a persevering effort, to free themselves
and future generations from this unhappy entanglement.

"Further, we consider it, upon Scripture warrant, to be the duty
of the Churches to follow after uniformity—not a uniformity to be
produced by pains and penalties, and legal enactments ; but by a

strict adherence to Scripture truth and apostolical practice. 'Now I beseech you, brethren, by the name of our Lord Jesus Christ, that ye all speak the same thing, and that there be no divisions among you ; but that ye be perfectly joined in the same mind, and in the same judgment.' Now, are Trinitarians and Arians joined in the same mind, in the same judgment ? They are divided about the very first principles of religion, about the great object of their testimony ; and while they remain contradicting one another, yet apparently forming one Church, they can only serve to increase the doubtings of the sceptic, or create suspicions in men's minds of their mutual insincerity. The great object for which Christ erected a Church was to bear witness of Him ; and except there be uniformity in that witness, I cannot discover upon what principles her testimony is entitled to acceptance.

" Finally, I believe we have Scripture authority for endeavouring to purify the Church from the errors in doctrine or in practice that may from time to time arise. The Apostle Paul addresses Timothy on his duties as a Christian minister. In 2 Tim. ii. 17, he impugns the erroneous doctrines of Hymenæus and Philetus, who had overthrown the faith of some ; and in the 21st verse he adds, 'If a man shall purge himself from these, he shall be a vessel unto honour, sanctified, and meet for the master's use, and prepared unto every good work.' To Titus Paul says, ' A man that is an heretic, after the first and second admonition, reject.' The Thessalonians he charges, ' Now, we command you, brethren, in the name of our Lord Jesus Christ, that ye withdraw yourselves from every brother that walketh disorderly, and not after the tradition which he received from us.' . . . .

" I have thus, sir, endeavoured to take and illustrate some of the Scripture grounds upon which we rest our cause. And I come now to exhibit the reasonableness of the means by which, under the good providence of God, we propose to advance the purity of this Church.

" The first of those means is, a scriptural, plain, and public declaration of the doctrines which we teach. This will apply to the examination of entrants to the ministry, and to the continuation of communion with those who are already ordained.

" A public confession of a Church's faith should never be a test to be imposed upon any man. But it is a public declaration to all men of what that Church believes, that they may know upon what terms, and in what professed principles, they enter her communion.

" As the Church I have already shown to be a witness for God, so
a public confession of her faith is necessary to let the nature of her
witness be known. In this way we know what the Church of Scotland
testifies, what the Church of England testifies ; and we are enabled thus
to judge into what communion we can enter with a good conscience.
I may be told that all this information may as well be received in
the present state of this Synod, for we all allow that the Bible is our
Confession. Granted. But I ask, what Bible is your Confession ? Is
it the Trinitarian Bible, which announces ' The Word was God ' ?
Or is it the Arian Bible, which announces ' The Word was
divine' ? Or is it the Socinian Bible, which has it, ' Reason was
divine' ? Answer me what Bible is our Confession, and then I shall
understand you.

" I am well aware that, in this age of liberality, the man who
stands up as the advocate of creeds or Confessions exposes himself to
a thousand hostile attacks. For the liberals of this age are only
liberal to themselves—with one exception, indeed. They are most
liberal of abuse to every man who dares to oppose them.

" Every man has a creed, for every man believes something ; and
a creed is merely what a man believes.

" The sole purpose of a creed, then, is to show what a man believes,
or what a Church believes. Everything beyond this comes under
the head of abuse. When we call upon a man for his creed, we
merely ask, what does he believe ? And I confess I see no principle,
either of politeness or religion, that forbids the question, nor any
principle of honesty that entitles any man to refuse a reply. . . .
The arguments urged against creeds seem to me reducible to the
following arrangement :—It has been argued that ' we wish to impose
a test.' There is a double fallacy in this. We impose nothing ; for
imposition implies power, with pains and penalties for refusing compliance. Then, in popular use, the word test signifies something to
be taken in order to qualify for office ; and which, if taken, the right
to the office follows. Confessions of Faith have been so abused ; but
any such abuse is far from our minds. Were a man to sign a
Confession of Faith again and again, I should not consider him one
whit better qualified for the ministerial office than before his signature. My conviction of the sincerity of his profession, the scriptu-
rality of his views, and the sanctity of his life, would, in my mind, be
his sole qualifications ; for the signing of a creed I consider not as a
test—I merely view it as a means of putting to a man this plain
question, What do you think ?

" The second argument against the use of any creed is derived from the danger of binding men to any uninspired phraseology. On this subject let me explain the practice of the Synod of Ulster. At an early period of the Synod's history it was found that some persons scrupled to admit certain phrases in the Westminster Confession. These scruples arose, not from opposition to the doctrines of the Confession, but from the phraseology in which some of them were expressed. The Synod, therefore, enacted, that persons, when required to make a declaration of their faith, might have liberty to explain, in words of their own, the sense in which they understood any particular phrases ; at the same time satisfying the Presbytery that they did not reject the doctrine, but merely scrupled at the phraseology. This order of Synod was called the Pacific Act, and has been the ordinary law in subscribing presbyteries down till this time. For my own part, I would not wish to bind any man to express his faith in any particular, uninspired phraseology. I would leave him to the free and unrestricted selection of his own words, where he could not adopt mine; but I would beg him to furnish me with such words as would clearly enable me to comprehend his meaning.

" But if you are willing to sanction a man's selection of phrases, why not be contented with mere Scripture phrases ? Here let me remark, that all the opponents of creeds and confessions would, I believe, at once surrender were Churches to accept their declaration of faith in mere Scripture phrases. And why are they not contented with such declaration ? Why ? just because it is no declaration. A confession in Scripture phrases is, indeed, a declaration of what God has said ; but not an account of the meaning man attaches to God's sayings. . . . . Had we asked Mr. Montgomery what the Bible had called Christ, he had answered rightly, ' The Son of God.' But we ask him not what the Bible says ; we ask him what he thinks the Bible means by ' Son of God.' . . . .

" To the use of confessions it has been ingenuously objected, that we require first to understand the Bible, and then we make a confession a rule for understanding the Bible, which we are presumed to understand before the confession was made. To this I answer—A confession is no rule for understanding the Bible ; a confession is a mere declaration of what we believe to be the meaning of the Bible.

" The same individual has argued, that by a confession we add to the Bible. Did the gentleman but weigh this charge, I am convinced he would retract it. His charge arises from his continual mistake about the nature and purposes of creeds. They are not made to add

to the Word of God, or to have any authority as the Word of God ;
they are merely intended to declare what we believe to be the meaning of the Word of God.   They are not to be considered an authoritative declaration of what God has said, but of what we believe to
be the import of His saying.

   " He has likewise charged us with an invasion of the rights of
private judgment . . . . I deny that the making of a Confession of Faith is an invasion of the rights of private judgment. It is
an exercise of private judgment. An individual comes to the Bible,
and by every means which God has bestowed upon him, he endeavours to ascertain its meaning. He propounds this meaning to
others; and on a similar examination they agree with him. This
agreement is a mere aggregate of private judgments. In their union
of private judgments, they determine that persons denying doctrines
which they hold to be fundamental and essential, shall not be considered of their company. Ah ! replies the objector, if you deny me
admission, you invade my private judgment. It may be so, reply
the others ; but if you intrude, you invade our private judgment.
We leave you undisturbed to the choice of your companionship ; nor
shall we intrude upon you farther than by our opinion, if you will
listen to it. If we cannot convince you of your error, and our correctness, we beg to part, and to part in charity. But surely if your
private judgment be to overturn our private judgment, this is not
liberality in sentiment, but tyranny over our consciences.

   " We are charged with claiming infallibility. I pause not to argue
the Church's infallibility. But I shall fearlessly announce that there
is a scriptural sense in which every true believer is infallible. This
I learn from Jesus Christ :—' And they shall be all taught of God.'
Now God must be an infallible teacher, and every one taught of Him
must, in the scriptural sense, be infallible. But in declaring our
creed, we claim not to be infallible interpreters of God's meaning,
but honest interpreters of our own. I do believe that every honest
man is able infallibly to declare what he believes, what he disbelieves,
or where he is in doubt. This is all that we, by a declaration of our
faith, propose to do. It is not fair to conjure up the phantom of
Romish infallibility, and charge us with all the enormities committed
under its guidance . . . .

   " Having now, sir, endeavoured to overturn a host of straggling
objections collected from different quarters, I come to engage with
the condensed phalanx which Mr. Montgomery has so powerfully
led on against us. Permit me, sir, to pause for a moment and pay

the tribute of my admiration to the splendour in which he has exhibited his array of argument. When last year he depicted the miseries of a minister's unhappy wife, whose husband came home to her, having avowed his real religious opinions, I could scarcely refuse a tear to the imaginary distresses of the admirable tragedian. But when this year, sir, he has summoned up the full energy of his powers, and given us scene after scene, in every possible variety, I was almost induced to forget the presence of the Moderator and Synod, and this crowded audience around us, and to believe myself transported to Arabia, and witnessing a modern exhibition of Aladdin and his wonderful lamp. I could almost fancy I saw him rub this lamp of wonders, while the first scene presented me with a lecturer on polemic theology.

" The lecturer began by announcing, with all due solemnity, this important proposition—' Religion is a matter entirely between a man and his God.' It sounds well. It served the lecturer to show that we, as a Synod, could, therefore, have no possible right to interfere in the matter. It is strange, sir, how nearly a proposition can approach to truth, and, after all, be untrue. That religion is a matter between man and his God, is a truth most certain; but that religion is a matter entirely between man and his God, is an assertion most unfounded. Were the lecturer's proposition true, I wonder how a minister would attempt to interfere in the religious instruction of his parish. Were the proposition true, I wonder why Paul has said,— ' Now, then, we are ambassadors for Christ; as though God did beseech you by us, we pray you in Christ's stead, be ye reconciled to God' . . . . Religion is not a matter entirely between a man and his God. There is a large portion of its outward instrumentality which is entirely a matter between man and man; yet regulated, in its ministration, not by the will of man, but by a strict conformity to the revelation of God. It is upon this principle that this Synod is bound, humbly, yet vigorously, perseveringly, and zealously, to interfere in the religious instruction of the people, to protect them from error, to furnish them with wholesome instruction in the truth.

" The second proposition announced by our lecturer was this,—' I will be accountable to no man in matters of religion, as no man can be accountable for me.' This is another of those splendid fallacies by which inconsiderate minds are led captive. 'Tis a bit of common glass, finely cut, and set as a jewel, deriving its play of colours from a little foil ingeniously placed beneath it. Take it asunder— the colours, and the beauty, and the value are gone. I shall separate this gem from its setting, that its true value may be ascertained. 'No man can be accountable for me.' This is the reason, the gem of the argument. Now, if by 'accountable' you mean that no man can be made a substitute for me, so that he may perish and I be saved, I freely admit its correctness. In this sense take it, and draw what conclusion you may. But our lecturer is too wise a man to exhibit such truisms to his pupils. In opposition, then, to the only other meaning he can have, I am ready to affirm, and to confirm it by the word of unerring truth, that men in certain circumstances are accountable for one another, and that too under the most awful penalties that the Divine Word has revealed. 'Son of man, I have made thee a watchman unto the house of Israel; therefore hear the word of my mouth, and give them warning from me. When I say unto the wicked, thou shalt surely die; and thou givest him not warning, nor speakest to warn the wicked from his wicked way, to save his life; the same wicked man shall die in his iniquity, but his blood will I require at thy hand.' Where is now the high-sounding proposition, that one man is not accountable for another ? God has spoken, and it is fled; and the sound of its terror shall be heard no more . . . .

" The other fragment of the lecturer's proposition,—' I will be accountable to no man in matters of religion,' is a bold, and open, and heroic announcement, yet totally inconsistent with the purposes of the gospel. I have already proved that the object of this gospel is to bear witness. Now, an unaccountable witness is rather a novelty in jurisprudence. It is unlike the conduct of Paul :—' I have not shunned to declare unto you all the counsel of God;' and it is only by this open and unreserved declaration that the apostle is able to say:—' I take you to record this day, that I am pure from the blood of all men.' Mr. Montgomery is also at variance with the advice of Peter:—' Be ready always to give an answer to every man that asketh a reason of the hope that is in you.' This advice clearly indicates an unrestricted accountability not only of our faith, but of the grounds and reasons upon which our hopes are rested.

" But as lectures are tiresome things, the lamp was rubbed, and the scene was changed . . . . We were transported to Spain, and found ourselves in the great square of Madrid. The bells were tolling sullenly from the steeples . . . . A dark procession was advancing with slow and measured steps. I saw prisoners whom they were conducting to execution. Their garments were painted with evil spirits and flames. I saw the rack, and the other instruments of torture. I saw the faggots they had heaped up to feed the murky fires of their *auto da fé*. I heard the prisoners groan and shriek in the midst of their tortures. I started as from a horrible dream; I exclaimed, What is all this? 'Oh!' replied a proud Castilian, 'It is merely a Presbyterian minister requested by his brethren to declare his real religious opinions.'"

After a few more such touches of irony illumined by Aladdin's lamp, he proceeds:—

"But the lamp is rubbed again, and lo! we are transported to the lofty mountains of Dungiven. The sun is riding high in the heavens; his beams are sleeping on the heath; peasants are pursuing their peaceful toils; the children are gathering the fuel for the ruddy bonfire of midsummer. The cattle are ruminating in quiet, or lowing to responsive echoes; and the clear blue sea sparkles in the distance, reflecting the beauties of the scene in the mirror of its placid bosom. The genius of the scene is rolling slowly along, enjoying at once the beauties of nature, and the comforts of his easy chariot; and his mind is indulging in all the reveries of the sublime, or soaring into the loftier contemplations of exalted piety. But mark how suddenly and lamentably the scene is changed. The contemplations of philanthropy are interrupted and disarranged; and the late placid face of nature assumes a sudden and unaccountable scowl, indicative of some mighty, and monstrous, and adverse agency. Can the muses of epic poetry or tragedy account for this wondrous change? Or, if there have arisen a muse of novel or romance, can she aid us in explaining the phenomenon? Yes, between them, somehow, they have discovered a solitary Calvinistic minister, plodding his weary way to the meeting of the Synod of Ulster, and nature has shrunk affrighted at his presence, and the genius of Arianism has participated in the discomposure. John Calvin, I have heard many a charge laid at thy door; and, from Pope, I have heard of 'Presbyterian sour;' but the master-charge of all remained for you, Mr. Montgomery, when you made the presence of a solitary Calvinist cast a gloom over the festivities of nature. If the thing be a jest, it is a very good jest. But Mr. Montgomery is no joker. If it be meant for a picture, 'tis a very good picture, and as fine a specimen of the creative as you would wish. But Mr. Montgomery avers that it is sober earnest, and real fact . . . .

"Having now, sir, endeavoured to dispose of that part of Mr. Montgomery's address which I would denominate the picturesque, I come to submit to you a condensed view of whatever can be considered argumentation.

" As the very front of our offending, we are accused of 'prescribing a creed' to our brethren. We prescribe no creed. We openly tell our own opinion. We say to those who wish to join us, 'What are your religious opinions?' If we cannot agree, we part as we met. We give our opinions openly, but we prescribe them to no man. I have already given you my views of what is called private judgment, and in my statement of principles this house appeared universally to acquiesce. I shall, therefore, only now add, that while I cannot recognise the use of private judgment as a right from God to think as a man pleases, without light from the revealed will of God, I do not therefore imply, that any man has right, or privilege, or power from God, to interfere by coercion with the private opinions of another. I disclaim such interference with any man, except by counsel, advice, or argument. I permit no such interference with myself, except when men come armed with the mere weapons of logical discussion, and scriptural argument. If, by 'private judgment' is merely meant that no public body has a right to prescribe opinions to private individuals, I most heartily assent to the proposition. But the same principle that refuses to the public body the right to prescribe to the individual, refuses to the individual the right to prescribe to the public body. My private, my individual opinion is, that we should not hold intimate church fellowship with persons differing from us on fundamental doctrines of religion. Mr. Montgomery thinks we should be united, though of the most essentially discordant materials. Whether must Mr. Montgomery or I surrender our individual opinions? My plan is, to leave Mr. Montgomery free to form his religious opinions, and to propagate them as he may, but not in my company, or under my sanction. Mr. Montgomery is determined to keep in our company, though not over agreeable, with the benignant wish, as he affirms, of converting us from our error . . . . Who now prescribes the creed in this case? I answer, it is Mr. Montgomery and his friends who wish to exercise over our faith such overwhelming hardships as will not even permit us to choose our own company . . . .

" But you must not inquire into our opinion, says Mr. Montgomery, for 'When creeds were formed, corruptions began.' This proposition is marvellously near the truth. Reverse the ends of the sentence and you have it perfect. It will stand thus :—When corruptions began in the Churches, then creeds were formed to counteract them. The corruptions of Arius preceded the Nicene creed. That the best and most scriptural creeds have formed insufficient barriers against error, is a fact I readily admit. But wherever they have been insufficient, the fault has been in the administration, not in the law. The Church of Geneva has been overwhelmed with neology; but not till after her ministers had begun, under the influence of Voltaire, to take the liberty of dispensing with her established creeds. Just the same was the case in the Synod of Ulster. In proportion as the Presbyteries insisted on subscription, in the same proportion did they retain their orthodoxy. In proportion as Presbyteries laid their formularies aside, in the same proportion were they overspread with Arianism. . . .

" Let us, says Mr. Montgomery, leave 'all disputed points : points trifling and unessential ; and let us come to an agreement upon undisputed, important, and fundamental matters.' . . . If our creed is to be formed of undisputed points, we must far excel those individuals who are characterized as scanty in creed. There is not a point in religion that has not been over and over again disputed. . . . .

" And, alas ! sir, is it come to this ? that the character of Our Lord Himself is announced as a point not essential ? Surely, the doctrine of His Deity is essential to the Bible, for 'the Word was God.' Surely it is essential to my salvation, for I require an Almighty Saviour. Surely it is essential to our worship, for men are commanded to 'honour the Son, even as they honour the Father.' Surely it is essential to our principles, for while the Bible demands of us to love the Lord our God, with all our heart and all our soul, the same word declares that the 'love of Christ constraineth us,' and 'if any man love not the Lord Jesus Christ, let him be anathema.'

Mr. Cooke wanted the immediate separation of Arian and Orthodox. This fact was generally known. Yet in his speech he advocated a moderate measure, which, when fully considered, was a compromise. At the close of his speech he gave his reason for so doing, while he declared his firm resolve to go farther at a future and fitting moment :—

" Why, it may be said, if such be my views, have I appeared as the mover of the amended resolutions of this year, which do not contemplate separation of our present constituency, but merely go to

erect a barrier against future inroads ? I shall render to this house
the reasons of my conduct.

"I do not think we have taken all the steps by which so
momentous a matter ought to be preceded. Our congregations have
not been addressed ; our eldership has not been sufficiently consulted ; we have given no admonition, we have proclaimed no fast,
as, in every religious emergency, our Scottish forefathers would have
done.   Now, all these are measures, I conceive, absolutely pre-
requisite ; therefore, until they shall have been attempted, or taken,
I do not conceive separation scriptural.

"I sincerely declare, that I am not only open to conviction, but
actually wishing to be convinced, that separation is unnecessary.
The man who attempts to reason me out of my present opinions,
has, I must confess, an opponent prejudiced in his favour.   I hope
particularly my friend Mr. Carlile will discuss the subject ; and if he
can convince me from Scripture, that Trinitarians, Arians, and Socinians, can form a scriptural Church, and cordially unite in licensing
and ordaining one another, I shall resign my present views, and
unite with him in preserving our present constituency.   But, as I
have yet heard no argument that convinces me of the propriety of
remaining in our present most admired disorder, I do hope that
something new will be produced ; and, above all things, that Scripture will be fairly and fully examined, and shown to give most explicit
testimony upon this subject, before I be expected to yield my judgment, or consent to the continuance of a nominal union, that only
proves how really we are disunited.

"I have rested for the present in the amended resolutions,
because they are in accordance with the opinions of men for whose
opinions I entertain the highest respect.   My own opinion is decidedly for separation.   Upon this point I most cordially concur
with the opinions delivered by my venerated friends, Messrs. Elder,
Dill, &c., and by my young friends, Messrs. Barnett, Brown, &c.
But when I see arrayed against us men, of whose orthodoxy I can
entertain no doubt ; men, of whose zeal I have seen most convincing
proofs ; when I see my friends, Messrs. Horner, and Hanna, and
Wright, and Morell, and Stewart, and Reid, willing to go no farther
than the present resolutions ; and when I know that the opinion of
Dr. Chalmers, whose name and praise are in all the Churches, goes
no farther, I must confess that, in face of this array, it requires a
man to have no little share of decision to hold his opinion without
faltering.   In face of it I do hesitate, but still my opinion is un-

changed ; yet I submit with deference, for a time, to the judgment of wiser and better men, that I may judge of the probable efficacy of their measures, by the result of a reasonable experiment.

" The object of my contemplated motion is to attempt a remedy for the evils that are found to exist in the constituency of this body.

" The principal evil I conceive to consist in the unnatural and un-coalescing admixture of our doctrines. . . . For a perfect church I look not till the Lord shall come with his saints ; but for a more perfect one than this Synod at present exhibits, I think, without much presumption, we may reasonably hope " . . . .

Delineating the character of the true gospel minister, he said :—

" A respectable minister, in whatever station he is placed by Pro- • vidence, must be a decided man. A minister of other character may be learned, and rich, and eloquent, and much a favourite ; but while, like the air-fed chameleon, he takes all the colour from the objects around him, and appears green, yellow, or grey, according to the objects he rests on, he is a most miserable specimen of clerical defection ; the mere creature of the circumstances by which he is surrounded. A respectable minister, like some of the bright gems, should give, not take, his colour. His character should not be moulded by the objects that surround him ; but he should endeavour to transfer his own moral image to the souls committed to his instruction. I would have him a man untaught in the school which whispers to a young minister, ' Do not be in a hurry to declare your religious sentiments ; time enough when you have got a congrega-tion, and learn the opinions that will please your people.' I would not have a man offensively intrusive, but gentle, yet decided in his principles and instructions. Without these qualities neither minister nor Synod can be truly respectable ; and to cherish, under the divine blessing, such a decision of character is one great object of the motion which I now wish to enter upon your books.

" Let me quote two passages of Scripture for the meditation of my brethren, and I shall relieve your patience by concluding this address. The first is a prophecy of the coming glory of the Church, indica-tive of her uniformity of opinion, testimony, and worship : ' Thy watchmen shall lift up the voice ; with the voice together shall they sing ; for they shall see eye to eye, when the Lord shall bring again Zion.'

" The other portion I shall repeat is in reference to the many exhortations we have received to study concord and peace. Many objects are to be sacrificed for peace; but peace, as well as gold, may be bought too dear. Therefore, when we look for peace, labour for peace, pray for peace, let us remember the words of the prophet,— 'I will give you peace and truth in this place.' In the promise of God they are united blessings ; and He will not bestow the one till we take it in conjunction with the other."

This remarkable speech made a profound impression. It confirmed waverers among the Orthodox. It showed the Arian party that their cause was lost, and that their connection with the Synod was already virtually severed. No attempt was made to oppose the notice of motion.

Mr. Cooke's labours in the pulpit and on the platform had roused the laity of the Church. The vast majority of them were Orthodox, and they pressed the Synod to defend the Church's faith. Memorials were presented from Cookstown, Knowhead, Ray, Donaghmore, Ballykelly, Omagh, Letterkenny, Raphoe, Stranorlar, and Boveva, praying for separation. The Arians attempted a counter demonstration, but only three congregations could be found to join in memorials. On hearing the memorials on both sides, the Synod resolved to postpone the consideration of them till next meeting. Matters were not yet ripe for final action, but the time was approaching. The minds, both of ministers and laity, were becoming leavened; and from certain indications of the feelings of the Arian party, Mr. Cooke was able to see, that, in all probability, he and those who acted with him, would be saved from an extreme measure by the voluntary withdrawal of their opponents.

It was not from the Arian party that Mr. Cooke had now most to fear. Some ministers of decided Orthodoxy opposed his measures. Among them were his earliest personal friends. Their plea was peace, and a desire to preserve the integrity of the Synod. Their hope was that the measures already adopted would prevent the spread of heresy. Mr. Carlile opposed him, but on different grounds. His orthodoxy was unquestioned, but he objected to creeds and confessions. The Scriptures, in his opinion, should be the sole creed of the Church. It was wrong to set up any other. It was the duty of ministers and Church courts to test all candidates for licence by the Bible, and " to use all due diligence, according to the circumstances of the case, to ascertain that the person who is under examination be conformed to that Standard." In regard to those already in the Church, who held Arian views, it was the duty of the Orthodox to separate themselves from them as individuals, and to endeavour to counteract their errors, but not to separate from them ecclesiastically.

" No man," he maintained, " who is not required personally to acquiesce in error, or to act contrary to his duty as a Christian or a minister, has any good ground for separating from the Synod. The idea of separating from others for the purpose of bearing testimony against them to the world, does not seem to me to be derived from the Word of God, but from the pride of the human heart. The only principle on which the Christian Church can ever be united is, that we unite with every man as far as we can, without denying some revealed truth, or violating some divine command. The Scripture principle of separation is to separate, for some specific work, from those who cannot, or will not, unite with us in that work, while we retain our connection with them in other particulars."

The letters in which these singular views were published were intended as a reply to Mr. Cooke's speech in the Synod, and to Mr. Paul's pamphlet on creeds. As might have been expected they produced little effect. The necessity for separation became every day more apparent. In a Church composed of such heterogeneous materials there could be no unity of action, and there could be no peace. Mr. Cooke's challenge was not, and could not be met :—" If he (Mr. Carlile) can convince me from Scripture, that Trinitarians, Arians, and Socinians can form a Scriptural Church, and cordially unite in licensing and ordaining one another, I shall willingly resign my present views, and unite with him in preserving our present constituency." Mr. Carlile's letters never touched the point.

Early in October an advertisement appeared in the Belfast newspapers, calling a meeting of those ministers and laymen throughout the province who disapproved of the enactments of the Synod. The meeting was to be held in the Arian place of worship, Belfast. The professed object was,—" Neither to advocate any peculiar system of theological opinions, nor to reflect upon the religious tenets of any denomination of Christians, but solely to devise the best means of maintaining the true principles of Protestantism, by endeavouring to frame such a temperate statement and REMONSTRANCE as may induce the Synod to return to the salutary regulations of their own Code of Discipline." The meeting was called for Thursday, the 16th. Two days before that date a letter was published, signed H. Cooke, Robert Stewart, H. Henry, commenting on the proposed meeting and its alleged object. It shows that, if the Arians were active, Mr. Cooke was watchful. After directing attention to the fact that the advertisement was anonymous, that the meeting, though called " Presbyterian," was not summoned by Moderator, Synod, or Presbytery, the writers say :—

" From the words of the requisition we should feel ourselves personally invited. For we are told, not only that the public will be freely admitted, but that it is expected many Calvinists, who are sincere friends of Christian liberty, will attend and take part in the proceedings. Now, as Calvinists, and sincere friends of Christian liberty, we feel authorised to attend this meeting, and take our share, however humble, in the discussions of the day. But, while we recognise the right of attendance and discussion derived from the announcement, we cannot forbear to remark, that the anonymous authors of the advertisement, who seem so anxious for Christian liberty, commence their proceedings with a curious specimen, inasmuch as, while they tell us ' that the public will be freely admitted, and that many Calvinists are expected to take part in the proceedings,' yet none will be ' permitted to interfere by vote except they disapprove of the late enactments of the Synod.' That is, any man may have liberty to agree with the requisitionists, but no man shall be permitted to differ from them. . . . .

" We now call upon the Presbyterians, who feel ' interested in the true principles of Protestantism,' to open their eyes and use their judgments. They are told that the meeting is to have no reference to any particular creed. Now, is not this too much for human credence ? For, when you reflect upon the place of meeting—one of the Arian meeting-houses of Belfast ; and when you consider the place of order for the subsequent dinner—that of the chief agent in Belfast for the Arian and Socinian press of England, Scotland, and Ireland ; then, will you not fairly conclude that, notwithstanding the implied invitation to orthodox attendance and participation in dis-cussion—that notwithstanding the profession of attachment to Christian liberty, and the true principles of Protestantism, yet the aforesaid meeting is to be neither more nor less than an assembly of Arian and Socinian ministers and laymen of the province, for the purpose of counteracting the endeavours of the Synod of Ulster to restore itself to those primitive principles of orthodoxy upon which it was originally founded ?

" We quarrel not with Arians or Socinians for making this attempt. We had expected it, and are not surprised. But we do deprecate the attempt to effect it under the colour of ' regard for the principles of Protestantism,' which are, and ever have been, as directly opposed to Arianism and Socinianism as light is opposed to darkness.

" We do, therefore, feel called upon to caution ' the sincere friends of Christian liberty,' the faithful adherents of ' the true principles of Protestantism,' against this wily attempt to undermine the truths of the everlasting gospel.

" We do not say, brethren, whether we or you ought to attend this meeting. We neither pledge ourselves, nor advise you, to attendance or absence. But we caution you to be upon your guard, lest any of you be entrapped into measures the nature and end of which you cannot learn from a meeting where none are to be per-mitted to interfere by vote but those who are already pledged to one side of the question. . . . .

" Again, therefore, we say, brethren, open your eyes ; use your judgments. We infringe not upon your Christian liberty, and we will stand or fall with the true principles of Protestantism. They are the principles of the Bible ; and neither artful sophistry, secret cunning, nor open violence shall ever prevail against them."

This bold, able, and timely letter created a great sensation. Mr. Cooke was already the most popular man in Ulster. His name was a tower of strength. But when it was appended to arguments so powerful, warnings so solemn, and truths so noble, it is not strange that it should have rallied round it the whole Orthodox sentiments of the Presbyterian Church.

The day of the meeting came. The house was crowded. All the leading Arians were present; and among the first to take their places were the Revs. H. Cooke, James Morgan, Robert Stewart, and J. Seaton Reid. The business was introduced by Mr. Porter, who explained the recent acts of the Synod, and the object of the meeting. He was followed by Mr. Montgomery, the theme of whose speech was the now celebrated letter of Messrs. Cooke, Stewart, and Henry. After reviewing its contents, he launched forth into a terrible philippic against Mr. Cooke. Leaving arguments and principles, with which he never cared to grapple, he raked up personalities, going back over many years in order to try to fasten upon his adversary some petty charge of inconsistency.

Mr. Montgomery no sooner resumed his seat than Mr. Cooke rose and demanded the right of reply. His appearance caused a storm of excitement. He was hissed, hooted, and ordered to leave. He stood firm, and refused to be put down by clamour. At length the chairman decided he should be heard, when the first resolution was formally before the meeting. When the appointed time came, he advanced to the side of his accuser in front of the pulpit, and said :—

"Mr. Chairman, I feel myself placed in circumstances peculiarly disagreeable. They are disagreeable, not because I regard the accusations of Mr. Montgomery, but because, in self-defence, I shall be compelled to make statements concerning others which I should rather, from feelings of delicacy, avoid ; and also because I may feel compelled to make such personal reference to Mr. Montgomery himself, as I should rather bury in silence than bring before the tribunal of a public meeting. Why, sir, it has pleased Mr. Montgomery to convert this public meeting into a tribunal before which to drag

private character ; and why you, sir, and this meeting have
pleased to tolerate such a line of procedure, it is not for me
determine.   But I must say, sir, the conduct of Mr. Montgomery
this day, though it has met the ready applause of a few of his many
admirers, can scarcely fail to excite very different feelings in the
minds of considerate and impartial men.   You call a meeting professedly for religious purposes, and your first proceeding is an attack
on private character.   But you I   followed your own course ; and
my business is, at present, to defend myself from the attacks which
have been made upon me.   I shall confine myself, sir, to repelling
the personal attacks of Mr. Montgomery. . . . . But if it
please God that I meet him at the next annual Assembly of the
General Synod, there I shall review and refute his arguments."

Mr. Cooke took up in detail Mr. Montgomery's charges and
insinuations, and he explained, and replied to them with such
effect, as to gain the approbation of even a hostile audience.
He then turned upon his calumniator, and in words, now of
cutting sarcasm, now of thrilling eloquence, he placed the acts
and policy of Mr. Montgomery and his followers in no enviable
light before the meeting.   Mr. Montgomery spoke in reply, so
did Mr. Porter ; but all their ability and tact could not counteract the damaging effect of Mr. Cooke's speech.

The object of these assaults on Mr. Cooke was only too
apparent.   He was the champion of orthodoxy.   His friends
trusted and followed him.   He was resolved never to rest
until he had freed his Church from Arianism.   No other leader
could be found.   No other man had the will, or, indeed, the
ability and courage for such a task.   His eloquence and his
indomitable energy specially fitted him for it.   If he, therefore, could in any way be set aside—if his influence among his
brethren could in any way be overthrown, Arianism might yet
maintain its place, or even regain ascendancy, in the Irish
Presbyterian Church.   Mr. Cooke was aware of this.   His
plans and purposes required him to meet all opposition—to
rebut personalities, as well as answer arguments.   He must
show his brethren that he was worthy of their confidence,
both morally and intellectually.   His character had been

assailed, and he triumphantly defended it. His consistency
had been called in question, and he satisfactorily established it.
The conflict in the Arian meeting-house raised him yet higher
in the estimation of his party, and contributed in no small
degree to the final overthrow of Arianism.

When the conflict ceased, Mr. Cooke and his friends withdrew. The Arians then passed a series of resolutions, one of
which was to the effect that *A Remonstrance* against recent
enactments in the Synod of Ulster in respect to Arian doctrines, be presented to the next meeting of that body, with a
view to obtain their repeal. The Remonstrance was a long
and elaborate document. It reviewed the Synod's overtures.
It denounced them as subversive of the great principles of
Protestantism, as opposed to the right of private judgment,
and as degrading to the character of the Church. Then, as if
its framers already felt the weakness of their cause, and
despaired of influencing the clear-minded people of Ulster,
they concluded with a threat :—

" We are, therefore, bound in duty to make a joint and firm effort
to have these obnoxious overtures repealed. But if we cannot get
this accomplished—if the Synod's overtures must be continued in
their present form—if the claim of exorbitant Church power, now
advanced, be persisted in—if the liberties of Christian ministers and
people continue to be trenched on, and the Holy Scriptures virtually
declared an inefficient rule of faith and duty—if these things must
be in the Synod of Ulster, then we declare that we can anticipate
nothing short of a schism ; and however we may deplore the necessity for such a step, it will, we think, become imperative upon those
ministers and congregations who value their religious character and
interests above the favour of the world, to form themselves into a
body, in which the liberties of Christians shall be more respected,
and where they may be permitted to show a becoming and undivided
reverence to our One Master, the Lord Jesus Christ, and to honour
the Word of God with the paramount veneration to which it is unquestionably entitled."

These were noble words ! and had the Presbyterian people
believed they fairly expressed the sentiments of the party,

they would have produced a great effect. But as it was known they were uttered by men who denied the Divinity of our Lord, the plenary inspiration of Scripture, and the historical truthfulness of many parts of God's Word, such language could impose upon no thoughtful man. The *Remonstrance* was the last effort of a vanquished party. It was eloquent and plausible, but dishonest. The document became historical, for it gave a name to the small body of Arians who separated, a few months later, from the Synod of Ulster.

The Remonstrance, accompanied by a short digest of the proceedings of the meeting, was published in the ' Whig,' then in a pamphlet, and again, in June, 1829, in all the Belfast newspapers. Every effort was made to give it the widest publicity. Its republication, in 1829, was especially designed to influence Presbyterians preparatory to the meeting of Synod, where it was known final action would be taken. But the leaders of the orthodox party were on the alert; and on the 23rd of June a letter appeared in those papers which had published the Remonstrance, containing an able review of it. It is subscribed " A Minister of the Synod of Ulster." Its style shows that it must have proceeded from the pen of Mr. Cooke. The writer explains the nature of the Synod's overtures, and defends them against the sophistical cavils of the Remonstrance. Referring to the oft-repeated cry of the overthrow of Christian liberty and Presbyterian privilege, he says :—

" Christian liberty and Presbyterian privilege are high-sounding terms; and it is no bad *ruse de guerre* in their Arian opposers to brand their orthodox neighbours with their invasion and destruction. The Presbyterian people are naturally and justly both fond and jealous of their privileges. And well they may. They were bought by many a year of persecution and blood, and retained with the death-grasp both in the field and at the stake. And shame upon the worthless hand who would sign away one jot or tittle of the noble inheritance ! But did Arians or Socinians purchase these glorious privileges ? No ! Presbyterians of Ulster ! your orthodox forefathers bought them, and transmitted them. And it is because your orthodox ministers and elders would now endeavour to protect you from an Arian and Socinian invasion, that they are branded as the destroyers of your liberties and your privileges. . . . .

" And, once for all, let it be clearly understood, that while Remonstrants openly call out ' Christian liberty and Presbyterian privilege,' their real object is to promote Arianism and Socinianism. When I examine the lists in the Remonstrance, I perceive the names of two or three who are, no doubt, Trinitarians, conscientious, and intelligent, and zealous ; but the great mass are decidedly Arian. The Belfast meeting, with a tincture of Socinianism, was perfectly Arian; and let them avow to the people that Arianism is their object, and they will add honesty to the other talents by which they support their cause. I blame them not for zeal in supporting and propagating their doctrines ; but I would pull down the false colours of ' Christian liberty' and ' Presbyterian privilege,' under which they fight; and I would hand over to them the banners of Arius and Socinus. Let them choose either ; or reject them both, and God will be with his own cause."

The letter concludes :—

" And now, Presbyterians of Ulster, the meeting of our Synod is fast coming on. During about eight months the Socinian and Arian members of our body have been both privately and openly at work. I blame them not for this. I admire—I would imitate—I would outwork their zeal. They have sent their Remonstrance into our congregations for signatures, and they thus hope to overwhelm the Synod by numerical influence. They have obtained signatures under the specious mis-statements of the Remonstrance. A few of these I have now endeavoured to refute and expose. The question comes to this—Are you to leave the door of your Church open to every Socinian or Arian who may choose to enter ; or will you man the walls and strengthen your defences, and compel them at least to climb before they gain farther footing.

" Two things you ought to do. The Arians are sending forward a Remonstrance with signatures from all their friends. Let orthodox congregations send forward memorials, calling upon the Synod to stand fast in the overtures of last year, and in the maintenance of the Examination Committee in full and unimpaired power. Then do not leave it to individuals to nominate who shall come as elders to the Synod. Every congregation has a right to hear publicly who is their elder ; and would they not do well to instruct their elder as to their views of his public duty ? If an elder be, as Remonstrants say, a representative of the people, let the people tell their representatives whether they wish for Arianism or Orthodoxy; for that is the undisguised state of the question.

"Elders of the Synod of Ulster, be at your posts. Be faithful again. Many of you last year witnessed a good confession for the Supreme Deity of your Lord. Forsake not the course through weakness or faint-heartedness; but be steadfast, immovable, and your labour shall not be in vain in the Lord."

This able letter produced a salutary effect. It roused the Presbyterians of Ulster. It opened their eyes to the skilful strategy of their enemies—a strategy that might have proved fatal. It showed them their own duty. Numerous appeals and warnings from orthodox men to their brethren appeared in the newspapers. Memorials were prepared in many of the leading congregations, praying the Synod to exclude heresy, and to guard the ancient faith of the church. It was evident that the crisis was approaching. Peace was no longer possible. The Old Lights would not yield the vantage-ground which the overtures of 1828 had gained for them; and the New Lights were resolved either to have them repealed, or to secede from the Synod. Mr. Cooke's policy was so far triumphant.

CHAPTER VIII.

1828—1829.

Renewal of Government Grant to Belfast College—Conditions stated by Lord
Leveson Gower—Resolutions of Synod and Correspondence with Chief
Secretary—Election of Mr. Ferrie to Chair of Moral Philosophy—Meeting
of Synod in Lurgan—Speech of Mr. Cooke and Resolutions on Belfast
College—Mr. Montgomery's Attack on Mr. Cooke—Cooke's Reply—Won-
derful effects of his Eloquence—The Arian Conflict virtually Closed—
Meeting of Arians—An Ultimatum—Meeting of Synod in Cookstown—The
Arian Ultimatum passed over in silence—Secession of the REMONSTRANTS
and formation of THE REMONSTRANT SYNOD OF ULSTER—Decline of
Arianism—Remarkable Progress of the Presbyterian Church of Ireland—
Appointment of Committee to superintend Training of Students—Mr.
Cooke's Speech in favour of Committee—The Class of Moral Philosophy—
Attacks upon Mr. Cooke—His great Popularity.

ANOTHER cause of discord had meantime arisen in the Synod
of Ulster. The Belfast College had never thoroughly gained,
nor had it deserved, the confidence of the Presbyterian Church.
Its managers professed great deference to the wishes of the
Synod. They presented to it an annual report. They permitted the Moderator to sit *ex officio* in their council. But
they were always suspected of Arian leanings, and the elections
of Professors had given just grounds for the suspicion. The
Government of the country had proposed to restore the annual
grant of 1500*l*., withdrawn in 1816, but only upon certain
conditions. They knew the feelings of distrust which the
Synod of Ulster entertained regarding the College. They
knew that the vast majority of the students were Presbyterians,
and candidates for the ministry. They wished to make the
Institution in all respects suitable as a place of training for the
clergy of the Presbyterian Church. It was but justice to do
so. The Episcopal Church had Trinity College, with its

princely revenues. Maynooth had been built and endowed for the Roman Catholics. The Presbyterians had hitherto to send their students to the Scotch Universities. Government now began to see that Presbyterians were not fairly treated; and they voted public money to Belfast College, on the condition that it should be a place for the academic training of members of the Presbyterian Church.

Before the Government communicated to the managers of the College their intention of renewing the annual grant, the Chief Secretary for Ireland wrote to the Moderator of Synod:—

" I am directed by the Lord Lieutenant to lay before you, as a governor of the Belfast Institution, the conditions under which His Excellency is disposed to make over the Parliamentary grant to that body. His Excellency conceives that he would not be justified in directing me to make a formal offer of the funds in question, on any particular terms, until the terms had been submitted to your consideration.

" It appears to His Excellency that he will be mainly justified in applying a portion of the public money to the support of the Belfast Institution, on the ground that it is now, or may be, a useful seminary for the education of the ministers of the Presbyterian Established Church in Ireland.

" With this principle in view, His Excellency is disposed to issue the grant, subject to the following regulations. Salaries are to be assured to the Professors on the scale and to the extent laid down by the Commissioners in their Report, viz., 1350*l.* is to be divided among nine Professors; of these nine, five are to be accounted religious Professorships, viz., the two Professors of Divinity, and those of Moral Philosophy, Hebrew, and Greek;—the last may be still open to consideration. The two Divinity Professors to be named, as before, by the Synods. The other religious Professors to be elected as at present, but joint certificates of their fitness for the appointment to be required from the Synod to this effect:—' We believe A. B. to be in all respects qualified for all such duties of the Professorship of ———— as are concerned in the instruction and preparation of youth for the ministry of the Presbyterian Church.'"

The desire of the Government was to give the Synod an absolute *veto* in the appointments to the religious Professorships, and to make this a condition of the renewal and continuance of the Parliamentary grant. The Moderator and his council considered the Chief Secretary's letter of sufficient importance to warrant him in calling a special meeting of Synod, which assembled in Cookstown on the 19th of November, 1828. The letter was carefully considered. Some thought the proposal of the Lord Lieutenant should be adopted, and that the Synod should insist upon a right of *veto*. Mr. Cooke, however, advised otherwise. He thought it might be humiliating to the managing Board. He therefore counselled the Synod to be satisfied if the Board should agree to concede to their Moderator the right of inspecting the testimonials of candidates for Professorships, and of officially advising the electing body what persons he considered eligible. This very moderate measure was adopted, unfortunately, as the result proved; and Mr. Cooke, ere long, had reason to repent of his moderation. The Synod's decision was communicated to the Chief Secretary, and excited some degree of surprise and dissatisfaction. Yet it was the basis on which the Parliamentary grant was renewed. Lord Leveson Gower's letter to the Moderator, containing the final decision of the Government, is as follows :—

"Dublin Castle, 8th December, 1828.

" Sir,—I have the honour to inform you that I have submitted to His Excellency's consideration your letter of the 26th November, as also a communication from the Rev. Patrick White, conveying the resolutions of a general meeting of the Synod of Ulster, which took place at Cookstown on the 19th of November.

" That meeting, as you are aware, was convened for the purpose of taking the opinion of the Synod on certain conditions which His Excellency had proposed to attach to the grant to the Belfast Institution, of the sum which Parliament has this year placed at his disposal for that purpose. Those conditions were framed with the view of securing the attainment of an object, which is considered by His Excellency one of so great public importance as alone to justify the appropriation of a grant of public money to the purposes of the Belfast Institution—I mean, the permanent utility of that seminary as a place of education for the members of the Presbyterian Church in Ireland.

" By directing me to obtain the consideration of the General Synod to the above-mentioned conditions, His Excellency conceives that he has fully evinced the anxiety which he feels to protect and to promote the interests of the Presbyterian Church; and he is gratified by observing, from the reply of the General Synod, how justly that body appreciates his motives in this respect. That body, however, has communicated to His Excellency a plain and unanimous expression of its opinion, that the interests of the Presbyterian Church in Ireland, as far as they are connected with the Belfast Institution, may be effectually protected by an arrangement of a different nature . . . .

" His Excellency is of opinion that he should not be justified in directing me to make any remark in the way of doubt or objection on a well-considered declaration of this nature, emanating, as it does, from a body so deeply interested in the soundness of its own conclusions, and so well qualified to protect that interest. He thinks that he should best continue to evince the same anxiety for the welfare of that body, which he has hitherto shown, by acceding to the arrangement which it suggests . . . .

" I have the honour to be, &c.,

" F. LEVESON GOWER."

" The Rev. the Moderator of the General
      Synod of Ulster."

Early in 1829, Dr. Young, Professor of Moral Philosophy in Belfast College, died. The election of a successor was appointed to take place on the 18th of June. There were many candidates. One of them was the Rev. James Carlile, of Dublin, a minister of the Presbyterian Church, a man of high character, of extensive scholarship, and proved by his writings to be eminently qualified to fill the chair. The representatives of the Synod of Ulster and Secession Synod agreed, after examining testimonials, to recommend the appointment of Mr. Carlile. But the electing body had a will of their own, and, by a majority of two, chose Mr. Ferrie. In a literary point of view no objection could be made to Mr. Ferrie. But there were other qualifications which the representative of the Synod was bound to press, and which the electors ought not to have overlooked. This was one of those Professorships which the Government had rightly termed religious. False principles in ethics must undermine religious truth. It was generally known that Mr. Ferrie held views on fundamental doctrines which were directly opposed to the Westminster Confession. It was believed that the fact of his holding those views, and of Mr. Carlile's being orthodox, had mainly decided the election. The electors were warned that Mr. Ferrie would not be acceptable to the Presbyterian Church; and the moderation of the Synod in refusing the power of *veto*, which Government had offered them a few months before, might have induced them to respect that warning. It is a remarkable fact that "A Member of Committee of the Synod of Ulster" —apparently Mr. Cooke himself—writing to the Belfast *News-Letter*, only a week after the election, says, "that it may eventually, and speedily, lead to the appointment of another Professor of Moral Philosophy in Belfast, I wish all parties concerned distinctly and timeously to understand." The words were prophetic.

The time for the annual meeting of Synod now approached. "The prospective meeting," says the Belfast *News-Letter*, in a leading article, "has already excited the interest proportioned to the importance to the subjects which are likely soon to engage the attention of that body." Even the great political changes in the government and constitution of the empire were scarcely so deeply felt in Ulster as the approaching ecclesiastical conflict. The Synod assembled in the Presbyterian Church, Lurgan, on Tuesday, the 30th of June. It was one of the largest meetings ever known. The Rev. Robert Park, of Ballymoney, was elected Moderator. The struggle began at once. Mr. Magill, of Antrim, moved that, " The Rev. Wm. Porter, being an avowed Arian, shall no longer be continued clerk to the General Synod of Ulster." The leaders on both sides felt, however, that this was a question of little moment. Greater questions must soon arise which would effectually dispose of the clerkship. The motion was therefore withdrawn.

On Thursday the reports on Belfast College, and the election of Mr. Ferrie, were introduced. It was now felt that the final struggle between Arianism and Orthodoxy had begun. The place of meeting was favourable to the Arians. They had many friends in and around Lurgan. These mustered in large numbers, and the spacious church was crowded in every part. Never before had the venerable body met in circumstances at once so exciting and so solemn. It is difficult for us, at this distance of time, to form anything like a just conception of the intense feeling throughout the province. For months previously Mr. Cooke had been labouring night and day: by night, keeping up a correspondence that seemed beyond the powers of any one man, besides writing reviews, circulars, and addresses; by day, travelling over the country preaching, speaking, and lecturing. On the 6th of June he wrote to Mrs. Cooke from Omagh :—" I have generally preached twice a day during some time past. I can sit or stand very well; but as to stooping, that is out of the question. My bones feel as if broken and dislocated by cars ten times rougher than Stewart's gig. This is literal truth; yet I rejoice in being able to dedicate my time and strength to Christ and his Church. We

serve a good Master. Oh ! to be able to spend and be spent
for Him."

It was after such exhausting labours Mr. Cooke appeared in
the Synod. He was still suffering, besides, from an old ail-
ment, which occasionally caused great pain and prostration.
But there was no outward sign of weariness. He was a man
of iron nerve and all-controlling will. When the case of Mr.
Ferrie came up for discussion he was calm, collected, watchful,
and ready as ever. The usual annual letter from the joint
Boards of the Belfast Institution was read. Among other
things it detailed the steps taken to fill the vacant chair of
Moral Philosophy. The synodical committee appointed to act
with the Moderator in examining the testimonials of candidates,
and advising the electors as to the parties considered eligible,
gave in their report. When the parties were heard, Mr. Cooke
reviewed the whole proceedings. He charged the synodical
committee with grievous neglect of duty in failing to inquire
into Mr. Ferrie's theological views, when doubts were cast
upon them, and in returning his name as eligible when they
suspected him of Arianism. He showed that the Orthodox
members of the committee had allowed themselves to be influenced, if not coerced, by the statements and acts of Mr.
Montgomery ; and that they were therefore largely responsible
for the unfortunate appointment. Referring next to the electors, he told them plainly that Mr. Carlile was, in point of
literary standing, by far the most eminent candidate, yet that
Arianism carried the day.

" I thought," he went on to say, " that between the Synod and the
managers of the Institution peace and harmony had been established
for ever. The Government would have put us as masters over them.
Our Moderator would have had only to take his pen and write *Veto*,
and their proceedings were annulled. But we said, nay ; we want no
influence over you save what is necessary for our own safety. We
claim no control over the choice of the proprietors save the right of
advice, and assurance that our religious principles will be respected.
Wherefore I maintain that a sense of justice and gratitude should
have constrained them to accept of Mr. Carlile."

He accused Mr. Ferrie of holding Socinian views :—

" That he is a Socinian is a matter of public rumour.   It has been heard echoing from the Highlands to the Borders.   Members of this House have heard it *vivâ voce*.   Others have proofs ready to be produced."

At the close of a speech of great power he moved a series of resolutions, which, after some explanations, he modified as follows :—

" That the duty of the election committee was to have examined the testimonials of candidates, and not to have declared any one eligible without sufficient evidence of his orthodoxy.

" That while the Synod disclaim every intention of exercising undue influence in elections to Professorships, they cannot but express their regret that the electors did not appoint the Rev. J. Carlile.

" That a committee be appointed to open a correspondence with the Secession and Reformed Presbyterian Synods on the subject of the late election ; and that a special meeting of Synod be called at Cookstown to receive the report of that committee."

Mr. Cooke's speech and resolutions brought matters to a crisis.   If his resolutions carried, the Arian party could not, with honour or consistency, remain in the Church.   The effect of their *Remonstrance*, too, which had not as yet been presented, would be greatly weakened.   They were, in fact, outgeneralled by the tact and talent of their powerful adversary. Their feelings were, on this account, all the more aggravated. The excitement in the house was intense, not only among the members of the Synod, but among the crowded audience.   The Arians knew that unless they could silence Mr. Cooke, or in some way destroy his influence, their cause was lost.   They resolved to make the attempt.   Mr. Montgomery was their leader and champion.   He had foreseen the conflict, and had come fully prepared for it.   He had gone back in his researches over the history of many years.   He had carefully culled out and arranged everything in Mr. Cooke's evidence, speeches, and general policy, which could be tortured into a semblance

of contradiction or inconsistency. He had fully twenty-four
hours to review Mr. Cooke's last speech, and he employed
them most diligently.

About one o'clock on Friday he rose to address the House.
He took his stand below the Moderator, in front of the pulpit.
His commanding figure was in full view of the members of
Synod and the audience. Mr. Cooke sat in a pew close to
him, and, next to the speaker, was the centre of observation.
Mr. Montgomery held in his hand elaborate notes, and the
ponderous Blue-book containing the report of the Royal and
Parliamentary Commissions. The moment he rose he was
hailed with enthusiastic cheers. It was clear that the vast
majority of the audience belonged to his party. It was clear,
too, from the triumphant looks of the Arian ministers, that
they expected a victory. Mr. Montgomery did not disappoint
them. In sentences measured, calm, persuasive, he related
the history of the question at issue. The outline was accurate;
but the narrative was so skilfully arranged—some parts brought
out prominently, others all but excluded—that the Orthodox
members of the Synod, and especially Mr. Cooke, appeared to
be relentless persecutors. He deprecated the introduction of
the question into the Synod, and modestly apologised for the
attitude which stern necessity compelled him reluctantly to
assume:—" I am not in this case the aggressor: I am not
conscious that I have been so in any other; but there is
nothing inconsistent with the principles of the gospel in
repelling accusations against public or private character, and
repelling them, too, with an open, honest indignation."

Having fairly introduced the subject, he proceeded to assail
Mr. Cooke. As he did so, his manner entirely changed. His
utterance became more rapid; his voice, though still musical,
became louder and deeper. His eyes flashed with indignation
as he glanced from time to time on his antagonist. Never,
perhaps, in the annals of debate, never in the whole history of
controversial warfare, were charges, grave and terrible, constructed with more consummate ingenuity, and pressed home

with such overwhelming power of oratory. Referring to Mr. Cooke's attack upon the deputies from the Institution, and the smile which, it seems, lighted up his face as he made it, Mr. Montgomery said :—

" I have heard of the vampire which fans its victim while it is sucking its blood, and such was the character of that smile. After the smile we had a laugh, but it was a laugh that foreran the dagger. I have, in common with other members of this house, been guilty of having been at the theatre; and I recollect having once witnessed Kemble's personation of Zanga in the tragedy of ' The Revenge,' and of having been struck with the expression of his countenance when, in the triumph of his feelings, he sets his feet on his fallen enemy. Such was the triumphant look with which Mr. Cooke seemed to re-gard the Institution when he fancied it had fallen, and he was trampling it under his feet. But then we are told that this arises from a love of truth, and a regard for the interests of the Redeemer. This would be tolerable if men's conduct did not betray their motives."

Mr. Montgomery's main point was to convict Mr. Cooke of contradiction in statements made at different times and for different purposes. He tried to show that his sworn testimony before the Parliamentary Committee was directly at variance with his assertions in the Synod. In fact, if proved, Mr. Montgomery's charge amounted to perjury. He exerted all his eloquence and ingenuity to establish the proof. He held in his hand the Parliamentary Blue-book. He quoted from it sentence after sentence. Raising the volume above his head and waving it in the face of the astonished audience, he ex-claimed again and again, with tremendous vehemence, " This, remember, is his sworn testimony—sworn upon the holy Evangelists." Then taking each sentence, and comparing it with Mr. Cooke's statements made in the Synod, and fresh in the memories of all, he said :—

" If Mr. Cooke have *sworn* the truth—yes, *if* Mr. Cooke have sworn the truth, it is impossible that his assertions made now, before

this Synod, can be true.   At that time, when the Parliamentary
Commission sat, his great point was to put down the Institution. It
answered a particular purpose then to give the Institution a stab by
holding up the orthodoxy of Glasgow Professors.   Now, it answers
a different purpose to deny their orthodoxy; and accordingly he
denies it."

His denunciations were absolutely appalling.   They sent a
thrill of horror through the assembly.   Once and again he
turned, in the midst of his vehement philippic, and with voice,
and gesture, and look, expressive of bitterest scorn, pointed to
his adversary, who sat before him, calm and motionless as a
statue, and exclaimed : "Who or what is our accuser ?   Has
the Almighty given any peculiar dignity of intellect or person
to Mr. Cooke, that he should speak so of us ? "

Towards the close the orator, with matchless skill, again
changed theme and manner.   The glance of scorn melted into
a smile of benevolence ; the voice of triumph gave place to the
mellow tone of touching pathos ; the flashing eye became
dimmed by a gathering tear-drop ; the lip, before curled with
indignation, now quivered as if with suppressed emotion.   In
language of classic beauty he alluded to the impending rupture
of the Synod.   He contrasted the stormy scenes of earthly conflict with the peace of heaven :—

"I trust," he said, " that when we have laid aside the garb of frail
mortality, when we have cast off the flesh with its passions, we shall all,
friends and foes alike, meet in that better and happier world, wondering
at our own sinful folly in having disputed, and excited strife, where
all should have been harmony and love.   I am weary of this contest.   .   .   .   If we cannot live together in peace, in the name of
God let us part in peace.   I have no fear as to consequences.
Some of my brethren may be injured ; but He that catereth for the
sparrow, will not let the children of the sufferers for conscience' sake
come to want.   The cause of God and truth will finally prevail ; and
though I cannot approve of the individuals who excited them, I feel
convinced that the storms which have raged among us will purify the
Church, and have their results in the triumph of those opinions which
I believe in my conscience to be true."

When he concluded the Synod, the whole audience, seemed as if under the spell of a mighty magician. When the enchanting music of that marvellous oratory ceased, there was, for a time, a stillness as of death. The intense strain upon the feelings needed a moment of rest. Then, thunders of applause burst from the assembly. They ceased, but were renewed again, and again renewed. The Arians were triumphant. The Orthodox thought their cause lost. Even the warmest friends and most enthusiastic admirers of Mr. Cooke hung their heads, or conversed in anxious whispers. Many supposed his character was ruined; all believed his influence was gone for ever.

Mr. Montgomery's speech occupied two hours and a half. At its close the Synod adjourned for half an hour. It was an anxious half hour. The only man who seemed calm and collected was he who had been the subject of that terrible philippic. He had no time to prepare a defence. He did not seem to desire it. Those who saw him as he joined in the conversation and merry laugh at the hurriedly-eaten dinner, thought he could not contemplate an immediate reply.

At half past four o'clock the Synod reassembled. The crowd was, if possible, denser than before. Mr. Cooke immediately rose amid profound silence. Not a voice ventured to greet him with an encouraging cheer. He stood in a pew beside the pulpit. Mr. Montgomery was seated before him, almost within arm's length. He began in calm and measured sentences to review Mr. Montgomery's speech. He admitted its surpassing ability. He lauded the splendour of its oratory and the overwhelming power of its invective.

" I rise, Moderator, to explain and clear away what I am forced to call the misrepresentations of Mr. Montgomery. I rise under difficulty—I had almost said fear. Never has this Synod, never has any assembly, witnessed such a display of forensic eloquence. What its effects upon others must have been I can well conceive, for even I, who was suffering under its stroke, could not refrain from giving it the tribute of my admiration; and as the dagger was driven home

to my heart, I felt it was wielded by the hand of a master. If I
fall beneath the stroke, I shall at least have the proud satisfaction of
knowing that the stroke was dealt by no unworthy foe.   .   .   .   .
Mr. Montgomery has compared me to a vampire.   I have never seen
the creature.   It is not to be found in the volumes of Buffon.   I
had supposed it to be fabulous ; but Mr. Montgomery appears to
have enjoyed some rare opportunity of inspection.   I could not even
have formed any correct conception of the fabled monster.   My
fancy could never have pictured those revolting—those inhuman
passions which it was made to personify.   Now, however, I am
enlightened.   I have got a new lesson in natural history.   Mr.
Montgomery, from the fertility of his own imagination—from the
dark chambers of his own dark heart, has drawn such a graphic picture of the vampire, and, by the waving and quivering of his outstretched arms, has given such a thrilling representation of the
monster at its work of death, that I could not repress the thought,
the horrid conviction, as I gazed on that consummate actor, and was
fanned by the motion of his hands—we have the living vampire
before us.   .   .   .   But I pass from these personalities.   I entreat,
I warn Mr. Montgomery never to repeat them.   He has tried to hold
me up to ridicule.   He has attempted to crush me under a load of
obloquy ; but he has not attempted to grapple with the question
before the house.   He gave us a specimen of that eloquence which
is sometimes soft as the evening breeze, or still and awful as the
dread hour when the vampire walks abroad ; and, anon, thundering
as the cataract, and splendid as the blaze of noonday.   But, though
he had a plain question before him, he did not once touch it.   All
will admit that he has eloquence enough to make the worse appear
the better part ; and yet, with all this, he never dares to enter on the
point at issue.   The great question before the Synod is, shall we
entrust our students to the teaching of an Arian Professor ? "

After some vivid flashes of wit, and some scathing touches of
satire, which made the house once more conscious of his power,
and drew forth, even from reluctant auditors, distinct expressions of applause, he proceeded to the main charge.

" Moderator, Mr. Montgomery has been pleased to take up my
evidence before the Commissioners, and he has dared to impeach me
of contradicting myself upon oath.   I now stand before you, sir—

before the bar of this house—charged with the foul crime of perjury. Oh! may it never be the fate, sir—may it never be the fate of a single individual in this vast assembly to lie for one moment under the stigma of so base, so terrible a charge! You will pardon, sir, the exhibition of feeling which I cannot suppress. You will sympathise with a man who stands charged with the crime of deliberate perjury. You will bear with him as he assails the foul impeachment—as he dashes to atoms the vile accusation—as he smites and shivers the atrocious calumny with the talisman of truth."

In uttering these words he raised himself to his full height; his whole frame seemed to dilate; his voice, clear as a trumpet, rung through the house; with a glance of proud defiance he looked for a moment on his accuser, and then stood nobly erect as if anticipating an immediate and unanimous verdict of acquittal. He was not disappointed. The audience felt the power of the great orator. They could not restrain their feelings. Tears burst from almost every eye in the assembly. They sprang to their feet; and their pent up emotions, their uncontrollable sympathies, burst forth in an enthusiastic and prolonged cheer.

No description could convey any adequate idea of the speech that followed. The charges of Mr. Montgomery were taken up in detail, and torn to shreds. His alleged contradictions were shown to be misrepresentations. His most powerful arguments were proved to be plausible sophistries. Mr. Cooke had no notes, yet not a point was overlooked. He had no documents, yet his marvellous memory enabled him to supply the designed omissions, to expunge the damaging interpolations of his adversary. His defence was clear, full, triumphant. The convictions of the Synod and the audience were won by the searching and incisive logic, and wonderful lucidity of the speaker; their sympathies and hearts were won by the resistless force of his eloquence. He swayed them as by the power of a mighty enchanter. They laughed, they wept, they cheered in turn. Every charge of Mr. Montgomery formed the theme for some happy repartee, or brilliant flash of wit, or scathing touch of satire, or burst of impassioned eloquence.

"Mr. Montgomery says I endeavoured to show that our students would be safer in Glasgow than in Belfast. I never endeavoured to do any such thing. Every time I was examined I testified in favour of a home education. The book he holds in his hand, and which he has flaunted before you, proves it. I pointed out, indeed, some advantages which Glasgow possesses over Belfast. I thought, and I still think, that there is a want of congeniality with Arian sentiment in Glasgow. The cold air of the north is not congenial to Arianism. Its germ arose out of the mud of the Nile. It cannot bear the healthy soil and keen air of a northern clime. Orthodoxy is the hardy mountain heath, which flourishes on bare hill-side and exposed upland. It courts the light of day. It bids defiance to the storm. It sports with the tempest, and it smiles upon the sunbeam. Arianism is the sickly exotic. It can only be forced by artificial heat. It takes root in the mud of intellectual and moral stagnation. It grows up among the seething population of a neglected city. But it droops and dies when exposed to the free blast of scriptural inquiry."

Thus was the imposing structure, reared by the subtilty and gilded by the eloquence of Mr. Montgomery, "dashed to atoms by the talisman of truth." Those who had cheered him while he spoke, who had hailed him victor when he closed, now almost pitied him as he sat under the terrible scourge of an injured and indignant orator. The house rang with peals of acclamation. The charges preferred against Mr. Cooke recoiled with double force upon the head of his accuser. When he resumed his seat the whole assembly rose, and by repeated rounds of applause, celebrated his victory. Those who were present have affirmed that they never felt till then the full power of eloquence; and that they never could have imagined the human mind was capable of such an effort, or that human language could have produced such an effect.

That speech virtually settled the Arian controversy in the Synod of Ulster. Although the final decision was postponed for a few months, the Arians from that moment abandoned the conflict, and eventually retired, without even an attempt at renewing the struggle. Mr. Cooke's speech occupied more than two hours, and when it closed the Synod adjourned. In fact, the excitement was so intense it was found imposible to take up any business.

When the Synod assembled again on Saturday, a number of explanatory statements were made regarding the acts of the Synodical Committee, and the testimonials of Mr. Ferrie. Evidence was also adduced as to his theological views. Mr. Cooke thereupon amended his resolutions, which were passed as follows :—

" That, whilst we entertain the highest respect for the managers and visitors of the Belfast Institution, and admit that in the late election of a Professor to the chair of Moral Philosophy, they acted strictly within the limits of the regulations existing between them and us ; yet, from certain doubts that have arisen respecting the religious tenets of the individual elected, we think it right to appoint a committee of our body, to communicate with the managers and visitors of the Institution, and to confer with the Secession and Reformed Synods on this subject, so important to the interests of the Presbyterian Churches in this kingdom ; and to report the result of these communications and conferences to the Synod.

" That a special meeting of Synod be held in Cookstown on the third Tuesday of August next, for the purpose of inquiring into the present circumstances and constitution of this Church, and of receiving the report of the committee."

Against these resolutions the leading Arians protested. It was of no avail. The Old Light party were triumphant; and Mr. Cooke would not yield a single point that might tend to compromise the orthodoxy of the Church, or the integrity of her Standards.

On the 30th of July the Arian ministers assembled in Belfast to consider what course they should adopt in relation to the approaching special meeting of Synod. After much discussion it was resolved that they should not attend it. They felt it

was useless to prolong the conflict. Every point had been
carried against them. Their leader had been signally defeated.
They were rapidly losing influence in the Synod, and over the
public. Mr. Cooke's crushing exposures of their favourite
pleas had opened men's minds to the true state of the question.
To attempt to renew the debate in the Synod would be vain.
To submit to its ruling would be humiliating. They, therefore, considered that the most dignified course they could
pursue would be to absent themselves from the meeting at
Cookstown, and to transmit their *Remonstrance*. They drew
up a lengthened " Address," deploring the strife which had for
years distracted the Synod ; deprecating farther discussion on
the doctrines at issue ; complaining of the Overtures of 1828 ;
and proposing the following as the only conditions on which
they would consent to remain in the Synod :—

"1st. That the Overtures of the year 1828 shall be totally repealed.

" 2nd. That the Code of Discipline adopted in 1825 shall resume
its authority as the law of the Synod, and be acted upon in good
faith, and agreeably to the liberal spirit in which it was enacted,
freely permitting licence and ordination according to the long-continued and general practice of our Church."

In case these conditions should not be granted, they asked
the appointment of a Synodical " Committee, vested with full
power to enter into an arrangement, with an equal number
upon our part, for a friendly and Christian separation." The
Rev. William Porter, Clerk of Synod, was appointed to present
the Remonstrance and Address. The Address was signed by
sixteen ministers and eleven elders.

The Synod met at Cookstown on the 18th of August. No
fewer than twenty memorials were handed in from different
congregations—some praying the Synod to adhere to the overtures ; others, to exclude from communion all persons denying
the doctrine of the Trinity ; others, to dissolve connection with
Anti-Trinitarians. Mr. Cooke's letter to the Presbyterians of

Ireland had been effective. It had roused the orthodox feeling throughout the province; and now even the lukewarm members of the Old Light party—the men who before were for peace at any price—felt that, if they would retain the sympathies of their people, they must stand boldly forward in defence of their principles.

When the memorials were presented, Mr. Porter read the " Remonstrance," and stated that he attended merely as Clerk of Synod, without intending to take any part in the discussion. In obedience to an order of Synod the " Remonstrance " was examined. It was signed by eighteen ministers, fifteen licentiates, one hundred and ninety-seven members of session, and three hundred and fourteen seatholders. At that time the entire Church contained two hundred and nineteen ministers, seventy-five licentiates, and about twelve hundred elders, and thirty thousand seatholders. The Synod listened to the Remonstrance and Address. The *ultimatum* they contained was passed over in silence. Mr. Cooke had attained his object. He was delighted at the proposed secession. It was just what he wished. No resolution of expulsion had been passed. Nothing had been done that could possibly be construed into an act of tyranny. The Synod had adopted measures necessary to secure the future purity of the Church. It had resolved to retain inviolate the antient Standards. To this the Arians would not submit; they, therefore, seceded. The Synod resolved, in compliance with the wish of the Remonstrants, to appoint a committee to arrange terms of separation. But specific instructions were given to it. It was enjoined that the negociations should be confined exclusively to the Widows' Fund and other matters of finance. A resolution was passed at the same time enjoining Presbyteries to take charge of any congregations, or parts of congregations, now under the care of Remonstrant ministers, but which might apply for the services of orthodox pastors.

The conference of the committees was held in Belfast on September 9th. There were present on behalf of the Synod

nine ministers and two elders, among whom were Messrs.
Cooke, Stewart, Seaton Reid, and Captain Rowan.   On behalf
of the Arians, there were ten ministers and eight elders.   The
latter submitted a paper, declaring their intention to organize
" a new Presbyterian Connexion ; " and demanding to be secured in certain specified " rights, privileges, and immunities."
Those having reference to finance, were readily agreed to.
One point, however, created discussion—" We require our
brethren of the Synod to declare that, on our ordaining a
minister in any congregation, now in existence, or which may
be hereafter erected, their Moderator shall, in all such cases,
annex his signature, in the usual manner, to the memorial for
Royal Bounty forwarded to him by such minister ; and shall,
on no account whatever, withhold his signature, when regularly
certified of such ordination." The Synodical committee refused
to commit their body to the recognition of any Arian congrega-
gation which might afterwards spring up.

This was the last act in the long struggle between the Old
and New Light parties in the Synod of Ulster.   Their official
connection was now finally dissolved ; and this important event
was brought about by Mr. Cooke.   He had resolved upon it
from the time he encountered Smithurst, in Killyleagh—from
the time, in fact, when Arianism began to assume an aggressive attitude.   At first not a single member of Synod thoroughly
sympathised in his views.   He stood alone.   He was opposed
by all the force of the Arian party.   He was opposed by a large
number of Orthodox men, who deprecated the division of the
Synod.   But, probably, the most harassing and intractable
opposition he had to contend with, arose from the waywardness,
the timidity, and, in a few cases, the cowardice of professed
friends.   He was opposed by the Press.   The columns of one,
at least, of the leading papers in Ulster were always open to
his adversaries ; but when he inserted letters, even though in
reply to attacks, he had almost uniformly to pay for them as
advertisements.   The speeches of his opponents were carefully
reported ; most of them were submitted to their authors for

revision, and not unfrequently for entire reconstruction. The reports of Mr. Cooke's speeches were generally so meagre and incorrect as to present only a caricature of his splendid displays of eloquence. His private correspondence shows the enormous difficulties he had to contend with in battling for the faith. His means were limited. His family was already large. His health was sometimes so shattered by anxiety and toil that life was despaired of. Yet his resolution was never shaken. His courage was sustained by faith in Christ. "I serve a great and good Master," he wrote to Mrs. Cooke, in the darkest period of the conflict : "it is for His honour I struggle. I must bear the cross if I would wear the Crown. I am willing, I am ready, to spend all, yea, everything, in His service." An indomitable will rose superior to all obstacles—all enemies. In this respect he displayed the characteristics of true genius. A tenacious and ready memory enabled him to use, whenever requisite, for defence or attack, the vast stores of his reading. An eloquence unsurpassed in power and brilliancy; a wit, playful and sparkling ; an irony which scathed everything it touched ; an oratory easy, graceful, and persuasive ; all united in giving him a mastery in debate, and enabling him to sway at will, the convictions, passions, and feelings of an audience. Thus gifted and inspired, Mr. Cooke triumphed.

The importance of the work he accomplished cannot be overestimated. Presbyterianism in Ireland had fallen asleep when he entered the ministry. The church, as a whole, was satisfied with a cold observance of the routine of worship. There was no power in the pulpit ; there was no energy in the Synod; there was no spiritual life among the people. Missionary work, whether at home or abroad, was never thought of. The church seemed indifferent to Christ's command and commission—"Go ye into all the world, and preach the gospel to every creature." Mr. Cooke believed that so long as Arianism existed in the church, life and power could never be developed. Others feared that disruption would be fatal to the church's social influence; and that Arianism, unrestrained by Orthodox energy and zeal, would spread over the land. Mr. Cooke's opinions were different. He had faith in the living power of a pure gospel. He had faith in the promises of God. He knew that the chilling dogmas of Arianism would not satisfy the wants of a thoughtful community. He, therefore, put forth all his energies to eradicate the Arian heresy. The result proved he was right. After all the cry about " Christian liberty," only seventeen ministers could be induced " to throw off the yoke " of the Synod. They met for the first time, as a distinct ecclesiastical body, in Belfast, on the 25th of May, 1830, and the following, among other resolutions, was passed :—" We now, in the name of the Great King and Head of the Church, solemnly associate ourselves, under the designation of the *Remonstrant Synod of Ulster.*"

The seceding ministers retained their endowments and their ecclesiastical buildings; but in many cases their people left them, and organized congregations in connection with the Synod of Ulster. Since their secession the Arians have slowly but steadily declined, both in numbers and influence. Reckoning the Remonstant Synod, the Synod of Munster, and the Presbytery of Antrim, the total number of Arian congregations at the present time is about forty, and some of them consist of only a few families. Their whole adherents, old and young, according to the census of 1861, did not much exceed 4000. These facts seem to show that it is only when concealed beneath the cloak of orthodoxy Arianism can make progress.

On the other hand, the career of the Synod of Ulster, since it was freed from Arianism, has been one of distinguished usefulness and prosperity. Ten years later it united with the Secession Synod, and formed the General Assembly of the Presbyterian Church in Ireland. It has now in its communion 630 ministers, 560 congregations, and above 100,000 families. It has studded many parts of Ulster with schools. It has established congregations and mission-stations in remote districts of the south and west of Ireland. It has

made noble efforts to provide for the spiritual training and
wants of the rapidly increasing population of the large towns.
In Belfast alone, twenty-two new churches have been erected
since 1830. It has missionaries labouring in Germany, Austria,
Spain, Italy, Palestine, India, and China, and in nearly all the
colonies of the British Empire. For this wonderful success
the Presbyterian Church is, under God, mainly indebted to the
talents and labours of Henry Cooke.

When the Remonstrants withdrew, the spirit of the New
Light party was not yet totally extinct in the Synod of Ulster.
Some remained who sympathised with their policy, if they did
not adopt their doctrines. Against these Mr. Cooke had to
contend. The great object he had in view was to preserve the
purity of the Church. To accomplish this the most watchful
care had to be exercised over candidates for the ministry. He
distrusted some of the Presbyteries; probably he distrusted
their wisdom more than their orthodoxy. To guard at once
against neglect and error, he had moved the appointment of a
synodical committee to examine all students. No man could
henceforth obtain licence to preach until he had passed that
committee. The Synod would see that its members, who were
appointed annually, were qualified for the responsible duties
assigned to them. When its reappointment was moved at the
special meeting of Synod in Cookstown, it was vigorously
opposed by a few. They argued that it infringed upon the rights
of Presbyteries, and upon the liberties of the people, and that
it was, therefore, unconstitutional. They raised again the old
cry of the evils of debate and party conflict in a Church. They
lamented and condemned the fierceness of that struggle which,
as alleged by one of the speakers, "caused the enemies of
religion to triumph, and entailed disgrace on the Synod." They
repeated, in fact, though in another form, the arguments embodied in the *Remonstrance*. Mr. Cooke replied with his
customary eloquence, and with overwhelming effect. He
showed from the whole history of the Church that great
reforms had only been brought about by great conflicts.

After referring to the life of our Lord, of the Apostles, of
Luther and Calvin, he continued :—

" Just so was the life of Knox, the apostle of Presbyterianism in
Scotland.   Controversy, oral and written—banishments and return-
ings—revilings, accusations, and imprisonments, mark the whole
course of his pilgrimage.   He followed his Master with the con-
stancy of a faithful servant; he encountered danger with the courage
of a dauntless soldier of the Cross ; and when laid in the narrow
tomb, he received from one of his worst enemies the noble eulogium,
' There lies he who never feared the face of man.'   Now, sir, if
Christ and His Apostles, and if the noble army of the Reformers,
had to encounter a host of troubles, and literally conquer peace,
what are we to expect in our days ?   Why, just that we, and all
who, by the grace of God, attempt to carry on a reformation work,
will have to labour through arguments, and difficulties, and troubles,
and endure all the tossings of the storm, before we anchor in the
port of rest."

Then, turning upon those who charged him with being the
author of strife, he said :—

" How, I ask, have these unhappy discussions originated ?   Why,
certainly, from the introduction of Arianism among us.   And how
have they been continued ?   Why, certainly by the declarations of
some of the Orthodox, that it cannot, or should not, be rooted out ;
or by the reluctance of others to join with their brethren in carrying into effect any specific plan of reform.   The Arians of this body
deserve credit for their union.   Like a military phalanx, they march
shoulder to shoulder ; but the Orthodox march in straggling divisions, and often, alas ! in hostile opposition.   In fact, the Arians do
not need to fight their own battles; it is done more effectually by
ourselves.   They could not fight their battles half so efficiently as
it is done for them by not a few of their Orthodox opponents.   I
mean not to intimate any want of talent among our Arian members
—that would be invidious and untrue ; but I mean to suggest to
some of our Orthodox brethren a review of the tendency of their
own measures.
" The general object professed by most of the Orthodox is to get
clear of Arianism.   To effect this prospectively the Examination

Committee has been devised.   And, however far I feel that it has come short of my own views, yet one thing is most certain—it has worked well.   It has rid us in one year of at least three or four Arian candidates.   I know it is likely to send some of our Arian probationers to England.   It has excited a more scriptural study among our students, and increased the confidence of our orthodox congregations."

Mr. Cooke then, with acuteness and logical power, replied to the various arguments:—

"Mr. Gray accuses the committee of infringing the rights of Presbyteries.   I would beg leave to ask, What is a Presbytery? and what are the rights of Presbyteries?   I answer, the geographical Presbytery is a delegation of the eldership, to whom is committed the care of a particular number of Churches.   Now, what has the Presbytery a right to do in those Churches?   Not everything they may please, but just so much as the whole eldership of the general Church may please to commit to their care.   Indeed the idea that one portion of a Church has any specific right to perform all the duties that may arise within a geographical district, must appear untenable.   Thus, to a local Presbytery are assigned certain duties ; yet are there certain functions which it is judged inconvenient for them ordinarily to exercise, and from these they are debarred until they receive the consent of the general eldership, or Presbytery, which we commonly call the Synod.   Just so, your committee is a particular delegation of the eldership, to whom is prescribed a particular duty, that of examination ; but who are debarred from the power of licence or ordination, because they have been appointed to no such duty. . .

"Mr. Hay tells us that the appointment of such a committee infringes on the fundamental principles of Presbyterianism.   Now, where are these principles to be found ?   In the Acts of the Apostles, and the Epistles.   And what are these principles ?   They are two. First, the absolute equality of pastors ; second, the power of delegation in Church courts.   By the first, it stands opposed to prelacy, which elevates one pastor above another.   Will any one show me how a committee receiving a special commission to perform a particular duty, and accountable to their brethren for its per- formance—will any one show me how they are made prelates ? Then as to the power of delegation in Church courts, what is the

Committee of Examination but one distinct example of the Presbyterian principle?

"But Mr. Gray assures us the committee is an invasion of religious liberty. No doubt, if the committee were not your committee; if they took their power from the State, and exercised it against your will, then you might call its acts an invasion of your liberties. But you made the committee; you can unmake it when you please; it is the creature of your own religious liberty, and I trust will be the efficient promoter of your religious reformation.

"There is, indeed, another case in which it might infringe your religious liberties. Were the committee guilty of a wrong act, or series of acts, there might be an infringement. But the committee inquires into the scriptural knowledge of your candidates. Can that act be pronounced improper? It inquires into personal piety. Where can be the evil in such research? It seeks to ascertain that a minister is not quite a novice in the gospel. I know not by what argument that can be demonstrated an evil. I dare boldly pronounce these acts amongst the best works ever undertaken by the Synod of Ulster, and the committee that shall faithfully perform them, the best benefactor of the Presbyterian Church. . . .

"In conclusion, I shall address myself to the serious charge so often adduced and so ably repelled—the charge that we have been guilty of a breach of faith. . . . While my brethren have traversed the indictment, I feel guilty. I think the Synod of Ulster in her efforts to purify herself from Arianism and Socinianism has been guilty of a breach of faith. Ay, and so was Luther, when the monk turned Reformer. And so was Calvin, when he cast off the trammels of that Church in which he had been baptized, that he might be washed with the true baptism of the Holy Spirit. And so was Knox, when the priest of the Church of Rome became the presbyter of the Church of Scotland—breaking an erroneous faith with man, that he might keep a true faith with God. Solemnly accused, I blench not at the accusation. Verily, we have been guilty in this matter. Watchmen on the towers of Zion, we have hung the trumpet upon the wall, and the enemy has climbed in while the city was unalarmed. We have enjoyed our comfortable watch-boxes of clerical repose; and angry were not a few, and still not a few are displeased, that their slumbers have been disturbed. Have we not continued to hear until this very hour woeful lamentations about the days of comfort, calm Synodical comfort, that were formerly enjoyed? If comfort any man had in former days, it must have been the comfort of the Mahometan dozing on a divan, and leaving the care of the world to Allah and the Prophet ; or the comfort of Gallio, enjoying his place and pension, looking out from his palace on the troubles of the world, and resolving to care for none of these things. . . .

"But perhaps it may be said that, under our circumstances, a compact, verbal or written, declared or implied, should be faithfully kept. This doctrine I flatly deny. There are two cases in which an agreement of any description ceases to be binding. One is when one of the parties violates the compact. This event can sever the most solemn obligations, and rend the tenderest ties. Such a breach of compact on the part of James roused the spirit of the land, and produced the glorious Revolution. The other circumstance which dissolves a compact is, the discovery of some deep immorality in the obligation. Thus Herod promised a kingly reward to a fantastic girl; she went to her adulterous mother, and her mother called for blood. Herod was sorry for the oath ; yet he murdered John the Baptist. Now, I do not hesitate to say he should rather have repented of his rash and sinful vow, than committed the double sin of adding murder to folly. Just so do I view the implied compact with the Arian members of the Synod. The thing existed in practice, and so far was a compact. But there was a radical immorality in it. To keep that compact with man is to violate our allegiance to God. When, therefore, our enemies cry 'breach of compact,' I reply 'reformation,' and, by the blessing of God, we will reform our Church. The Lord, in Revelation, calls upon some of the Churches to remember from whence they had fallen ; to repent and do the first works. The first work of our Church was the work of advancing evangelical truth. We are now returning to that work, and no obstacle shall be able to retard our progress. We are embarked, indeed, on a troubled ocean ; but Christ is in the ship, and His hand is at the helm. He points to the glorious day-star in the east of our horizon. Our night may be in storm and sadness ; but in the morning joy shall arise."

This noble speech carried the convictions of the Synod. When the motion for the appointment of the committee was put to the House, seventy-four ministers and all the elders voted " Appoint," while only three ministers voted " Not." Dissentients never again ventured to measure their strength with Mr.

Cooke.   Now, for a period of forty years the committee has
been in operation, and the result is an orthodox Church, and a
faithful and highly-trained ministry.

There was still one subject which excited the fears of Mr.
Cooke.   Most of the candidates for the ministry were being
trained in Belfast College, and were thus under the care of Mr.
Ferrie.   During the eighteenth century a semi-sceptical philosophy, taught in the Professor's chair in Glasgow, had been the
chief source of error in the Presbyterian Church in Ireland.
Now the danger was much greater, for a powerful Arian party
in Belfast would naturally desire to infuse their dogmas into
the minds of young men ; and, if Mr. Ferrie's philosophical
opinions tended, as was believed, to Arianism or infidelity, his
influence would be all the more dangerous.   Mr. Cooke, ever
watchful, moved that the College Committee be directed "to
take such steps as they may deem most effectual to inquire
into the religious sentiments of Mr. Ferrie, and his fitness
for the office of Professor."   The motion was carried by acclamation.

The separation of the Synod did not secure that peace
which the Arian party seemed so very anxious to obtain.
On the contrary, secession intensified animosity.   Mr.
Cooke was attacked by the whole force of the Remonstrants.
In private letters, in meetings of committee, in Presbyteries, in the press, he was assailed with uncontrolled viru-
lence.   The *Whig* in Belfast, the *Evening Post* in Dublin,
and the leading Radical papers in England and Scotland,
charged him with undermining popular rights, and striking
at the root of civil and religious liberty.   Except in a
very few instances, when special charges were preferred,
he took no notice of his assailants. His opinions were
before the world.   His principles were boldly and fairly
stated.   His policy was clear to all.   He had gained the
grand object of his ten years' conflict—the freedom of his
Church from Arian heresy.   The vast body of the Presbyterian people fully endorsed his principles, and appreciated

his successful labours.   Dr. Killen says with truth:—" The popularity enjoyed at this period by the pastor of Killyleagh was such as perhaps has never been attained by any other minister of any denomination in this country."

CHAPTER IX.

1829—1831.

MR. COOKE was not less distinguished for pulpit eloquence than for power in debate. It was admitted that no such preacher had ever appeared in the Presbyterian Church of Ireland.· And his fame was not confined to Ireland. Wherever he went in Scotland and England, crowds flocked to hear him. The demands upon him for charity sermons, and other public services were incessant. As far as time and strength permitted, he freely responded to them. He never refused to go where duty seemed to call. In great bodily weakness, often in great pain, he journeyed far to serve the Church. " I am not my own, I am Christ's," he wrote to one who had pressed him to preach. " I am overwhelmed with work here ; but if I can advance my Master's kingdom, I dare not refuse to go to you. God has done great things for us ; we must show our gratitude by consecrating all we have to Him." This intensity of love to Christ, and devotion to His cause, contributed largely to his success as a pulpit orator. Every one felt he was in earnest. His reasoning was manifestly the expression of deep conviction ; his enthusiasm was as manifestly the outpouring of a full heart. Many, and among them some who now hold the highest places in the Church, have stated that they never knew what preaching was—they never were able fully to understand the power of the pulpit, until they heard Mr. Cooke.

Having been invited to preach, on behalf of a local charity, in Berry Street Church, Belfast, he selected as his text the words of Solomon, " Righteousness exalteth a nation." The sermon produced an impression on the minds of many of his hearers which is to this day fresh as ever. A gentleman, who was present (a Covenanter), has thus described the effect made upon him by one magnificent burst of eloquence :—" Mr. Cooke spoke of the greatness of England. He said some would place the glory of our country in her ships, bearing the red-cross flag to every coast, as a symbol of liberty—a refuge for the oppressed, a sanctuary for the enslaved. Some would place England's glory in her armies, winning victories for freedom in well-fought fields in every country of the world. ' But,' he added, ' if I were to choose a chaplet to bind around the brow of Britain, I would cull it of the flowers which Mercy planted when Wilberforce stood in the senate of the realm, and pro-claimed that slavery was no more.' The words went through me like an electric shock. I sprang to my feet, and was just on the point of crying ' hear, hear !' when my wife caught me, and recalled me to a sense of my true position."

After a sermon preached in the New Church, Coleraine, on May 3rd, 1829, an admiring hearer wrote the following critique. Cowper's well-known words are first quoted :—

> " Would I describe a preacher, such as Paul,
> Were he on earth, would hear, approve and own,
> Paul should himself direct me. I would trace
> His master-strokes, and draw from his design.
> I would express him simple, grave, sincere ;
> In doctrine uncorrupt ; in language plain,
> And plain in manner ; decent, solemn, chaste,
> And natural in gesture ; much impressed.
> Himself as conscious of his awful charge,

And anxious mainly that the flock he feeds
May feel it too ; affectionate in look,
And tender in address, as well becomes
A messenger of grace to guilty man.
Behold the picture ! Is it like ? "

" Mr. Cooke in the pulpit yesterday reminded me of this
description, and, perhaps, in his parochial ministry, seldom goes
beyond it. He knows how to rein in his transcendant talents to
the simplicity of the gospel ; but, like St. Paul, he does upon
fit occasion rise into a sublimity astonishing even to those acquainted with his powers. He is eminently qualified for preaching public sermons. His extensive information, his wonderful
memory, his correct taste, enable him to collect whatever air,
or earth, or ocean can supply to illustrate his subject. But,
above all, his piety, his devotedness to his Saviour—'the
Mighty God, the Everlasting Father, the Prince of Peace'—
have stamped upon him such a character of authority, energy,
and gentleness, that he might indeed make a Felix tremble,
and ' almost persuade ' a careless multitude to become
Christians. He is not a theatrical preacher. Of stage trick,
or stage effect, all who look upon his pale, yet manly and
expressive countenance, will acquit him. His is no vulgar or
stormy vehemence ; no rant, no studied attitude. He rises
calm, serene, dispassionate, as if conscious that the eye of
Jehovah is upon him. But as his mind expands, as the
interest is awakened which he wishes to excite in his fellow
man, he deems it not beneath him to use for the best purposes,
those marvellous gifts with which he is so richly endowed.
The most beautiful imagery, the choicest words, the most
appropriate scriptural quotations, are enforced by gestures at
once natural, graceful, and commanding. Those who can
imagine the unstudied eloquence and action of St. Paul when
he said ' Would to God ye all were as I am, except these
bonds,' can fancy how he raised his hands, as if seeking to
shake off the bonds of mortality. Such were some of the
striking actions of Mr. Cooke. He seemed, in his highest

flights, like a blessed spirit about to soar heavenward, and draw, by irresistible power, all after him."

An attempt was made to induce Mr. Cooke to remove to Dublin. On the 12th of October, 1828, a unanimous call was presented to him by the congregation of Mary's Abbey. Appended to it is the following note, in the handwriting of the venerable Dr. Horner, the senior minister:—" The above call meets with my most cordial concurrence." Though great influence was brought to bear upon Mr. Cooke, though the wants of the capital, and the wide field of usefulness that would be there opened up for his commanding talents, were pressed upon him, he felt it his duty to decline the invitation. It is probable that friends in Belfast were chiefly instrumental in preventing him from going to Dublin. Belfast was the centre both of Arianism and Presbyterianism. The ablest men of the New Light party were located there. Their power over the leading merchants, and surrounding gentry was great. An Orthodox leader was required in the pulpit, and on the platform, to counteract Arian influence. When the Church of Fisherwick Place was erected, some wished Mr. Cooke to be its minister. The Rev. James Morgan, however, was happily placed over that new congregation, and his zeal, piety, wisdom, and talents, have, by God's blessing, made it a model church. After Mr. Morgan's settlement, the friends of Mr. Cooke resolved to build a new church specially for himself. They chose a site in May Street, and the edifice was completed in October, 1829.

" The new church," says the Belfast *News-Letter* of that date, " is one of the most splendid, and even magnificent, structures for Presbyterian worship, in Ireland. We have seen nothing equal to it, in point of symmetry and beauty, among the meeting-houses of any class of dissenters in this country, and, regarded as a public edifice, it is an ornament to Belfast, and highly creditable to the public spirit and taste of those gentlemen under whose management it has been erected."

The opening services were conducted by Mr. Cooke, on

Sunday, the 18th of October. Though the admission was by ticket, and though every effort was made on the part of the managing committee to prevent undue pressure, the streets around the church were filled hours before the time appointed for worship. When the doors were opened, every seat and passage was immediately occupied. The aisles, the vestibule, the portico were thronged with an eager crowd. The excitement became intense when it was found that no more could gain an entrance. Hundreds grouped themselves before the doors and windows. The leading nobility and gentry of Down and Antrim had come to hear the great pulpit orator ; but many of them, including the Marquis of Donegal, were forced to leave, not being able even to approach the door.

Mr. Cooke's text was Psalm lxxxvii. 3—" Glorious things are spoken of thee, O City of God." A local paper says :— " After an eloquent introduction descriptive of the privileges and glory of the Jewish dispensation, and the circumstances in virtue of which peculiar honour was ascribed to Jerusalem, Mr. Cooke applied the doctrine of the text to the case of the New Testament Zion, to the statement of its distinctive privileges, and the consequent duties of its denizens. The subject was illustrated in a masterly manner, and with that earnestness and power of persuasion for which Mr. Cooke is distinguished. We do not attempt an outline of this able discourse, simply because, in our limited space, we would be unable to do justice to it ; and to offer any·lengthened eulogium on the merits of the preacher as a man of first-rate talents and an orator, would be little short of affectation in regard to one whose celebrity is not confined to this country."

A few days after the opening of the church, a unanimous call from the congregation was presented to Mr. Cooke. It was accepted. To separate from his attached flock in Killyleagh was a sore trial. He had won the affections and the confidence of all classes. Especially did he feel the pain of separating from his bosom friend, his wise and long-tried counsellor, his fearless and chivalrous assistant in all battles for the faith,

Sydney Hamilton Rowan. But Captain Rowan knew, as others knew, that the Church required Mr. Cooke's services in Belfast. To him the call of duty was paramount. He would permit no private feelings to interfere with the interests of Christ's kingdom. He therefore not only approved of the call, but he plainly told Mr. Cooke that he must accept of it.

Mr. Cooke had announced that he would deliver his farewell sermon in Killyleagh on Sunday, November 8th. The day was not allowed to pass in peace. On the previous Sunday a large handbill was posted on the gate of Killyleagh Church, stating that the Rev. Henry Montgomery would preach within the bounds of that parish, on the succeeding Sunday at twelve o'clock. This was not all. Attached to the handbill was a written challenge, calling upon Mr. Cooke to meet Mr. Montgomery face to face, if he dare ; and to refute his arguments from Scripture, if he could. The announcement was most embarrassing. It was doubtless intended to be so. On seeing the handbill, Mr. Cooke decided on his line of action. He gave public notice that he could not attend at the hour specified, as it was the time appointed for preaching his farewell sermon. He added that he should avail himself of the best information he might be able to obtain regarding Mr. Montgomery's statements and arguments, and that he would reply to them at seven o'clock on the evening of the same day, in his own church.

Mr. Montgomery preached at Derryboy, on the outskirts of the parish of Killyleagh. His text was Matthew v. 11, 12, " Blessed are ye, when men shall revile you, and persecute you, and shall say all manner of evil against you falsely, for my sake. Rejoice, and be exceeding glad; for great is your reward in heaven; for so persecuted they the prophets which were before you." His sermon occupied nearly two hours and a half. He attempted to defend the Arian doctrines from the charges which, he alleged, had been brought against them by certain of his fellow ministers of the Synod of Ulster. He then changed from defence to assault. He accused Trinitarians of persecution, of stirring up strife, of preventing people from living together in love. He arraigned their doctrines as anti-evangelical, as comprising a system of false confidence, as bewildering the mind with the notion of a Deity compounded of three persons. A full report was taken and handed to Mr. Cooke at five o'clock, and at seven he preached to the largest congregation ever known to have assembled in Killyleagh. There was a double interest connected with the service. It was his last appearance as minister of the congregation; and it was known he would reply to his great Arian antagonist. It was just an occasion to bring out all his powers. He selected for his text Jude 3, "I exhort you that ye should earnestly co ntend for the faith which was once delivered unto the saints." After a brief introduction setting forth the leading principles of "the faith," he took up in order Mr. Mont-gomery's assertions, arguments, and charges. He showed that Arianism was subversive of the fundamental doctrines of Christianity, while the truths set forth in the time-honoured Standards of the Presbyterian Church, embodied all the grand principles of life, and love, and liberty. For three hours he held the audience spell-bound. He concluded with an appeal that touched every heart. In Killyleagh, Arianism received its first decided check when Smithurst was silenced; and in Killyleagh, it received its final overthrow, in so far as con-cerned the Synod of Ulster, when that overwhelming reply was made to Montgomery. The people, in bidding farewell to their beloved pastor, had the proud satisfaction of knowing that he, during the ten years of his ministry among them, had been the means, under God, of accomplishing the greatest work ever achieved for the Presbyterian Church in Ireland.

Mr. Cooke was installed minister of May Street, on the 24th of November, 1829. The Rev. (now Professor) Henry Wallace preached upon the occasion. In the evening, says the *News-Letter*, "Nearly eighty gentlemen sat down to dinner in the Royal Hotel; Captain Rowan, of Killyleagh, in the chair. After the cloth was removed the chairman intimated that no toasts were to be given. Mr. Cooke stated his reasons for not attending any dinner on such an occasion, where toasts were to be drunk. With the decision of the chairman, who acted according to the directions of the committee of the New House, and the sentiments of Mr. Cooke, the company seemed much gratified."

May Street Church soon became celebrated. The fame of Mr. Cooke drew to it crowds of earnest auditors. The like was never seen before in Belfast, nor indeed in Ireland. The Church was the centre of attraction for the inhabitants, and for strangers. Men of all sects and parties filled its pews and aisles. Members of the bar, when the duties of the circuit brought them to Belfast, went to May Street to hear pulpit eloquence, such as they never heard elsewhere. One of the brightest ornaments of the legal profession, the Rt. Hon. Sir J. Napier, has given a graphic sketch of Dr. Cooke, in 1833:—

" Carrickfergus being so near to Belfast, we generally have a Sunday to spend in the latter place, when I invariably go to hear Dr. Cooke preach. The body of the people of this town are sturdy, sterling Presbyterians ; Arianism is confined to a section of wealthy merchants. . . . This withering creed, that partially rejects the great and sublime manifestation of the love and grace of God, and in which the sickly light of reason is made to supply the glorious splendour of revelation ; the heat of sectarian prejudice acts as a substitute for the glowing warmth of that heaven-born truth, which is worthy of all men to be received ; this mixture of the pride of intellect and vain philosophy, has been encountered by Dr. Cooke, with the spirit of a David, and the power of a Samson, and paralyzed by the vigour of his gigantic intellect, under the direction of Him to whom all power is given. The newspaper press, which, of course, will always please, not regulate, the popular appetite, was made the bow from which arrows were shot at the Doctor, but it was shooting at the sun. There he stands, like a majestic cliff, from which the raging billows are thrown back with an angry surge, impotent and crest-fallen. As he

ascends the pulpit-stairs, you trace the lineaments of a Crom-
wellian spirit—energy, determination, and vigour. The forehead is bold and fine ; the countenance, sombre and solemn ;
the pronunciation, slow and measured ; the method, logical
and copious ; the eloquence, ornate and vigorous ; the demonstration, powerful and persuasive. There is an inclination to resort to fanciful analogies, and quaint conceits ; but
withal there is a mighty pouring forth of gospel truth, em-
bellished with the graces of rhetoric and the power of logic.
Have you ever seen a lowering cloud, dark, heavy, and
slumbering ; now it rolls with the peal of the thunder ; now
the lightning flashes from it, illuminating, and sometimes
burning ; the rain descends ; the atmosphere is purified, the
sun again bursts forth with placid and genial warmth, and ' the
shepherd's heart is glad.' This will illustrate the power which
Dr. Cooke possesses over his audience. The most exquisite
imagery drops unconsciously from him. I remember hearing
him discourse upon the unchristian passion of anger ; and as he
was describing the tranquillity of the christian's bosom, he proceeded thus :—' The storms of dissension may roar around
him ; the tempest of unholy zeal may burst over his head with
raging fury, and roll on in awful violence ; his spirit remains
calm, still, and quiescent as the peaceful slumbering of some
lovely lake, embosomed in a valley, which the winds of heaven
never stooped to ruffle.' "

Some years later, Professor Witherow heard Dr. Cooke for
the first time, and has embodied the following account of the
scene and circumstances in his eloquent lecture on " Three
Prophets of Our Own."

" A report that the Doctor was to preach on the sin of theatricals, drew me one evening to May Street Church. I was in
attendance a little before the hour appointed, but found the immense place of worship quite full—every seat occupied, so that I
with difficulty found standing-room in the aisle. The Doctor
entered dressed in his Geneva gown and bands, and ascended
to the pulpit with all the dignity of a monarch mounting the

steps of a throne, and all the stern gravity of a judge about to
pronounce sentence of death; and the people, for lack of room,
crept quietly up the stairs after the preacher till they gained
the summit, and outside the pulpit door stood on a level with
himself. The text of the evening was so rivetted in my
memory that I will never forget it; it was, 1 Cor. xv. 33, 'Be
not deceived; evil communications corrupt good manners.'
When he commenced, I soon found that he had been preaching
on the same subject the preceding Sabbath; that a report of
the sermon, and an elaborate answer to it from an anonymous
correspondent signing himself 'Thespis,' had appeared in the
Northern Whig, and that to this newspaper critique he was now
giving a public reply. On this occasion the Doctor was in a
position for making a display of the peculiar talents of which
he is so eminent a master. He had the excitement arising
from an immense audience, a novel subject, and an antagonist;
and never did preacher acquit himself better than he did that
night. He reiterated his arguments against the theatre, took
up Thespis and tore his reasoning to shreds, and even the
magnates of the Belfast press—' the people down in Calender
Street '—did not escape without due castigation. The force of
the speaker's reasoning and the vehemence of his utterance—
the power of that full-toned voice, whose lowest whisper could
be distinctly heard in the most distant seat of the gallery, and
whose thunder-peals the moment after, made the ceiling ring—
the contempt that he made the audience feel for the arguments
of his adversary, and his passionate appeals to the assembly,
satisfied me that I had never heard an orator before, and that
the one to whom I then was listening was more than worthy
his brilliant reputation. The streams of irony, and eloquence,
and argument, that flowed that evening from the pulpit of May
Street, and blended all together in one burning flood of fiery
declamation, were as irresistible as a cataract from the hills.
In the midst of the sermon all the gaslights in the house were
simultaneously extinguished, whether from design or accident
is unknown to me; and for nearly fifteen minutes the church

was in total darkness, with the exception of whatever light
emanated from four candles that burned upon the pulpit, and
that served only to make the darkness visible. But the
preacher did not stop, nor even falter. Like a hurricane at
midnight, on he thundered through the gloom ; and when the
gas-lamps were relighted, he concluded with a splendid pero-
ration. That night is memorable to me, being the first time I
ever was made to feel the power of eloquence ; and it is memorable to more than me, for the theatricals in Belfast received a
shock that evening, from which they have not yet recovered.
Since that time I have had an opportunity of hearing many
able speakers from different parts of the kingdom, yet I must
confess that never on any occasion have I met with one, who
could command an audience, sway the passions of a multitude,
or demolish an antagonist with the same facility as Dr. Cooke.
And on this point I hazard my opinion with the more confidence as in some other respects, I have never been one of his
blind and bigoted admirers.''

For a period of eighteen years, Dr. Cooke conducted three
services every Sunday in May Street Church. At each service there was a sermon or lecture, seldom less, and generally
more, than an hour in length. Yet the spacious building was
always crowded ; and the auditors seemed never to weary. His
expositions of Scripture were characterised by great breadth
and grasp of thought, and acute analytical power; his illustrations were marked by originality and poetic beauty; his practical applications of truth were pointed and deeply impressive.
He was especially distinguished in the pulpit for the wonderful
tact and power with which he brought the lessons of God's Word
to bear upon the engagements of everyday life. No popular
error was overlooked ; no social abuse evaded his keen eye ;
no political corruption, no mercantile immorality, escaped the
scathing touch of his satire, and the fire of his indignant denunciations. The politician, the lawyer, the merchant, the
agriculturist—every man, in fact, in every sphere, had his
duties developed in language so clear, and enforced in terms so

persuasive, that he could not fail to profit. Dr. Cooke was no mere theorist, either in the pulpit or in the study. He was preeminently a man of action. He had no patience with cold and barren intellectual display. To overthrow error, to defend and establish truth, to enlighten, elevate, ennoble man—these were the grand aims of his life. His transparent honesty, and whole-hearted earnestness in this work, were the main secrets of his unrivalled and continued popularity. He made every hearer feel he was in earnest. No man could possibly sit passive under his preaching. His descriptions of the frivolities of fashionable society, and of the vices that so largely prevail in great cities, were life-pictures. They stood out before the audience as stern and appalling realities. His words of warning and rebuke pierced the heart like a sword. His appeals melted strong, hardened men to tears. The fervour of his address, and the eloquence of his language, were largely aided by his magnificent voice, by the dignity and grace of his person, and by his gestures, which were easy and yet singularly striking. No man of his day could command an audience, whether from pulpit or platform, like Dr. Cooke. The intellect, the heart, the imagination, were all alike under his control ; he could move and sway them at will, as by the wand of a mighty magician. When its pulpit was occupied by such a preacher, none will wonder that May Street became celebrated. His connection with it continued unbroken for thirty-nine years, and was only severed by death.

The struggle for the truth in the Synod of Ulster had been watched by thousands in the United States of America. The Presbyterian Church in that country was founded by an Irish Presbyterian minister. A large proportion of its members were Irish by birth or descent. They felt a deep interest, therefore, in the controversy waged in the land and Church of their fathers. Mr. Cooke's name became a household word. When he triumphed, his American brethren were not slow to tender their congratulations, and convey a tribute of esteem to the victor. At a meeting of the Board of Jefferson College,

in April, 1829, it was resolved that the degree of Doctor in
Divinity should be conferred upon the Rev. Henry Cooke.
The letter communicating the intelligence of this unsolicited
and unexpected honour is dated October 21st, 1829.   It states
that the degree was conferred on account of high attainments
in literature and science, and zealous earnestness in the promotion of evangelical truth.   During his whole life, even when
other honours were showered upon him, Dr. Cooke prized,
perhaps more highly than all, this recognition of his services
on the part of the great American nation.   Even until within
a few years of his death he fondly cherished the hope of visiting the far west, and tendering to its noble people his thanks
for their sympathy with him in his work, and for the reward
they bestowed.

The Orthodox party in the Synod of Ulster had long felt the
want of a journal.   Hitherto they had no public organ through
which to make known their views to the people of Ireland, or
to defend them when assailed.   One of the leading Belfast
papers, *The Whig*, was under the control of the Arians.   It
advocated their opinions.   It lauded their liberality.   It re-
echoed their plausible cry for freedom of thought.   It gave
full publicity to their letters and speeches.   It reported with
scrupulous care everything in their favour.   But, as a general
rule, it suppressed everything opposed to Arianism.   Where
it was not possible, or prudent to suppress, it presented facts,
statements, and arguments in such a way as to leave an
entirely false impression on the public mind.   *The Whig*, in
fact, was then characterised by intense antipathy to orthodoxy.   During the ten years of the Arian conflict it in-
dulged in the bitterest invectives against Henry Cooke.   The
old *News-Letter* had more of independence ; but it had not a
little of the Gallio spirit—it " cared for none of these things."
The Guardian, to some extent, adopted the views of Mr.
Cooke, and not unfrequently came generously forward to defend his character, and to administer a stern rebuke to his
assailants.   Still, *The Guardian* had so much of High Church

leaning, that it could not be relied upon for advocating Presbyterian principles.

Under these circumstances it was resolved to establish a new periodical. Its design and character were sufficiently indicated by its name, " *The Orthodox Presbyterian*." " In its pages," the Prospectus says, " the precious truths of the Gospel shall be faithfully maintained—the principles of the Reformation vindicated—the cause of vital godliness advocated, and the distinguishing tenets of Presbyterianism explained and defended." Dr. Cooke was one of its chief promoters. Its first number appeared just at the time when he was removing from Killyleagh to Belfast ; and it contained a very able and opportune article on " Presbyterianism," which displayed to great advantage his nervous style and logical mind. He continued for years a regular contributor to its pages. Some of its most telling papers, including all those on education, were the products of his pen.

The magazine accomplished a good work for the Synod of Ulster, and for evangelical truth. In it, for the first time, the masses were fully informed of the real state of the Presbyterian Church. Misrepresentations were set aside, and charges of interference with popular rights were dissipated. The acts of the Synod, designed to preserve the constitution and protect the spiritual interests of the Church, were clearly explained. A paper appeared in the number for October, 1830, on " The Synod of Ulster," which removed many false impressions, and showed how soon new life and power were being developed after the expulsion of the Arian heresy. Referring to a resolution to appoint a committee to correspond with the Presbyterian Churches in Europe and America, with a view to closer ecclesiastical connection, it is said :—" We presume it is already known to many of our readers, that by the friends of evangelical truth, both at home and abroad, there has been felt and expressed the deepest interest in the late struggles of the Synod for the promotion of truth. The most encouraging letters have been received from England, Scotland, and

America. Strangers who have visited this country from all
these places have assured us of the warmest sympathy of the
Churches with which they are connected. And already arrangements have been made by a Presbyterian Synod in England,
and by the General Assembly in America, to enter into correspondence with the Synod of Ulster . . . While the
Synod appeared indifferent to the deadly heresies that had
crept into her communion, she was frowned upon by the
Christian Churches of other countries, and would soon justly
have become an outcast from their fellowship ; but since she
has roused herself from her lethargy, and stood as a witness
for the truth, the countenance of Christendom begins to shine
upon her—the hand of Christian fellowship is stretched out to
congratulate her, and she is invited to join her counsels with
the followers of the Lamb in other places, for mutual encouragement and support."

It appears, too, from the same paper that missions were
already beginning to occupy their right place in the minds of
the ministers, and in the deliberations of the Synod :—" The
Church is manifestly a missionary institution. It is an association of Christians for their own edification and the extension
of their principles. And from the beginning it will be found
that the spirit of missionary zeal in the Church has been a
sure criterion of its internal prosperity. The pulse of missionary life beats in exact proportion to the health and vigour
of the spiritual character. To take an example from the
history of our own Church :—When first our fathers settled
in the land, they were borne by the impulse of missionary zeal
from county to county, nor did they rest until the entire province was supplied with an effective ministry. At that period
error was unknown among them. In a later age, when error
was making silent progress, the Church appeared to have
fallen into a complete lethargy. . . . In our own
times, since zeal has been revived for maintaining the doctrines
of the Cross, it has shown itself also in its exertions to propagate them. And the passing of the Overtures for the main-

tenance of truth in the body, has been accompanied with the establishment of the Presbyterian Missionary Society." Thus early did Dr. Cooke begin to see the good fruits of his battle for truth.

When the Arians found themselves excluded from the Synod, and their peculiar doctrines prevented from making " silent progress" by the energetic measures of Dr. Cooke, they attempted to advance their cause by other means. Wherever a congregation was divided in sentiment, the Arian members endeavoured to appropriate the ecclesiastical buildings. The Synod was forced, in 1830, to establish a general fund for assisting in the protection of congregational property and the rights of ministers. In no less than five places the Remonstrants had seized upon the churches, and refused to allow a poll to be taken in the congregation as to how the property should be divided.

A case of peculiar hardship occurred in Clough, County Down. A dispute having arisen there regarding the settlement of a minister, a section of the people seceded to the Presbytery of Antrim, a body which, for more than a century, had no connection with the Synod of Ulster. The seceders laid claim to the *Regium Donum*, and attempted to gain possession of the church by force. The Orthodox party were assailed when engaged in worship. The minister was, on one occasion, assaulted in the pulpit. On another occasion, a riotous mob, composed partly of Arians and partly of Roman Catholics, tried to break in the church doors during the time of service, and were only dispersed by the appearance of a body of police. The policy of the civil authorities was somewhat strange. Instead of protecting the people when assembled for public worship, the police actually drove them from their meeting-house; and the Lord Lieutenant threatened that, unless, before a certain date, all disputes between the parties were settled, he would withdraw the *Regium Donum*. This was certainly a new way to settle a question of title. One would have supposed that a court of justice alone could

have decided which party had a legal right to the building.
To punish either or both for claiming their right was an act of
tyranny.

It was in this state the matter came before the Synod.   Dr.
Cooke had thoroughly investigated it.   His speech was in
some respects one of the most important he had ever
delivered.   After giving a clear outline of its history, he
proceeded to criticise the action of the civil authorities, and
the threat of the Lord Lieutenant.   He stated that the Presbyterian Church had rights, and that within her own sphere
she was free.   She would permit no man and no authority to
interfere with her decisions.   She would never submit to the
dictation of the State in matters purely ecclesiastical.

" The congregation of Clough are told that unless after twelve
days they settle a most complicated legal case by arbitration, or
otherwise, the royal grant will be withdrawn.   I regard the twelve
days' declaration of Sir William Gosset as one of the deepest importance, not because it involves the interests of one of our congregations, our minister and his family; but I fear the threat here hung
out *in terrorem* is only the commencement of a plan for a more
extended stripping of our poor Presbyterian churches.   But though
the Government that threatens one should strip the whole, and turn
us out naked on the cold green hills of Ulster, the God who ' tempers
the wind to the shorn lamb' will also temper the storm to your
capacity of endurance.   Our fathers were respectable in their deep
poverty, before the grant was received; their sons will be respectable
should it be taken away.   Do I, then, dread the withdrawal ?   No,
I do not dread it.   I say to the Government, with the most loyal
respect, Take it from us if you will, and give it to Maynooth or to
the Arians.   The poor pittance of which our minister and his family
may be deprived will indeed be a sorry addition ; but because it will
arise from the deprivation of an orthodox minister, they will regard
it as the *opima spolia.*   And I will say honestly and fearlessly to the
Government, If you think it right to deprive one minister of his
endowment, you need not pause there, for I trust there is spirit
enough in the Presbyterian body to say and to feel—If you deprive
one, you must deprive us all.   We will not stand calmly by, and see
a poor brother openly robbed.   .   .   .

" The endowment was granted, but the Government took it back. And why did they take it back ? The allegation was that it must be suspended till the location of the minister should be settled. Well, then, who are to settle our discipline, and pronounce upon the regularity of our ordinations ? Is it the Government ? No, indeed ; they are denied the power by the Canons of the Church. We alone can settle the question. A legal question we are ready to submit to lawyers ; a mercantile question to merchants ; but an ecclesiastical question, respecting the settlement of a minister, we submit to neither. . . . . I am a Presbyterian of the old school, and will not consent that the laity become the ecclesiastical judges of the clergy. The Church of England groans because her discipline has been absorbed into the civil courts, and lawyers exercise the functions which belong of right to her ministers ; and shall the Presbyterian Church surrender into the hands of merchants the highest case of their ecclesiastical jurisdiction ? It cannot be. The question here to be judged is one purely ecclesiastical, and by judges ecclesiastical it must be determined. To consent to a mercantile arbitration over an ecclesiastical appointment, were a specimen of pure Erastianism against which our Church has ever most decidedly protested. . . .

" In all things temporal we will render to the King an undivided loyalty and a prompt obedience ; but in all things spiritual Christ is our King, and in the spiritualities of His Church our loyalty and our obedience are for Him alone."

He concluded with the following stirring words :—

" Our fathers bought our privileges and our liberties dear, and their sons will never barter them for golden fetters. One tittle of our church discipline we will never surrender, though a king come in person to make the demand. Misrepresented, we will appeal to facts ; injured, we will appeal to the law; misunderstood, we will appeal to the good sense and good feeling of our rulers. And if, withal, we should haply fail, there is still another earthly tribunal, at which, under Providence, you are sure to be heard. You will appeal to the feelings of the people, who will not leave your minister and his family to want, because Arianism has stepped in and deprived them of their birthright."

This speech was worthy of the days of Knox. It is a sufficient answer to all the Voluntary charges of State bondage preferred, before and since, against the Presbyterian Church of Ireland. It shows that Church was ever free, and that it was not afraid in days of danger to proclaim and defend its freedom. The speech was received with enthusiasm. It made a profound impression. The Synod at once resolved to lay the whole case before the Government, and respectfully demand redress. It is enough to say that Dr. Cooke was again successful. His arguments and his eloquence were irresistible. The Church of Clough was retained, and the *Regium Donum* was restored to the minister.

In Belfast Dr. Cooke found no repose, and little peace. He had a host of difficulties to contend with, and a host of enemies to meet. Some little idea may be formed of his labours from a letter written at this period to his dear Christian friend, Dr. Malan :—

"BELFAST, 12th July, 1830.

"My dear Brother in Christ,—Since I saw you at Tollymore Park I have been removed to Belfast. It is a place of much difficulty, but of much hope. It is the head-quarters of the Arian and Socinian heresies in this country. Both by preaching and publishing they are straining every nerve against the truth; but, by the blessing of God, we are endeavouring to counteract them in both ways. One of their chief aims has been to misrepresent the state of religion on the Continent. . . . If you can send me anything illustrative of the past and present state of religion in Geneva, or elsewhere, it would be extremely acceptable. . . Above all, pray for me. You are ever in my heart before the Lord. May He have you in His holy keeping.

"Yours in Christ,

"H. Cooke."

Dr. Cooke was not left without encouragement and sympathy. From Lords Roden, Mount-Cashell, and Dufferin, from Doctors Chalmers and Wardlaw, and from many other men distinguished in the Church and in the world, he received cordial letters of congratulation. His success was acknowledged throughout Evangelical Christendom to be a victory gained for truth. Among those who rejoiced in the reformation of the Irish Presbyterian Church was Edward Irving. Dr. Cooke had wished Mr. Irving to conduct the opening services of May Street; but family affliction prevented him. He promised, however, that as soon as possible he would visit Belfast. Accordingly, on the 27th of August, 1830, he wrote to Dr. Cooke :—

"My dear Friend,—The Lord has removed to Himself the cause of long anxiety and watching, and my wife and surviving child are, by His goodness, so far restored as that I can now leave home to fulfil my engagements. So I have resolved to set out for Ireland on Monday first, and to proceed to Powerscourt, where my wife and child are to rest with Lady Powerscourt till I return home. Now my wish is to come to Belfast either the second or the third Sabbath of September. My object is, besides fulfilling my engagements to you and other friends, to give myself to preach in the open air to the people. I know not how the Lord may prosper it; but this is my desire. A time of great trial for the truth's sake is now come. God grant you grace to be faithful. It will be needed. Farewell.

"Your affectionate and faithful friend,

"Edward Irving."

Dr. Cooke's home labour was great; but it did not prevent him from doing something for the Church abroad. He had wide sympathies; and wherever a way was opened for advancing his Master's kingdom, he spared neither time nor toil. Thoroughly Presbyterian in feeling and convictions, he yet felt the deepest interest in the prosperity of other evangelical denominations. His eloquence and influence were always at their service when any Christian object was to be promoted. In the spring of 1831 he visited Liverpool, Manchester, and London on behalf of the Irish Evangelical and Bible Societies. It was a time of great political excitement. The elections were going on. He was a keen observer; and his comments on passing events, contained in letters to Mrs. Cooke, show with what clearness he read the future :—"I have seen all manner of sights since leaving you. First, an election-chairing at Liverpool, with ' Ewart for ever.' . . . Manchester was much the same, and so was the whole route to London. The people are all *Reformers;* and, sooth to say, their good temper and orderly behaviour entitle them to reform. But, through all the reform, I see the downfall of the Established Church. There is a deep-rooted antipathy to her honours, and posses- sions, and proud exclusiveness, that will soon appear in her overthrow. I should regret this event—partly because I do not wish to disturb things that are established—partly be- cause, that when the Church is robbed, it is a question whether the spoil will go to better men—partly because I believe the hatred of the Church is just covetousness and envy on the part of a vast majority of those who would fleece her ;—but mainly because the principle of Establishments is Scriptural, and the Church now established, with many serious blemishes, is sound at the bottom. All this you will, perhaps, say is no small confession from an Irish Presbyterian. In truth, I wish the Church to keep all she has ; only I would earnestly and solemnly counsel and even warn her to divide it better, and to work more for what she gets, and to reform her glaring abuses. If she be deaf to counsel—if she prove inaccessible to reform—I will prophesy, though I do it in sadness, that she will be spoiled of her possessions ; and then the spoil will go to a worse."

This is a remarkable letter, especially when read in the light of recent history. At the time it was written most men would have pronounced it the record of a dreamy imagination. It was not so. It was the conclusion of a thoughtful and far-seeing intellect. Dr. Cooke's ecclesiastical principles never changed. His views regarding Church establishments remained the same to the last hour of his life. On many occasions, in after-years, when the subject was brought up by current events, he gave utterance to the same feelings and the same fears.

CHAPTER X.

1831—1834.

THE important question of National Education was introduced to the public by the celebrated Letter of the Right Hon. E. G. Stanley, Chief Secretary for Ireland. It is dated October, 1831. The object of the Government, which Mr. Stanley represented, was professedly to surmount the religious difficulty, hitherto the main barrier in the way of any general scheme for the education of the Irish people. Prejudices deeply rooted, and principles strongly held, had to be overcome, or wisely accommodated. " The system of the new Commissioners was designed to banish even the suspicion of proselytism, and, while admitting children of all creeds, to interfere with the tenets of none. It was to be based upon the plan of association in literary instruction, but separation in religious." The Managing Board was to be " composed of men of high personal character, including individuals of exalted station in the Church ; " and it was " in part " to be composed of " persons professing different religious opinions." Christians of all denominations might apply for educational grants; but, it being one main object to unite in one system children of different creeds, the Letter states that the Board would regard favourably applications for aid proceeding from— " 1st. The Protestant and Roman Catholic clergy of the parish; 2nd. One of the clergymen, and a number of the parishioners professing the opposite creed; or 3rd. Parishioners of both denominations." The Board was instructed

" To require that schools should be kept open for a certain number of hours on four or five days of the week, at the discretion of the Commissioners, for moral and literary education only ; and that the remaining one or two days should be set apart for giving, separately, such religious education to the children, as may be approved by the clergy of their respective persuasions. They will also permit and encourage the clergy to give religious instruction to the children of their respective persuasions, either before or after the ordinary school hours, on the other days of the week."

Another important duty was assigned to the Board.

" They will exercise the most entire control over all books to be used in the schools, whether in the combined moral and literary or separate religious instruction ; none to be employed in the first except under the sanction of the Board, nor in the latter, but with the approbation of those members of the Board who are of the same religious persuasion with those for whose use they are intended."

It may be observed that of this Letter there are two copies : —one in the Irish Office, which is doubtless the original; the other printed in the report of the Board. They do not correspond in all points. In the latter there are some very remarkable and suggestive changes and omissions. The changes show an early determination materially to alter the constitution of the Board, and wholly to exclude the use of the Bible as a class-book. In the original copy the following paragraph occurs :—

" Although it is not designed to exclude from the list of books for the combined instruction such portions of sacred history, or of religious and moral teaching, as may be approved of by the Board, it is to be understood that this is by no means intended to convey a perfect and sufficient religious education, or to supersede the necessity of separate religious instruction on the day set apart for that purpose."

This paragraph is omitted in the copy of the Letter printed by the Board. Again, the original Letter provides "that the Board shall be composed of men of high personal character, including individuals of exalted station in the Church;" while the Board's copy reads—" It appears essential that a portion of the Board should be composed of men of high personal character, *and* of exalted station in the Church." These are serious changes, and betray a strong desire to modify official documents, and to conform them, as far as possible, to the views of a certain party.

The Presbyterian Church was deeply interested in the scheme of education. Immediately after the publication of Mr. Stanley's Letter, a special meeting of Synod was convened. It assembled at Cookstown, on the 11th of January, 1832. The first session was spent in private conference and deliberation. On the succeeding morning Dr. Cooke moved a series of resolutions, embodying the views of the Synod on elementary education, and their objections to the scheme developed by Mr. Stanley. The resolutions were unanimously adopted. Their main points were as follows :—

" That it is our deliberate opinion and decided conviction that in a Christian country the Bible, unabridged and unmutilated, should form the basis of national education (as we learn from Deut. vi. 6, 7 ; Psalm cxix. 9 ; John xvii. 17 ; 2 Tim. iii. 14—17) ; and that, consequently, we never can accede to any system that in the least degree interferes with the unrestricted possession and use of the Scriptures in our schools.

" That we have heard, with deep regret, that His Majesty's Government have proceeded to erect a Metropolitan Board of Education, vested with complete control over all schools and teachers receiving public aid, and an entire control over all school-books, whether for literary or religious education.

" That such an entire control, as, by the constitution of the

Board, the Government have vested in the hands of one member of
this body over all school-books employed by ministers in the religious
instruction of such children of their congregations as may attend the
national schools, cannot, in our opinion, be transferred to, nor be
exercised by, any one, without innovating on the constitutional principles of, and creating supremacy over, a Church, the absolute
parity of whose ministers is, and ever has been, one of her distinguishing and essential characteristics.

"That we cannot contemplate without peculiar disapprobation
that part of the proposed system which requires any members of the
Synod that may be called to the Board, to 'encourage' religious
teachers in the inculcation of doctrines which they must conscientiously believe to be directly opposed to the sacred Scriptures."

The Government felt that the consent of the Presbyterian
Church was necessary to the success of any scheme of national
education for Ireland. They were, therefore, ready to hear
objections, and consider suggestions, regarding the system
proposed by Mr. Stanley. In deference to the views of the
Synod, certain explanations were published by the Board during
the spring of 1832, which, in some degree, removed the objectionable points. Still the Church was not satisfied; and, accordingly, at the meeting of Synod in July, 1832, the Government Committee were instructed to correspond with the Irish
Office upon the subject. A remonstrance was prepared, and
presented by deputation to the Chief Secretary in Dublin, on
the 1st of September. It demanded, on behalf of the Synod,
a right to read the Bible, by such as might desire it, during
school hours. This was laid down as the necessary basis of all
negotiation. Should it be granted, the Committee had power
to effect an arrangement regarding other points at issue;
should it be declined, the Synod would refuse its sanction to
the proposed plan of education. The views of the Synod were
embodied in seven propositions. The Government declined to
accede to them; but it became evident from the conversation
and correspondence which ensued, that, if the phraseology of
the resolutions were changed, and certain modifications introduced, a satisfactory arrangement might be effected. With

this hope Dr. Cooke, on behalf of the Synod's committee, reduced the seven original propositions to three, as follows :—

"I. That persons of all denominations shall have the right, either jointly or separately, of applying to the Board for aid.

"II. That patrons of schools, on making application for aid, shall fix the ordinary period of school hours, and shall have the right of setting apart such portion or portions of said school hours as they may deem sufficient, for reading the Holy Scriptures.

"III. That all children, whose parents or guardians may so direct, shall daily read the Holy Scriptures during the time appointed by the patrons ; but that no compulsion whatever be employed to induce others to read, or remain during the reading."

These propositions were presented to His Majesty's Government in London, in May, 1833, by a deputation, of which Dr. Cooke was a leading member. They were again rejected ; and, in his official reply, the Chief Secretary for Ireland states :— " It will be impossible for me to recommend to His Majesty's Government any modification of the established system that would strike so entirely at the principle of that system as would the adoption of these propositions."

Meantime the education question had excited the liveliest interest in Ulster, and indeed throughout Ireland. A large section of the Protestants looked upon the Government scheme as tending to favour the claims and advance the designs of Roman Catholics. The determined efforts to exclude the Bible from the schools, and to afford encouragement for the teaching of the dogmas of Rome, were calculated to excite alarm. One paragraph in Mr. Stanley's Letter was specially obnoxious to conscientious Protestants. It says the Board " will require that a register shall be kept in the schools, in which shall be entered the attendance or non-attendance of each child on divine worship on Sundays." The Commissioners of Education were thus made virtually guardians of Roman Catholic children, to see that they attended regularly to their duties as members of the Papal Church. And under such a system Protestant patrons and schoolmasters would have been compelled to act as wardens of Papal superstition.

The Orthodox Presbyterian, in its first notice of the new scheme, says :—" We do not hesitate to denounce the report of the bill as the most cunning, the most daring, and the most specious attempts that have been made against Protestantism since the day when James II. sent his ambassador to Rome to reconcile the nation to the Pope."

Dr. Cooke, who wrote these words, and who had battled so long against Arianism, now came prominently forward as the champion of scriptural education. He announced that he would preach upon the subject on Sunday, the 15th of January, 1832. May Street Church was crowded long before the hour of service. His text was Proverbs xxii. 6 : " Train up a child in the way he should go ; and when he is old he will not depart from it." The sermon produced a wonderful effect upon the popular mind. It was published, by request ; but, like all Dr. Cooke's published sermons and speeches, it conveys no adequate idea of the power of the discourse as delivered by the impassioned orator. In it, however, he enunciated great principles, and exposed the errors of the educational scheme with such clearness and logical force that his words carried conviction.

" The whole subject of education seems reducible to one single question—What is the way in which God has commanded the teacher to train, and the child to go ? The prophets of the Old Testament, the apostles of the New, the fathers of the primitive ages, and the heads of the Reformation, the National Churches of Scotland and England, with all the other evangelical Churches of these kingdoms, unite in one reply,—train up a child in the way of all Scripture, which is able to ' make him wise unto salvation, through faith that is in Christ Jesus.' "

After developing the duty and necessity of discussing such a question in the pulpit, and thus endeavouring to impart correct knowledge on a subject of paramount importance to

the great body of the Christian people, he went on to
say :—

" Two objects present themselves before us : first, to ascertain
the Scripture principle ; second, to examine the Government plan
of education. The principle of education we find frequently discussed in the Bible ; from which authority it will appear, that the
Bible, without mutilation or addition, forms the only divine basis of
family or national education. . . . . From Bible teaching
three principles are clearly deducible : first, that the duty, together with all the privileges and responsibility of teaching, lies with
parents ; second, that the Holy Scriptures alone have received the
authoritative sanction of God for the education of children ; third,
that all Scripture is alike inspired of God, and is, without deduction
or mutilation, to be employed in the training of Christian children,
and the perfecting of Christian men.

" How far the Government plan of education comes short of these
scriptural principles, a brief review will abundantly demonstrate.

" To understand the true bearings of the plan, we must go back
to some of the fundamental principles of the Reformation. The
original difference between the See of Rome and the Protestant
Churches commences about the Bible. The Church of Rome affirms
that the Bible derives all its authority from her ; the Protestant
Churches affirm that it derives all its authority from God. The
Church of Rome affirms that she is the sole depository of the Bible ;
the Protestant Churches affirm that it is, and ever has been, the
Word of the Spirit committed to all the Churches,—nay, to the
Churches' enemies, whom it rebukes and condemns. The Church of
Rome affirms that she is the sole interpreter of the Bible ; the Protestant Churches affirm that the Spirit of God, speaking in the Word,
and in the consciences of His people, is the only competent interpreter. . . . . The Church of Rome affirms that no man has a
right to possess or to read the Scriptures, but under her sanction ;
the Protestant Churches affirm that all Scripture is the common
legacy of Christ to the Churches, and that every man is free to
possess, and bound to read, study, and determine, on the ground of
his accountability to God. Now, if the Church of Rome be right in
all these positions, then the Government plan of National education
is right in all its details. But if the Protestant Churches are right
in all their positions, then the Government system is constitutionally
and incurably diseased in every member of its body. Lend us your

attention while we examine the Government plan, which Infidels admire, Roman Catholics tolerate, and Protestants detest.

" The first essential feature is, a supreme, despotic Board. Three parts Protestant Establishment ; two parts Roman Catholic ; one part Unitarian ; one part Church of Scotland.

" The Board is vested with complete control over all teachers. By this usurpation it robs every father in the kingdom, who may send a child to one of the Government schools, of all right to choose a schoolmaster for his children.

" The Board is invested with entire control over all school-books, whether for literary or religious instruction. That the Bible has ever been the chief Protestant school-book, every child can tell. But here is a Board with entire control over it. . . .

" The Board appropriates four days in the week to what is termed literary and moral education ; and the two remaining days are set apart, one for religious instruction of Protestants, and the other of Roman Catholics.   The plan is illusory, impracticable, unjust, wasteful, and demoralising. . . . .

" Another most unholy portion of the plan enjoins upon Protestants not merely to permit, but absolutely to encourage the teaching of Popery, Unitarianism, and every possible form of apostacy and infidelity.   To what the liberalism of this generation will next extend, it is impossible to foretell.   But surely it is not presumptuous to say, that when men have come publicly under such an obligation, there is no visible limit to future concessions.

" We do not arraign the motives of our rulers.   We admit, and we believe, their plan has been intended for the public good.   But as all human councils are liable to err, so we believe our rulers have erred.   They have regarded the wisdom of men more than the authority of heaven.   They have consulted with changing expediency more than with permanent principle.   Their ears have been disturbed by the clamorous demands of Rome, and they would purchase quiet for the land by a great Protestant sacrifice.   We must respectfully answer them,—the sacrifice cannot be made. Demand anything but our Protestant principles, and to the utmost of our ability we will render compliance.   We will pay our tribute ; we will lift up our prayers ; we will give our loyalty ; but we will retain our Bibles."

On the Tuesday following the delivery of this sermon, a large and influential meeting was held in Belfast.   Dr. Cooke, in a speech of great power, thus described the new scheme of education :—

" The proposition of the Government is this : We pray you do, for concession's sake, give up your principles ; we pray you, do resign your differences with Rome ; and, oh ! do give up that troublesome thing you call conscience, and just take out of the Bible whatever keeps you in opposition to Popery. I am grieved to the soul that Government have not thought of a better plan than one which would quench the spirit of free-born truth. . . . . No, if we are to have a plan of education, let it be a plan that will leave us in possession of our Bibles. . . . . Let us have the Bible unexpurgated by the Index of Rome."

Dr. Cooke supported his views of the Romanising tendency of the scheme by some startling facts. The first school in Ulster taken under the care of the Board, was a Roman Catholic school in Belfast. In it was a lesson-book called " The Grounds of Catholic Doctrine," which assigned the following, among other reasons, why a Roman Catholic cannot embrace Protestantism :—" We are convinced that they (the Protestants) are schismatics and heretics, and consequently that they have no part in the Church of Christ, no authority to preach the Word of God, no share in the promise of Christ's heavenly kingdom." Extracts from the Bible were recommended by the Board. Dr. Cooke stated that he was not opposed to extracts if fairly made ; but he was opposed to them if made for the purpose of suppressing any great fact or doctrine.

" Of this we have a notable example in the case of a school-book of Extracts, which has already received the unreserved approbation of a member of the Education Board. The example we select is the narrative of the Lord's Supper. This begins, in the Extracts, with Matthew xxvi. 26, ' And as they were eating, Jesus took bread, and blessed it, and brake it, and gave it to the disciples, and said, Take, eat ; this is my body.' But, instead of going on with the narrative in Matthew, which would have overturned the doctrine of Rome, in denying the cup to the laity, the extractor dexterously forsakes the narrative of Matthew, which says, 'Drink ye all of it,' and subjoins Luke xxii. 20, in which it is merely said, 'Likewise also the cup after supper, saying, This cup is the new testament in my blood which is shed for you.' Now, this we call, not an extract, but a mutilation, because it purposely breaks off a part of the truth.

"In a book of Scripture Extracts, drawn up by Mr. Carlile, and published by the Board, a new translation of the Ten Commandments is given, in which ' graven thing,' the rendering of the Douay version, is substituted for ' graven image,' and the word ' worship ' for ' bow down.' The Commandments are divided, besides, not into ten, but into seventeen parts. In the same book a note is appended to the extract from Genesis iii., to the effect that, in verse 15, the Latin vulgate reads *ipsa*—'*She* shall bruise,' instead of ' It shall bruise ' ; thus making this passage refer to the Virgin Mary."

At a meeting held on the twenty-first Anniversary of the Brown Street Schools, Dr. Cooke, in moving a vote of thanks to the Educational Society for Ireland, said :—

" I do not approve of everything in the society ; but I do approve of its uncompromising adherence to Scripture education . . . . So far as it honestly and simply acts upon this principle, I would call upon every one who loves the Bible to give to the society his countenance and his prayers. We should recommend its claims to the attention of the Legislature ; and in the cause of education the voice of Ulster deserves to be heard. . . . . Let us call upon them by our cultivated fields. Our fathers found the hills a succession of barren heaths ; their religion and their toil clothed them with verdure. They found the country covered with unprofitable woods, and intersected with impassable morasses ; their industry and their education have rendered it a productive garden. The cause of education may be retarded by the withdrawal of public patronage ; but the plant can never be blighted by the frowns of modern Liberalism. It has struck its root deep into the principles and habits of the people ; and, by the blessing of Providence, it will spread and flourish with increasing fruitfulness, till the wish of the pious monarch shall be realised, and every child in these realms shall be able to read his Bible."

Dr. Cooke's 'aim was pure and patriotic. He believed Scripture truth and morality to be a necessary basis of sound

education. He believed ignorance of the Bible to be the main
source of Ireland's miseries. He believed the Government of
the day to be inclined, in deference to the wishes of the
Church of Rome, to exclude the Bible from National schools.
He, therefore, opposed the Government scheme, and sought
to have it remodelled in such a way as to make it acceptable,
not to Roman Catholics merely, but to the Protestant people
of Ireland. Unfortunately his object was misunderstood by
some, and misrepresented by others. He was charged with
being a political partizan; with trying to overthrow a Whig
ministry; with attempting to perpetuate Church and State
abuses. Some ministers of the Secession Church unhappily
joined in the opposition. They passed a series of resolutions
branding, not directly, but by implication, the statements of
Dr. Cooke, and the overtures of the Synod of Ulster in regard
to the Education scheme, as "false and calumnious." In
reply, Dr. Cooke analyzed, with his wonted acuteness, the
whole scheme as originally developed in Mr. Stanley's Letter,
and subsequently explained in a letter of the Education Board.
He exposed the inconsistencies and contradictions of these
documents. He showed that there was a deliberate attempt
made to deceive the public, to rob the Protestants of Ulster of
a Scriptural education while professing to grant it.

"We pity from our hearts the men who are tied down to drudge
in this system of deception. We like to call things by their right
names ; and, therefore, there are some parts of the foregoing documents that we must denominate either cunning evasions or down-
right untruths. . . . . We are not possessed of that penetrative
faculty which enables us to know that when Mr. Stanley says 'complete control' he means no control ; or that when he says 'all books
of religious instruction,' he means none. This attainment in philology seems reserved for the Board, who appear determined to
instruct the public in a new meaning for words. We hate special
pleading, wherever it appears. If the Board think Mr. Stanley was
wrong, let them honestly tell us so ; and let them not affix meanings
to his words that they know in their consciences his words will not
bear. . . . . The Board tells us what they understand by

'encouraging' different religious teachers; and if we can believe them, they understand by it no encouragement. Now this is most dishonest. It is nothing to us what they please to understand by it; the question is, What does it mean? We would have no equivocation, no forced and unnatural meanings which words will not bear."

It was thus Dr. Cooke endeavoured to expose the dishonest attempts of the Board to cloak the real character and tendencies of the Educational scheme. He was opposed; but he was accustomed to opposition. He was misrepresented and vilified; but that mode of controversy was not new to him. He saw the duty he owed to his Church and to his country, and he never swerved from it. He was not alone in his opinions. The leading men in the Churches of England and Scotland agreed with him. Probably there was not a single man of thought or position in the Evangelical Churches of the empire who entirely approved of the Government scheme. Dr. Chalmers, in addressing the Presbytery of Edinburgh, said :—

"The Government had fallen into the error of their predecessors, of making Catholics parties in the negociations. Instead of treating with Catholics or Orangemen, they ought to have adopted a plan founded on the principles of truth, and not departed from it to serve either party. His view of what was right was, that a daily Bible-class should be made part of the system. There ought to be no compulsion in any system of this kind; and Government, in rectifying one error, had fallen into another, in excluding the Bible-class. They had made a concession which was not necessary—they had made a temporising concession, an unworthy surrender of the moral to the numerical. Though Government might find that the multitude was against, they ought to have known that truth was with them; and that though the priests might rebel, the people in the end would find it to be their interest to send their children where they would be educated." . . . .

Still more emphatic were the statements of Principal Lee. He was at a distance from the scene of strife. He could not be biassed by Irish parties or prejudices. He had studied the

measure, and was in confidential communication with some of
its leading promoters.   Yet, referring chiefly to the published
letters of Mr. Carlile, the leading defender of the Board and
exponent of its views, he thus writes to Dr. Cooke :—

" I cannot help owning that I was bitterly mortified and grieved
to observe the style in which Mr. Carlile expressed himself, not only
in a printed letter of which I received several copies, under cover of
Lord Melbourne, but in a still more confidential communication to
one of his like-minded friends here . . . . Mr. Carlile says,
' If you deduct political opposition to the present ministry, Orange
antipathy to Roman Catholics, and High Church jealousy both of
Roman Catholics and Dissenters, I am firmly persuaded that you
would withdraw five-sixths, more probably nine-tenths, of the
hostility to us (the Board).' I tell him that he labours under a
strong delusion, and that he cannot know what he says, and whereof
he affirms. There is not much wisdom in confident assertions which
cannot possibly be built on the result of extensive, impartial, or un-
prejudiced inquiries. I know nobody who opposes the plan from
any such motives, but I do know many who support it because they
wish to strengthen the hands of the present Ministry, and because
they expect their measures to effect the demolition of establishments,
and the removal of old land-marks which our fathers set . . . .
My creed is this :—The souls of men are alienated from the life of
God through ignorance, and they are brought to eternal life only by
that knowledge which the Scriptures supply."

The question gave rise to a sharp and somewhat painful
controversy between Dr. Cooke and Mr. Carlile.   Mr. Carlile
was a member of the Synod of Ulster, and a Commissioner of
Education.   Originally all the commissioners were unpaid ;
but in consequence of the pressure of business, and the in-
ability of the general body of commissioners to give proper
attention to it, Mr. Carlile was appointed Resident Commissioner, with a salary of 400l. a year.   He thus became to a
large extent an embodiment of the Education Board.   Every
point came under his consideration ; and the issue on each
question mainly depended on his decision.   He promoted with
a zeal that amounted to enthusiasm, the Government scheme.
He tried to press it upon the acceptance of the Synod of

Ulster. His explanations of objectionable rules were ingenious, if not convincing. When the Synod presented its
propositions to the Government, Mr. Carlile endeavoured to
persuade the Board that they might be adopted without any
compromise on their part; while, on the other hand, he
endeavoured to persuade the Synod that the laws of the Board
violated no principle held by the Presbyterian Church. The
task was a difficult one. Most men would say it was impossible; and, in attempting to perform it, Mr. Carlile exposed
himself to the keen criticisms of Dr. Cooke and others. The
Synod, after careful consideration and long debates, refused to
accept Mr. Carlile's explanations, or to endorse his views.
The scheme of the Board, notwithstanding all glosses, and
changes, and letters of explanation, and pleadings on the part
of Mr. Carlile, was rejected almost without a dissentient
voice.

Such was the state of the Education question when the
Synod met in June, 1833. It was then again taken up and
discussed at length. Mr. Carlile defended the Government
scheme. He brought serious charges against the Moderator
and Dr. Cooke, who had been the leading members of the
Synod's committee, and of the deputations to Dublin and
London, and who had drawn up the Three Propositions
presented to the Government. Dr. Cooke replied. He reviewed the leading points in the negociations. He exposed the
strange and often crooked policy of the Board. He charged
Mr. Carlile with being the chief cause of the difficulties the
Synod had to encounter. Referring to the controversy about
the " Scripture Extracts," he said :—

" When your deputation had the honour of waiting on Lord Grey,
we submitted the Three Propositions with which you are already acquainted, and we chiefly insisted on the great cardinal point—the
free use of the Bible during ordinary school hours for all who might
choose it. In answer to our earnest requests, Lord Grey replied :—
' Surely you have the Bible in the schools at all hours ; for you have
the Extracts during ordinary hours, and the whole Bible before and

after' . . . . We then stated that in our opinion the Extracts formed a most objectionable school-book, and were more obnoxious to Protestants than any other part of the system. At this statement Lord Grey expressed some astonishment, and asked upon what principles the objections were founded. We replied that we did not object to extracts honestly made, nor even to new translations learnedly considered, but that we objected, among other things, to some of the notes appended to the book, and in particular to the one in Genesis, which contained at once a philological untruth, and a theological heresy. I did more than testify against the note in Genesis. I referred to the imperfect and erroneous manner in which the Extracts presented the great Protestant doctrine of justification by faith; and I did not neglect to refer to the new translation of the Ten Commandments provided for the National schools, which I freely characterised as appearing to be constructed, like the note on Genesis, to favour the doctrines of popery."

Referring to a statement of Mr. Carlile that Dr. Cooke was the main instigator of the crusade against the National Board, and that if he should keep silent there would be little danger of public uneasiness on the subject, he said :—

" Never did ignorance utter a more unfounded response. I use the word ignorance respectfully, when I say that Mr. Carlile is profoundly ignorant of the state of Ulster. Notwithstanding all the respect and love of his brother ministers, he has not the confidence of the people of Ulster. They are alike suspicious of his judgment and of his plans, and would laugh at his pretensions to give a report of their feelings. True, indeed, the people of Ulster will not agitate, but they will think—they will feel. They will think and feel that their opinions are despised, their petitions rejected, their privileges assailed; and their minds will, by slow but sure degrees, be loosened and alienated from their cherished attachment to England. All this, indeed, is not literal agitation. The water remains unruffled, but it is embittered to the very bottom, and the new system of education is the wormwood from which that bitterness is derived. I will, therefore, speak it before Mr. Carlile, and entrust him to repeat it in the ears of His Majesty's ministers, that Protestant principle deserves to be respected; Protestant feeling deserves to be cherished—even our stubborn Presbyterian prejudices are not to be despised; for the day may not be far distant when England may need them all."

Mr. Carlile had assailed *The Orthodox Presbyterian* and its articles on Education.   Dr. Cooke replied :—

" With the article in the number for June, the editor had nothing to do ; I take the accountability entirely upon myself.   With the exception, I believe, of one single notice of the question, I am the sole author of every article on education that has appeared in the work.   With the first sentence in the present number Mr. Carlile seems to be particularly offended. . . . . I repeat it for his benefit. ' Protestants, beware! for now is the trial of your principles.   Protestants, be firm! for your final victory is certain.'   To this I will add the last sentence also—' If Presbyterians and all other true Protestants do not inconsiderately go to the new scheme of education, the new scheme of education must shortly come to them.' "

Mr. Carlile had charged Dr. Cooke with attempting to tyrannize over the Synod, and to assume the place of an arrogant dictator.   He had called upon the members to resist usurped authority, to throw off a galling yoke.   Dr. Cooke replied :—

" To my elder brethren I need not appeal.   They remember the time when this Synod was really trammelled.   They remember when a large part of the Presbytery of Route were suspended for an honest exercise of private judgment.   Where was Mr. Carlile then, when I and my now accused friends were writhing in the trammels of an Arian dictatorship?   He left us to fight the battle and gain the victory, and now he comes into the field, and accuses us of being leaders.   For myself, I never have been a leader.   I did, indeed, join my brethren in the forlorn hope that mounted the breach, and wrested the citadel from the opponents of evangelical truth.   And where was Mr. Carlile then?   In the ranks of the enemy, contending against us inch by inch, and worth, for their purposes, a whole battalion of their chosen troops, because he professed allegiance to our principles, yet fought against our measures of reform.   During the time of this conflict, I, no doubt, took an active part.   I was often in the post of danger, because more cautious men declined it.   During that conflict I received many a thrust and many a shot ; but, thank God, they were in front, and I never turned my back against the enemy.   But now that the warfare is over, have I ever encroached upon the liberties of this House ? . . . . Yet Mr. Carlile cries, 'free yourselves from trammels.' No! Mr. Carlile, this house will continue to be trammelled ; and I tell you how. It will be trammelled by the Bible ; it will be trammelled by common sense ; it will be trammelled by unyielding honesty; it will be trammelled by Protestant principles; it will be trammelled by evangelical truth. And now, to prove the truth of my announcement, and to demonstrate how little envy is excitable in this Synod, I shall do what I did not propose to do ; I shall move the resolutions of Synod upon the whole education question. I shall move the Three Propositions submitted in London by your deputies. I shall move them as rendered at once more definite and extensive by the suggestion of my friends Mr. Wallace, Mr. Hamilton, and Mr. Huston ; and I foretell, for Mr. Carlile's satisfaction, that every proposal I make shall be carried. Let him tell this to Lord Grey, let him tell this to Mr. Littleton, and let him tell this to their misinformers, who prophesied a change of mind in this Synod. The mind of this Synod has undergone no change. But let the system of education change to meet our principles, we will receive it of the Government as a most generous boon, and it will serve to rivet an attachment to England, and loyalty to the king, as it will increase the means of that civilization and religious instruction, for which Ulster has been distinguished since the date of its settlement."

Dr. Cooke concluded by moving the following resolutions, which were unanimously adopted :—

" I. That after examining the various documents, in which the new system of National Education was originally described, and subsequently modified, the mind of this Synod concerning it, as expressed and embodied in the resolutions of January and June, 1832, remains unchanged.

" II. That we feel most anxious to obtain from His Majesty's Government such modifications of the system as may enable our ministers and people, without compromise of principle, to avail themselves of Government aid, in the establishment and support of Schools.

" III. That having considered the Three Propositions submitted to His Majesty's Government in London by our deputation in May last, and approving and adopting the principle of them, we agree to submit them anew in the following modified form :—

" Prop. 1. That the ministers and people of this Church, without the necessary concurrence of the ministers or members of any other Church, shall enjoy the right of applying to the Board of Education for aid to schools, by a statement of the constitution and regulations of the schools, accompanied with an engagement to adhere to them. But in this proposition we recognise the right of the Board to consider the regulations, and decide accordingly.

" Prop. 2. That it shall be the right of all parents to require of patrons and managers of schools to set apart for reading the Holy Scriptures, a convenient and sufficient portion of the stated school hours, and to direct the master, or some other whom the parents may appoint and provide, to superintend the reading.

" Prop. 3. That all children, whose parents and guardians so direct, shall daily read the Holy Scriptures during the period appointed ; but that no compulsion whatever be employed to induce others either to read, or remain during the reading.

" Prop. 4. That every use of school-rooms be vested in the local patrons or committees, subject, in case of abuse, to the cognizance of the Board.

" IV. That our Moderator and clerk, with Drs. Hanna and Cooke, Messrs. Stewart, Hay, E. Reid, John Brown, Park, Morgan, Gray, and Barnett, be a Committee, to submit these propositions to His Majesty's Government, and respectfully and earnestly to urge their consideration.

" V. That whilst we entertain a well-founded hope that His Majesty's Government will be pleased to adopt the modifications proposed by this Synod, we do, in the meantime, and pending the negociations, exhort our ministers, elders, and people, still to abstain from all connection with the Board ; and we do hereby declare, that, whilst we desire not to interfere with the private judgment of individual brethren, yet no member of this Synod, at present connected, or who may in the meantime connect himself with the Board, is to be understood as acting in our name, or under our authority and sanction."

Dr. Cooke was frequently assailed on the platform and through the press for demanding a free Bible in the National schools. His views on this point were often, indeed generally, misunderstood or misrepresented by those opposed to him. At a meeting of the subscribers to the Brown Street School,

Belfast, the subject came under discussion, and he embraced the opportunity of explaining his views.

"In seeking the privilege of the free and unrestricted use of the Scriptures in schools, we have been described, no doubt, as seeking a thing most utopian and absurd ; and, indeed, I confess that, if by free and unrestricted use of the Scriptures I mean constant and uninterrupted, the attempt would be chargeable with all the absurdity alleged. The use of my limbs is free and unrestricted. But do I therefore conclude that I may walk into every man's parlour ? The use of my voice is free and unrestricted. Do I therefore conclude I may bawl into every man's ear ? The use of the Bible is free and unrestricted. Do we therefore conclude that any scholar may read it uninterruptedly from morning till night, occupy the whole time of the master, and prevent the other studies of the school ? We never dreamt of such a monstrous absurdity. What, then, do we mean by the free and unrestricted use of the Scriptures ? Tell me what you mean by the free and unrestricted use of ' Gough's Arithmetic.' You mean that a boy may just use it as long as his parent directs, and as often as his teacher can afford to attend to him. I ask no more freedom for the Bible. But while I deny any limit to freedom, do I admit no limit to the use of the Bible ? I do. I admit the will of parents, who stand in the first place of accountability, to be one limit ; and I admit Christian charity, so far as it can act without surrender of any Christian principle, to be another limit. But any such limiting power to kings, parliaments, or boards, clergy, patrons, or committees, I utterly and determinately deny."

On another occasion, at a meeting of the friends of the same school, Dr. Cooke gave his opinion of the National Board:—

"To the Board of Education, as originally constituted, I have hitherto professed, and I do now profess, the most determined and unqualified hostility. My hostility was produced by several circumstances in its constitution and principles ; but chiefly by the following :—
1. It demanded of me, and of every other Protestant, that in order to get into the highest rank of probable favour, we must seek and obtain a co-signature and alliance with the Roman Catholic priesthood. That to get into a lower grade of probable favour, we must crave the signatures and alliance of the Roman Catholic people ; while not a solitary spot for favour was recorded for the unrecognized Protestantism of the land. Now, to united education I profess

myself a friend; but to purchased favouritism I profess myself an enemy. 2. The Board required, that having formed this compulsory alliance, Protestants must surrender to the Board the right of sending the Roman Catholic priests into their school-houses, both before and after school hours ; and the Protestants must guarantee to encourage him to teach, then and there, his peculiar doctrines. 3. The Board required that one or two days in each week should be set apart for separate religious instruction, by which fifty-two holidays in each year must be introduced, which could have no other effect than to accelerate the demoralization of all classes of the community. The Board represented all power to dictate the plan of education as emanating from themselves, and finally vested in the patrons; and totally excluded all mention or recognition of parental authority. 5. The Board totally excluded the Bible from the ordinary school hours."

At a subsequent date, in reviewing the political aspect of the question, he said :—

" The present Ministry found the Protestants of Ireland in the full and free possession of the Bible in all their schools. This possession their fathers had enjoyed from the time that the Reformers rescued their heavenly patrimony from the usurpation and tyranny of Rome. And it was reserved for the nineteenth to restore the usurpation of the fifteenth century. It was reserved for the men of the march of intellect to order the stand-still of implicit obedience, and for the diffusers of useful knowledge to patronize the reign of ignorance. In obedience to the Romish priesthood, the Bible of God is ordered out of every Protestant school, and Protestants there are who sell themselves to see the order obeyed."   .   .   .   .

The determined stand made by the Synod of Ulster, under the leadership of Dr. Cooke, was felt by the Government. Many changes were effected in the rules of the Board ; official explanations were given which tended to modify objectionable points. When the unanimous decision of the Synod in 1833 was reported to the Government, it was felt that a crisis had been reached. The Government must yield or break entirely with the Presbyterian Church. A report was spread that matters were about to be adjusted. It was affirmed that the

Commissioners of Education had been instructed, and were prepared, to adopt the Synod's Propositions. Even Dr. Cooke for a time supposed that he had triumphed; and in July he thus wrote :—

"The Synod of Ulster has done itself immortal honour by the part it has acted on the subject of education. It has earned the character of a faithful witness for Christ. Had it not been for the noble stand which it has made, we have little doubt our National schools would this day have been deprived of the light of God's Word. By its faithfulness, however, there is now some prospect that the Government will yield. Some of its most distinguished members have allowed that the principle for which the Synod has contended is the right one. Among these is Mr. Spring Rice. A deference is now paid to the opinion of the Synod, which, a short time ago, was not at all to be anticipated ; and only let it remain firm, and we have no doubt its just demands will be granted. Nor is it a small gratification to observe the influence which the example and conduct of the Synod appear to have had on other religious bodies. We may be mistaken, but our fear is, that if the Synod had yielded, they would not all have kept steadfast. Whether this be the case or not, it is now, however, delightful to behold that testimonies have been borne to the necessity of a Scriptural education, and, consequently, to the condemnation of the Board, by almost all the Protestant Churches in the three kingdoms. Will the Government be so mad as to withstand such a testimony ? We think not. They have learned that it was no mere political feeling that animated the Synod of Ulster, but that it was a deep-rooted conviction of the anti-Scriptural character of the Board ; a conviction neither to be frightened into submission, nor flattered into compliance. . . . . Mr. Carlile took a deep interest in modelling the resolutions. The resolutions were unanimously adopted ; and we think the Synod may calculate on their being recommended to the Government, by whatever influence Mr. Carlile may possess. . . . . Our rulers are not unreasonable ; they needed to be rightly informed ; this, to a considerable extent, has taken place."

Dr. Cooke was disappointed. He had placed faith in the professions of public men, and he was deceived. The commissioners, it is true, formally accepted the Synod's Proposi-

CH. X.]   DECEPTIVE POLICY OF THE BOARD.   257

tions.   Earl Grey wrote to the Moderator on the 30th of
July :—

"I have read, with great attention, the four resolutions extracted
from the minutes of the Synod of Ulster, and, I am happy to say, I
see nothing in them which may not be agreed to, as in perfect
accordance with the general principles on which the new system of
education is founded. I trust, therefore, that, all objections being
now removed, we may look forward to the full attainment of those
benefits for which that system was introduced."

The proceedings of the Government were most remarkable.
In May, 1833, the Chief Secretary for Ireland rejected the
propositions offered by the Synod's committee, because he
considered them "to strike entirely at the principles of the
system." The Synod at its meeting in July, reappointed the
committee, including Mr. Carlile, the resident Commissioner ;
and the committee changed the three original propositions
into four, without, however, in the least changing their principle ; and those four propositions were accepted by Earl Grey
in August, as "in perfect accordance with the general principles on which the new system of education is founded." Proceedings so inconsistent, so contradictory, appear to indicate
that the Government were influenced, not by regard to justice,
but by some secret agency which it was not prudent to avow.
The worst has yet to be told.   Dr. Cooke thus describes it in
his examination before the Committee of the House of Commons in 1837 :—

"The Synod and Commissioners seemed to me to be like persons
that proposed to come to peace, but were drawn up with their armies
opposite, and in hostility to each other ; and they agree to make
peace while holding the armies in the same position ; but the one
army in the meantime, in the night, turns the flank of the other.
The Commissioners took a little time in giving an answer ; and they
took care in the meantime to make a new system, by which they
turned every point we brought forward ; and they stood ready to say
that they admitted the propositions ; but, then, the propositions were
made for the old system, and not the new one.   We should have

required to make new propositions before we could meet their new system."

The Commissioners, in fact, formed new regulations so ingeniously as to neutralise the whole force and bearing of the Synod's resolutions, and then, having done so, they passed a minute to the effect that they " were of opinion that the propositions of the Synod did not contain anything inconsistent with the principles of the system of education committed to their charge." The trick was clever. Ordinary people could scarcely see through it. The Presbyterian public would naturally be gratified to find their propositions formally adopted. But such a crooked policy was scarcely worthy of a Board, established by Government for conducting the intellectual and moral education of the youth of Ireland. Dr. Cooke explained its bearing in regard to one point :—

" As we understood the original regulations of the Board, persons who were officially connected with the school, applied for the school (to be supported by the Board) ; it might be the Rector, or the Presbyterian minister, or the Roman Catholic priest ; but we considered the system as making the persons who had so applied the official overseers of the school. Now we negociated for a right to apply to the Board by ourselves, and consequently, a Roman Catholic priest had no right to interfere in the government of our schools. . . . . But we found the Board had made a new rule that completely destroyed our proposition, for, before they accepted it, they made a regulation that the Roman Catholic priest was, *ex officio*, visitor of the school. . . . . It was made immediately before the answer from the Board. It was made intermediately between the construction of our four propositions, and the professed acknowledgment or recognition of those propositions."

The whole objections of the Synod's Committee to the new regulations of the Board were very clearly and emphatically stated, as appears from the following letter, dated 18th February, 1834, and addressed to T. F. Kelly, Esq. :—

" The letter of the Board of Education has been submitted to the Committee of the General Synod of Ulster ; and I have been instructed by them to return the following reply :—When the Synod submitted their four propositions, it will be obvious that they were intended as the sole basis on which they proposed to put the schools under the management of the Board ; yet, while His Majesty's Government have fully and unreservedly complied with these propositions, the Board has appended to them such conditions as not only to neutralise, but destroy them. The correctness of this will appear from the following contrast :—1st. The Synod requires, in proposition first, that their ministers and people shall have the right of applying for aid, by a statement of the constitution and regulation of the schools, accompanied with an engagement to adhere to them. In addition to this the Board demands an answer to queries, thereby annexing a new condition, annulling the Synod's right . . . and rendering their propositions perfectly nugatory."

Dr. Brown, the Moderator, mentions another point :—

" With respect to the reading of the Scriptures, we thought we had secured to the people of our persuasion the right of having the children taught during the whole of the stated school-hours to read the Scriptures, and we found by the new instructions given by the Board, that there were four hours during which the Scriptures could not be read."

In fact, Dr. Cooke saw that the Synod had been grossly deceived in this whole transaction. Their views, even as stated in the propositions, seem to have been misrepresented to the Government. Mr. Carlile endeavoured to make it appear that the Synod had obtained all it originally contended for when its propositions were adopted ; and it was broadly hinted that the continued opposition of Dr. Cooke proceeded from political partizanship. Some ministers of Synod were thus misled, and advocated union with the Board. The Board encouraged them in a way that must appear strange to disinterested men. The Presbyterians objected to certain queries, which the Board now put to all applicants for aid. Those queries involved the very points at issue between the Board and Dr. Cooke. Mr. Carlile recommended the Board, while still retaining the query-sheet, and making it formally a part of its laws, not to press mem-

bers of the Synod of Ulster for answers to the obnoxious
questions! The Board agreed; and then a concession was
made to members of the Synod, such as no others were permitted to participate in. The result of this wily policy is
stated by Mr. Kelly in his examination before a Committee
of the House of Commons in 1837 :—

"Though the Synod, as a body, have professed to break off from
any connection with the Board, the members of the Synod, as individuals, have from time to time applied and received aid ; and in
regard to them this question has, for the reason stated, always been
suffered to remain unreplied to."

The whole subject was again brought before the Synod at its
annual meeting in Derry, in June, 1834. The skilful manœuvre of the Board had not deceived the Synod, but it had
won over a party in it; and they moved,—

" That it is the opinion of this Synod, that the ministers and people
of our Church, if they see fit, may now make application for aid out
of the funds for national education, strictly adhering to the propositions which were agreed upon at last meeting of Synod, and which
have been subsequently approved by the Government and the Board
of Commissioners."

Dr. Cooke strongly opposed the motion. He criticised with
cutting irony the strange and crooked policy of the Commissioners. He showed that they were attempting to gain over
the Synod by a trick. He denounced the whole transaction as
unworthy of a public body, and deserving the reprobation of
the country. He moved, as an amendment, the following
resolutions :—

" 1. That ever since the blessed Reformation, in all the common
schools of Evangelical Protestants, but especially in the schools of
the Church of Scotland, and in those of the Synod of Ulster and
other Presbyterian bodies in Ireland, children have enjoyed the free
and unrestricted use of the Holy Scriptures, and have been, until

lately, generally accustomed, where their parents so directed, to learn to read in the sacred volume.

" 2. That the authoritative exclusion of the Bible from the National schools during ordinary school hours, seems to have originated, not from any desire of Protestants, but out of deference to the opinions and objections of the Roman Catholic hierarchy, who have always discovered such jealousy and dread of the sacred Scriptures, that wherever they have had the power, they have denied their unrestricted use to the laity in general, and to children in schools in particular ; and farther, that experience demonstrates, that, in whatever country the use of the Scriptures has, in any wise, been restricted, the progress of Protestantism has been proportionably retarded, and the domination of the Church of Rome extended and confirmed.

" 3. That for the above, amongst other reasons, the Synod, as a witness for the Lord Jesus, and the Word of His Truth, did, in the years 1832 and 1833, most explicitly declare their disapprobation of the system of national education, and did earnestly seek to have it reformed ; but that, from the correspondence of our committee with the Commissioners, and from their report to the Government, it appears that the original system remains unchanged, and, consequently, the reform sought by the Synod still unattained.

" 4. That this Synod, therefore, now renews its exhortations to the ministers and elders of this body to refrain from connecting themselves with the Board ; and resolves to continue to employ every means to obtain from His Majesty's Government such a *bonâ fide* recognition of our propositions as will enable our people, without surrender of principle, to obtain for their schools a portion of the public funds."

The debate was long and keen. It continued from eleven o'clock on Friday forenoon, till two o'clock on Saturday morning. The question at issue was not the merits of the national system of education abstractedly considered, but simply whether the Board had fairly acceded to the Synod's propositions of the previous year. Mr. Carlile was the principal defender of the Board. He placed its policy and its acts before the Synod in the best possible light. Most of those who now joined him, had been from the first, and still were, opposed to the system as a whole ; but they were willing to accept the aid the Com-

missioners, in violation of their own rules, were ready to give
them. Dr. Cooke was again triumphant. His amendment
was carried, though only by a small majority. Mr. Carlile
protested, but it was in vain. The Synod broke off all negotiation with the National Board.

CHAPTER XI.

1830—1835.

DR. COOKE's political principles were formed at a very early period, and were never changed. The effects produced upon his mind by the dark scenes of '98 have already been detailed. He was then led to regard with the strongest feelings of horror and detestation the revolutionary sentiments and acts of the United Irishmen. Everything tending to disturb settled government or excite popular passion, he looked upon as radically wrong. He was opposed to tyranny; but he could see tyranny in a revolutionary mob, as well as in a crowned despot. He was an ardent advocate of liberty, civil and religious; but he carefully distinguished between real liberty, and the licence of anarchy on the one hand, and of infidelity on the other. He was an enthusiastic admirer of the British Constitution; but he was ready, wherever a flaw could be detected in it, or a bulwark made more firm, to effect reform.

At the commencement of the present century Dr. Cooke's politics were not popular in Ulster. The revolution in France and the wide diffusion of French Republican literature had created exaggerated notions of popular rights, and had given

rise to a spurious liberalism. Belfast was the stronghold of
the Volunteers, whose feelings and aims were essentially de-
mocratic. After the rebellion of '98, the principles which led
to it were still held, and zealously propagated by leading men
in the town. The Arian party in the Synod of Ulster adopted
them, and the influence and eloquence of some of their ministers tended to spread them among the Presbyterians of Ulster.
The statement of a distinguished member of Synod was probably correct that, during the first quarter of the present
century, nine-tenths of the Presbyterians of Ireland were
Whigs. About the year 1830 a marked change began to be
perceptible, more perhaps among the laity than the clergy.
Constitutional views became popular. A powerful re-action set
in against the Radical politics of Arians, and the aggressive
demands of Roman Catholics. There can be no question that
this change was mainly owing to the energy, the eloquence, and
the commanding influence of one man;—and that man was
Dr. Cooke.

Dr. Cooke's politics were not a mere sentiment; they were
an inspiring power. They were based upon settled convictions
of truth and duty. They were held with unyielding tenacity.
They were advocated with uncompromising enthusiasm. They
were wedded to his religious principles, and were therefore
developed in the pulpit as well as on the platform. They
entered largely into the whole plans and acts of his public life.
Their origin and their nature he himself explained to one of
the largest and most influential meetings ever held in Ulster:—

"I mean to state on what political ground I stand. First,
then, I am not a Whig. The time was when I would have been a
Whig, when Whigs had religious as well as political principles, and
when Whiggery would have abhorred the serpent contact of infidelity. But, now that the foul serpent has coiled itself around
Whiggery, I repudiate the name Whig. Neither am I a Tory; for
though, as Whigs have grown worse, Tories have grown better, yet
have they some things about them, as a political party, which I dare
not adopt or approve. The mere party distinctions of Whig and
Tory I regard not. Whatever party shall adopt scriptural principles

of legislation; whatever party shall pursue reform without destruction; whatever party shall adopt as its motto 'popular liberty,' without licentious anarchy; whatever party shall stand unflinchingly by the bulwarks of the Constitution, in the time-honoured architecture of King, Lords, and Commons; whatever party shall reverence religion, and protect its scriptural rights and measures—they shall command my feeble voice. But whilst I reject alike the name of Whig or Tory, I decidedly avow myself a Conservative. But of what am I conservative? Why, of everything that is worth conserving. I am conservative of the rights of property. I am conservative of abstract and general Protestantism, whatever may be the form of the Church in which it is contained. Let the lamp be fed by the oil of the sanctuary; let the light be brilliant and fill the whole house; and I do openly profess that I love the light for its own sake, regardless of the form of the lamp in which it is hung out. Yet I am no latitudinarian either in doctrine or in Church government. I have my prepossessions, my preferences, my convictions. Yet, above all, I desire to have that brotherly kindness and charity, those bonds of perfectness, whereby the various members of the great Protestant body, 'being knit together in love, may grow up and make increase to the edifying of themselves in love.' Finally, I am conservative of the Bible."

In another part of the same speech he said:—

"Amongst the principles of a Conservative are these: to protect no abuse that can be proved; to resist reckless innovation, not rational reform; to sacrifice no honest interest to hungry clamour; to yield no principle to time-serving expediency; to stand by religion in opposition to every form of infidelity."

Such a political creed, when fairly enunciated, could not fail to gain ground among a thoughtful people. It is wrong to call it Toryism. Its enemies, when they could not withstand its influence, fixed upon it that opprobrious name, so as to make it distasteful to Presbyterians. It is not Toryism. It combines what is noblest and purest in all the schemes of politics. It is eclectic of everything calculated to promote the common weal. It is Conservatism, but Conservatism with those limitations which Dr. Cooke stated so clearly and forcibly. It is Liberalism, but Liberalism shorn of its Radical and revolutionary tendencies.

When Dr. Cooke removed to Belfast he was the acknowledged leader of ecclesiastical reform, and his success was
brilliant. He soon assumed the lead in political reform also.
He advocated his political principles with an eloquence that
had never been surpassed. He gathered round him a powerful
party. On the platform and through the press his views were
expounded and defended with a persuasive power that was
irresistible. People seemed to regard him with a kind of
veneration, and to follow him with an ardour that approached
to enthusiasm. His views of the connection between religion
and politics were strong and decided. He held that a clergyman was still a citizen, and ought conscientiously to exercise
all the rights of citizenship. He held that, within due limits,
it was his duty to try to mould the political sentiments, and
guide the acts of those within the sphere of his influence. He
ever laboured to convince by reason, but never to influence
by fear or favour. A political opponent was not, therefore, an
enemy. Some of his warmest and most cherished friends
through life were diametrically opposed to him in politics.
His high principle, his untarnished honour, his genial *bonhomie*,
his warm and loving heart, secured for him the esteem and
affection of men of all parties.

Dr. Cooke took up his residence in Belfast at a critical
period of its political history. The borough had long been
under the control of a party of ultra Liberals. No man had
hitherto ventured to gain the suffrages of its electors until first
approved of and nominated by the Liberal dictators. Matters,
however, were beginning to change. A number of talented
and influential young men resolved, if possible, to shake off the
bonds of political slavery. A Conservative opposition was
organized, chiefly by the exertions of Mr. Richard Davison
and Mr. William Cairns. Dr. Cooke gave them the benefit of
his counsel, and the aid of his eloquence. He soon became
the life of the party, and he held his place for more than thirty
years. The cause he advocated triumphed. The Radical
nominees were defeated in 1832, and Lord Arthur Chichester

and Mr. James Emerson Tennent were returned as the first Conservative members for Belfast to the British Parliament. Dr. Cooke's influence was not confined to Belfast. It spread over the north, especially among the Presbyterian yeomen; and ere many years Ulster became one of the most intensely Conservative sections of the United Kingdom.

Dr. Cooke's wide sympathies and enlarged views of Christian truth and duty often led him to unite with the members of other denominations, for the promotion and defence of a common Protestantism. Episcopalians, Methodists, Independents have often felt and gratefully acknowledged the power of his advocacy. Those who did not know him, or who could not comprehend his principles, have sometimes charged him with sacrificing his Presbyterianism at the shrine of Episcopal favour. His life and labours form a noble protest against the calumny. No man was ever more devotedly attached to the simple Presbyterianism of his fathers. He never forgot, he never ignored, he never degraded it. In whatever society he moved, on whatever platform he stood, he let it be known what he was. Soon after his settlement in Killyleagh, while yet a young man, he was asked to take part in a meeting at Downpatrick on behalf of the Bible Society, under the presidency of Lord Roden, and in company with the leading men of the county. Dr. Daly, afterwards Bishop of Cashel, in his speech referred to Dr. Cooke, and expressed his delight at having the countenance and aid of his "dissenting brother." When Dr. Cooke rose, he too, in graceful sentences, gave thanks to God that Christian men of different communions could thus meet for a common object on a common platform. He congratulated Dr. Daly on his liberal sentiments and Christian charity. "But," he said, "for myself I repudiate the name dissenter. I am no dissenter. The Presbyterians of Ulster were never connected with the Episcopal Church of England or Ireland. The Presbyterian Church of Ireland is a branch of the Church of Scotland. From it I hold my orders; and as one of its ministers I stand before you this day." The declara-

tion was received with great applause. Dr. Cooke was congratulated by all parties on his manly, and yet courteous explanation
and defence. Lord Roden and Dr. Daly were ever afterwards
among his warmest friends. Throughout his whole life he
showed the same independent spirit. In Exeter Hall, when
in the midst of High Church dignitaries, and surrounded by
the titled aristocracy of England, whenever occasion required
or opportunity offered, he avowed his convictions on ecclesiastical polity. In Lambeth Palace, when enjoying the splendid
hospitality of the Archbishop of Canterbury, and occupying a
seat beside the Duke of Wellington, the subject of Church
government being raised, he maintained the scriptural parity
of Christian ministers with a boldness and power, and, at the
same time, with a taste and courtesy, which excited the admiration of all present. Instead of lowering his Church and
" dragging it in the mire before a contemptuous hierarchy," as
some hot-headed orators accused him of doing, Dr. Cooke, by
his commanding talents, and far-reaching influence, contributed
to raise it to a position in Ulster and in the empire, to which
it had never before attained.

In the year 1834 the state of Ireland became alarming. The
passing of the Reform Bill, instead of calming the Roman
Catholics, as was triumphantly predicted by its advocates,
seemed rather to increase discontent and agitation. The
Whig ministry of the day were charged, and with some degree
of justice, of truckling to Popery, and seeking to conciliate the
priesthood by the degradation of Protestantism. Ulster was
excited to its centre. The descendants of the men who had
fought for religion and liberty at Derry, Aughrim, and the
Boyne, feared that those dear-bought privileges were about to
be wrested from them. A requisition, signed by the leading
men of Down and Antrim, was presented to Lord Hillsborough,
High Sheriff of Down, requesting him to convene a meeting
of the inhabitants for the purpose of considering the state of
public affairs, and petitioning Parliament. He complied, and
the result was one of the most influential meetings ever held in

Ireland.   It assembled at Hillsborough on the 30th of October,
1834.   The chair was occupied by the High Sheriff.   Round him
on the platform were the heads of the leading families in the
province.   In the large field in which the platform was erected
were assembled more than forty thousand of the gentry and
yeomen of Down and Antrim.   The place of meeting was
historic.   Hillsborough, the seat of the Hills, was the scene of
many a fierce struggle in the early days of the Ulster settlement.   In its old castle William III. slept on his way from
Carrickfergus to the Boyne, and there he wrote the celebrated
letter which secured the *Regium Donum* to the Presbyterian
Church.

The attitude which Dr. Cooke might assume towards the
proposed meeting had been a subject of deep anxiety to many,
and of intense interest to the whole Protestant community.   A
large number of the Presbyterian clergy looked upon the
meeting with no friendly eye.   They seemed to regard it as a
demonstration in support of Tory politics, and High Church
ascendency.   They were, therefore, opposed to it both politically and ecclesiastically.   Dr. Cooke was warned against
attending it.   He was told that if he did so he would compromise his Church, and peril his position as leader of the
Synod.   But Dr. Cooke was not a man to be moved by warnings or fears.   He would never stoop to court popularity by
the sacrifice of principle.   A sense of duty alone could sway
him—duty to his God and his country.   Among the promoters
of the meeting were some of his most attached personal and
political friends.   They saw the difficult and delicate position
in which he was placed, and in a spirit of honourable self-
denial, they did not even ask him to attend.   They laid the
object of the meeting before him, and left the decision entirely
with himself.   The following letter from Lord Roden shows
the deference and consideration with which he was treated :—

"Tollymore Park, 26th Oct. 1834.

" My dear Friend,—I can sincerely assure you that my

heart overflowed with gratitude and my eyes with tears at the receipt of your kind and affectionate letter this morning. I was perfectly aware of the reason of your not replying sooner, and I should have been equally certain of the wisdom and soundness of your decision if I had not received any reply at all till after the meeting. But I cannot express how thankful I am that your mind has been led to make the decision you have announced to me. I have only to press upon you that if there now exists, or if there should exist at any time between this and the 30th, any doubt on your mind as to the course you ought to pursue, that you will not allow any consideration for me to induce you to take a contrary course, or even to bias your mind on the subject. I need not tell you how grateful I shall feel to my blessed Master if he allow me to be supported by one of His dear ministers, who has so boldly stood out for His honour. But were I to proceed alone, I should still feel that I am engaged in His service. I cannot but think the exertion I have been permitted to make in rousing my Protestant brethren to a sense of their real ills, is of my glorious Master; for how otherwise could it have been possible to have got together for this one object all those names you see signed to the requisition, so opposed to us before in all our politico-religious views. But so it is, and to the Lord be the praise!

"I perfectly agree with you in what you say about your Presbyterian views, and no man could ask you for more than what you voluntarily offer yourself; at least I am sure I would not. And it is because you are a Presbyterian, and a dear brother in Christ, that I am anxious to have you with me in our common cause. I have carefully drawn up the resolutions, to which no friend to the Constitution of this country, or to the religion of Protestants, I think, could object. The Committee have allotted the last resolution to me; and if you will second me in it, I am sure they would feel happy, and I should feel proud. I enclose you a copy of the resolutions, which, I hope, you will approve. As it is important they should not be known before the meeting, I send them to you in confidence. . . .

" Before I conclude, I have only again to say, my very dear friend, don't let any expressed wish of mine guide you, or weigh against your own better judgment; for I would even rather not have you, than that, after you had been there, anything should give you cause of regret for the line you had adopted. Be it as it may, I commend you to the Lord our great Master, who is the wisdom as well as the righteousness of His people. Many, many thanks for your prayers. Write me a line here by return of post, and believe me always,

" Most affectionately yours,

" RODEN."

Dr. Cooke had formed his resolution. His line of duty was, to his mind, sufficiently clear. He would take his stand upon the platform of a common Protestantism. Whatever men might say, whatever results might follow, he would act fearlessly as conscience dictated, and attend the meeting.

The first resolution was moved by the Marquess of Downshire; he was followed by the Marquesses of Donegal and Londonderry, the Earl of Clanwilliam, Lords Castlereagh, Dufferin, Arthur Hill, and the Earl of Roden. But the speech of the day was that of Dr. Cooke. " Never before," says one who was present, " had I an opportunity, such as I then enjoyed, of perceiving the manner in which a true orator, who understands how to construct his sentences, and to use his organs of speech aright, can become audible to an enormous multitude. Members of Parliament, men used to military command, lawyers, and others, were speakers on this occasion, but only in their immediate circle were they heard. During the morning the eyes of the spectators were fixed upon one noble form, who sat in his usual calm, statuesque repose. At length he rose. It was a raw and gusty day. There was a leaden canopy in the heavens, and the people were chilled. He lifted his hand gently, and as he uttered his voice in apparently commonplace tones, he was at once audible in the outer circle of the vast assembly. Standing, as I did, at the farthest

verge of the great concourse, I found with delight and wonder
that every word, and even the gentlest inflections of his voice,
were distinctly heard during all his masterly oration. This
speech was a memorable incident in his history."

He began by explaining why he was present. An explanation was necessary. He knew well the outcry some of his
brethren in the Presbyterian Church would raise against him.
His explanation was clear, logical, unanswerable :—

"As this is a meeting where great political questions are discussed, the interference of ministers of the Gospel will by some be
condemned. I must, therefore, vindicate myself from such shallow
and hypocritical cavils. Shallow cavils I call them, and shallow they
are ; for there is not a prophet in the Old Testament, nor an apostle
in the New, that ever evaded a political question—that ever tamely
surrendered a political right, or shrunk from teaching rulers, as well
as subjects, their various and reciprocal duties. Hypocritical cavils,
I call them, and hypocritical they are ; for never are they adduced
except when the Christian politics of ministers condemn the time-
serving expediencies of the world ; and then, forsooth, there arises a
cry deprecating all clerical interference with politics as a descent
from a higher office, or an unwarranted intrusion into forbidden
ground. Such shallow, hypocritical cavils I shall ever treat with the
contempt they deserve. I am, nevertheless, most willing to admit,
that there are departments of politics with which ministers of the
Gospel should never interfere ; to the politics of mere partizanship,
the strivings of worldly men for place, and not for principle—to these
they should never descend. 'Touch not, taste not, handle not,'
should be their motto and their practice.

"But there are two departments of politics where I hold it to be
the bounden duty of every minister to interfere. The first department embraces the teaching of the relative duties of rulers and
subjects. This is well defined and permanent. It forms an integral
part of the Gospel commission, and has equally been discharged by
prophets and apostles. The second is of a more indefinite and un-
certain character, and I endeavour to explain it thus : a minister
may, and must, interfere with politics whenever politics interfere with
religion. Such a crisis, I believe, has now arisen ; and I pity the
faithless watchman who sees the enemy coming in like a flood, and
will not blow the trumpet and rouse the sleeping garrison. The

thoughtless may wonder, the incredulous may deny, the bold may disregard, and the abettors of anarchy may affect to despise, when I declare it to be my deliberate and fixed opinion, that never, in the history of Ireland, was Protestantism in greater danger than at this hour.

" I have made my election to serve under the banners of our common Protestantism ; and this declaration will require me to explain how I, as a Presbyterian, and standing by all the religious and political principles of my Puritan fathers, can in anywise undertake the defence of a Church not governed by presbyters, but by prelates. I know it is possible that by some my attempt at explanation, or, if you will, vindication, will be supposed hopeless. Let me bespeak their candour and their patience ; and, above all, I entreat them to open that old almanac, history, and read to learn, and wait to judge, before they pronounce sentence.

" First, then, allow me to state, that I stand here as a Presbyterian, supporting and adhering to every principle of Presbyterianism, in doctrine and Church government. Were my appearance here to imply my surrender of one jot or tittle of the doctrines of the Church of Scotland, I should hold myself unworthy to be called her son. Did my appearance here imply that I surrendered the humble temple of Presbyterianism to ruinous dilapidation, or more splendid reconstruction, I should hold myself unworthy of a sentinel's post upon the lowest of her venerable watch-towers. But I surrender not my own post, I betray not my own charge, while I cheer forward another column of our noble Protestant army, who, though differently officered and differently dressed, yet wield the same weapons of truth, and serve under the same banners. (Cheers.) And if any one condemn me for affording them that cheer ; if any one think I should leave them to their fate, without sympathy for their sufferings, or encouragement in their conflict, I would again entreat such an one to recur to the old almanac of history ; and, before he condemn me for uniting in defence of our general and common Protestantism, ask himself would he condemn our Presbyterian forefathers for uniting in a similar defence within the walls of Derry, or at the passes of Enniskillen ? Common danger produced that union.

" But while I appear before you as a Presbyterian, I wish it to be distinctly understood that I do not appear as a representative, but merely as a sample of the Presbyterian Church. Representation implies always election, sometimes instruction, occasionally delega-

tion. In none of these senses can I be considered as a representative
of my brethren; they have not chosen, they have not instructed,
they have not sent me. I alone stand accountable for the sentiments
I utter. I believe, however, that I know and speak the religious
and political sentiments of the great majority of my brethren; and
if there be any who question this statement, our annual meeting will
afford them an opportunity of bringing the subject to a public trial.

"There are two great points on which the Churches of Scotland and
England are agreed, and in which the Synod of Ulster most cordially
concurs. First, they agree in doctrine. And, though this is a point
whereon some may differ from me, yet I declare I never could discover an essential discrepancy between the Westminster Confession
and the doctrinal parts of the Thirty-nine Articles. Second, they
agree on the principle of establishments, though they differ in the
details of the arrangement. Whenever, then, I require an answer to
any man who may please, as, no doubt, many will please, to assail or
revile me for joining hands with the Church of England, I will point
to her Scriptural Articles, to her glorious testimony for the truth as
it is in Jesus; and I will tell my accusers that it is for the sake of
these heavenly things, and not for the sake of her worldly endowments, that I say, ' Peace be within her walls, and prosperity in her
palaces.' Believing farther, as I do, that it is the duty of every
Government to establish the Christian religion, and also, when
possible, to endow its churches, I feel also that I stand upon
common ground with the Church of England, though we erect our
temples with different orders of architecture. And whilst I would
defend the Church of England, not for the sake of the form without,
but of the truth within, I yield not my conviction of the apostolic
architecture of Presbytery, but will defend it to the very frieze and
cornice of its temple.

"There is another reason why, as a Presbyterian, I feel bound to
speak. I know that both in high and low places the Presbyterians of
Ulster have been represented as unfriendly to the United Churches of
England and Ireland. The truth of this insinuation, or assertion, I
openly and positively deny. There are, no doubt, Presbyterians, so
called, who hate the Church of England for the very reasons for
which I respect her. They hate her, and they hate her liturgy,
because they both testify to the truth. But what are these amongst
the hundreds of thousands of Ulster Presbyterians? A few drops in
a bucket; a few feathers in a scale. They would not, if the province
were raked for their collection, make a fraction of this noble meeting.

. . . . The real state of the case, then, I believe to stand thus :—The Presbyterians of Ulster, who correspond to the Church of Scotland, believing their own Church government to be apostolic, neither agree with prelacy on the one hand, nor with independency on the other ; but they bear charity to the Christians of both forms, and exercise towards others the forbearance they claim for themselves.

" I have another reason for my decided goodwill to the clergy of the Established Churches ; I happen to know them well. I know personally and intimately a number of the clergy of England ; and, to use the words of a late celebrated individual, I know a line of Irish clergy from Carrickfergus to Cape Clear ; and though in that lengthened line there are lights and shadows of varied personal and ministerial character, yet truth compels me to say, that in no denomination of Protestants do I know a greater proportion of learned, faithful, laborious, and zealous heralds of the Gospel of salvation."

In urging union among Evangelical Protestants in the face of a common danger and a common foe, he uttered these noble sentiments :—

" Take warning from the fact that your opponents have long been firmly banded and united. The priesthood and laity of Rome, the Socinian, and the Infidel, form a threefold cord that is not easily broken ; and while this cord has been twisted together, and labelled with destruction, Protestants have been uncombined in loose and separate threads, ready to be snapped asunder by the effects of the weakest hand. This state of disunion must continue no longer. The advice of the dying father to his sons must be weighed and applied. He was afraid that, after his death, his sons would fall out by the way ; so he took a quiver of arrows, and delivering them one by one to his heirs, he required them to break them to pieces, and the work was done. He took another quiver, and calling for a cord, he bound the arrows together, and delivered them to his youngest son, and bade him break them ; the feeble boy attempted it in vain. They passed in succession round the family ; and the eldest and the strongest tugged and toiled to break them, but could not succeed. Thus, said he, my sons, disunited you will be destroyed, but combined in affection you need fear no enemy. Protestants, you are the quivers. Remain asunder, look upon each other with suspicion, repel one another with sectarian antipathies, let the one look on with apathy or satisfaction till the other is laid prostrate ; do this,

and then I tell you, you will be broken in succession, till nothing but
splinters and fragments remain to tell of your existence. Presbyterians, I speak to you. The days are gone by when in Ireland
Wentworth unleashed his bloodhounds on the track of your fathers;
when Laud, papist at heart, forged chains at once for their consciences and their liberties. The days are gone by when a Lauderdale plotted, and, upon the mountains of Scotland, a Dundee
executed, the purposes of a bloody and heartless tyranny. Let us
thank God that these days are gone by; and let us not stand, like
moody magicians, conjuring up the ghosts of departed jealousies or
injuries; but let our common faith, and our common dangers, unite
us for common protection; and, united thus, though the powers of
earth, and the powers of darkness, frown with equal hate upon our
compacted ranks, they will never make a breach in our array; but
they will flit around us as fierce, yet as innocuous, as the Chasseurs
of Napoleon galloped round the irongirt squares of Wellington upon
the memorable field of Waterloo."

He concluded as follows :—

" Let the dangers with which you are threatened lead you nearer
to the God of salvation, and render you more familiar at a throne of
grace, looking for grace to help you in time of need. The great
fault of Protestants, the fault for which they have suffered, and, if
they discover it not and amend it not, for which they will suffer
again, is their trusting in princes and men's sons, and not in the
living God. Experience of the past should have taught us that we
could trust our destinies to no man, to no individual, to no party.
The scenes that are every day occurring around us should teach us
how little the bare name of Protestant is to be trusted, where our
lives and the destinies of the empire are thrown into the scale against
the ambition of office. . . .

" In conclusion; you may, if you will, call this a small meeting;
yet upwards of sixty thousand Protestant men, educated, peaceable,
united in one sentiment, is somewhat of a fair array. But though I
call this meeting small for the present, I see in it the germ of much
future increase. The acorn is planted, the bud has sprung forth,
and the hour is coming when, like the father oak that adorns the
forest, it will shoot its roots into the soil, it will seize the rocks in
its embrace, it will lift up its fearless head, it will spread abroad its
mighty arms, it will sport with the whirlwind, and repose when the

storm has gone by. I trust I see more in this meeting than a mere eliciting of public opinion, or a mere gathering of the clans. I trust I see in it the pledge of Protestant union and co-operation. Between the divided Churches I publish the banns of a sacred marriage of Christian forbearance where they differ, of Christian love where they agree, and of Christian co-operation in all matters where their common safety is concerned. Who forbids the banns? None. Then I trust our union, for these holy purposes, is indissoluble, and that the God who has bound us in ties of Christian affection, and of a common faith, will never allow the recollections of the past, or the temptations of the present, to sever those whom He has thus united.

"A parting word to the aristocracy whom I have the honour to address. The people have nobly done their part to-day. I am much deceived if the voice of this meeting be not heard through the length and breadth of the land. Its echoes will reverberate both in Windsor and Westminster; its temperance will satisfy the reasonable and the loyal; and its power will awe the destructive and the factious. Let but the nobility and landed aristocracy of Ulster continue to cherish and co-operate with their tenantry, and they need not build them moated towers and battlemented castles. Like Sparta they will need no walls; their surest defence is the gallant hearts that surround them. We are threatened, no doubt, with the overthrow of our hereditary nobility, and I am not surprised at the threat. The coolness of the House of Lords has, of late, more than once, so tempered the hot zeal of the Commons, and so baffled the schemes of the great Dictator, the man who, like Warwick the king-maker, may justly be called the minister-maker, that I am not surprised he longs to hurl them from their hereditary places, and supply the vacancy with a few elective joints of his own tail. But let the nobility look around them on that plain; there are the supporters of their arms; there are the men who will never suffer a blot on their escutcheons. And if the danger come, which may Heaven in its mercy forbid; but if, I say, the danger come, there are the heralds who will adopt, with one heart, the motto of a nobleman who has this day addressed you, and proclaim with trumpet voice to the vanquished assailant of your honours, *Metuenda corolla draconis.*"

No description could convey any adequate idea of the enthusiastic applause which followed this noble speech. The vast crowd seemed almost frantic with excitement. And the excitement was increased by a scene which occurred upon the platform. Dr. Cooke's eloquent allusion to the Marquess of Londonderry, and the happy introduction of his well-known family motto, made the veteran spring to his feet, and bow to the speaker. His brilliant achievements, under Wellington, in the Peninsula, and at Waterloo, were still fresh in the memory of all; and his breast, as he stood there, was covered with the decorations he had won on many a field of victory. The scene was a remarkable one, and the assembly cheered, with equal enthusiasm, the warrior and the orator.

Just as he had anticipated, Dr. Cooke's presence at the Hillsborough Meeting gave great dissatisfaction to many of the clergy of his own Church. The dissatisfaction was largely increased by the inaccuracy of the report of his speech, which was reproduced in the leading journals of the empire ; and by the injudicious, and sometimes absurd comments of the Conservative press. He was described as Moderator of the Synod of Ulster, Head of the Church, Representative of the whole Presbyterians of Ireland. The enthusiasm of Protestants was so great, that they did not always stop to ascertain facts, or even to read the speaker's words. He was assailed, as usual, by the Radical press, which was not slow to take advantage of the blunders and exaggerations of Conservative journals. He was reproached in private letters by old and cherished friends. To remove the misapprehensions which prevailed, he published an authentic report of his speech. Of course, those who differed from him in politics, were not satisfied. But the vast majority of the Presbyterian people of Ulster sympathised with his views ; and at no period of his history was he more popular than after the Hillsborough Demonstration.

The meeting was a great success. It inspired the Protestants of all sects and classes. It roused the people of Britain to a sense of the dangers of Ireland. It contributed largely to the overthrow of a time-serving Ministry ; and it saved the country from obnoxious measures, and acts of daring lawlessness, which might eventually have led to civil war.

While taking such a prominent part in the great events of the day, guiding the public mind both in religion and politics, Dr. Cooke had to endure private sorrows which keenly touched his tender heart. A large debt had been incurred in the building of May Street Church. A few of its managing committee, and especially one, who differed widely from the Doctor in politics, and whose temper was probably soured by the triumphs of a party he abhorred, agreed to press Dr. Cooke to employ his spare time in collecting funds for the removal of the debt. This was a work by no means congenial to Dr. Cooke's tastes and feelings. Yet he undertook it. On this unpleasant mission he went to London, in May, 1835. The first to welcome and aid him was his friend, Lord Roden. His mission was successful. But many of his Belfast friends were indignant that such a task should be put upon him. " I think it is too hard," wrote Mr. Cairns, " that you should have to expend your influence, and lay yourself under obligation, in accomplishing an object in which you have only a temporary interest."

While he was in London, his two oldest sons, who had for some time been in delicate health, became dangerously ill. It was a sore trial. Duty to his Church detained him ; but strong parental affection made him long to be home. His anxieties and sufferings were great. His letters to Mrs. Cooke, and to his children, are tender and touching. They show the affectionate heart ; but they breathe the spirit of the true Christian, commending his beloved ones, with implicit faith, to the care and keeping of his and their Heavenly Father. He writes on the 17th of May ;—" My dearest hope, my earnest and constant prayer is, for the salvation of myself, my wife, and my children." A strange dream, caused, no doubt, by mental anxiety, still further troubled him. He thus describes it in a letter to Mrs. Cooke :—" The first night of my arrival, I dreamt of my being at some lake, not large, but with muddy

waters; and I possessed the ridiculous power of traversing it
in a basket, as a matter of amusement to you and others
present. But in the midst of my frolic there came a cry that
John was drowned. I imagined I had the power of summoning
his body from the bottom. I saw it rise. I stretched out for
it in agony. It eluded my grasp. I brought it up, but could
not keep it up. I had a notion that, but for sleep which
overpowered me, I might have prevented his drowning. Oh!
the agony of that thought! Never, never did I feel such
mental torture. My son, my son, my son was lying dead in
the water. I awoke in such anguish as enabled me, more than
anything I ever before felt, to appreciate the agonies of Jesus
my Saviour, when He bore our griefs and carried our sorrows."

On the 26th he again wrote to Mrs. Cooke :—"When I got
Catherine's (Miss Cooke) letter, and Dr. Ferguson's to-day at
three, I had just returned from an effort to arrange my plans,
and I had been much encouraged by the kindness of friends.
By my letters from home all was dashed to the ground. I read
them, and I remembered my terrible dream about my dear
boy. My heart was like to break. . . . I am nearly
distracted between conflicting views. The Lord direct me for
the best. The Lord pity you. As for me, why should a
living man complain; a man, for the scourge of his merciful
God, his Heavenly Father! I am unworthy of the least of
His mercies; and I only pray to Him to deliver us from the
evil. The Lord spare my son! The Lord show me the work
of grace in his heart; and then, let Him who gave take away,
if He will. Only let me hope to meet him with his Saviour.
I will bow and weep. The good Lord spare my son! I wrote
him a letter. Perhaps it was too severe. It was one of reproof
and advice, but of hope. I wish you to see it, and to talk with
him of its contents. . . . My heart is bleeding, and my
eyes are running over with tears. The Lord be merciful to
us, and lift upon us the light of His countenance! Last night
I was expounding the fourteenth chapter of John. Read it,
and learn its worth. Oh! how I require the cure of heart-

trouble. The Lord send me better news! I wish to stay, if stay I can, to serve my congregation. . . . But the Lord's will be done."

On the 29th he wrote to his son :—"I have been much encouraged by the accounts I have heard from Thomas [his oldest son], and your uncle [Mr. O'Neill]. Put your trust in the Lord. Call on his mercy. Jesus is able to heal both body and soul ; and he will not cast out any that come to the Father by Him. I wrote to you in solemn admonition. I see now how needful it was to admonish, as we know not how soon we must all appear before the judgment seat of Christ. This is our joy, that we have Jesus an High Priest, touched with our infirmities ; and able to succour us, as he is God, and above our infirmities. The blessedness of knowing Jesus Christ as God manifest in the flesh, is beyond all other blessings. To know Him and the Father is life eternal. Hear His voice, my son. Be one of His following sheep. He will give you eternal life. And though the earthly house of this tabernacle be dissolved, you have a building of God, an house not made with hands, eternal in the heavens."

On the 2nd of June he concludes an affectionate letter to Mrs. Cooke, in these sorrowful, yet hopeful words :—" God is good ; therefore I will trust in Him. His mercy endureth for ever ; therefore I will pray to him. May He keep and bless you ! In the danger of poor John, I have nearly forgotten my poor Thomas. ' Misfortunes love a train ;' so I have found it. Well, the Sun of Righteousness will yet shine out upon us, and we shall rejoice together."

On June 6th he again wrote to his son John :—" Your letter every way gave me great pleasure. That your health is improving is so far well ; but that you are sensible of your sin is better. The Lord grant you repentance and remission through the blood that cleanses from all sin. I am also glad to find your anxiety not to distress mamma ; yet in all things be simple and true. Never conceal, and never exaggerate, is the true plan. Truth, simple truth, is always best. It has been good for you to be afflicted. I trust the Lord meant it, and will overrule it for good. Blessed be His holy name!

"I went yesterday to Uxbridge; spoke an hour to a meeting for the Irish Society, and got twenty pounds collection. I preach three times to-morrow; I preach on Wednesday, Friday, Sunday, Monday, Tuesday, Thursday, Friday, Sunday; with a meeting on Wednesday 17th, at Stamford, in Essex. And on my way home, I have a meeting every day till I reach Liverpool. . . .

"I have no news here, except that O'Connell seems the god of this world. He rides in the chariot of power unresisted; and Rome, in his hands, seems fast rising again to supremacy. We are determined to give him work on the 20th, as probably you will have learned from the papers. The eyes of the Protestants are closed, and they will not see; their ears are shut, and they will not hear. We must rouse them by exploding Rome's own artillery under their nose; and, if they sleep on, it will be the sleep of death. Popery on the one hand, and Radicalism on the other, with sleeping Toryism between, are the banes of the land. Conservatism and Orangeism are alike mere worldly things. They are not the things can save a land. Protestantism, intellectual and spiritual, the Protestantism of the Reformation, of the Puritans, the genuine Protestantism of the Covenant, is the only thing under heaven that can save us from a return of the days of Charles or James II. I trust this feeling is working its way into the vitals of society, and that yet this country is not to be given over of man, or deserted of God. Presbyterians in particular have sadly degenerated from the state of their fathers, in piety, family prayer, church-going, attendance on ordinances, and zeal against popery. The spirit of liberalism has infected many of them like a leprosy; and they must either have it scourged out, or turned out, for it will not go out. I trust we shall be able to consider these things with faith in God who rules over all; with love to men, His creatures, yea, to them who are our enemies; yet with an ardent desire for the conversion of all men from the error of

their ways, and the salvation of our country from the dangers
with which it is threatened. The Church of England and
Ireland has sinned much, and it will suffer much. I see it
in the distance. It must pass through the furnace, that it
may be purified. Yet, in that Church there is still a world
of spiritual life. Indeed, I think it contains the most spiritual
men I meet. Dear Mr. Simons, of St. Paul's-cross, the holiest
man I ever met, is praying for you. And the prayer of a
righteous man, a man made righteous by the righteousness
of Christ, availeth much. The Lord keep you, and restore
you, prays your father."

The nature and object of the meeting in Exeter Hall, referred to in the above letter, will be best understood by the
following advertisement, which appeared in the leading London
and Dublin papers, on the first and second weeks of June,
1835 :—

" To the Protestants of Great Britain and
Ireland.

" The undersigned having recently discovered by authentic
and unquestionable documents, which they have reason to
believe have never met the public eye, that the standards
adopted and the principles inculcated by the Roman Catholic
Hierarchy of Ireland are of the same intolerant and persecuting
nature at this day that are well known to have characterised
their Church in former times, do feel it their painful but imperative duty to stand forward and produce, before Protestants
of all denominations, unanswerable testimony on this subject.

" They make this public address to Protestants, for the purpose of giving them an opportunity of judging on a question
of vital importance to every one who values the right of conscience, and the security of property, of liberty, and of life;
and also for the purpose of affording to the Roman Catholic
bishops in general, and to Doctor Murray, Roman Catholic
Archbishop of Dublin, in particular, as specially implicated in
the charge, an opportunity of meeting it in public, in their own

persons, or by any of their clergy, or by any Roman Catholic layman, duly delegated and authorised by them.

" They accordingly give notice, that three or more of their number, purpose, with the gracious permission of Divine Providence, to attend at Exeter Hall, on Saturday, the 20th of June, instant, at twelve o'clock, and submit and illustrate the documents to which they have above referred. (Signed)

" H. R. Dawson, Dean of St. Patrick's,
" Robert Maude, Dean of Clogher,
" Richard Murray, Dean of Ardagh,
" J. H. Singer, D.D., F.T.C.D.,
" Henry Cooke, D.D.,
" Rev. Robert Daly,
" Rev. Horatio T. Newman, &c., &c."

Mr. O'Connell was specially invited to attend, on the ground that he had thrown down a challenge to Protestants, and had said it would be his " delight to grapple with no-Popery hypocrites." It was expected that a number of Roman Catholic clergy, or some persons delegated by them, would appear to defend their Church against damaging charges. The excitement in London was tremendous. Twelve o'clock was the hour appointed for the meeting, but long before that time every seat in the hall was occupied. Among those who crowded the platform were Lords Roden, Galloway, Bandon, Mandeville, and Ashley; the Honourables F. Bernard, J. A. Maude, F. Maude, R. H. Plunkett, Sir F. Stapleton, J. W. Stratford, J. King; Sir Harcourt Lees, Sir Robert Shaw, Sir George Rose, Sir Robert Bateson, Sir E. S. Hayes; Right Hon. F. Shaw, M.P.; W. Ewart Gladstone, M.P. The chair was occupied by Lord Kenyon. The Rev. R. J. M'Ghee was the first speaker, and he gave in detail the documentary evidence, proving that Dens' " Theology" was the book adopted by the Roman Catholic Bishops of Ireland, " as containing those principles which they approve for the guidance of the priesthood." He showed at length the character of the book. He proved that

it was intolerant and immoral; that it enjoined the persecution
and even extirpation of heretics. Dr. Cooke followed, and his
theme was the Bull *Unigenitus*. Before grappling, however,
with the " notorious and furious Bull," he referred in a style of
racy humour to the challenge given to Mr. O'Connell, and to
certain charges which had been brought against himself by the
Romish and Radical press.

    " We invited (to this meeting) the most influential in point of
learning, when we invited the whole priesthood ; we invited the
most influential in point of acuteness, when we invited that man
whose talents entitle him to the respect of the public. I should
have felt great delight, having once or twice been honoured by
the special favour of the honourable and learned gentleman, in
having an opportunity of bandying the compliment. I have no
idea that I possess the powers of his head, the wisdom of his mind,
or the legal tact of making the worse appear the better cause. In
these things I could not compete with him ; but I would compete
with him in courtesy and kindness. The weapons of my warfare
should not be carnal ; they should be a reference to his own
Scriptures. It would be a reference to truth and to principle I
would employ as the weapons of the warfare in which I should
delight to engage with him.
    " I have farther to notice an attack in the public press. We have
been treated as persons who have come over here for the purpose, not
of ministers of peace, but of ministers of ill will. I fling back the
accusation upon those who bring it. I ask these gentlemen is that
[holding up the Bull *Unigenitus*] a peaceful document ? I ask them
is it in the vocabulary of their peaceful object that heretics should be
confiscated as to property, and that they should be consigned to the
tender mercies of the Inquisition ? I tell you that to have peace so
long as the doctrine of war is hugged to the bosom of the Church of
Rome is utterly impossible. We will have peace with the men, but
with the principle I do proclaim an unchanging war." . . .

    After some interruptions caused by Roman Catholics in the
body of the hall crying for fair play, and charging the speaker
with misrepresentation, and the meeting with partiality, Dr.
Cooke said :—

" The papers have already stated that we were coming before
a packed jury; but I shall now give them another challenge. Let
them meet us in Dublin ; half the tickets shall be given to Roman
Catholics and half to Protestants ; and with a jury thus equal we
pledge ourselves to make them ashamed or afraid of Dominus Dens.
Though I know pretty well the character of the men by whom we
shall be met ; and though, from what I have encountered before, I
have but little stomach for the fight, yet I have no doubt we shall
meet them shield to shield and man to man ; and, with numbers
thus equally selected from both sides, we shall win the day. Let
them meet us by their clergy, with their learning and research ; and
by their respectable laity, who have rank, and character, and talent ;
let them thus meet us, and we will plead the cause of liberty against
domination, of charity against separation, of protection against in-
carceration, and of saving men, body and soul, instead of delivering
them over to the power of the secular arm."

On returning from the meeting to his hotel, he wrote to Mrs.
Cooke :—" I have merely time to say I am alive after a two
hours' speech at Exeter Hall. Dan did not appear ; so, as the
newspapers were twitting us about attempting to evade him,
I challenged them to name their time and equal men, either in
London or Dublin. What they will do we shall see. I do
think this day has lighted anew the candle of the truth in
England, which no time will extinguish."

Two days latter he gave his son a graphic account of the
scene. " It would have given me great delight to have had
you with me on Saturday. We had a splendid meeting. The
great hall was crowded. We had but three speakers—M'Ghee,
O'Sullivan, and my poor self. M'Ghee is the greatest speaker
I ever heard. He electrified me. He bore me away. He
overwhelmed everybody with admiration of the man, and conviction of the truth.

" O'Sullivan was a cataract tumbling from a mountain.
M'Ghee, a thunderbolt, flashing and laying prostrate.
O'Sullivan in winding up, almost made me start to my feet,
by one awful picture of Rome, rising as a dead body, with

all the noisomeness of the grave, and with all the activity of a demon.

"I do believe that if ever Protestants will be roused, Saturday blew the trumpet-note, at once of war and victory. May the Lord restore you, and make you valiant for His truth: so prays your father."

Dr. Cooke's expectations were verified. The meeting at Exeter Hall roused the Protestant feeling of England. The Bishop of Exeter, in a powerful speech called the attention of the House of Lords to the exposure of the Roman Catholic system made by the speakers, and to the effects of such teaching on the exciteable population of Ireland. The Roman Catholic Hierarchy became alarmed. They knew that an enlightened British public must condemn such a system. Dr. Murray, Archbishop of Dublin, wrote to Lord Melbourne, the Prime Minister, apparently denying the charges regarding the adoption of Dens' " Theologia" as a text-book for the clergy. It was only apparently, for the language he used was studiously obscure ; and evidence was subsequently adduced which showed that the statements made in Exeter Hall were correct.

On Monday, the 22nd, Dr. Cooke again wrote to Mrs. Cooke :—" Yesterday I preached three times, and twice addressed communicants ; having for the first time in my life seen, and partaken of communion, in the manner of the Church of England. As to forms, I care not unless they be imposed. Then I rebel, and justly too, against man's authority, in favour of my Lord's sole supremacy. To day I have preached once in private, and will again in the evening. To-morrow I preach twice, also, and give, in the last of them, my farewell sermon. On Thursday I hope to escape."

Before leaving London he received the following touching letter from one of Ireland's truest friends. It was accompanied by a ring which Dr. Cooke ever afterwards cherished among his choicest treasures. It bears the motto, *Nulla pax cum Roma*.

" Blackheath Park.

" My dear and honoured Friend,—I herewith transfer to your hand the signet that has long adorned mine ; and in so doing, I fulfil a wish formed from the first day of its being in my possession.   The Lord has graciously given me the principle of 'No peace with Rome,' together with a sincere desire to act it out in every possible way. But to you He has vouchsafed both opportunity and power to wage a war of extermination against His accursed foe; and oh ! how thankful I am that your day is thus lengthened for that purpose. I have very often, at the Lord's Table, after receiving the cup of blessing, which the monster Popery would rend away, renewed my sweet vow over that ring, and put up the reiterated prayer that it might be my happy privilege to my last breath, to testify against Rome, and to labour for the souls she holds captive in her net.   Often and often have you been the means of cheering me on in some puny effort against her, and for our own dear Ireland ; and, perhaps a glance at this little ring, may sometimes speak encouragement (for which of God's servants does not occasionally need it ?), by reminding you of the wide, deep, permanent effect to be produced by the testimony you are called on to bear in this most righteous cause. Already the very foundations of Satan's throne in dear Ireland, are shaken by means of that testimony ; and if it be not yours to behold in the flesh the full triumph that will yet crown the conflict, you will share it in the Church above.

" Never will you have cause to regret the expenditure of your time, strength, health, yea life, in this cause ; never even in time will you regret it ; and will you in eternity ?

" As a member of the Episcopalian Church, I most heartily thank you, dear brother, for your catholic advocacy of the common cause. The man who would interpose a bar, whether a belt of mountains or a wisp of hay, between the sister Churches, ought to be made ashamed : and, I know nothing better calculated to do it, than the line of conduct which you, by God's grace, pursue.

"Therefore, go on. Never slacken your efforts while you have a word to speak, or a hand to raise, until the word is spoken to your country at large :—'Arise, shine, for thy light is come!' I pray God keep you steadfast, immovable, always abounding in His work ; and I pray that you may very long be spared to us, and give us a practical exposition of *Nulla pax cum Roma.*

"With all respect and gratitude, I am,

"Your affectionate friend,

"CHARLOTTE ELIZABETH."

He reached Liverpool on the 26th, almost worn out with unceasing labour, and intending to sail direct to Belfast. But he found that he was already advertised to preach on Sunday, the 28th. He felt deeply grieved by this arrangement, of which he had received no notice. He longed to be back with his suffering children. He required rest for himself both in mind and body. He forwarded a letter to Mrs. Cooke, explaining the cause of his delay :—"The will of God be done, both in crosses and crowns. To me this is a cross ; but I am bound to thank God it is so light."

He got home in time for the annual meeting of Synod which was held in Belfast. Matters of great importance affecting the welfare of the Church, and the efficient training of its ministers, were to come before it ; and he was expected, and, as usual, prepared to take a leading part in the deliberations. The prelections of Professor Ferrie continued to excite distrust and dissatisfaction : Complaints were made by students, that the principles developed tended to undermine the truths of Revelation, and to foster a spirit of scepticism. These complaints became at length so numerous and so strong, that the Synod was forced to take notice of them ; and a committee was appointed to inquire into the doctrines taught in the class. That committee, after careful investigation, recommended the Synod "to direct the students under their care not to attend that class so long as it is conducted by the present Professor." The Synod directed accordingly; and in order to provide for the training of the students, Dr. Cooke and Mr. Molyneux were appointed to lecture during Session 1834-35, the former on Ethics and Natural Theology, the latter on Metaphysics. The arrangement gave entire satisfaction. The prelections of Dr. Cooke were distinguished by originality of thought, lucidity of arrangement, and remarkable beauty of style and illustration. The students were often electrified by bursts of eloquence, as the sublime problems of Christian ethics were passed in review. An enthusiasm new and unparalleled was infused into the cold routine of academic training. The Professor's chair became the centre of intellectual life, the stimulator of new energies and aspirations. Great additional labour was required to prepare for the class-room; but Dr. Cooke was equal to it. His public services in the church suffered no diminution. He took as prominent a part as before in every great political movement. Many wondered how he was able to overtake such an amount of work. The secret lay in the resources of his mind, and of a memory that never forgot anything. His old habits of study largely aided him. He always rose at four in the morning, and wrote till seven. Then he spent from half an hour to an hour in his garden. Breakfast came at eight, and was followed by an unceasing stream of visitors, continuing usually till noon. This was the time of greatest worry and annoyance. People called to consult him on every conceivable subject. Now, it was a peer, or member of Parliament, on politics; now, a deputation on Church matters; now, a servant out of place; now, a poor widow, trying to recover some remnant of her husband's property. His wonderful sagacity, his vast influence, his tender heart, his genial sympathy, made his house a centre of attraction. His purse, too, was ever open. He could not resist an appeal for help. Many a distressed family was relieved, and many an unfortunate minister and struggling young man, was saved from exposure, perhaps from ruin, by his generous liberality. He was often imposed upon. His papers show that not a few, of whom better things might have been expected, took advantage of his noble generosity, to obtain from him sums which he could ill spare, and which they apparently never thought of repaying.

When receiving visits he had always an open book before him, in the perusal of which he occupied every spare moment. His power of abstraction was remarkable. He could read, and think, and write, amid the din of conversation, with as much ease and freedom as if alone in his study. From twelve to three, when he had no meetings to attend, or visits to pay, he retired to the vestry of May Street Church, where he had a few works of reference, and where none could get access to him. There he generally wrote his letters and prepared his sermons. Four was his dinner hour. After it, he was usually free from systematic work, though never idle, and seldom taking part in conversation, except when strangers were present, which was very often the case, for his hospitality was proverbial. When alone with his family he read current literature. Every new work which appeared on history, geology, chemistry, and political economy, was eagerly devoured. These were his favourite subjects during spare hours. He retired early, but read or wrote in his own room till far on in the night. He slept little ; never more than five hours, including, in latter years, a short siesta after dinner. He had an iron constitution, which seemed to be braced, not worn, by severe and protracted mental toil.

He read quickly, marking with signs of approval or dissent, such passages as struck him. He did not care for reading borrowed books ; he bought all he required, and not unfrequently gave them away to some friend after perusal. He rarely made separate notes on any book or subject which he studied, but his perceptive power was so quick, and his memory so retentive, that he was able to master a subject or book in an incredibly short time.

His lectures on Ethics and Natural Theology created a sensation in Belfast. They were so highly appreciated that the members of his class resolved to unite in a public expression of admiration and thanks. At the close of the Session they presented him with a splendid gold watch, bearing a suitable inscription. The address which accompanied it was read by Mr. (now the Reverend) John Meneely, whose devoted friendship through life, and unremitting care and attention during his last illness, were a source of high gratification to Dr. Cooke himself, and can never be forgotten by his mourning family. The Synod of Ulster, at its annual meeting in 1835, unanimously agreed, " That the warmest thanks of this Synod are due to the Rev. Dr. Cooke, and the Rev. H. W. Molyneux, for the readiness with which, at an important juncture, they undertook the instruction of the students of this Church in Moral Philosophy; for the zeal, ability, and success with which they discharged the duties of that office ; and that it be referred to the Committee of Overtures to consider what suitable mark of gratitude it is in the power of the Synod to confer upon them."

A somewhat painful experience had now shown the accuracy of Dr. Cooke's prediction regarding Mr. Ferrie's appointment to the chair of Moral Philosophy. It was a fatal mistake. It involved both the Synod and the Institution in great difficulties, and to none was it more painful than to Mr. Ferrie himself. The subject came up for discussion in connection with the College Committee report, in the Synod of 1835. The question was one of extreme delicacy. It was admitted on all hands that Mr. Ferrie was an able and earnest man. It was admitted that during the first three Sessions his lectures were, on the whole, sound. He had followed the system of Brown, and of other Scotch philosophers. But influenced by the Millian analysis, he afterwards changed his system, and introduced principles which would lead, in their full logical development, to atheism. This was proved in the public papers. It is a remarkable fact, that the first to expose Mr. Ferrie's erroneous teaching, was the Rev. Dr. Bruce, who, under the signature of

"Erasmus," declared that his doctrines were at variance with the first principles of religion. Mr. Ferrie defended his system; but a writer, who signed " Presbyterian," with great acuteness and erudition, showed its atheistical tendency.

The Synod had now a painful duty to discharge. It had suffered in former times, its very existence had been perilled, by the erroneous teachings of philosophical and theological professors. Dr. Cooke determined that no effort should be spared to secure the sound and efficient training of candidates for the ministry. During a keen debate he spoke plainly and forcibly. He condemned the Managing Board of the Institution for having elected Mr. Ferrie, in opposition to the expressed wishes of the Synod. He condemned them for attempting to shield him when convicted, by the testimony of his own students, of teaching doctrines calculated to undermine the foundations of faith in God's Word. His speech carried the house. The Rev. P. Shuldham Henry, now President of Queen's College, moved a resolution which was unanimously adopted : " That this Synod do not see any cause to alter the decision of the special Synod at Cookstown, by which students under the care of this Church are directed not to attend the Moral Philosophy Class in the Belfast Royal College, so long as it is conducted by the present Professor."

Although Arians had been forced to withdraw from the Synod of Ulster, and although by the organization of the Theological Committee, and a careful oversight of the training of students, a barrier was raised against the re-entrance of heresy, it was felt that the safeguards of the Church were not yet sufficiently established. The Law passed in 1825 did not make subscription to the Confession of Faith imperative on candidates for ordination. It merely provided that the Presbytery " shall ascertain the soundness of their faith, either by requiring subscription to the Westminster Confession, or by such examinations as they shall consider best adapted for this purpose." The alternative was thought by many to be a dangerous one. It left a power in the hands of a

Presbytery which, through laxity, or declension from high Gospel truth, might prove fatal to the Church. The celebrated Overtures of 1828, though they secured adherence to the fundamental doctrines set forth in the Westminster Standards, went no further in regard to subscription than the Law of 1825. The subject was brought before the Synod in 1829, and again in 1832, by the Rev. (now Dr.) John Brown, of Aghadoey. But it was not till 1835, that a final decision was come to. The question was introduced by overture, and after a long debate, the following resolution was passed, and has since been the law of the Presbyterian Church in Ireland :—" Whereas doubts appear to exist respecting the meaning and extent of the resolution of last Synod, not to sustain any exceptions opposing the doctrines of the Confession of Faith ; and whereas it is most desirable in itself, and indispensable to the renewal and maintenance of ecclesiastical communion with other Presbyterian churches, to adhere to an unqualified subscription of the Westminster Confession of Faith :—This Synod do now declare, in accordance with the resolution adopted at the last annual meeting of this Body, that they will not, from this time forth, receive any exceptions or explanations from candidates for the ministry ; and require, that all who in future wish to become licentiates or ministers of this Church, shall subscribe its Standards in terms of the formula agreed upon at Monaghan in the year 1832, which is as follows :—I believe the Westminster Confession of Faith to be founded on, and agreeable to, the Word of God, and as such I subscribe it as the confession of my faith."

CHAPTER XII.

1835—1836.

Agitation against Ecclesiastical Establishments—Dr. Ritchie arrives in Belfast— Discussion on "Voluntaryism" between Drs. Cooke and Ritchie—Effects of Dr. Cooke's Eloquence—Defeat and Flight of Dr. Ritchie—Letter of Mr. William Cairns—Report of the Discussion and Reviews—Re-establishment of Ecclesiastical Communion between the Synod of Ulster and the Church of Scotland—Dr. Cooke's Speech in the General Assembly—His Reception in Scotland—Degree of LL.D. from Trinity College—Mission to Scotland on the Education Question—Controversy with Mr. Massie—Conclusion of the Clough Case—Presentation of Plate to Mr. Macrory.

AFTER the passing of the Reform Bill a determined attack began to be made upon the Ecclesiastical Establishments of Great Britain. The attack was directed by a great political party. It was soon felt that the Church was in danger. Abuses could not be cloaked. Friends were, unfortunately, not always judicious in their line of defence. They would not acknowledge defects or anomalies, and they would not submit to reform. Enemies, on the other hand, were united, determined, and noisy. They agitated the country, and besieged the doors of the Legislature. Commissions of inquiry into the state of the English Church were appointed. The leading Minister of the Crown seemed ready to grant whatever the popular voice might demand.

The Scotch Establishment did not escape. It was assailed by a party which had sprung from its own bosom. The Seceders had, strangely enough, engrafted Voluntaryism upon the ecclesiastical principles of the Erskines, and now tried to overthrow the Church of their fathers. The leader of the Voluntary crusade in Scotland was the Rev. Dr. Ritchie, of

Edinburgh. He was qualified for the office : he was fluent in speech, practised in debate, popular in address, and filled with anecdotes illustrative of the abuses of ecclesiastical establishments in general, and that of Scotland in particular.

Voluntaryism had never flourished in Ireland. Hitherto it had a hard struggle for bare existence. A few of its enthusiastic adherents in and around Belfast believed that the day of its regeneration had come, and they sent for Dr. Ritchie. It was the spring of 1836. Arrangements were made by the Belfast committee to celebrate his advent by a soirée, to be held on the 15th of March. The evening came, and the hall was crowded; for it had got abroad somehow that Dr. Cooke would be present. The assembly was not disappointed; Dr. Cooke, having written a polite note stating his intention, appeared upon the scene. After tea, and a number of minor speeches, Dr. Ritchie rose. His address was such as might have been expected from a man who anticipated an easy victory. It was sparkling, plausible, and shallow. Evidently he did not know the opponent he had to deal with. He despised the opposition, and he suffered for it. As soon as he had finished, Dr. Cooke rose. His appearance was the signal for a storm of hisses and cheers. It was soon manifest that more of Dr. Cooke's friends were present than had been desired by the projectors of the soirée. The chairman refused to hear him; but he persisted, and his friends enthusiastically applauded. He said Dr. Ritchie had invaded Ireland; he had come to assail a principle which was dear to nine-tenths of the Protestants of Ulster; he must, therefore, be prepared to discuss its merits. To refuse would be cowardice. His very presence in Belfast was a challenge; his speech that evening was a challenge; and now he, Dr. Cooke, was there to accept the challenge, and meet him in fair and open controversy. The excitement was intense. There was no escape for the Voluntary party, even had they desired escape. Dr. Cooke spoke briefly, but effectively. He ridiculed Dr. Ritchie's assault on establishments. He showed that it was illogical and childish; and he concluded by describing, in terms of racy humour and caustic sarcasm, the Voluntary crusade in Belfast.

It was arranged that the question at issue should be discussed. For that purpose a meeting was convened for the evening of March 17th. The friends of Voluntaryism were to speak first, and Dr. Cooke was to reply. On the morning of that day, Dr. Cooke, whose health had been in a delicate state for some time, took seriously ill. When the appointed hour arrived he was with difficulty conveyed to the large hall, which was crowded in every part by an excited audience. Religion and politics combined to rouse the people of Belfast almost to a state of phrensy. Dr. Cooke's political principles were, if possible, more offensive to the Voluntary leaders than his views regarding ecclesiastical establishments. They had been gaining ground, besides, in Belfast and Ulster. His eloquence and influence had contributed to place them in the ascendant. Unless his career could be checked the power of Radicalism must soon cease; hence the intensity of feeling manifested by the friends of Dr. Ritchie; hence, too, the enthusiasm of those who stood by Dr. Cooke.

The chair was occupied by Dr. Tennent; and the nature of his views may be gathered from the few introductory words he addressed to the audience. He observed that " the meeting was called by the friends of religious liberty; yet, though their title and their object were both so excellent, it was possible, it was even understood, there was likely to be opposition. He hoped, however, the meeting would hear, with patience and impartiality, whatever might be advanced. He himself was not present to speak, but to hear what might be advanced by others capable of explaining the great principles of the meeting. One of these great principles—it might be called the sumtotal of their principles—was this, that no man should be called on to pay for the religious instruction of another, against the light of his own conscience. He stood, and would ever stand, upon this principle; and he trusted the meeting would concur with him in its adoption."

Dr. Cooke was thus manifestly in the enemy's camp. He could expect no favour, and he might get scant justice; but he did not shrink. The crowd and the enthusiasm roused him; and though he had before him a host of adversaries, he boldly faced them all.

The Rev. Mr. McIlwaine, from Ohio, opened the discussion by pronouncing a glowing eulogy on Voluntaryism and its results in America. He was followed by the Rev. John Alexander, a Covenanting minister, who stated that, while he believed establishments in the abstract were scriptural, he was opposed to all existing established Churches. Next came the Rev. Mr. McIntyre, the representative of a small body of Seceders. At length Dr. Ritchie addressed the meeting :—

" Mr. Chairman,—It is necessary, before proceeding to the subject in hand, to justify myself from the charge of invading a hitherto peaceful town. I deny that I invaded it. I came by special invitation. I came to Ireland for the good of the land. Ireland, of all countries in the world, most needs universal reform. Examine the map of Europe, and you will find no country so badly governed for the last three hundred years. It is a country of which it may be said, especially when I view its religious establishments, that iniquity is established by law. In a country constituted like Ireland no nuisance can be greater than the present Law Church, which provides for a contemptible minority out of the pockets of the overwhelming majority; and not merely out of the pockets of the majority, but out of their toil, and sweat, and blood. These things are the relics of wicked and unpopular Governments; but now, under the administration of Lord Melbourne, the nation possesses the best and most popular Government that ever ruled its destinies. They will not spare antiquated abuses under the name of ancient institutions."

After this political exordium, he entered at length on the abuses of the Scotch Establishment, relating numerous and absurd anecdotes, which afforded great amusement to the audience. He defended the policy of Voluntaries in uniting with

Papists and infidels in attempts to overthrow the national Churches. Turning at length to Ireland, he said :—

" With respect to the *Regium Donum*, I look upon it, as a previous speaker has said, as degrading the Synod of Ulster to the level of Maynooth, and as fettering and enslaving her ministers and congregations. One of my objects is to free that Synod from its present trammels, and to raise it in public estimation. A similar good will I feel towards the Established Churches of Scotland and England. Our object is not to destroy, but to purify; to emancipate the Churches from the iron grasp of the State, and to send them forth into the world, depending upon nothing but their own resources, to sink or swim, according as they lose or retain the affections of the people. Above everything, we should wish to rescue the Synod of Ulster from the system of *Regium Donum*, were it merely on account of the man (Lord Castlereagh) by whom it was chiefly augmented—a man of whom it has, as I think, been justly said, that the best action of his life was that by which it was ended."

It was half-past ten o'clock when Dr. Ritchie concluded, and Dr. Cooke rose to reply :—

" I am bound to thank the managers of this meeting for the privilege of reply, while I entreat the candour and sympathy of the audience, on account of bodily weakness, as it is known to my friends that I have literally risen from a sick bed. I more particularly crave the candour of my audience, as, while my antagonists have come in the full feather of preparation, I am without time or opportunity to arrange a thought or consult an authority. That my antagonists were fully prepared is manifest from what the meeting have heard. Mr. McIlwaine led the van as a sharp-shooter, with a well-charged Indian rifle; Mr. Alexander, the first line, with the heavy artillery of Selden, Blackstone, and Coke upon Littleton ; then came Mr. McIntyre with four well-trained squadrons of heavy dragoons, but as expert and alert as a cloud of Don Cossacks. Dr. Ritchie himself, the general of the field, brings up the rear ; and for my own part, when I observed the ' squalling, snoring, and roaring boys ' he has collected and drilled, I could scarcely believe their leader a Scotchman, or his troops the plaided hosts of his

native hills; but I took the whole division for my own dear countrymen, and imagined I saw General Doyle and the *Fagh-a-Ballaghs*
hurrying on to Talavera, and replying to a peal of French artillery
with a peal of Irish laughter, and answering heavy lead with light
wit."

Dr. Cooke's plan was clear and effective. He commenced
with a few general observations, to throw light upon the insidious character of the attacks on Establishments, and to
expose the strange operations of the Belfast Voluntaries. He
then reviewed the speeches of his opponents, meeting argument
with argument and stories of abuses with cutting irony and
withering sarcasm. In venturing on such a mode of controversy Dr. Ritchie mistook his ground. Unwittingly he put a
weapon in his adversary's hand, which was dexterously turned
against him, and wielded with the skill of a master. Towards
the close of his address Dr. Cooke defined establishments,
freeing them from the haze in which Dr. Ritchie had enveloped them; he then defended them by clear and convincing
arguments drawn from the Word of God.

The skill with which Dr. Cooke, in his introductory remarks,
gained the ear of an adverse audience, shows the practised controversialist and accomplished orator :—

"Should Dr. Ritchie triumph in argument as he has done in wit,
and carry even involuntary conviction to every mind, I shall,
rejoice ; for no one should be grieved at any of the triumphs of
truth. I trust there is not a minister in any Protestant Establishment or endowed Church in the land that would prefer the paltry
possession of pounds, shillings, and pence to the gain of godliness
and the book-keeping of a quiet conscience. Let Voluntaryism first
succeed in renouncing every principle of the early Puritans, the
persecuted Covenanters, and the original Secession ; let them next,
like Claverhouse, the prince of Voluntaries, harry and spoliate the
Establishment; and let the mothers in Israel, when expelled from
their manses and their glebes, have again to call, like her of An-
crum, ' God's will be done ! Fetch the creels again to carry the poor
bairns.' Still, I trust there are ministers, and wives, and children,
who, in the spirit of their martyred fathers, will take joyfully the

spoiling of their goods, and 'possess their souls in patience,' till the God that permits the storm shall send better days."

Referring to Dr. Ritchie's assault upon the Church of Scotland, and a most virulent attack upon Dr. Chalmers, Dr. Cooke said :—

"Are these fair and honest specimens of Scotland's ministers and Scotland's congregations ? Supposing—admitting—them to be true, still what are they ? They are just as if I should attempt to write the history of the Ulster gentry, and draw the materials from the annals of ' Castle Rack-rent '—an individual picture too true to the original, but, as a general description of the landlords of Down and Antrim, at once a fictitious and a libellous caricature. Above all, what are men to think of the system which depends for its zest upon holding up to ridicule the incomparable Chalmers ? The man who, with the eagle wing of a genius at once soaring and sanctified, ascended the highest heaven of contemplation, and then descended again to earth, telling of the heart-beatings, deep and intense, with which the inhabitants of the higher, resting in peace, gaze upon the worshippers of the lower sanctuary, still struggling in war ; the man who, from the loftiest aspirings of science, descended to the lowest concerns of everyday existence, penetrated to the lanes and garrets of the city of his habitation, that he might return with mind full fraught with the story of the misery and destitution he had witnessed ; the man who first roused the mind of Scotland to the glorious enterprise of Christian aggression upon the regions of popular ignorance ; the man who, still unwearied, labours to increase the number of Scotland's Churches and ministers. Yet this man, at once the honour of his country, of Christianity, and of human nature—this man must be caricatured in his projects of Christian benevolence, and represented as a mere visionary, unworthy the favourable consideration and confidence of a Board of Church Commissioners."

The semi-political character of the meeting was only too apparent. Dr. Ritchie admitted it ; and Dr. Cooke here turned upon the political partizan with tremendous effect :—

"Another general feature of this meeting, more especially exhibited by Dr. Ritchie, demands animadversion before I can come to close quarters with my reverend opponents. I mean the line of procedure by which Dr. Ritchie has converted a proposed religious meeting into a political club. Dr. Ritchie, as if to ensure the identification of a Voluntary and political meeting, has first lauded the Melbourne Administration by name, as the best of all possible Governments, the best that England ever saw. Well, doctors differ on more points than physic. But what business has my Lord Melbourne, as a politician, to be dragged into a meeting professedly called for religious purposes? Next followed the praises of Radicalism and agitation. Now, who does not know that agitation is just a discreet name for Daniel O'Connell, and that Radicalism is but another word for the destruction of the House of Lords? Ay, if my reverend friend and his confederates do once succeed in letting loose the fierce democracy, they will soon realise Dr. Ritchie's splendid picture of Radicalism. The roots, the aristocracy, sustaining at once both the trunk of kingly power and the wide-spreading branches of the populace; the roots giving stability to every part of the national tree; let them be grubbed by the Radical mattock, and hewn through by the Radical axe, and trunk and branches will tumble together, and the whole shall be trodden down by the iron heel of another Cromwell, canting in the name of civil and religious liberty, while he is forging the chains of despotism to shackle and enslave his country. And agitation, too, must have its apotheosis! and, because, it is a sombre subject, must be enlivened by the accompaniment of a dairy-maid and a churn-dash. Yes, my reverend friend and his co-mates on this platform may talk of the militant attitude of an Establishment, as if they had studied under Harry Hotspur himself; and they may tell of 'guns, and drums, and wounds;' but I shall fearlessly tell them, that the real blood-shedder in Ireland is agitation. The insatiate Moloch demands the sacrifice, and the blood is shed by his worshippers to appease his appetite."

In replying to the arguments and statements of his opponents, Dr. Cooke made skilful use of Franklin's maxim —" When you have got a good principle go through with it." The chairman, had affirmed, in his opening speech, that " no man should be called upon to pay for the religious instruction of another against the light of his own conscience."

" The plaudits with which the sentiment was received," replied Dr. Cooke, "justify me in attributing it to the whole party of which the chairman is a distinguished leader. Well, let it pass with this observation, if it be a good principle go through with it. And let it be applied first to that precious protégé of the best of all possible Governments, the National Board of Education. That Board supports, or did support—for there is no telling to what reforms public opinion may compel private shame—that Board supports, or did support, the Friary and Nunnery Schools in Galway, the Jesuits' School at Clongowes, with others such in Dublin and elsewhere ; and yet Protestants, against their consciences, are compelled to pay their quota of the assessment ; and not only is the chairman silent on the subject of this oppression, but, if report tell true, he was one amongst the very first to become a patron and defender of the system ! And surely, never did the tenderest Voluntary conscience more shrink from either giving or receiving a church endowment than do hundreds and thousands of Protestant consciences revolt against the support of a Popish school. A Popish school held within the very precincts of a nunnery, a monastery, or a chapel; with nuns, monks, and lay brothers for teachers ; with Doyle's Catechism for a school-book, teaching small stealing, or small lying, to be venial sins, and angel-worship or staff-worship, to be holy and righteous services. Yet strangers must be convened from the ends of the earth, meetings must be called, and tea and oratory must flow in equal streams, and all the fair faces of the town must be summoned to preside over the libation, and all the tender hearts must be taught to palpitate in gentlest sympathy over the agony of a Voluntary conscience, if compelled to pay a farthing for Protestantism; yet the self-same parties cheer on the men that despise the petitions, trample on·the liberties, and exult in the tortures of a Protestant conscience, when compelled to make payment for Popery. I shall bring the chairman's applauded sentiment a second time to Dr. Franklin's test. 'No man,' says the chairman, 'should be compelled to pay for the religious instruction of another against his own conscience.' Admirable sentiment ! Maynooth to wit. Some nine thousand a year is annually voted by the British Parliament, for the exclusive education of Roman Catholic priests in the precepts of Delahogue and the mysteries of Peter Dens. What tender Voluntary conscience has shrunk ? What Voluntary soirée has assembled ? What Voluntary orator has cried aloud ? What Voluntary petition was presented, to abate that national nuisance ? None, none. Let

Voluntaries, then, be silent on the subject of a tender conscience; for no conscience can be tender till it has learned to be impartial."

Mr. McIlwaine had lauded the American Churches; he had described in glowing colours their wonderful success; and yet, he said, they had never received, never desired assistance from the State; they would not have prospered had they done so; they would "consider legal endowment degrading, polluting, or destructive."

"Pray," said Dr. Cooke, in reply, " do any of those devoted, humble, voluntary, endowment-abhorring ministers, of whom Mr. McIlwaine has spoken—do any of them reside in the slave-holding States ?"

Mr. McIlwaine at once acknowledged that many of them did so, and received, besides, stipends from slave-holding masters. With cutting irony, Dr. Cooke replied :—

"Well, well! The delicacy of some ministers, like the delicacy of some appetites, is truly wonderful! Some men faint at the smell of cheese : others, to the attar of roses prefer the perfume of ripe Stilton. *De gustibus non est disputandum;* nor shall I infringe the canon. Still I may be permitted to admire that ecclesiastical *gourmanderie* which rejects State endowments as abhorrently as tartar-emetic, yet can swallow and digest the bones, sinews, liberties, and souls of slaves."

This keen retort excited the wrath of Mr. McIlwaine and his friends. Mr. McIlwaine cried out, in high indignation, " This attack is ungenerous." A gentleman beside him gave utterance to a very audible *hiss.* Dr. Cooke, however, had the ear of the meeting. The great majority felt that he ought to have fair play; and the cry was raised, " Put out the man who hissed." But Dr. Cooke interfered; and by a happy home-thrust restored the good humour of the audience.

" I am not certain," he observed, "that it was a hiss at all ; nor is there any special proof that it was intended for me, or my conscience-searching statement. But if it were a hiss intended for me, I beg to assure the meeting I am quite prepared for such politeness. I have been hissed a hundred times by—a goose."

This was followed by a peal of laughter, and Dr. Cooke was not again interrupted while he administered a sharp and merited rebuke to his Transatlantic antagonist :—

" My American friend has called my allusion to slavery ungenerous; and let him call it so if he will; but in Ireland men are accustomed to say, Be just before you be generous. My observation was just, for it was a thorough-going application of the great Franklin's principle. But my observation was not merely just; it was generous, too. I am one of those who have always thanked Providence for American Independence. England and America, under one Government, would have unbalanced the freedom of the world. America, no doubt, like England, has her faults ; but, like England, ' with all her faults, I love her still.' But, if ever it be my lot, as I wish it may one day be, to visit America, I shall devote myself exclusively to my religious duties, and I shall keep studiously aloof from all her political parties. I shall neither spout on her platforms as a Federalist nor as an anti-Federalist. I shall admire her Jacksons and her Clays, but refuse to be either Jacksonite or Clayite. I shall visit her as a citizen of the world, and return without having identified myself with any of her local individualities. It was generous, therefore, when I gave a lesson to American ministers, and admonished them to avoid galling their neighbours. Let American ministers come to Europe, to give and receive the helps of mutual faith ; and not, like our present worthy visitant, to commingle their voices with the shout of the Radical, or the crash of agitation. . . . Why, after having, accidentally or purposely, identified himself with agitators and Radicals, in a public meeting, and joined to denounce some of the long-cherished institutions of the land—why does he exclaim against all reference to the unreformed American institution of slavery, and denounce the allusion as unfair or ungenerous? But again I affirm the allusion was most generous. It was generous to the slave-master, whom I would rouse to self-examination, through the twitchings of public opinion, expressed, not by those who hate and would rob him, but by those who pity the false position in which the errors of other days have placed him, and who would say to

America, as they said to England, 'Pay for breaking the chains your
own laws have riveted.' Above all, it was generous to the American
character, in which there is so much to admire, with a few things to
regret ; and, more especially, that deification of self, and supercilious
contempt of other Governments, with which America's children
often dance round the cap of liberty, and chant the hymn of Independence, while the chains of their slaves rattle like the castanets
of a *figurante*, and the deep groans of their captives respond, in
melancholy accompaniment to the shrill-voiced treble of the public
joy. My reference to American slavery is called ungenerous; I
rejoice it was called so. The patient cries loudest when the surgeon is adjusting the broken limb. But where was the cry of ungenerous when the previous speakers were feeding the Church
Establishments, like cannibals, on human blood, and denouncing
them, not only as the neglecters, but the despoilers, of widows
and of orphans! Who raised the cry of 'ungenerous' then? Who
offered to move a tongue in defence of the calumniated and the
absent? Calumniate Scotland's ministers, and you are cheered.
Calumniate Ireland's ministers, and you are huzzaed. But touch
only the garment of American slave-holding, and your conduct is
instantly denounced as disgraceful and ungenerous. Oh! may I ever
be covered with such disgrace! May I ever be guilty of being so
generously ungenerous!"

The effect of his speech was overwhelming. The audience
were completely carried away by the power of his eloquence.
His antagonists had laid themselves open to his criticisms ;
and he used his advantage with unsparing hand. When the
meeting became impatient or noisy, a flash of wit, or a brilliant
repartee, restored good humour. Through the long night the
people remained, and the orator continued to speak with a
freshness of illustration and a force of argument that seemed
inexhaustible. At length, when the morning light began to
stream in through the windows, he said :—" I now trust that,
in mercy to me and to themselves, the meeting will adjourn.
If Providence and health permit, I pledge myself to return
and resume the subject where I left off." The meeting
adjourned accordingly.

At six o'clock on the succeeding evening the doors of the

hall were again thrown open. Admission was by ticket. In a few minutes the place was crowded. The excitement was even greater than on the previous night. It had gone abroad that the Voluntaries had the worst of the battle. They, therefore, mustered in force, as if resolved to gain by numbers what they lost by argument. It was alleged that unfair means had been used to prevent the free and impartial distribution of tickets. To this Dr. Cooke referred in strong terms in his opening speech :—

"I denounce the conduct of the Voluntaries to their faces, and arraign them of corrupt practices in plotting to pack this meeting."

Dr. Cooke had, during the day, been supplied with some American papers, which described in touching terms the spiritual destitution prevailing in many of the Western cities and villages. From these he read a number of extracts, some of them giving a sad picture of Ohio, the very State from which Mr. McIlwaine had come. The effect on Mr. McIlwaine, on his brother Voluntaries, and on the audience can be easily imagined, especially when, at the close of each telling fact and painful revelation, Dr. Cooke exclaimed, " Oh ! but the Voluntary system, we are told, works well in America ! "

Having, by a torrent of argument, wit, and sarcasm, overwhelmed his assailants, he proceeded to define and defend his own views of establishments :—

" The first proposition I lay down and defend amounts to this, that every State is bound to make Christianity the law of the land, and enact no law contrary to its letter or spirit. In my second proposition I distinguish between establishments and endowments ; and, though I must maintain that every State is bound to make such provision as is requisite or in its power ; yet as circumstances may be supposed where maintenance is not needed, or where a Government has nothing to give ; in such a case the duty of establishment exists in full force, but the duty of endowment is modified by the circumstances.

"To save trouble to my antagonists, I shall make three distinct reservations. First, I take nothing to do with particular forms of establishment. I do not come here to advocate Prelacy, Presbyterianism, or Independency. I discuss establishments, not forms of Church government. Second, I must set it down as a point, that I do not come here to defend the abuses of any establishment, any more than I would defend the conduct of individual ministers, who are frail and sinful like other men. Nor do I come here to defend every Act of Parliament by which establishments are recognised or maintained. Parliaments, like other councils, may err; and their object may be legitimate, when special enactments may be indefensible. Third, I do not allow of the captivity of the Church by the State. To a certain degree I am myself supported by the State; but were Government to demand one single concession of the liberty wherewith Christ hath made His Church free, I would fling back their gift as a polluting bribe, that disgraced, though enriched, the unworthy acceptor. But whatever aid the Synod of Ulster receives, she receives it without compromise of principle or surrender of liberty. The people are free; the ministers are free. They may be calumniated and said to be enslaved by those who are ignorant of facts, or speak falsely for interested purposes; but there lives not the man who dares look the Synod of Ulster in the face, and point his accusing finger to any plague-spot of her slavery. I stand now before the men who have brought the accusation; I pronounce it a calumny, and I dare them to the proof."

Dr. Cooke then proceeded at great length to lay down and enforce his arguments and proofs, and he succeeded in triumphantly establishing his several propositions. In the course of his speech he had occasion to mention an Act of Parliament to prevent legalised violations of the Sabbath, passed when Lord Castlereagh was Prime Minister, and promoted by him. This recalled to Dr. Cooke's mind the unseemly attack made upon the memory of that great statesman in the close of Dr. Ritchie's speech, and it inspired one of the most magnificent bursts of eloquence ever heard by any audience. The meeting was electrified. Paid reporters were present to take down the speeches; but in the midst of this sublime passage their excitement became so intense that they dropped their pencils, and sat trembling, with eyes riveted on the speaker. When it was concluded they tried to recall the words; others aided them; Dr. Cooke himself was subsequently asked for his assistance: it was all in vain. The published report is fine, splendid; but it is cold and feeble compared with the grand sentences as they flowed from the lips of the impassioned orator. He spoke of "that great man whose slumbering ashes have been so unfeelingly disturbed : "—

"Oh!" he exclaimed, "is there no lapse of years will wear away the perennial hate of party? Will the coffin and the grave afford no protection against its vampire appetite? Will the stroke by which mysterious Heaven extinguishes the lamp of reason, extract no tear of pity from the eye of iron-hearted man? Will it form the very text upon which theological partizanship shall utter its unfeeling commentaries of exulting sarcasm and unappeasable hate? Charity! charity! where is that mantle with which thou hast been wont to cover the multitude of a neighbour's transgressions? Is it now the office of the loudest advocate to tear the mantle aside, and expose to the rudest gaze the errors of both the living and the dead; the errors of a mind exhausted with the toils of thought; the error of the frenzied hour when reason reels and lunacy is in the ascendant? Oh! might not the act of that unhappy hour be consigned to the recesses of oblivion, or charitably be supposed to lie beyond the verge of accountability? Might not, in such a case, the 'accusing spirit, as he flew up to Heaven's chancery with the account, blush as he gave it in, and the recording spirit drop a tear upon it, and blot it out for ever?' In heaven it might be so, where mercy tempers justice. And on earth shall there be no mercy? Shall the commissioned advocate of reform, who assumes all humanity for his client, not only assail the errors of the living, but, hunting amidst the tombs of the dead, shall he, like another Old Mortality, be seen, with steeled chisel and incessant mallet, deepening those records of human frailty or of mysterious judgments which the winds and the rains of heaven were mercifully providing to obliterate?"

He quoted at some length the proofs of the Divine origin of establishments recorded in the Old Testament. They were

clear and conclusive, and consequently not palatable to Dr.
Ritchie and his friends, one of whom, with considerable
evidences of irritation, cried out, "Go to the New Law—
that's all Mosaic." "Go to common sense," retorted Dr.
Cooke, turning quickly upon his rude interrupter, "and that
will be a new journey for you. Go to good manners, and that
may be a new acquaintance. Go to patience, and that will be
a new virtue." Every interruption, in fact, he turned against
his assailants. Every attempt to confuse him, or put him
down by clamour, he, with consummate tact and skill, converted into an instrument for pointing his own keen satire,
and securing the attention, if not always the assent, of his
hearers. When closing he said :—

"I am happy that I do not now, as last night, stand alone in
front of so many formidable foes. The Rev. Mr. Wilson, of Towns-
end Street, is by my side ; near me stands my learned young friend,
Mr. Blackwood, of Holywood ; and in front sits Mr. Gibson, a
valiant son of the Covenant. Voluntarious deputies may, therefore,
be sure of opponents. I last night considered it my duty to stand
forth and bear testimony in these days, and tell those unthinking
men, whose watch-word is 'separate Church and State,' that they
were speaking of a subject they had never studied and did not understand. I feel it also to be a singular privilege, that I have been
able to bear testimony to the principles of my forefathers, the
honoured Covenanters of Scotland. By their principles I stand, and
maintain that our Lord Jesus Christ is Lord of heaven and earth,
King of kings, and 'Head over all things to His Church.' I rejoice that there still exists in these days a stern and unyielding
Presbyterian band, who, like their own banner of true blue, neither
blanch in the rays of the sun, nor rend with the blasts of the storm.
If, in the heat and hurry of argument, I have uttered a word calculated to give offence, I am sorry for it ; and I beg to assure my
opponents that, if such a word has escaped my lips, it has not come
from the heart. And if I have occasionally made use of sarcasm,
who was the first to set the example ? I knew something of the
mode of warfare adopted by my chief opponent, and was determined
from the outset, that if I heard raillery for reasoning, and ridicule
for argument, I should try to convince my reverend opponents they

had chosen a game at which two could play. If all had been plain, blunt argument I should have confined myself to argument; but it was my duty to return whatever fire the enemy gave, and, if possible, to point his captured artillery upon his own ranks. I have shotted, however, my last discharge with such heavy argument, that I long to see my opponents attempt to return the fire. I have raised up a scriptural fortress, and taken post on its high towers; and I know those walls will remain unscathed when the agitations of Voluntaryism are sunk into the calm of exhaustion, and the roar of its artillery is hushed into everlasting silence."

Dr. Cooke spoke for five hours. Dr. Ritchie's reply occupied three, and Dr. Cooke's rejoinder about an hour. Point after point, objection after objection, was brought forward by Dr. Ritchie with much tact and skill: but each argument and statement was placed under the knife of a logical anatomist, cut in pieces, and held up a subject of surprise and laughter to every thoughtful man. A charge that has been more than once preferred against those Presbyterians who venture to defend establishments, was thus met by Dr. Cooke:—

" Dr. Ritchie makes an ingenious attempt, by quoting from the Scots' Covenant, either to compel me to renounce its established principles, or to bind me hand and foot to the extirpation of Prelacy; consequently, to embroil me in warfare with the Church of England, or convict me of inconsistency in being its friend. A dilemma is always the best or worst argument. In the present case Dr. Ritchie's horns would not be able to suspend a fly. I could extricate myself by affixing my reverend friend in my stead; for, when a Voluntary has the effrontery to accuse an Establishment-Presbyterian of consorting with Black Prelacy, let him retort, and accuse the Voluntary of consorting with Red Popery. Is not the Voluntary Seceder bound to extirpate Popery? If not, what Original Secession principle does he retain? But I will not attempt to escape in this way, though it effectually silences the Secession Voluntary; but will meet the question directly. The Covenanters vowed to extirpate Black Prelacy; so does Dr. Cooke. Had I lived in the days when Black Prelacy rode rough-shod over the liberties and lives of Presbyterians; and when, with the exception of the sainted Leighton,

it numbered in its ranks in Scotland scarcely a man of worth or
piety, I should have felt it my duty, by every constitutional means
and legal effort, to labour to abate or remove the nuisance.   And,
were the Prelacy of to-day of the same colour, and pursuing the
same course, I would meet it with the same opposition, and labour
by the same means for its removal.   Nay, were Presbyterianism to
be dyed in the same vat, I should feel it a duty to resist its claims
till it had washed its garments.   Prelacy, I admit, has not changed ;
but it is notorious prelates have.   The system of Church government remains unchanged ; but the character, piety, zeal, and
efficiency of the clergy have risen, and are rising every hour.   This
gives room for mutual forbearance on points of government and discipline, and gives a stimulus to brotherly kindness in matters of
truth and godliness. . . .   Dr. Ritchie has ingeniously, rather
than ingenuously, extracted one paragraph in which the Covenanters
were bound to extirpate Popery and Prelacy.   Now, extirpate is an
ugly word, for it may be misrepresented as referable to men, and not
to opinions; and Dr. Ritchie seems to have produced it in that sense.
If it refer to men, it is obnoxious; if to opinions, it is inoffensive.
For, taking extirpate to apply to opinions, it is a strong but most
harmless word.   I judge that, in this sense, every Prelatist holds
himself bound to extirpate Presbytery, while he is at the moment
the sincere, warm friend of Presbyterians ; that is, being convinced in his own mind that Bishops are superior to Presbyters, he
feels bound to propagate that opinion, and extirpate the opinion of
clerical equality.   And in all this, we may say, there is error; but
yet there is no persecution."

After this last speech the debate continued in brief addresses
and replies till six o'clock in the morning.   The scene is thus
described by an eye-witness :—" We were present at Dr.
Cooke's special request, and seated at his feet on the platform.
We had a full view of the audience, and witnessed the over-
powering effect that his magnificent oratory produced.   In his
usual style, he commenced by clearing his way, and gradually
it was found that he was building up a mighty argument.
From time to time he would take up one or other of the
sophistries which lay beside the truth he was establishing.
He would hold them up before the audience for their ridicule,
and with the strength of a giant he would tear them into frag-

ments and cast them aside. Then, as if relieved, he would burst into a corruscation of wit and humour, and with a brilliancy of fancy he would lift his audience up into an atmosphere of poetic beauty. As he concentrated his colossal sentences, piling member upon member, as his voice rose in majesty through the hall, until the summit of the climax was attained, it was a striking scene to witness the spell-bound listeners leaning forward, breathless, electrified, and at length when the sense was complete, as if the soul was satisfied, falling back in a mass to rest. . . . Never in any assembly had we beheld such an overwhelming power of mind in its highest development, producing its normal effect on the intellect of a multitude. It was as if the wand in the hand of a mighty magician had been swaying the audience to and fro, according to his will."

The concluding scene and the result of the debate are sketched with graphic power by a writer in the *Orthodox Presbyterian:*—" When the formality of speech-making was over, then came the tug of war, when Dr. Cooke demanded the answers of the Voluntary to a few questions. Here he shut him up completely. He reduced his argumentation to a complete absurdity. And the debate closed, leaving a deep impression on the mind of every impartial witness, that the cause of Voluntaryism was indefensible, and that Dr. Ritchie had received such a castigation, as the man merited who came to disturb the peace of the Churches and ministers of another country. So complete was his discomfiture, that, with a few exceptions, the very men who invited him, whether ashamed of the cause or its advocate we know not, fled from the scene of action before the debate was terminated. The time is not yet come when the people of this country will not require a law to protect the Sabbath day from violation, and forbid the practice of polygamy; but both the law of the Sabbath and of marriage are learned only from Revelation, and if legislated for by the Government of the country, the principle of an establishment is admitted."

When the meeting broke up Dr. Cooke's friends gathered round him, and carried him home in triumph amid the enthusiastic plaudits of a crowd of followers. The victory was decisive. Dr. Ritchie was literally overwhelmed with a flood of argument and splendid declamation. His Voluntary crusade in Ireland was at an end. He left abruptly, and returned to Edinburgh; but the tidings of his defeat followed him, and was hailed with delight by the Church of Scotland. The victory gained in Ireland was a victory for establishments. The influence of the little noisy party that had brought Dr. Ritchie to Belfast was overthrown, and political Voluntaryism received a blow from which it never recovered. Dr. Cooke was now the most popular man in Ulster. His fame spread over the kingdom. The principles he had defended with such distinguished success were common to the Established Churches of the empire, and their leading men were not slow to acknowledge his services.

From London, Mr. William Cairns, one of Dr. Cooke's most esteemed and most talented friends, wrote :—"I have not been able to find time sooner to congratulate you on the discomfiture of the Voluntaries, or that extraordinary collection from all parts of the political and religious compass which assembled in Belfast under that name. I have had no sufficiently intelligible account of the proceedings, but am waiting for it with anxiety, and particularly long to see some one qualified to relate what occurred ; and I feel in the meantime unspeakable satisfaction at the result.

" I last night witnessed Sir Robert Peel's superior powers as a public speaker in the House of Commons, and his triumph over the sophistries of Mr. Sheil, who, in a speech of much eloquence, but most afflicting to the ears, appeared as the mouthpiece of the Ministers in support of the third reading of the Irish Municipal Corporations Bill. . . . He made honourable mention of you in reply to some observations on the political interference and language of Priest Keough; but he qualified what he said with so much complimentary acknow-

ledgment of the justice of the high opinion which was entertained of you by your own Church, and the influence which you
possess, and ought to possess in it, that you could not have
found fault with what he said. He associated with you the
Bishop of Exeter."

An authentic report of the discussion was published, and
had an enormous sale. It was reviewed by some of the leading
periodicals, and Dr. Cooke's powers as an orator and controversialist formed the theme of general admiration. *The Church
of Scotland Magazine* says:—" We were previously aware of
Dr. Cooke's preeminent powers as a controversialist and
debater; but our perusal of this report has increased our
admiration an hundredfold. His speeches exhibit a freshness
and strength, both of thought and expression, peculiarly characteristic. There are frequent bursts of impassioned eloquence. His power of instant retort is admirable; his sarcasm
most biting and well applied; and, though he spurns vulgarity,
and descends to nothing like personalities—nothing that ever
giveᴗ unnecessary offence to the feelings of any—yet sometimes
we could not help pitying his opponents in their unsuccessful
attempts to lure him off from the contested ground. Yes, we
did pity his opponents, or rather his prey, in their vain
endeavours to escape, by leaping, and doubling, and burrow-
ing, and all their other peculiar arts. Dr. Ritchie had come by
special invitation, longing to deliver misruled Ireland. His
speech we do not think it necessary to refer to; it was just the
old and oft-repeated tale. . . . Dr. Cooke fights each man with
his own weapons. He takes up his antagonists one by one,
apparently without the slightest effort; and having amused his
audience with them for a little, lays them to rest with inimi-
table composure." In the course of a trenchant article *Frazer*
thus writes:—" The coarse jests of Dr. Ritchie, spouted in
every meeting-house in the north of England and Scotland,
the lame and pointless assaults of the Potterrow Voluntary on
all that is ancient and sacred, were laid hold on by Dr. Cooke,
and turned with such dexterity and force against their unhappy

utterer, that the pity of the audience was elicited for the man,
and their contempt and indignation poured on his cause.
Never, certainly, have we read arguments so appositely put,
wit and anecdote, and genuine humour, made more subser-
vient to the best and holiest of causes, than in the speeches of
Dr. Henry Cooke, reported in this pamphlet."

Dr. Cooke's triumph in the Voluntary controversy had an
important ecclesiastical result. The Presbyterian Church of
Ireland is a daughter of the Old Kirk of Scotland. But she
was long a degenerate daughter. The Arian heresy had largely
corrupted her ministry. She had forsaken or forgotten her
old honoured Standards, and the Church of Scotland would not
acknowledge her. Now, however, by the efforts and talents of
Henry Cooke, Arianism had been expelled, and subscription to
the Westminster Confession had been made imperative. The
way was thus open for the restoration of communion between
the Churches, and Dr. Cooke's defence of the establishment
principle proved the immediate cause of accomplishing the
desired end. The Synod of Ulster entered into correspondence with the Church of Scotland. A deputation, consisting
of Dr. Cooke and others, was appointed to attend the meeting of the General Assembly, in May, 1836. The Assembly
resolved that " the ministers of the Synod of Ulster may
hold ministerial communion with the Church of Scotland."
The Moderator announced this decision from the chair to the
deputation, when Dr. Cooke, at the request of his brethren,
returned thanks to the Assembly for "the favourable reception which had been given to their application." In his
speech he brought out some interesting and important facts
connected with the state and history of Presbyterianism in
Ireland :—

" I feel bound to address our thanks to the God of our fathers
who has spared us, and honoured us to behold this high day, when
my brethren and I are publicly and officially recognised, true sons of
the Church of Scotland. . . . While obeying my fellow-deputies in
conveying their thanks, and the thanks of the Synod of Ulster, to

this venerable assembly, may I be permitted to trespass for a short time in glancing at the history of Presbyterianism in Ireland. The Presbyterian settlement commenced about 1611, and from that time till 1642 continued, by a peculiar ecclesiastical comprehension, to constitute a part of the Established Church of Ireland. We learn from authentic documents contained in the "Life of Livingstone," that the Scotch Presbyterian ministers who emigrated to Ireland acknowledged the Irish Prelates as Presbyters, joined with them, in that character, in the act of ordination, being permitted to model the forms of the Service-book according to their own views of discipline and Church government. In this state of mutual forbearance and charity, the two branches of Protestantism continued till a few years previous to 1641. At this time our Presbyterian fathers were, through evil counsels, expelled from their churches and exiled from their people ; but Presbyterian order and worship continued uninterrupted through the zealous labours of the regimental chaplains who accompanied Munro. By these the first Presbytery in Ireland was constituted at Carrickfergus, in June, 1642 ; and from this little seed sprung up the General Synod of Ulster, now embracing in its jurisdiction twenty-four Presbyteries, and extending its ministers and its congregations into every province of the kingdom. But as the ministry of the chaplains was necessarily confined to the neighbourhood of the garrisons, the destitute condition of the country parishes was, in 1642-43, brought before the venerable Assembly of the Mother Church, and a mission of six ministers, including Livingstone, Baillie, and Blair, was deputed to Ireland, by whose indefatigable labours the lamp of the gospel was kept burning in those dark and troublous times. It is, perhaps, not unworthy of remark that, in the earnest petition addressed to the Scottish Assembly, our Irish forefathers expressed an humble hope, that 'the day might come when a General Assembly in Ireland might return the firstfruit of thanks,' for the seed of the plants they then begged from their mother's garden. This day, their hope—I had almost said their prophecy—stands realized; and the mission your fathers commenced, by the loan, as the petition expressed it, of six, now returns you the firstfruit of thanks from a General Assembly of two hundred and fifty ministers, with large and flourishing congregations. Through the period of our history, like most other Churches, we have been assailed by divers doctrines ; but, from the first, our fathers have continued to recognize either the Scots' or Westminster Confession, as the exhibition of their faith. Our records anterior to the Revolution

are lost ; but in a protest by one of our ministers, he testifies that
he subscribed the Westminster Confession in 1688, and that such he
had always heard to have been the law and practice, from the original
organization of our Synod.   In 1698, 1707, and upon various other
occasions, our Synod continued its adherence to the same Confession;
and now, as you have heard, confirms that adherence by a constitution, which, I trust and believe, will remain immutable through all
the fortunes of our future history."

Referring to the endowments of the Presbyterian Church in
Ireland, he made the following important statement :—

" It may be gratifying to this venerable Assembly to learn, that
the kindness of the Government in granting endowments continues
to keep pace with the necessities of our people.   The Government
know that our Scottish forefathers were planted in the wildest and
most barren portions of our land, where the malediction of O'Neill
was pronounced upon the man who would cultivate a field or build a
house.   The Government know it was the most rude and lawless of
the provinces, where resistance retired, as to her fortress ; and the
Government know that Scottish industry has drained its bogs, and
cultivated its barren wastes ; has filled its ports with shipping, substituted towns and cities for its hovels and *claghans*, and given peace
and good order to a land of confusion and blood.   The Government
know, that while nearly twenty regiments are required for the three
southern provinces, the northern province is garrisoned by three."

His closing sentences were graceful and eloquent :—

" Some of our fathers, more observant than we of the times, and
the signs of them, might, perhaps, have drawn encouraging omens
from the circumstance of finding in the chair a Scotchman (Dr.
Macleod), with an Irish tongue and an Irish heart.   I see, on your
left, a venerated brother, who was, I believe, the first to awake attention to the gospel might that slumbered in the Irish tongue.   Others
have since laboured in the same cause; and to yourself, under Providence, Ireland will soon be indebted for a gift that will awake her
music and her poetry to the strains of the gospel.   The shamrock-
wreathed harp of my country has hitherto responded to the *coronach*
of sorrow or the record of blood ; by you it will be entwined with the
roses of Sharon, and your hands will awake its chords to the strains

of mercy and love. You have visited our country, not to spy out the nakedness of the land; but you have returned with the best bunches of our Eshcol-grapes, encouraging others to come over and help us; and you transmit, by them, the strain and the harp with which David expelled the demon visitant of Saul, as an antidote to the discords of our country, and as the anticipated celebration of our victory and peace. In the name of my brethren who have deputed me to the office—in the name of the Synod of Ulster, which we here represent, I return to you, and this venerable Assembly, our deep-felt thanks. After years of separation we are reunited; and though in different lands, and in different outward circumstances, we form, in spirit and communion, one Presbyterian Church. And, if it be the will of a mysterious Providence, that, in these days of rebuke and aggression, your venerable edifice should be assailed by the storm; or if, in times to come, some new and fiery trial should await you, may the God who attracted Moses to the vision of Horeb, and showed him the emblem of the Universal Church—the Bush in unscathed verdure subsisting in the devouring flame—may He still dwell with you— your protection and your glory; and may the page of your history, as it tells of your labours, your victories, and your faithful contendings, ever continue to append to her imperishable records the motto of your Church's effigies—NEC TAMEN CONSUMEBATUR."

The Voluntary discussion had made Dr. Cooke almost as popular in Scotland as in Ireland. His eloquence produced a marked effect upon the Assembly; and the services he had rendered to a common cause, gained for him the utmost respect. He writes to Mrs. Cooke, from Glasgow, on the 2nd of June:—" Mr. Carmichal will inform you that my remaining here has been, in some sense, much against my will. But two reasons have weighed with me. First, as we are now in communion with the old Mother in Scotland, Principal Baird has expressed a strong wish that I should preach before the magistrates in Edinburgh, in the Cathedral, as a public memorial of the reunion of the Churches. Second, Mr. Carmichal has got churches for me to preach in, and get collections for him. . . .

" I have been greatly pleased with my visit. If Dr. Ritchie had clapped me into Dr. Hanna's doublet, and stuffed me out with straw, he could not so speedily have made me a great man. The sayings of the discussion are in every mouth; and I stand acknowledged champion of the Church of Scotland. The Irish *shillelah* has cracked the cranium that presented its impenetrable thickness to the Scottish battle-axe. In fact, I have succeeded in what I sought—to paint a ridiculous party, and make them truly ridiculous. The Scots argued with them; I laughed at them. A light wit has effected more than the powers of heavy argument. Under all the circumstances I have been greatly caressed. I would have had little more to ask for, had you been with me, and my poor boys well; and Jenny—my dear, dear Jenny, living. The happier I am, she is the surer to rise to my mind; and my tears are ready to start at the moment of my greatest joy. God's will be done!

" On Saturday I had an express invitation from his Grace, the Commissioner, to attend his levee, for I had not gone before. I attended, and was received with marked respect. I had the honour of a long chat; and then an invitation to dinner, and to coffee in the evening with Lady Belhaven. In the drawing-room, before dinner, his Grace spoke to the Moderator to give me a chair near his seat; so I was located just opposite the Lord Provost of Edinburgh. There, with near three hundred guests, in the princely hall of the Stewarts, my humble name was toasted from the vice-regal throne, and the music of the attending band awaked in my honour. The Moderator, beside whom I sat, whispered me his wish that Dr. Ritchie, and the Belfast ' Rads,' had just got a peep in at the window. I told him it was all well; but that if John Knox had not fought, we should not have dined. Had Knox dreaded the power of the Queen, we should not have received the smile of a king. In the evening I attended Lady Belhaven's soirée. When I was stealing away, her Grace observed me, and crossed me at the door to give me a pressing invitation to visit her at home." . .

Dr. Cooke and his fellow-deputies received the thanks of the Synod of Ulster, at its annual meeting. It was a subject for congratulation that the Presbyterian Church of Ireland, which had been so long labouring under the incubus of a deadly heresy, was now freed from it; and that as a token of her hard won freedom, she was once again received into the bosom of the mother Church of Scotland. It was an earnest of better times; and Dr. Cooke, who had been so largely instrumental in achieving this position, lived to see those better times.

But a still more remarkable recognition of his services yet awaited him. It came from the Provost of Trinity College, Dublin.

"PROVOST'S HOUSE, Feb. 9th, 1837.

"REVEREND SIR,—It is with the most sincere pleasure that I have undertaken to convey to you, the unanimous wish of the Board of Trinity College, that you would do us the favour of accepting the honorary degree of LL.D. in this University, as the expression of our admiration of the talents with which you have so successfully cleared from heterodoxy, the branch of the Protestant Church in Ireland, over which you preside, and of the ability with which you have defended the Establishment against the attempts of those, who, under the pretence of purging its corruptions, would deprive it of the means of support. . . .

"I have the honour to be, Sir,
"With the highest esteem,
"Your very faithful servant,
"BAR. BOYD."

Such an honour conferred upon a minister of the Presbyterian Church, by a University under Episcopal rule, was extremely rare. A similar honour was given a short time previously, to Dr. Chalmers, by the University of Oxford.

If Dr. Cooke's defence of Establishments had gained for him the grateful acknowledgments of Churchmen, it had also exposed him to the unceasing hostility of Voluntaries. He was assailed from every part of the three kingdoms. No opportunity was missed of attempting to refute his arguments, and to

set aside the great principles he had developed. His assailants
even stooped to misrepresentation and personal abuse. In
January, 1837, he and Dr. Stewart, were deputed to visit Scotland, to awaken an interest in the Scriptural schools which the
Synod of Ulster was engaged in establishing in Ireland. A
great meeting was held in Perth. The scheme of the Synod
was explained, and the defects of the National System of Education were pointed out. While Dr. Cooke was speaking, he
was repeatedly interrupted and contradicted by Mr. Massie, an
Independent minister. To prevent unseemly confusion, the
chairman consented to hear Mr. Massie, when Dr. Cooke had
finished his speech. He was heard; and he charged Dr.
Cooke with uttering "a foul slander and calumny," against
the National Board. Dr. Cooke, in reply, pledged himself to
substantiate, by unquestionable documentary evidence, every
statement he had made. In due time he enclosed his proofs
to the Rev. Mr. Lewis, of Perth ; but before they could be
published, Mr. Massie renewed his attack through the Press,
and charged Dr. Cooke with having violated his pledge. Dr.
Cooke replied in a letter, which was widely circulated in Scotland and Ireland. He explains the origin and nature of the
controversy :—

"About the end of January last, I was told that a report of a
public meeting in Perth, at which Dr. Stewart and myself attended,
had been published in Belfast, and, I naturally supposed, the abuse
uttered at the meeting by Mr. Massie. As my custom is, I let the
matter pass in silence. . . . I will state my reasons. . . . First,
were I to reply to every slander with which I have for many years
been successively assailed, I should find time for little else. I do
believe, according to the Scriptures, that the devil is the father of
lies and slanders, and that it is often part of his policy to detach
ministers of the gospel from assailing his kingdom by occupying them
incessantly in defending themselves. Upon this scriptural principle
I have acted, and will continue to act so long as I am personally concerned, and will depart from it only in the present instance when
silence might injure some public interest of the Church. Secondly,
I have submitted hitherto in silence to many false accusations because

I was convinced that, if God did not enable me to live them down, no human ability could write them down.   Truth is unity, falsehood everything but infinity.

" Thirdly, studiously avoiding to read newspaper attacks, and patiently sitting down under their multiplied accusations, I know I may have appeared to some afraid to meet them.   Now, I must honestly plead guilty to the last part of this charge.   I have been, and I still am afraid to read even the most groundless slander.   And why ?   Just because I am afraid to be made angry.   I pray to God, ' Lead me not into temptation ; ' and if I expect him to lead me one way, I must not lead myself another.   This is a practical truth I would that Christians did more deeply consider.   I know not any temptation much greater than to hear and to read unmerited abuse.

" But why do I now come forward to meet Mr. Massie ?   Because, not contented with one attack, he has repeated it, and brings against me the tangible charge of violation of my public pledge—a charge which, if true, affects my ministerial usefulness.   The case then ceases to be my own.   The Church is concerned."

Dr. Cooke proceeds to reply in detail to Mr. Massie's charges, and he does so with his usual ability and success.   His answer to the accusation of violating a public pledge, brings out some strange, but characteristic, phases of the policy and practice of the National Board of Education :—

" The document I promised to send was not the private written instructions to inspectors.   The document I promised to send was the rule for ' excluding ministers from preaching even in school-houses they had built '—the sole point on which Mr. Massie offered me the shadow of contradiction.   Now, the promise of transmitting that document I made in Perth on Thursday, the 13th January; and on the 17th I received it from Belfast at Glasgow, and transmitted it to Perth to the Rev. Mr. Lewis, with the expectation and request that it should be published immediately.   As to the fact of written private instructions having been, at one time, given to the Inspectors of schools, the only evidences I can give are my own eyes and my own veracity, supported by the testimony of Mr. Massie's friend, Mr. Carlile, who cannot and will not deny it; with that of the astonished Inspector who showed them to me in Dublin, and whose name and honourable character Mr. Carlile well knows, together with the whole

Synod of Ulster, to whom I stated the fact in presence of Mr. Carlile, and who must well recollect his angry charge against me for speaking in public of a private document. That these once private instructions have since been published and printed, is no denial of my previous discovery. In fact, I compelled their publication by discovering and denouncing the part that prohibited the Bible during four hours each day."

Mr. Massie had sneered at Dr. Cooke, for joining with his Protestant brethren at the Hillsborough meeting. He represented him as a renegade Presbyterian, because he proclaimed the banns of marriage between the Protestant Churches of the empire. Dr. Cooke replies :—

" Have I accused Mr. Massie for slandering me ? . . . . No. I thank him for the allusion. The remembrance of it is delightful. . . . Nay, I think the bare repetition of it may do him good even now ; and, therefore, so far from calling him slanderer for bringing it up before the meeting, I shall repeat it, with thanks to him for furnishing the opportunity. My words are these, ' Between the divided Churches I publish the banns of a sacred marriage of Christian forbearance where they differ ; of Christian love where they agree ; and of Christian co-operation in all matters where their common safety is concerned.' Am I slandered when this is repeated? No. I glory in being author of the proposal, and I now challenge Mr. Massie, with every one of his most liberal friends, though shielded in the threefold antipathies of most brazen Voluntaryism, to say they dare forbid the banns. I tell them they dare not. It was a scriptural, it was a holy purpose of marriage, on which, though bad men of all classes must frown, the good of all sects and denominations must cordially rejoice."

Another point in the Board of Education's crooked policy, he brought out with great force :—

" In relation to Mr. Massie's quotation from the propositions of the Synod of Ulster, submitted to Government for the improvement of the Board, and which, misled by the Board, he declares to have been granted by the Commissioners of Education, I have only to remark that the statement of their being granted is totally untrue. Had they been so, the whole Synod of Ulster would now be in connexion with the Board. With this untruth Mr. Massie is no way charge-able. It lies at the door of the Board. They published to the world that the propositions had been granted; and, as I have done already, I stand before the public again to say and to prove their statement untrue. I say, it was impossible for the Board to grant the Synod's propositions ; because, after receiving them, the Board delayed an answer, and then added two new rules that rendered the Synod's propositions null and void. Of all the acts of the Board I have ever looked upon this is the worst."

The deep interest which Dr. Cooke took in the celebrated Clough case, and the important services he rendered to that congregation and to the Presbyterian Church in Ireland, have already been noticed. The congregation of Clough was obliged to enter on a protracted law-suit; and every plan and plea which ingenuity could devise was tried, to rob the people òf their property. The bearings of the point at issue were very wide. If the Arians should succeed in gaining the church at Clough, many others might be claimed and seized ; no congre-gation of the Synod of Ulster, in fact, could feel secure in the possession of its ecclesiastical property.

At length, in 1836, the Government Committee of the Synod were able to report, that their cause had triumphed; and they stated that much of the success was to be ascribed, under God, to the zeal and ability of the solicitor for the con-gregation, A. J. Macrory, Esq. It was thereupon moved by Dr. Cooke, and unanimously resolved :—" That this Synod, impressed with a deep sense of obligation to A. J. Macrory, Esq., for his generosity in acting gratuitously as solicitor for the congregation of Clough, in the recovery of their property, and in defence of the rights of this Church. . . do resolve to re-quest his acceptance of some testimonial of their gratitude." An influential committee was appointed to carry out the wishes of the Synod; and Dr. Cooke, at their request selected a magni-ficent service of plate, and a Bible, which were publicly pre-sented to Mr. Macrory, at the annual meeting in 1837.

CHAPTER XIII.

1836—1839.

Notice of Motion in the Synod on Protestant Defence—Meeting in May Street
Church—Speech of Rev. Hugh McNeile—Dr. Cooke on Protestant Union—
Sermon on National Infidelity—On the Signs of the Times—Religion and
Politics—Conservative Banquet—Dr. Cooke's Speech— His Views on Con-
servatism and the Church of England—On Religious Establishments and
Protestant Unity—Ethical Principles developed in his Class Lectures—
Monument to Samuel Rutherward—Sermon at Anwoth—Speech at Stranraer
—Fundamental Principle of Establishments—Description of Dr. Cooke at
Exeter Hall—Freedom of the City of Dublin—Severe Accident—Addresses
of Congratulation on his Recovery—Letter from Lord Roden.

THE passing of the Reform Bill, the establishment of the
National System of Education in Ireland, and other proceedings of the Legislature, created an uneasy feeling in the minds
of a large number of Protestants throughout the empire. It
began to be feared that, by undue yielding to the aggressive
demands of Popery, the principles of the Reformation would be
sacrificed, and the Protestant Constitution of England endangered. Under this impression Protestant Associations were
organized in many of the leading cities. Their object was
purely defensive. They asked no new powers. They laid
claim to no exclusive immunities or privileges. They were
conservative in their aim. They were designed to protect and
preserve, by all legitimate means, the Protestantism of the
Throne and Constitution. Dr. Cooke deemed the subject of
such importance, that he brought it under the notice of the
Synod of Ulster, at Belfast, in 1837, and gave notice of motion
to the following effect :—

" That whilst we hold that the ministers, elders, and lay members of our communion are, under every consideration of prudence and obligation of duty, as much as lieth in them, bound to avoid all connection with the factious and partizan politics by which these and other countries are so much disturbed ; and to avoid, on all occasions, the putting forth of themselves or individuals in a representative character, without specific commission from their brethren ; yet we also hold it to be their undoubted and inalienable privilege to express their personal opinions, at any proper or suitable time or place, on any or every question of constitutional politics, without being liable to reflection or censure in any of our Church Courts ; and in these times of trouble and rebuke, when the glorious principles of civil and religious liberty, advocated and supported by our Puritan forefathers, are threatened by the conjoint assaults of Popery and Infidelity ; and, especially, when the important doctrine of the duty of kingdoms and nations, as such, to acknowledge and support religion, is so openly assailed, we hold it to be our specially bounden duty to defend these principles, and to co-operate, for these objects, with all our Protestant brethren, who hold the common faith and truth as it is in Jesus."

His action did not stop with this, nor was it confined to the Synod. He gathered round him the leading men of Belfast and Ulster, and they agreed that a meeting should be held in May Street church, for the purpose of inaugurating a Protestant Defence Association. Thursday, August 31st, 1837, was the day fixed. Long before the hour appointed, the street in front of the church was filled with an eager crowd. When the doors were thrown open, every seat in the spacious building was immediately occupied. The leading clergy and gentry of Belfast and the surrounding country were present. The chair was occupied by the Rev. A. C. Macartney, and the first speaker was the Rev. Hugh McNeile, who thus explained the object of the assemblage :—

" It is impossible to conceive any occasion for which a public meeting can be convened within the precincts of the British Empire, of deeper importance to the temporal and spiritual interests of its inhabitants of all denominations, than that for which we are this day assembled. It is not to create or foment divisions among our fellow-countrymen, as is slanderously reported, and as some affirm that we intend. No, it is with far different objects that we are met together. These objects may be fairly classed under two heads:— 1st, to combine in one Christian brotherhood of self-defence all who truly love true religion and genuine liberty; all who sincerely advocate the free circulation of the unmutilated and unadulterated Word of God; all who assert and defend the right of private judgment; all who venerate the inviolable sanctity of an oath; all real loyalists who maintain the unrivalled and universal supremacy of the King or Queen of England within these realms, and renounce, adjure, and detest any allegiance whatever to any foreign power or potentate, ecclesiastical or civil. This is the direct object of our Protestant Association, considered in its scriptural foundation, and in its national exercise. Our second object is, to address ourselves with earnest affection to those of our fellow-countrymen who have the misfortune still to labour under anti-scriptural and anti-national prejudices; who are denied the free circulation of the pure Word of God, and the right of private judgment; who are taught that oaths, under certain circumstances, may and ought to be violated; and who are commanded to yield their first and highest allegiance to a foreign ecclesiastical authority."

Referring to the services already rendered by Dr. Cooke to the cause of Protestantism, and to the abuse that had been heaped upon him from many quarters, Mr. McNeile said :—

" There is not, perhaps, a man in the kingdom to whom this more forcibly applies than to our valued brother and faithful champion of Protestantism, Dr. Cooke, a man who is at once the subject of eulogy and the butt of calumny—eulogy from all that is noble, and calumny from all that is base, in the society of his fellow-countrymen. How eminently it has pleased God to qualify him for the position in which he is situated! Our Lord Jesus Christ is represented in Scripture as standing among the candlesticks or Churches, and holding the stars or ministers in His right hand. This speaks the ready adaptation of the stars to their respective candlesticks. When the appointed time was come for sending the Gospel message to the polished Athenians, He had a fitted messenger ready, not an unlettered fisherman of Galilee, but a classical student, a pupil of

Gamaliel, versed in the secular learning of the Greeks. The same adaptation of means is manifest throughout the whole history of the Church. Calvin would have failed in Germany, and Luther in Geneva. In Scotland, Cranmer would have been denounced as a temporiser with Popery. In England, Knox would have caused a reaction by a want of courtesy to the Queen. Among the mountaineers of the high Alps, Dr. Chalmers would have been useless; and in the Professor's chair in Edinburgh, Felix Neff would have been absurd. And we may truly affirm that Paul was not more suited to the Athenians, Luther to the Germans, Calvin to the Swiss; that Cranmer was not more suited to the moderation of England, or Knox to the single-eyed determination of Scotland; that Neff was not more precisely the man for Alpine hardships, or Chalmers for the Professor's chair, than Cooke is, and has been, for the Orthodox battles of the Synod of Ulster, and the Protestant awakening of the town of Belfast."

Dr. Cooke was the next speaker. When he appeared, the whole assembly rose to their feet, and continued cheering for several minutes. He began his speech by stating his reasons for appearing there that day, surrounded by men of another Church :—

"A common danger should lead to a common defence. Union and charity can only tend to elevate the universal Church. In the present generation, while Churches which agree in all fundamental points are accused and decried for uniting, the world is striving to unite all who agree in no one common point, but the overthrow of Protestant and evangelical truth. All who reject Christ are combined; and I call upon all who receive Him to adopt a counter-combination. . . . If England, and Scotland, and Presbyterian Ulster would arise in the strength of zeal, and love, and Christian decision, we should find instrumentality enough in existence, and success would be certain."

In the pulpit as well as on the platform, Dr. Cooke developed and enforced his great principles of Christian union and co-operation. On the 15th of July he preached on "National Calamities the Consequence of National Sins," selecting as his text the words of Amos : " Shall there be evil in a city, and the Lord hath not done it ? " With skilful hand he sketched the sins of Britain : worldliness, drunkenness, Sabbath-breaking, neglect of education, political and religious strife; and to these he traced the calamities which were then afflicting the country:—

"If any evil is endured in the nation or individual; if it be found in the whole city, in the splendid streets where the rich dwell; if it be found in the extended marts of commerce, where merchandise is continually exposing its wares and accumulating its profits; or in the dark and dreary lanes into which misery and poverty retire to hide themselves; or if it be found in those wretched garrets, the last resort of unfriended humanity, where they are open to the winds and rains of heaven, and where the poor, all uncared for, sleep but rest not; whether there be evil in one or another part of the city, or in the whole city—' the Lord hath done it.' If it be a calamity that has come to the treasury of a nation, and closed up the fountains from which it was supplied—that comes to the health of a nation, and lays its hundreds and thousands on beds of pain—' the Lord hath done it.' So that, whatever be the condition of the land, in sorrow and in suffering, the Spirit of God distinctly informs us, it is the Lord hath sent it, it is the 'Lord hath done it.' "

His remarks on education were most appropriate and instructive. They show how his thoughtful mind and clear perception reached to the root of the nation's ills :—

"There is not a portion of this land that is not suffering from one sin—the neglect of the education of the people. What is the great cause of the multiplied calamities of the land, but that the people have not been taught to know God? And just at the very time when the nation was beginning to awake to some sense of education, then a blighting form of education is presented, forced on the land, the tendency of which is to deliver the children of Ireland, bound hand and foot, into the power of their spiritual rulers, with an impenetrable barrier placed between them and God's eternal Word."

On the 20th of August he preached to his congregation on "The Signs of the Times." The sermon was printed, and in the preface he says :—

" The Lord's message to Ezekiel (iii. 17) comes with equal force to every minister of the Gospel. The message declares his awful responsibility, and demands unbounded faithfulness in his office. Let ministers and people hear it : 'Son of Man, I have made thee a watchman unto the house of Israel; therefore hear the word at my mouth, and give them warning from me.' . . . Two departments of ministerial duty are here presented : the one, to warn the wicked, that he may repent ; the other, to warn the righteous, that he may be roused to watch and pray against temptation and sin."

In this discourse Dr. Cooke traces fully the connection between religion and politics. He shows how far a clergyman is justified, and in duty bound, to interfere in and direct the current of public events; and how far a king or government is justified, or bound, to interfere in religious concerns. In illustrating the false views generally entertained on this subject, he says:—

" Let us take a few of those principles which are most confidently asserted and most eagerly propagated.

" Of these perhaps there is none that so much assumes the dignity of a first principle as the assertion that religion and politics should be kept totally separate. This broad principle includes within its verge a variety of subordinate parts. First, it implies that even Christian kingdoms, as such, have no concern with the avowal, or propagation, or maintenance of Christianity. Secondly, that even Christian kingdoms, as such, have no concern with the discountenancing or eradication of superstition or idolatry. Thirdly, it implies and avows that, in the choice of legislators and rulers, their religion is to be totally disregarded ; that the most faithful servant of Christ may be unworthy of the Christian's support, and the most avowed infidel the object of his confidence and choice. And these, be it remembered, are not our imaginings, but the avowed deductions of those who adopt the broad principle upon which they are apparently based. But upon what lower and deeper principle is the basis itself supported ? Ordinarily, upon one single text: ' My kingdom is not of this world.' And what then ? Though Christ's kingdom be not of this world, by what logical perversion is it thence inferred that the kingdoms of this world owe to Christ neither allegiance, homage, nor service ? In all the annals of false reasoning there is not a more impotent conclusion. 'My kingdom,' saith Christ, 'is not of this world.' And why is it not? To show you why it is not, let us see what Christ's kingdom is. The Apostle informs us, 'The kingdom of God is not meat and drink, but righteousness and peace, and joy in the Holy Ghost.' These three principles are not of this world. They are principles that come down from above, from the Father of lights and of mercies. But because they come down from above, are the kingdoms of this world under no obligation to adopt, propagate, or maintain them? Is it come to this, that because a principle is not of this world, therefore this world has no concern with it? Is truth of this world? Is love of this world? Is holiness of this world? No; they must all come down from above; but surely, the loftiness of their origin, instead of diminishing their claims upon the men of this world, and the kingdoms of this world, is the very circumstance by which their claims to universal acceptance and patronage are most clearly evinced and irresistibly enforced. . . .

"Now, the highest of all authorities, and the best of all examples, is God's. Does God, then, confine himself to the revelation, exposition, and enforcement of religious doctrine and duty, as distinguished from political principles and civil interests? . . . What is the second Psalm but a description of the combined rebellion of Jews and Gentiles against Jesus, as King of kings; and a lesson of true political instruction to the kings and judges of the earth? Hath God the Son, either when preaching by the Spirit, or when manifest in the flesh—hath He ever drawn a line of distinction between religious and political things? Hath He ever confined Himself to the religious, to the exclusion of political instruction? He hath drawn no such line in His teaching; He hath authorized no such exclusion by His example. In one sententious aphorism Our Lord hath compressed the politics of the Universe ;—' Render unto Cæsar the things that are Cæsar's, and unto God the things that are God's ; '—a sentence the more remarkable because in one breath it delivers the sum and substance of every doctrine and duty both of religion and politics. Would to God that kings would be wise, that the judges of the earth would be instructed—that rulers would read and study the unchanging and universal politics of the Bible, instead of the ephemeral and partizan politics of the world—that they would learn their political creed and duties from the Son of God, who on these, as on every other subject, spoke as never man spoke—that they would combine religion and politics as He has combined them;

nor, what He has thus joined together, dare any longer to put asunder. Nor hath the Spirit of God, in His unlimited varieties of communication, deviated, at any time, from the example of the Father and the Son; but, in revealing the deep things of God, hath carefully inculcated the political relations and duties of men. Take one example out of many with which the historical and prophetical Scriptures everywhere abound. Take Nehemiah ix. throughout. It relates, and comments on a great political revolution, its causes, and its consequences; and, what is peculiarly worthy of remark, it is in the very act of worship—that act in which ' the Spirit Himself helpeth our infirmities'—yet, in that very solemn act, the Holy Spirit makes the political sins, both of rulers and people, the subject of confession, record, and instruction.   .   .   .   History nowhere furnishes an example of a more patriotic statesman, a more energetic reformer, a more valiant general, a more pious man than Nehemiah. He stands before us the model of a highminded and disinterested politician, whom God raised up, that he might exemplify to succeeding genera- tions the inseparable connection between sound national policy and deep personal piety: that, from the school of worldly principles and selfish motives, he might conduct the political student to the school of the Spirit, without whom, let men devise and build up as they may, still ' nothing is strong, nothing is holy.' ''

His reference to the power of the Press, and the evil use sometimes made of it, was appropriate and forcible :—

" We have contended, not for any secular purpose, to establish the right and duty of Christian ministers to study and expound political principles and doctrines. We contend for it because it is both a spiritual right with which they are endowed, and a spiritual function to which they are appointed. We contend for it, however, not because we would monopolise it, but because we would resist the monopoly which the Liberal politicians of a liberal age are endeavouring to establish in their favour. We contend for this right, not because we would transfer to the pulpit the functions of the press, but because we would not yield to the usurpation of the press one legitimate and hereditary right of the pulpit. We contend for it, because, without meaning any offence, beyond what an unwelcome truth may perchance convey, we do believe that the press is, of all tyrants, the most to be resisted, and, of all teachers, least to be trusted. Yes, it is to be resisted, just because it is generally a secret tribunal—an irre-

sponsible inquisition, where the accuser seldom dares to confront the
accused; where the tutored witness is submitted to no cross-exami-
nation; where the accuser often concentrates in his own person the
various and irreconcilable functions of accuser, witness, jury, and
judge; and adds, not unfrequently, that of the relentless and
hardened executioner, gloating over the tortures of his victim, and
feeding on the price of his venality and his injustice. That this
description is not universally applicable to the public press is cause
of great thankfulness to Almighty God. Yet, a public journal that
dares to be distinctly religious in its news—that knows no party but
Christ, and no politics but those of the Bible—still remains a rare
phenomenon amidst its local companionship—at once the glory and
the shame of the land."

The concluding appeal to ministers was eloquent and impressive:—

"And ye, ministers of the Gospel, a word more especially to you.
In these days, when men seem as ignorant of the contents of civil
history as of the policy of the Bible, you will be told you are neither
called nor competent to expound political principles, or defend
political rights. But we tell these ignorant men that the ministers
of the Gospel have been the real liberators of Europe. Who freed
Saxony and the other members of the Smalcaldic League from the
iron fangs of the Pope and the Emperor? The gentle Melanchthon,
the unbending Luther. Who freed Scotland? Was it the chivalry
of her nobles—the hardihood of her peasantry? No, but the
learning of her Melville and the thunder of her Knox. Who
created the imperishable fortress of England's liberties? Not the
patriotism of her Commons, nor the power of her nobility, but the
patience and boldness of her Puritan fathers. Those mighty men
were not enchained by the puling sentimentalism of these days, or
by that fear of man which ever bringeth a snare. Remember, ye,
that your commission is, as theirs, not from men, but from God;
that it is not narrowed by any authority, but extends, like theirs,
over the wide dominions of your Lord and Master. Remember how
your Lord conjoined in the same rebuke every religious error, and
every political error, when he charged his disciples, 'Take heed,
beware of the leaven of the Pharisees, and of the leaven of Herod.'
So charge upon this generation to beware of the leaven of Rome
ecclesiastical, which teacheth self-righteousness, as the Pharisees;

and to beware of the leaven of Rome political, which enforceth a yoke as Herod. And whether these things be introduced under a Protestant name and disguise, or whether in their own proper Romish name and garb, describe with equal truth, warn with equal faithfulness, and denounce them with equal authority—if ye would be faithful witnesses for the crown and kingdom of your only Lord and Saviour."

The effect produced by this sermon was wonderful. It stirred Belfast to its centre. It roused the slumbering energies of the Protestants of Ulster. Dr. Cooke was now a recognized political leader. He had long been an ecclesiastical leader. It was remarkable that those whose council he guided in the Synod of Ulster, were, to a large extent, opposed to him in politics. Many of them wrote against him, and spoke against him, as a politician. Yet this did not affect his ecclesiastical position. The services he had rendered, and was still rendering, to the Presbyterian Church, prevented his influence from waning.

The state of public affairs, especially the noisy agitation of O'Connell, and the ominous acts of a time-serving Ministry, made Dr. Cooke resolve still farther to consolidate that Protestant party which he had been mainly instrumental in organizing. The leading nobility and gentry of Ulster were, therefore, invited to a political banquet, on the 19th of October, 1837. It was the most influential assemblage hitherto seen in Belfast. It had been arranged that the speakers should be limited to fifteen minutes; but when Dr. Cooke's turn came, his eloquence entranced the audience, and kept them spellbound for more than an hour. "We speak without affectation," says the *Ulster Times*, "when we say that we account it at once the most fortunate and the most honourable circumstance in our short career, that our columns have been the medium of presenting to the world so noble a monument of genius, dedicated to the noblest purposes, as the speech of Dr. Cooke. Whether we regard the clear and sagacious exposition of the state and prospects of the empire, viewed on Christian principles; the evangelical spirit which labours to compose all differences between Christian men, and inspire them with mutual confidence for the rescue of the Commonwealth; or the outbursts of eloquence, exceeded neither in ancient or modern literature, by which the whole is enforced, we are equally lost in admiration."

The speech suffered greatly from the difficulty—indeed, the impossibility of fully reporting it. The enthusiasm it excited affected the reporters as well as the audience, and some of the noblest passages were lost. Speaking of the difficulties and dangers that threatened Protestantism, he said :—

" But if we must constitutionally ˷strive for our civil and religious liberties, 'tis not five years will tire either our patience or our exertions, nor ten times five, nor ten times ten. And if within that period we be all gathered to our fathers, by the blessing of God we shall leave those behind us who know the worth of British liberty— who feel that if it be worth the having it is also worth the holding— an inheritance, of which the threatener is unable to deprive us, and we will not, in five years of hopeless endurance resign; but which we will maintain with the indomitable spirit of our fathers in the perennial fee-simple that lies in 'No Surrender.' We have sound Protestant principles, we have true Protestant hearts; above all, we have humble and secure dependence upon the mighty God of Protestantism; and whatever threats, whether of legal prosecutions or brutal force, may be hoarsely thundered from the high walls of Derrynane, or sweetly squeaked from the shrill and discordant sparrow-pipe that chirrups in the groves of Tipperary—still will the spirit of Irish Protestantism remain with heart unaffrighted, with arm untired, with faith unsubdued, with loyalty unchanged, with ranks unshaken, adopting as its motto of patient endurance of injuries, and ardent hope of redress, the words of Luther when arraigned before the Diet of Worms :—' Here I take my stand ; I can do nothing else, and God be my help.' From Protestantism alone does our civil constitution derive its power of perpetual renovation. It flourishes alike in the sunshine and in the shade ; it blooms in the brightness of the parterre, and it ripens in the gloom of the dungeon ; it repays the hand that protects it by its loveliness and its fruitfulness ; and, like a medical plant of our gardens, it defies the foot that tramples it, and grows the more vigorously the more it is depressed. . . . Conservatism is now in deep waters, simply because Toryism required to be washed. From these deep waters of danger and struggle Conservatism will finally emerge. I foretell it as confidently as I anticipate the rising of the sun to-morrow, that so long as it allies itself with the truth, and the propagation and holiness of genuine, not nominal, Protestantism, Conservatism must finally triumph in every conflict. But so sure as darkness is ever succeeding, and, for a time, subduing and displacing the light, so sure must Protestantism stand prepared for successive and unremitting assaults, and its endurance and its efforts continue, not for five short years, but for perpetuity. . . . Protestantism is no sapling of yesterday, yielding to every blast, or uprooted by any rude hand. Protestantism is the oak mocking at the storm. Its branches may be tossed around it; but its roots defy the assault. And when the storm is hushed to sleep, as if by the music of its own howlings, the oak remains as an unsubdued monarch protecting beneath its shade, and gracing the landscape with its beauty."

Returning thanks specially for the toast which had been proposed, and enthusiastically received,—"Dr. Cooke and the Church of Scotland in Ireland,"—he said :—

"It is the first time I ever heard this form, and, I confess, it is the form in which it should always have been put. Our Mother Church of Scotland is a noble vine. Planted in the land of the mist and the mountain, she sends out her goodly boughs to the ends of the earth. She gathers luxuriant clusters on the sunny banks of the Ganges ; she plants her hopeful shoots in the islands of Australia; she edifies, in her simple but impressive service, the negro of the West Indies; she clings with her fruitful tendrils amid the forests of North America. What she is in Ireland you all know . . . . I have sometimes been taunted with undue partiality to the Church of England and Ireland. Little care I for these taunts. I am not unduly partial to these Churches; I am not partial to them at all. I repeat it—I am not partial to them, but I am friendly to them. I practise not their forms, but I wish to imitate their virtues. I wish to reform their abuses, and I wish to correct my own. My early impressions of the Established Church in this country were far from favourable. They were drawn from the days of Claverhouse and Strafford, and from the living death that, at the time of my boyhood, had deeply pervaded the Protestantism of Europe. A

change came over the spirit of my dream when I first heard her advocates in the Bible and Missionary Societies. Since that time my
knowledge of her sons has extended, and my friendship has been
increased and confirmed. Right well I know it is a favourite object
with our common enemies to foment jealousies between the members
of the Established and Presbyterian Churches in Ireland. . . .
Heartily would I aid to work reform in the Establishment, but I will
not assist to cut it down. . . . I am not ashamed to say my affections are not narrowed to one Church. I prefer my own; I cling to
her and defend her ; but I love every Church of which it can be
said that her ministers and her people love the Lord Jesus Christ in
sincerity."

His concluding remarks on the struggle which he anticipated
between Romanism and Protestantism in Ireland, are as just as
they are eloquent. They would not be out of place as hints to
all denominations of Protestants at the present moment :—

" I confess I entertain serious apprehensions of the struggle; but
I deny that I ever dream of defeat. Ireland indeed is the battle-
field of the constitution, and Ulster—not the Thermopylæ, where
the bravest stand to die—Ulster is the Marathon, where the invaded
stand and conquer. I do not mean to attach to the members of the
Church of Scotland in Ireland any undue value ; but it is my conviction that, were any circumstances to obliterate this moment, or
pervert the Presbyterianism of Ulster, the union of the three kingdoms is not worth a twelvemonth's purchase. But so long as the
Presbyterians of Ulster retain the genuine principles of the Mother
Church, so long will the union of the kingdoms remain indissoluble,
and the war-whoop of Repeal, that now again begins its ominous
under-growl, will be despised as a bugbear that might frighten
children, but could not for a moment disturb the repose of men.
Now, amongst the other grounds on which I rest my hopes is this
important fact, that whilst the Secession in Scotland, and the Presbyterianism of England, have largely degenerated into Radicalism,
the Synod of Ulster, the Secession, and the Covenanters of Ireland,
have, almost to a man, retained the genuine Establishment principles
of the Mother Church. True, they differ in their Church order from
the Establishment of this kingdom ; but the genuine and scriptural
principles of an Establishment they retain inviolate. An error on
this subject is fatal at once both to religion and politics : fatal to

religion, for, whilst I do not mean to say that all Voluntaries are Atheists—far from it—yet I do not hesitate to say that the principle of Voluntaryism, carried to its full extent, necessarily terminates in national Atheism ; fatal to politics, for the moment politics are separated from religious direction and restraint, that moment they degenerate into Radicalism, and Radicalism into destructiveness. Then comes a military despotism; and a Cromwell, a Robespierre, or a Napoleon, whilst they restrain the fiery elements of faction, extinguish at the same time the last embers of expiring liberty."

An intense desire to unite the different sections of evangelical Protestants in defence of a common faith, and in opposition to a common foe, was one of the·leading aims of Dr. Cooke's life. His heart was so large, his views of truth so broad, his love of fundamental Protestant principles so deep, that he was led to overlook those minor points which divided the Protestant Churches of the land. Carried away by a noble enthusiasm, there can be no doubt he sometimes spake and acted in a way which gave offence to many of his Presbyterian brethren; while, on the other hand, there can be as little doubt that his liberal spirit and commanding advocacy, were, sometimes at least, taken advantage of by other parties, to promote their own selfish or sectarian purposes. But Dr. Cooke, himself, cared little for this. He saw it, he felt it, and he lamented it ; but he was not influenced by it farther than that it forced him to give, on public occasions, still clearer and more emphatic explanations of his views and principles. He was often mis-represented ; he was sometimes branded as a traitor to Presby-terianism ; but they knew little of Dr. Cooke, who could, with honesty, prefer such charges. Never was there a more ardent admirer of the ecclesiastical polity of Knox ; never was there a more determined champion of the doctrinal system of Calvin ; never was there a more faithful son of the Church of Scotland. But he was not a sectary. His preference for his own Church did not make him denounce and anathematize others. He would cordially unite with evangelical brethren of all denominations for the furtherance of a common object. Whatever reproaches

bigotry might heap upon him, whatever misrepresentations intolerance might conjure up, he would, in the face of them all,
resolutely follow what he believed to be the path of duty. His
principles and policy were never more plainly stated than in
his speech at a Protestant meeting held in Manchester, on
September 26th, 1839, where he appeared again on the same
platform with that veteran defender of Protestantism, the Rev.
Hugh McNeile :—

" I regard the Church of England with respect and affection, not
because I think that it possesses any advantages of Apostolical
descent, or Apostolical order, over my Mother Church of Scotland.
I believe the Church of England to be Apostolical, and I believe the
Church of Scotland to be just as Apostolical as she. The Church of
Scotland is Presbyterian by distinction, but she is Episcopalian by
principle. I am an Episcopalian, Paul being my witness. Humble
though I be, I hold myself to be as much a bishop as the Archbishop
of Canterbury. His diocese is a province, mine is a parish. The venerable Archbishop hath several suffragans, and many presbyters ;
mine are some six in number, whom I scarcely hope to increase beyond a dozen. Why, then, should I be jealous of the Church of
England ? I have all she has in quality ; there I stand her equal.
She has more in quantity, and that is the sole difference that I
acknowledge. Am I, then, to aid in pulling down a Church that is
nobly and successfully doing God's work, solely because the order of
that Church gives one man a wider diocese than the order of the
Church of Scotland allots to me ? For my own part I am contented
with what I have ; and, instead of thinking it too little, I constantly
feel it to be too much. . . . My affection to the Church of
England rests, no doubt, upon other grounds. I rest it mainly on
the scriptural purity of her doctrines, piety of her prayers, and the
holiness of life and conversation that I have so often discovered
among her ministers and people. . . . And if any ultra members of the Church of England will not, on the same principle, yield
their affection to the Church of Scotland, I pity their sectarian
narrowness, but I will not be tempted to contract my own brotherly
affections to their shrivelled dimensions ; and should any of them
deal out to us the last sweepings of their charity, and, because
they think we have no bishops, no orders, deliver us over as Samaria
to the uncovenanted mercies of God, why I just tell them the Church

of Scotland is a Church ordered with bishops, presbyters, and deacons ; and if they refuse to concede to us the title of Church, I shall take it at the hands of Paul, and be contented with his certificate of ordination, should theirs be niggardly withheld. But the best of the sons of the Church of England will not now so unkindly deal with the Church of Scotland ; nor did the noblest of her founders, nor the brightest of her ornaments, formerly deal so with her. Cranmer, and Hooker, and Stillingfleet, and Wake, not to mention others as great as they, have not hesitated to acknowledge the Apostolic orders of the Church of Scotland. . . . In the face of the polemics of either party I call them kindred Churches. And I exhort them, in these evil days, to remember that soon they may have need to count that kindred, and to claim mutual assistance. . . . The Church of England is built more splendidly than that of my Mother; must I, therefore, undermine her deep foundations, and bring down her sculptured minarets? Her Gothic windows drink in the sun through stained glass; mine through plain. Must I, therefore, collect pebbles to demolish those rainbow beauties? The Church of England robes her ministers in a surplice; I wear a Geneva gown; must I, therefore, in the zeal of ecclesiastical tailorship, tear her garments to rags? She reads her prayers from a fixed Liturgy ; we follow extemporaneous thought and feeling ; must I, therefore, fling her Liturgy to the winds, or bury it in the earth, or commit it to the flames? Or, what might be more magnanimous still, because the Church of England employs a fixed Liturgy, the Church of Scotland extemporaneous prayer, shall we seize upon her Liturgy, and liberally compel her either to pray as we do, or not to pray at all ? Let the Protestant Churches—and under the scriptural name of Churches I include all Churches that avow and maintain evangelical truth, however differing in outward forms—let the Protestant Churches only learn to pray for one another, and they will not fail to love one another; and if they learn, as I know some have learned or will soon be taught, to love together, I can fearlessly foretell that over superstition and error they will soon become conquerors together."

He concluded with a solemn injunction to union :—

" Protestants, I speak it with sorrow, the great reason of all our dangers is to be found in our divisions. . . . We stand divided in the outward forms of our Churches ; but, Protestants, is it necessary we should be divided in heart? I think it is not. I judge by myself. I confess I am no great Liberal; but I do most honestly declare that I do pray for the Church of England as sincerely as I do for the Church of Scotland. . . . We are encircled by common dangers, and those that are building up Popery affect to look down upon us as pigmies;—

> " We petty men creep
> Under their huge legs, and peep about
> To find ourselves dishonourable graves."

Rome has the great advantage of being a huge monarchy, guided by politics, not by religion; for it can mould itself to any form of religion—its politics alone do never change. There is only one parallel in history to the position in which we stand. The little States of Greece, so long as the Persian Empire kept on the other side of the Hellespont, warred with and weakened each other; all the good they did being to teach each other the use of the sword and the shield. At last Persia invaded Greece, and she had the advantage of Greece being divided into petty states, while Persia had all her forces concentrated under the guidance of Xerxes. What was the consequence? One state met her at Thermopylæ; there, few and alone, they met her, but she conquered, and the Spartans fell. Another met her at Marathon, and Persia was conquered in turn. But what was the consequence of these gigantic inroads? The States of Greece united under Alexander; they compelled Persia to recross the Hellespont; they pursued her; carried the war into her own country, and swept the Persian Empire from the face of the earth. The Church of Rome thus makes her attacks on Protestantism; she threatens first the Church of England in Ireland, because she sees that it is small in number and comparatively weak; perhaps she may lay her low; but if she do, it will but rouse the bold hearts of the Marathons of Protestantism, and the tide will yet be rolled back over the continent of Christendom, and obliterate every vestige of the superstitions by which it has been disfigured, and break every chain of the bondage in which it has been bound. Yes, the time is coming when united Protestantism, having learned by the injuries which it has sustained, the evils of division—when united Protestants, having learned to forbear when they differ, and to love when they agree—will go hand in hand, with one purpose, one soul, one faith, one baptism, one Lord over all, one God, one great object in view, one right of truth, which they shall bear before them, one sword of the spirit, which they will valiantly wield ; and like those once divided, but now united, States of Greece, they will carry the inextinguishable lamp of truth, and the victorious banner of liberty, to those very ends of the earth that Rome has bedarkened and enslaved."

During Session 1837-38, Dr. Cooke again, by special request of Synod, took charge of the class of Moral Philosophy. At its close the students testified their high appreciation of his services by presenting him with a Bible. In the address which companied it, they say :—

" The course of morals through which you have conducted us, was not founded on the vain and barren speculations of fallen man, but on the eternal foundation of God's love to the sinner through the cleansing blood of a Crucified Redeemer. Your prelections have been distinguished by clear and convincing argument, by attractive and powerful eloquence, and by strictly scientific analysis, congenial to your masterly and philosophical mind. The extended induction of facts by which you philosophically investigated the real condition of our fallen humanity, indicated a mind trained to those habits of close, yet extended observation, by which every department of human life becomes a subject of investigation, and ministers to the illustration and evidence of the Oracles of divine truth."

Dr. Cooke's philosophical and ethical principles are indicated in his reply :—

" I accept it (the Bible) as an appropriate memorial of a course of instruction in which philosophy and revelation have been considered neither as independent, nor rival, nor antagonistic powers, but as confederate auxiliaries in one common cause, and concurrent guides in one common investigation. To me, nothing can appear more preposterous than to represent the philosophy of Christians as unconnected with the Christian Revelation. By philosophy, I simply understand what the word means—the love of wisdom ; and I have yet to learn that the love of wisdom forbids you and me to inquire at any oracle by which truth can be discovered. On the contrary, the true love of wisdom must not only commission, but impel us to visit every region where a new discovery promises to reward our research, and in a world confessedly overwhelmed in deep intellectual and moral darkness, to borrow every light that providence affords. In the use of Scripture, however, in our ethical course, I have felt it my duty to proceed, not dogmatically, as the theologian is entitled to do, but inquisitively, as a philosopher ever should do. By this distinction I mean, that, when referring to Scripture, I had never employed it without investigating the rational evidence, from the analogies of nature, by which its discoveries were illustrated, its statements confirmed, and its dictates enforced. Scripture is to philosophy what the higher forms of calculus are to science—an abbreviated form of investigation, a more potent organ of discovery. But the discoveries of the higher calculus in science are not the less demonstrable, because by the lower forms of calculus they could not have been attained ; and the discoveries of Revelation are not the less philosophical, because reason unassisted, and dispositions depraved, could not have educed them from darkness without a light from heaven. This last observation contains one point in particular to which we are all bound to attend. Ethical philosophers, with a very few exceptions, have not only neglected, but determinedly refused, to cultivate the very first field of legitimate inquiry. They have set out expressly to discover and propound the rules of human life, and yet they have obstinately shut their eyes against all observation of the moral nature of the being they propose to govern. Plain men will be surprised to learn that what is called philosophy pretends, or affects to consider man as what he was when he came forth from the hand of his Creator. His mind it represents as a mere *tabula rasa*, without the blot or record of evil-inclination—at once, by pure reasons within, or perceiving utilities without, a law or law-giver to itself, and a moral picture of the Being who endowed it with all its attributes. . . . This first blunder in ethical philosophy must necessarily be fatal to all its inquiries and conclusions. I have told you, accordingly, not to examine man as an inhabitant of an imaginary moral Utopia, but as the actual everyday being we invariably find him. We have found him weak in judgment, and depraved in inclination. We have seen that in this condition, he could not have come from the hand of his God. We have inquired how he became what we find him to be, and we have philosophically retired upon the historic record, for whilst mere reason possesses no power of discovering any historical event, but can barely search for testimony, yet, having found it, she can subject it to the various and infallible tests of its credibility and accuracy ; and from it, when so tested and confirmed, she can draw a demonstration of truth on principles as strictly philosophical as if the entire discovery had originally been her own. We have found man, moreover, longing for restoration, and we have equally seen cause philosophically to retire upon the record which, whilst it tells of the past, anticipates his recovery ; and the wondrous plan of God for achieving this glorious consummation, we have discovered in Christ crucified ' the wisdom of God,' though ' to the Greeks foolishness,' and ' the power of God,' though ' to the Jews a stumbling-block.'

" In closing the ethical department of our studies, I felt bound to examine with you the grand modern sophism of man's non-accountability for his belief, and carefully avoiding to involve you in any metaphysical labyrinth, I endeavoured, by an induction of facts, to demonstrate that every human opinion is uniformly, necessarily, and inseparably connected with certain consequences. . . . Nor do I believe it possible to furnish an example of opinion or belief disconnected with some consequences, penal or beneficial. This being demonstrably true, man's non-accountability for his opinions or belief vanishes into a mere verbal show, having a form of philosophy without a particle of truth."

The continued opposition of the Synod of Ulster to the teachings of Professor Ferrie, caused great dissatisfaction to the managers of Belfast College. Various attempts were made to compel the attendance of the Synod's students, and a threat was thrown out that they would not otherwise be regarded as entitled to a General Certificate. This threat was met at once by Dr. Cooke, who declared that he would move in the Synod that a General Certificate be not considered a necessary qualification for ordination. A special meeting of Synod was held in Belfast on the 29th August, 1838, for the purpose of inquiring into the state of the College, and especially the teaching in the class of Moral Philosophy. After a long discussion, the matter was left in the hands of a committee, with Dr. Cooke at its head. All negotiations with the Managing Board of the College proved vain. Mr. Ferrie remained Professor, and Doctors Cooke and Molyneux continued to lecture on ethics and metaphysics.

The multitude and variety of Dr. Cooke's home duties and
labours did not prevent him from responding to earnest calls
for his services in other lands.   In the summer of 1838,
the people of Anwoth, in Gallowayshire, resolved to erect
a monument to the memory of Samuel Rutherford.   As one
means of promoting so good an object, it was agreed that
a sermon should be preached in a suitable locality, so that
all classes might have an opportunity of hearing it and joining in the work.   Dr. Cooke was selected as the preacher,
and Sunday, the 9th of September, was the day appointed.
He became the guest of Sir David Maxwell, of Cardoness.
The place chosen for the service was in every respect suitable.   It was in front of Boreland House, facing a semi-
circular recess in the side of a low hill.   A platform was
erected in the centre, and on it was set the old oaken pulpit
in which Rutherford had so often preached when minister of
the parish.   The vast audience ranged themselves in front;
some on benches and chairs, but most on the green grass
which covered the slope; while along the crest of the ridge
behind were drawn up the carriages of the gentry.   It was a
grand scene.   The day was beautiful.   The sun shone in full
splendour on a landscape of unsurpassed richness.   Autumn
gave its mellow tints to the woods, and its golden hues to the
cornfields.   In front of the congregation were the meadows of
Boreland, divided by the links of the sluggish Fleet.   Beyond
spread out the demesne of Cally, the turrets of its princely
mansion rising out of dense foliage, and hundreds of deer
sporting on lawn and forest-glade.   To the left lay the gray
ruins of Cardoness Castle, and away in the distance stretched
the long line of the Anwoth hills.   To the right, the Fleet
was seen flowing into the sea, while the lofty summit of Cairn-
harrow formed a noble back-ground.

The text was, Psalm lxxxix. 15, 16, "Blessed is the people
that know the joyful sound: they shall walk, O Lord, in the
light of Thy countenance.   In Thy name shall they rejoice all
the day: and in Thy righteousness shall they be exalted."

A reporter says, " The subject was treated in a manner at once clear and comprehensive. His language was well chosen. It was by turns forcible, pathetic, and poetically beautiful. . . . At the conclusion of the sermon, which occupied two hours in the delivery, the Doctor's voice was as clear and as distinct as at the beginning, nor did he evince the slightest symptom of fatigue. Not a syllable was lost on the vast assemblage. He evidently possessed and exercised the gift of riveting the attention of the audience, to an extent that weariness or bodily fatigue are, for the moment, entirely forgotten, and the whole soul is wrapt in the speaker. Various calculations were made as to the numbers congregated on Boreland Bank, but that nearest the truth seems to be, to estimate them at between six thousand and seven thousand. . . . In every sense of the word, the celebrated sermon on Boreland of Anwoth, will be long remembered on the banks of the Fleet."

The writer's description of Dr. Cooke's person is interesting :—" The appearance of the learned Doctor of Belfast, is striking at first sight. He may, apparently, have numbered fifty-five summers [his age was only fifty]. He may stand five feet ten in height, and he is of spare habit of body. His features are broadly marked. His hair, which is very slightly tinged with grey, is closely shaded back from his massive brow; and when engaged in prayer, with his arms reverently folded over his breast, we could almost believe we listened to the seraphic tones of one of the rapt seers of old—or, when lighted up afterwards by the fire of his subject, it were little stretch of fancy to conceive him the prototype of one of the stern, eloquent, unbending fathers of the Covenant."

During a subsequent visit to Scotland, Dr. Cooke was invited, while staying with his old friend the late Sir Andrew Agnew, to address a meeting of the " Stranraer and Rhins of Galloway Church Extension Society." He there stated, with wonted clearness, his views as to the fundamental principles and the practical advantages of ecclesiastical establishments :—

"I must recollect that my chief business is to maintain that the sanctuaries you may raise by the sacrifices of your liberality, are entitled to the aid of the State ; and that upon this aid their full efficiency greatly depends.   I lay it down as the ground-work of my argument, that the discovery of truth is the great object of every intelligent being.   Truth is an attribute of God himself.   Truth is one of the glorious titles of our Lord.   Truth is the only emancipator of the enslaved spirit.   Truth is the instrumental sanctifier of the impure heart.   It is the only merchandise worthy to be purchased ; it is the only possession that never can be sold.   But though truth cannot be sold it can be propagated ; and I lay it down as a sound principle, that what a man believes to be truth—man's truth, God's truth, he is by all appropriate means in his power, bound to foster, propagate, and sustain.   With the man who locks up truth, as the antiquarian holds curiosities, rarely to be shown, except to the uninitiated ; or with the man who holds truth as a mere fashion of dress, to be put off, or put on, according to climate, or custom, or country—with such a man I do not argue.   But with the man who holds truth to be the highest acquisition of the intellectual man, and the instrument of holiness to the spiritual man, even with such would I reason.   And I would ask him,—do you not hold that you are bound to propagate truth amongst your children, your friends, your servants, and, if such there be, your enemies ?   Do you dare to resist that ordinance of sovereign wisdom which speaks thus, 'Withhold not good from them to whom it is due, when it is in the power of thine hand to do it.'   And if you dare not resist the ordinance in your own person, then I ask by what perverted logic will you dissuade others from endeavouring to propagate the same truths that you have acknowledged you are bound to propagate ?   Above all, with what countenance of consistency will you actually oppose the efforts of others to aid in accomplishing a work in which you are bound to co-operate ?

"If then, the Articles of the Established Church embody truth, as is admitted by all Protestants, and if the object of that Establishment be to maintain and propagate the truth, your contribution to that Establishment is neither more nor less than your contribution to maintain and propagate the truth.   Disrobe the question thus of the logical mystery, and the conventional offensiveness that the word Establishment now conjures up around it, and look upon it as it really is—as a mere question concerning the maintenance and propagation of acknowledged truth, and I will venture to hope that it

will be an efficient remedy against the sensitive tenderness of conscience, which would wrest from the Church of Scotland her present
endowments, and resist the additions judged necessary for the wants
of her increasing population."

Dr. Cooke's noble efforts in defence of the fundamental principles of a common Protestantism were known and recognised
throughout the United Kingdom. Wherever he was announced
to speak or preach, crowds flocked to hear. In Ireland he was
the leader of his own Church, and the chief of a great and
powerful Protestant party. In Scotland, perhaps no stranger
had ever hitherto attained to such popularity. The General
Assembly accorded to him marks of regard which were
altogether exceptional. The position he held among ecclesiastical magnates in England, may be gathered from the following graphic sketch by a writer in *Frazer's Magazine* for
1838. Its author was manifestly familiar with the scenes
referred to, and competent to describe them :—

"The Rev. Henry Cooke, D.D., the Presbyterian Minister of Belfast,
is one of the most talented speakers which any platform ever presented, and his person is well calculated to give effect to his
speeches.

" He has a tall, commanding figure, very spare, but firmly compacted ; short dark grey hair, a long thin face, an aquiline nose, a
projecting brow, deep-set grey eyes, and a compressed mouth ; his
profile altogether is not unlike that of the Duke of Wellington.

" His appearance, when silent, is one of the most deceptive I ever
saw. You would think he had no more talent, or even intellect, than
a dry tree or a wooden statue. He sits motionless with one knee
put over the other, and his whole frame, as it were, doubled up ; his
eyes fixed on the ground, or wandering over the audience, with an
imperturbable vacancy of expression, as though he had not, nor ever
had, nor ever would have, one single idea in his possession. While
thus meditating, many have been the guesses among the auditory as
to who that ' dry-looking old gentleman' could be ; and on the name
of Dr. Cooke being announced, many a look of astonishment has
been raised to see him rise in answer to it.

" He coolly looks round, and begins his address in a slow, hard,

North Irish brogue, in which those who wish to imitate him will
succeed best by speaking with their teeth closed. He steps at once
into the argument with which he is prepared to defend the position
which he has assumed as his subject-matter. They are always
logically put, clearly illustrated, and triumphantly sustained.

"Whether he most excels in argument, declamation, or description,
I cannot say; he is as incontrovertible in the first as he is solemnly
impressive in the second, while few can surpass his dry, quaint
humour and striking point in the third.

"None but Mr. Beamish or Mr. Stowell can contend with him in
the telling of an anecdote. Those of the former are decidedly more
pathetic, but less vivid in their reality; the latter gives a story with
far more laughing zest and broad comedy, but wants the irresistible
ludicro-solemn slyness of Dr. Cooke; while no man but himself
ever acted his facts with such perfect truth by one or two movements.

" He has full possession of that secret of genius, the production
of the greatest quantity of effect by the smallest quantity of means,
and nowhere does he manifest this more completely than in his action
while speaking.

" He uses very little of it, but that little is always exactly of the
right kind, and exactly in the right place; moreover, two or three of
his quiet gestures will convey as much meaning as twenty from most
other men.

"I once saw him act an anecdote, in which he personated to the
life the surprise of a poor Irishwoman on finding an unexpected
bundle in her cabin—her curiosity as to its contents, her peeping in
at one corner, her stealthily opening it, her discovery of a cloak in
it, the unfolding of the cloak, and, finally, the putting it on; and
all this was done by a few slow, quiet movements of his hands, and
of a small book which he held in them.

" The story ended by the good woman's being informed by her
husband, that the cloak was a present for herself, purchased with his
quarter's salary as reader to the Irish Society, an employment to
which she had been greatly opposed.

" Few who heard this part of the tale will forget the look of
delighted simplicity with which Dr. Cooke cast up his eyes, and
clasped his hands just below his chin, while, in a deep and fervid
tone, he gave his final exclamation, ' Ough, bless ut, then, for a
darrlint of a Soceeity!'

" This is but one among many things of the kind which I could relate of this extraordinary man. In debate and discussion he is said to be invincible ; and certainly, to judge from his usual speeches, one would guess that at times, when extraordinary exertion is required, his genius would rise with the occasion. There is a unity of design, and a completeness of execution, in all his addresses which invariably leave a satisfactory impression on the mind ; whatever his subject may have been, he has made you understand it, and (unless you be of the prejudiced class) he has made you believe it also.

" Nor is he one of those cold, dry reasoners, who only convince the judgment without touching the feelings. He has a fund of pathos at his command—not the common-place weeping sort of pathos, but that deep, tragic kind which awes while it stills the heart, and ends in solemnity, not in mere transient emotion. Many of his appeals on behalf of his country are of this class, and produce an unrivalled effect whenever they are made.

" The absence of Dr. Cooke during the two last seasons has been a great loss to the May Meetings ; I know not whether he may have superiors, but I am quite sure that, in his own line, he has no rival and no substitute."

But the most remarkable tribute rendered to the talents and triumphs of Dr. Cooke—perhaps the most remarkable ever accorded to a divine and religious controversialist—was that which conferred upon him the freedom of the City of Dublin. The gratifying intelligence was first communicated in the following letter :—

"Town Clerk's Office, Dublin, 6th Feb., 1839.

" Rev. Sir,—In the performance of a very pleasing duty, we beg leave to acquaint you that the Corporation of Dublin, in Common Council assembled, this day resolved as follows :— ' That the freedom of this City be granted to the Rev. Doctor Cooke, of the Synod of Ulster, in consideration of the zeal which he has long manifested in support of pure religion.

" We have the honour to be,
" Reverend Sir,
" Your most obedient,
" Very humble servants,
" Archer & Long,
" Rev. Dr. Cooke, &c.   " Town Clerks."

In May, 1839, Dr. Cooke met with an accident, which, it was for a time feared, would terminate fatally. In driving to a meeting of Presbytery, his horse fell, and, in addition to other injuries, the thumb of his right hand was shattered. Having wrapped it up, he proceeded to the meeting, took a leading part in the business, and returned home. There, however, inflammation set in, and his sufferings became intense. The first surgeon in Dublin was summoned to see him. Amputation was decided on, but Dr. Cooke resisted. Eventually the thumb was saved, though much disfigured, and rendered useless for life. When his danger became known, the sorrow and consternation throughout the Church and the country were profound; and when the danger was at length averted, and health partially restored, the expressions of joy were proportional. At the annual meeting of the Synod, held on the 26th of June, the following resolution was passed :—" That this Synod, feeling deep gratitude to Almighty God for the recovery of the Rev. Dr. Cooke, a beloved and esteemed brother, from a recent dangerous sickness, do now resolve that supplications be offered with thanksgiving, that the dispensation with which he has been visited, may be sanctified to him and to the Church at large."

During the sittings of the Synod, he was still weak and suffering; yet he took a leading part in the debates. So soon as the meeting closed he was ordered to England for change of air. His recovery was then more rapid, and on the 8th of August he wrote to Mrs. Cooke from London :—" On Saturday last, I had to walk through the streets some seven or eight miles, and expected to be quite knocked up, but, thanks be to God, I found myself almost quite restored by the exertion. The extreme heat of the air, and dryness of Hampstead, have set me on my legs again, so that I feel a new man. Indeed, I feel so much restored, that I think it likely, that, after another week, I shall be home with you.

" Poor Haldane ! [his youngest son, then a child] I wish I knew how he is. When I yesterday saw little Samuel in his shirt, in the National Gallery, I thought of poor Hally. I have heard Lord Brougham sweep the filth off the Whigs, and nearly the whiskers off Lord ——; but, unless our gracious little Queen furnish me with a cushion, I do protest against ever entering the gallery of the House of Lords again. I proposed to Dr. Stewart to go down and ask the Lord Chancellor's wig for me to sit on; it would have been of more use to me than to him.

"I shall stay here till Monday, the 19th, to try to get thoroughly well, which the dry air is effecting rapidly. If not then well, I shall sail immediately after for the Netherlands."

On his return to Ireland, he was entertained by the inhabitants of Armagh, who presented him with an address of congratulation on his restoration to health. The chair was occupied on the occasion by General Sir Thomas Molyneux, and the Tontine Rooms were crowded with the clergy and gentry of the city and county. The enthusiasm manifested on the appearance of Dr. Cooke, is described as exceeding anything previously witnessed in the city.

The Presbyterians of Downpatrick resolved to commemorate their joy at his recovery, and their high appreciation of the services rendered by him to their Church, in a still more substantial manner. They presented him with an exquisitely painted miniature of John Knox, set in a massive medallion of Irish silver, ornamented with emblematic figures, *in relievo*, and studded with Irish amethysts. The whole was surrounded by a rich frame of Irish oak, with carved wreaths of the shamrock, rose, and thistle. This chaste and beautiful testimonial bears the following inscription :—" Presented to the Rev. H. Cooke, D.D., LL.D., by the Presbyterian Congregation of Downpatrick, on his recovery from illness, 1839. Phil. ii. 27."

The numerous private letters which he received from esteemed and honoured friends, were, if possible, even more gratifying than these public testimonials. Among them is one from Lord Roden, breathing the same feelings of ardent friendship and deep piety which always characterized him. At the

close he says :—" I was indeed in the greatest anxiety when I
heard of your accident, and wrote to my friends in the neighbourhood to send me frequent tidings about you.   It was my
chief comfort to know that you were in the Lord's keeping, and
if it was His pleasure to remove you, while it would be such a
cause to the Church for mourning, as regarded herself, it would
be to the glory of the power of Jesus, and it would be to the
endless bliss of His dear servant.   I often long to fly away, as
I find life sometimes a great weight and burden ; but my
Saviour knows what is best; and His people are His instruments ; and He uses them according to the counsel of His will.
God bless you, my dear friend.   A thousand thanks for your
prayers for me.   Believe me always your affectionate friend.

" Roden."

CHAPTER XIV.

1837—1840.

National Education in Ireland—Education Scheme of the Synod of Ulster—Dr. Cooke opposes the National Board—Parliamentary Commission in 1837— Dr. Cooke's Evidence—Changes in the Rules of the Board—The Rev. P. S. Henry appointed Commissioner—Important Results — Negociations with Government—Interview of Synod's Committee with the Lord Lieutenant— The Board abandons objectionable Rules—Basis of Agreement with Synod of Ulster — Dr. Cooke's Principles and Policy triumphant — Assailed by former Allies—Letter to the Rev. Hugh McNeile—Desire for Peace frustrated —Controversy with Mr. Gregg.

In 1839 the important question of National Education was again brought before the Presbyterian Church by Dr. Cooke in a new phase. The strange and crooked policy of the Board had compelled the Synod to break off all negotiations with it in 1834. So long as the same counsels prevailed in Dublin, and the same influence continued to work, it was felt that all hope of a just or amicable settlement was vain. The Synod, therefore, resolved, mainly at the instigation of Dr. Cooke, to organise an education scheme of its own. The fundamental principles of the scheme, as contradistinguished from the National Board, were as follows :—

" The plan of education provides that the Bible shall be free in all the Synod's schools during every school hour. It shall, like the light of heaven, be open for every eye that is not shut against it ; and all who attend the schools may read in it as much, and as often during the day, as may be thought consistent with their advantage and the other duties of the school. The children of our communion shall daily read such proportion of Scripture, and learn such portion of our Standard Catechisms, as parents, with the concurrence of the Church Session, may advise ; but when the children of other communions attend our schools, they shall be at perfect liberty to read the Scriptures or not, as their parents or guardians direct. . . . Our system of education will be strictly scriptural, and at the same time catholic, forbearing, and charitable. . . .

" It is known that the Synod disapproves of and highly condemns the system that would exclude the Scriptures during school hours, and thus oppose the circulation of God's Word ; yet it has been affirmed that our principles merely lead us to introduce the Bible for the use of our own communion, and such others as may demand access to the Word of God. . . . The Directors would beg leave most respectfully to submit that such a principle has never been laid down by this Synod, nor adopted in the practice of our schools.

" If it be anti-scriptural to exclude the Word of God from our schools, it is maintained that the Church is ignorant of duty, and lamentably deficient in the service of the Lord, if it content itself with merely making provision for the scriptural instruction of the members of its own communion. It is the duty of the Church to bring the Word of God to bear on all who may be ignorant of its blessed tidings. It is bound in the first place to use its energies in removing every obstacle to the circulation of the Scriptures, and then, whenever an opportunity is found, to offer the message of eternal life. If it be rejected, the Church has fulfilled a duty ; but until the offer has been made, the Church has been negligent of its responsibility to God, and careless respecting the condition and future prospects of immortal souls."

As a deputy from the Synod Dr. Cooke explained and advocated this scheme in England and Scotland. He was successful, and the scheme increased year after year in popularity. Suitable school-books were prepared. An annotated edition of the Westminster Shorter Catechism was edited, at Dr. Cooke's request, by Captain Hamilton Rowan, and proved eminently useful. While pleading the cause of the scheme, Dr. Cooke continued, wherever he went, to expose the false principles and strange acts of the Irish National Board. At a great meeting held in Liverpool, in February, 1839, he denounced the National system as opposed to the Word of God, and to the fundamental principles of Protestantism. He showed that it was designed, by an unworthy sacrifice of truth, to conciliate Roman Catholics. He showed, besides, that in this respect it had been a signal failure. The leaders of the Papal Church in Ireland had already become so distrustful of the system that they had written to Rome for instructions, and it now depended on the will of the Pope whether the National Board would be continued or not.

A few months afterwards, at a Protestant meeting in Manchester, Dr. Cooke explained the radical evils of the National system, his dissatisfaction with the changes which had been made in it, and his continued distrust of its management, as already stated.

The National Board and the Government came at length to feel that some change was necessary. The whole system was in danger. The Presbyterian Church refused to adopt it, and were working out with vigour and success a scheme of their own. The Roman Catholics threatened to throw it overboard. Some concessions must, therefore, be made to satisfy the conscientious scruples of Protestants. Committees of Inquiry were appointed by both Houses of Parliament in 1837. An immense mass of evidence was collected and printed; but little good was effected. Dr. Cooke was examined at great length. His stedfast objection to one of the principles of the Board, which was represented to be "fundamental and unalterable," was brought out fully in reply to a question put by Mr. Gladstone :—

" Would you object altogether to the separate instruction of the Roman Catholic children in the school, and to allowing the Douay Version to be used in their instruction ?

"*Answer*. To the separate instruction in Roman Catholic doctrine I object *in toto*, for that makes me a party to its inculcation. To the use of the Douay Version in any form I would object, unless I had an opportunity of testifying against its errors in translation and its tremendous notes. If Romanists would not take King James's Version from me, I would not give the Douay Version in its place. But if the Douay Version they must have, let them have it with my testimony against it, and with this testimony I conceive I should have done my duty."

The rule of the Board to which the question referred was that which required in all schools, vested or non-vested, under Presbyterian management or not, that a day should be set apart each week for religious instruction, on which " such pastors, or other persons as are approved by the parents shall have access to the children, whether those pastors shall have signed the original application or not." This really made the patrons and master of the school agents and helpers of the Roman Catholic priest in the performance of his spiritual work. Against this Dr. Cooke protested in the strongest terms; yet the regulation was retained in the revised rules of 1838. A salutary change, however, was introduced which allowed the Scriptures to be read, and religious instruction given, during any of the school hours. This change removed one great barrier in the way of Presbyterians.

Another change took place in 1838, which had an important effect upon the relations of the Board to the Synod of Ulster. The Rev. Mr. Carlile retired from the Board, and the secretary, Mr. Kelly, resigned his office. The Rev. P. S. Henry, minister of the Presbyterian Church, Armagh, was appointed Commissioner in the room of Mr. Carlile. Her Majesty's Government felt the necessity of attempting to conciliate the Synod, and the way was now open to accomplish that object. The Ministry had long thought that Mr. Carlile's influence in the Presbyterian Church would eventually induce the Synod to agree to the rules of the Board, especially after the important modifications made in 1838. They were disappointed; and as the Roman Catholic prelates began to show signs of withdrawing their patronage, it was felt that the adhesion of the Presbyterians was necessary to the very existence of the National system.

The Synod of 1839 instructed the Directors of their schools to apply to Her Majesty's Government for pecuniary aid. Drs. Cooke and Stewart were consequently commissioned to proceed to London for that purpose. They had interviews with the leading members of the Cabinet. They were received with marked respect; but they were informed that no aid could be given to schools in Ireland except through the National Board. Dr. Cooke urged that the rules of the Board were such as to preclude all possibility of obtaining or accepting aid from that quarter. The Government stated in reply that the representatives of the Synod would now find an anxious disposition on the part of the Board to meet their views. Dr. Cooke was pleased and surprised at the statement. He knew, besides, that he could rely on the wisdom and friendly assistance of the new Commissioner, Mr. Henry, whose appointment opened the way to a solution of all difficulties. He, therefore, with the consent of the Directors, at once opened a correspondence with Mr. Henry, who expressed confident hope in the practicability of a reconciliation, and immediately communicated on the subject with the Lord Lieutenant and the Board. His Excellency expressed a wish that a deputation from the Synod should proceed to Dublin and confer with himself and the Commissioners on the points at issue. Drs. Cooke and Stewart, Mr. Morgan, and other leading men, were appointed, and were prepared with a written statement of their objections to the rules of the Board, and of the conditions upon which the Synod would consent to accept aid. His Excellency, who was thoroughly acquainted with the whole subject, stated freely, at the opening of the interview, that the Query-sheet, formerly sent to each applicant for a grant, and which contained the objectionable rules, had been altogether withdrawn. He said that patrons might now have such religious instruction given in their schools as they wished, provided no compulsion were used to make children attend. That there might be no misunderstanding for the future, and that there might be something more definite than a mere statement of abstract rules and principles, which past experience led Dr. Cooke to distrust, it was arranged that an application should be made to the Board for aid towards a school, the actual circumstances and rules of which, as laid down by its own managing committee, should be stated; that the Board should come to a decision upon it, without waiting for, or seeking, any previous reference to the local superintendant, or to any other parties; and that the Board's action in regard to it should be the sole standard for all future applications and grants.

Immediately on this arrangement being made, the deputation withdrew, for the purpose of preparing the model application. It was a difficult and most responsible task. The principles which the Synod of Ulster had all along laid down as fundamental, had to be carefully and jealously guarded. Each point had to be stated so clearly that there could be no possibility of misunderstanding, and no just ground of complaint for the future. Dr. Cooke knew well the ordeal he would have to pass through as the prime mover in all past and present negotiations. He knew that many who had joined him in opposing the National system, but whose views were not so clear, and whose principles were not so well defined as his own, would be likely to misunderstand, if not misrepresent, his policy and conduct. He had, however, the clear logical mind of Dr. Stewart, and the sagacity of Mr. Morgan, and the caution of Dr. Brown, and the experience of Mr. Henry, to aid him. The application was drawn up on the 24th of January, 1840, for Curren school, under the patronage of Dr. Stewart, and its rules were stated as follows:—

" The school is under the management of a committee chosen by the parents of the children.

" The times for reading the Scriptures and for catechetical instruction are so arranged as not to interfere with or impede the scientific or secular business of the school; and no child, whose parents or guardians object, is required to be present, or take part in those exercises; and no obstruction shall be offered to the children of such parents receiving such instruction elsewhere, as they may think proper.

" The school opens in the summer at half-past nine, A.M., and continues till half-past five, P.M., with the interval of one hour, from one till two, for dinner. In the winter it opens at ten and continues till three. In both summer and winter it is held during six days of the week. The school is open upon all days of the week to the public of all denominations, who have liberty to inspect the registry, witness the mode of teaching, and see that the regulations of the school are faithfully observed ; but no persons, except members of the committee, and the officers of the Board, are permitted *ex officio* to interfere in the business or management of the school. The books used, in addition to the Scriptures and the Westminster Catechism, are those sanctioned by the Kildare Place Society."

The application was received by the Board, and its petition immediately granted. The grant was made also with the express, and recorded stipulation, that all similar applications from members of the Synod of Ulster should be granted, so far as the funds of the National Board might allow. An official copy of the application was asked by the Board, and was given by the deputation, and thereafter it became the model and the law which regulated the connection between the Board and the Synod. The deputation in presenting their report to a special meeting of Synod, held in Belfast, in April, 1840, were fully justified in saying :—

" Your deputation have thus the satisfaction of submitting to their brethren that aid has been obtained for their schools, not only without any compromise of principle, but in perfect harmony with the principles on which the schools of the Synod have hitherto been conducted. 1. Protestants can apply for aid to their schools, without any reference to, or union with, any other denomination. This was not the case in the former rules of the Board ; for though Protestants might have applied by themselves, the Query-sheet afterwards required the reason why reference to others had been omitted. 2. The Query-sheet, of which several of the questions and regulations were exceedingly offensive to Protestants, has been totally withdrawn ; and aid for our schools is granted simply on our own statement of their constitution and regulations. 3. The schools, as Protestant schools have ever been, are open to the public ; but none, except the applicants, are recognised as *ex officio* visitors. This is a valuable improvement upon the former regulation of the Board, which empowered others to be *ex officio* visitors in every Protestant school, to which regulation every Protestant applicant was required to submit. 4. The Bible is free during school hours, and the extent of its use subject to no control but the will of the parents expressed through committees of their own free choice, and the greatest convenience of the attending scholars. 5. The Westminster Catechisms are also free during school hours ; a privilege not enjoyed even under the Kildare Place Society. 6. There is no concession of any day in the week for separate religious instruction, as the former regulations of the Board, in every case, required. 7. No one has a right to demand admission to teach in our school-houses, as the former regulations of the Board required and enforced. 8. In return for aid to our schools we are neither required to make, nor have we made, to the Board any concession of any Protestant principle or practice. In relation to other denominations we neither recognise, promise, nor guarantee, instruction in their peculiar creeds ; we barely stipulate, that, when parents object, we, acting upon the Protestant principle of liberty of conscience, and following the immemorial practice of our schools, will neither require nor compel their children to read our Bibles nor commit our Catechisms ; and that if the parents so direct, we will not obstruct their seeking instruction elsewhere. 9. We have secured to our schools and the children of the Protestant communions, the great principle which our Synod, learning from the Scriptures, so early adopted, and has so faithfully maintained, viz., That religious and secular learning should form the united and inseparable parts of a Christian education. Thus all that the Synod ever asked has been granted, and all the principles of our own system of education have been maintained."

When the report was read, it was unanimously resolved :—

"That the Synod cordially approve of the report and proceedings of the Directors and the Deputation, and return them their marked thanks for the fidelity with which they have executed the important commission entrusted to them, and the success which has attended their efforts."

Dr. Cooke was thus at last triumphant after a long and hard struggle. He had gained every principle for which, from the outset, he contended. He had never yielded one iota either to the entreaties of professed friends, or the assaults of open and determined foes. He had exposed with unsparing severity the false principles hitherto maintained by the National Board, and the crooked policy by which it had attempted to force them upon the acceptance of the Synod of Ulster. He had shown that the changes insisted upon by the Synod, as a basis of connection, were just and scriptural. His conduct from first to last had been open, honest, consistent. To him the Presbyterian Church is indebted for those great advantages she has derived from the National system of education; and to him Ireland is indebted for the preservation of that system, either from utter ruin on the one hand, or the rule of Ultramontane despotism on the other.

Dr. Cooke was assailed just as he had anticipated. He was assailed by some who had been trying to serve their own purposes and advance their own party interests, by his eloquent advocacy and commanding influence. He was charged with having " betrayed the cause of Protestantism," with having " sold the pass," with having " stipulated to teach Popery." It was a sore trial to be thus maligned by the friends whom he had served. He replied in temperate and dignified language, showing with the precision of mathematical demonstration, that he had made no sacrifice of Protestantism; that in his negotiations he had preserved the sound scriptural principles all along contended for by his Church; and that, after all, the result of the arrangement effected, was not the connecting of the Synod with the National Board, nor was it the sanctioning on the part of the Synod, through its deputies, of the general rules of the Board; but it was simply and solely a consenting to accept for the Synod's schools, through the Board as a channel, a National endowment, in accordance with rules and regulations laid down by the Synod and accepted by the Board. Farther than this Dr. Cooke never went; and farther than this, under his leadership, the Presbyterian Church never went.

Never, perhaps, during his long public career had Dr. Cooke's large-hearted charity been so severely tested as now. But it did not fail. He met argument with argument. He met misrepresentations with facts. He met groundless charges of betrayal with indignant denial. But he never was betrayed into an unkind or uncharitable word against the Church to

which his traducers belonged. On the contrary, even when
stung by calumny, he embraced every fitting opportunity of
inculcating his old and loved theme, "Protestant peace and
Protestant union." At a public entertainment given to him and
Mr. Molyneux at the close of the College session of 1839-40,
he said in his parting address to his students :—

"I would impress upon your minds that while you are Presbyterians you are Protestants ; while one is your Christian name the other
is your surname. I shall tell you an anecdote of the best times of the
Presbyterian Church, and when it was most tried. In a particular
locality in Scotland there lay a beautiful valley, and in it an humble
church, whose pastor had as good a head as ever rested on Presbyterian
shoulders ; he was a Covenanter. A stranger in humble garb applied
at the Manse one afternoon for shelter, and was hospitably welcomed.
During the evening, the minister being out, his wife assembled the
servants and began to catechise them. While so engaged, she
asked the stranger ' How many commandments are there ? ' ' Eleven, '
was the reply. Astonished at his ignorance, she told him how awful
it was for a man of his age to be so ill informed. He quietly, yet
solemnly, replied, ' Did not our Saviour say, A new commandment
give I unto you, that ye love one another ? ' He then retired to
bed. On his return home the minister was told what had occurred.
In the morning, when going forth for his customary walk, his attention was arrested by solemn words of prayer ; and listening, he
heard most earnest supplication for unhappy Ireland. When it
ended, the stranger came forth from his retirement. The mystery
was now solved. ' Tell me,' said the minister, ' are you not Archbishop Ussher, come to mingle your prayers with the Presbyters of
Scotland ? ' It was he. Then they joined in prayer ; and Ussher,
Ireland's mitred prelate, on the following Sunday, preached in the
pulpit of Samuel Rutherford, the Scotch Covenanter."

It was by members of the Established Church Dr. Cooke
was attacked on account of his recent policy in regard to
National Education. He was extremely anxious to avoid controversy, because he knew it would tend more and more to
divide the two great sections of the Protestant Church in
Ireland, and thereby to injure the cause of truth. With this
view he wrote privately to the Rev. Hugh McNeile, who had

been drawn into the controversy. He strongly deprecated all discussion and correspondence on the subject; but he plainly stated, at the same time, that unless the calumnious attacks made upon him were stopped, he would be compelled to retaliate. Referring to a letter written by Dr. Stewart, in reply to published communications from the Rev. Mr. Drew and Mr. McNeile himself, Dr. Cooke says :—

"I must confess I think it has demolished your arguments. Still you are right when you judged, and say that you thought me an enemy to the 'hodge-podge' character of the Board, and, on this subject, I never did nor do I now, differ from you ; I am just as much opposed to the 'hodge-podge' of the Board as to the 'hodge-podge' of both Houses of Parliament, yet I receive the pay of that Parliament, and I trust I have a good conscience. From the same Parliament, with all its 'hodge-podge,' the Church of England willingly and thankfully receives money for churches, universities, societies, and bishops.

"Ah! you will say, but the Parliament requires no unprotestant concession ; I answer, Neither does the Board. Where is now the Popery-acknowledging Query-sheet ? Gone to the fire. Where are now the fifty-two days in the year for separate religious instruction ? Melted into the three hundred and sixty-five without note of such distinction. Where is now the claim or concession of the right of the Popish priest, as such, to visit, *ex officio*, a Protestant school-house ? The claim is not preferred ; the concession is not made. Where is now the arrangement for teaching Popery elsewhere ? Not in our 'Bond.' We'd sooner have given a pound of our dearest flesh. Where are now the ordinary school hours during which Bibles were authoritatively excluded ? Their very name is buried, and no authority but the direct or delegated parental interference to regulate the times of their being read. Could a Protestant Board give more, or ask less ? If so, what ? "

Referring to the charge so frequently and persistently hurled against him and his friends in the Synod of Ulster, that they had deserted the Established Church and selfishly sought their own ends, he thus writes :—

"Hear our defence, and then say what Church is deserted and betrayed for selfish ends ? Before ever the deputation of the Synod of Ulster presented their application to Government in 1833, they

waited successively on the Bishops of Exeter and London, stating that
as a deputation of the Presbyterian Church in Ireland, they desired
to cooperate with the Established Church ; but having no recognized organ to whom they could officially apply, they had been
advised to wait on some of the more prominent of the Heads of the
Establishment, to submit their proposals for their inspection, and to
beg their kind counsel and suggestion, and to declare their willing-
ness and determination to proceed not a step without their concurrence.   During lengthened interviews with the two first prelates,
they fully explained their propositions, and obtained their unqualified
approval ; and after explaining them to his Grace of Armagh, he requested a day for their consideration, after which they were returned,
with a letter of unqualified concurrence and approbation. . . . .
All this was known to every one of our assailants ; it was stated in
open Synod ; published in the newspapers, related on platforms in
company with some of the very men who now accuse us of deserting
or betraying the Established Church. . . . . God grant me patience
and forbearance and meekness to meet men of another spirit. I have
been maligned, misrepresented, abused, and I have borne it without
a word of public retort. I shall bear a few days longer ; and then
patience will have ceased to be a virtue. But, alas ! When I defend
myself I must smite the Societies [the Kildare Street, the London
Hibernian School Society, &c.]. Would that I could escape this
dilemma ! But I feel there is no such possibility. . . . . I see
that even you make light of Presbyterian aid. . . . . But if you
make light of the passive resistance our people gave to O'Connell on
the tithe question, I think you treat us with something that is either
mere forgetfulness, or that is akin to ingratitude. Had we joined
the ' Appropriation ' outcry, where had been the livings of the
Church ? With things forgotten. You know me too well, I trust,
to think that even ill-treatment will change my principles of universal Protestantism, or narrow my heart to my own shell. But let
ministers controvert, and the people will quarrel. Let O'Connell
know that we are divided, and the Devil will soon find him some
popular wedge which he will drive home into the trunk of our glorious
tree. I have made up my mind that whatever the Papists and
Infidel press write of slander I will bear ; but if the Protestant press
and clergy assail me or my poor Church again, I draw the sword."

This strong and touching remonstrance was written on the
5th of March. It was in vain. The suicidal policy was per-

severed in. Dr. Cooke was at length forced to make a public defence. He did so at the Synod, and at various meetings. He challenged his opponents to a fair and full discussion of all the points at issue. He defied them to prove by honest investigation and fair argument, that he had ever changed his policy, or that he had ever yielded a single principle of sound Protestantism.

Yet still the ungracious and ungrateful attacks of members of the Established Church did not alter Dr. Cooke's views or general line of conduct. His feelings toward that Church sprung from a deeply-rooted principle.

"I will not," he said, when defending himself against unworthy calumnies ; "I will not identify the Church of England with a fraction or a faction. Certain ministers of that Church have assailed this Synod. What business, I ask, have they with the Synod of Ulster ? I have known a man made a chaplain for abusing me ; but I still wish to maintain, as I have ever wished to maintain, Protestant peace."

It is quite true that these attacks produced no effect upon Dr. Cooke's generous and noble nature ; but it is just as true that they did produce an effect on the Presbyterian public. They contributed, and that in no small degree, to alienate the sympathies of many Presbyterian ministers, and of thousands of their people, who might otherwise have stood by and aided the Church of England in her day of trial.

Dr. Cooke himself did not write much in this unhappy controversy ; but his friend Dr. Stewart published a number of telling letters defending the character of Dr. Cooke, proving his perfect consistency, and maintaining the wise and honest policy of the Synod of Ulster. Unfortunately the small party in the Church of England persisted in their opposition. They employed all the powers of the press to disseminate their misrepresentations of Dr. Cooke. They printed and circulated gratuitously, pamphlets and letters, setting forth their own superlative purity, and the grievous defections of the Synod of Ulster. Dr. Cooke was again forced, in self-defence, to state his views in relation to the National Board, and to show from the undeniable testimony of his own published evidence before Parliamentary Committees in 1825, 1833, and 1837, that his principles and policy remained unchanged from first to last. In May, 1840, he published the following statement in the *Ulster Times*, as a preface to one of Dr. Stewart's letters :—

" So much am I willing to sacrifice for peace, that, though my friend, Dr. Stewart, has so generously come to the rescue of my character, yet would I decline availing myself of his sword, were it not that the calumnies of the *University Magazine* have been so industriously circulated in Belfast and its neighbourhood. Yes, sir, it is a fact, that, not contented with the magazine's own circulation, its false and calumnious article was printed as a tract, and not only sold 'dog-cheap' to those who would buy, but pre-paid at the post-office to ensure acceptance, and scattered gratuitously through the drawing-rooms of the rich and the garrets of the poor.

" I say not a word of the revilings of the *Evening Mail*, and other journals. With one exception, they make no pretensions to religious character, and, as acknowledged party papers, claim the prescriptive right of an ambassador—a man, according to Rochefoucault, sent out to tell lies for the good of his country. But the magazine has well-founded pretensions to literary, and therefore should have to honest, character ; and the *Examiner*, from its name of *Christian*, binds itself to truth and charity. Yet, of my calumniators in both I will deliberately say, and can incontrovertibly prove, that they knew, when they penned their calumnies, that they were both dishonest men. . . . . The writers, who, I find, accuse me of changing, from dishonourable motives, my views on the education question, and who, consequently, must have examined my evidence in 1837, I do distinctly and deliberately accuse of knowing their own falsehood and dishonesty. I have never changed one fragment of an opinion on the subject either of the Board or their system. The Brown Street Committee can witness we never sought for more than our own system, and which amounted to no more than this—the recognition of the right to fix our own hours for reading the Scriptures, and being bound simply and solely by our own rules. And my printed evidence, which has, I find, been tortured in a manner so unworthy of theologians, bound to truth alone—this printed evidence, when not garbled, will demonstrate that, so far from differing now from my former self, so as to give my calumniators room for their exclamation, *quantum mutatus ab illo*, I held in 1840 the self-same opinions I recorded in 1837, and which were the self-same opinions which I held and promulgated in 1833."

The controversy remained dormant till February, 1841, when it was unfortunately revived by the Rev. T. D. Gregg, who, during a visit to Belfast, published a strong and irritating letter, in which he accepted the challenge given by Dr. Cooke some months previously. The acceptance was somewhat tardy, and the point at issue besides was dexterously changed. Dr. Cooke at once agreed to meet him; but insisted on confining the discussion to the point originally stated. The time was most inopportune. O'Connell had carried his repeal agitation to Belfast, and had just been driven away in disgrace by Dr. Cooke. To divide the ranks of Protestants at such a juncture was felt by all thoughtful men to be suicidal. The friends of repeal were already exulting at the prospect of a division in the Protestant camp, and they exerted all their powers through the Roman Catholic press to fan the flame of discord. Under these circumstances the leaders of the Protestant party resolved, if possible, to prevent the discussion. A public meeting was held, and a deputation appointed to wait upon Dr. Cooke and Mr. Gregg, and request them to abandon their proposed discussion. The result was stated in an advertisement which appeared in the *News-Letter* of March 5th :—

" We, the undersigned, having been appointed a deputation to communicate to the Rev. Dr. Cooke, and the Rev. T. D. Gregg, the resolution unanimously adopted by a most influential public meeting, held here on the 1st instant, strongly disapproving of the proposed discussion between those gentlemen, and earnestly desiring that it should be abandoned, cannot but deeply regret that Mr. Gregg should have declined yielding to the wishes of that meeting. And, at the same time, we feel called on to express the satisfaction we experienced from the manner in which Dr. Cooke received the deputation, and the desire he manifested to sacrifice his own feelings in deference to them. And he having placed the matter entirely in our hands, we beg to state it as our decided opinion, that (notwithstanding the

steps since taken by Mr. Gregg), for the sake of Protestant peace
and union, Dr. Cooke should not enter on this discussion.

    (*Signed*) " JOHN CHAIN, Dean of Connor.
             A. C. MACARTNEY, Vicar of Belfast.
             DANIEL MCAFEE, Wesleyan Minister.
             DAVID HAMILTON, Presbyterian Minister.
             JOHN MCNEILE.
             ANDREW MULHOLLAND.
             JAMES GODDARD.
             JAMES BLAIR."

    Dr. Cooke acted wisely. Nothing could be gained by a dis-
cussion. He had already triumphantly answered all the
calumnies of his assailants. The consistency of the Synod of
Ulster from first to last was established by unquestionable
documentary evidence. Men might hold different views as to
the general policy of the National Board. They might condemn some of its rules; they might complain of the glaring
and lamentable inconsistency of its acts; but every intelligent
man must admit that the course pursued by Dr. Cooke was
manly, honest, and scriptural. He laid down at the first the
terms on which he would consent to accept aid for the schools
of the Synod of Ulster, and not until those terms were fully
granted, did he agree to receive a single shilling on behalf of
the Synod's schools from the National Board.

    The Synod of Ulster fully approved of Dr. Cooke's procedure,
and, at the Annual Meeting in 1840, passed a unanimous vote
of thanks to Doctors Cooke and Stewart and the Rev. P. S.
Henry, for their zealous and successful labours.

CHAPTER XV.

1840.

ONE of the most important events in the history of the Presbyterian Church in Ireland occurred in 1840. In that year a union was effected between the General Synod of Ulster and the Secession Synod; and this happy union was one of the results of Dr. Cooke's great reforms. The Seceders were descendants of the men who, under the leadership of the Erskines, left the Church of Scotland in 1733, on account of the evils of patronage. They had ever remained faithful to the principles and traditions of their distinguished forefathers. Their cause prospered in Ireland. Their ministers were noted for piety and devotion. Their Church was never tainted with those errors which unfortunately prevailed in the Synod of Ulster. Unqualified subscription to the Westminster Standards had always been their law. After the Synod of Ulster was freed from Arianism, Dr. Cooke looked forward to, and laboured for, union with the Seceders. When the subject came before the Synod by memorial, in 1839, he said :—

" The first reason in favour of the desired union is, that our
Mother Church of Scotland has been wooing back some who had
separated from her, and her daughter, the Synod of Ulster, ought to
follow the example. Unlike their Scottish brethren, the Seceders of
Ireland have adhered to the Confession of Faith, as a whole, without
reservation or exception, as it had been originally adopted by the
Church of Scotland. The Seceders of Ireland are not Voluntaries.
The Establishment of Scotland is anxiously watching the movements
of the Synod of Ulster, and for the satisfaction of its members it is
necessary for me to state that the Seceders of Ireland are not, like
the Seceders of Scotland, prepared with axes and pickaxes to destroy
the foundations and break down the walls of the Church of Scotland. Hence, in seeking union with the Seceders, the Synod of
Ulster is not seeking union with a body of Church destructives . . .
There is no difference in principle between the Synod of Ulster and
the Secession Synod, but simply in matters of detail ; and if the
parties meet in goodwill, humility, and prayerfulness, I have no
doubt that every minor difference will be adjusted. . . . . Seceders have never relinquished the Covenants ; and, at no distant
period, I also look forward to union with those commonly called
Covenanters, as well as with the Secession body ; and then in Ireland, and throughout the empire, the Presbyterian community will
present an unbroken and resistless phalanx. The proposed union
will take away from Presbyterianism the stigma of endless divisions
now attached to it by Roman Catholics. On a former occasion, the
Synod lost seventeen Arian congregations, instead of which seventy
Orthodox have been generated ; and now it is likely to gain one
hundred and fifty more by its connection with the Secession Church.
In another point of view union is important ; I mean in a political
point of view. It has been usual for ministers to disclaim all connection with politics ; but, for myself, I avow the fact that I am a
politician ; and in this respect the Presbyterian Church has miser-
ably neglected its own interests. It has no representative in Parliament. . . . . An echo from the South lately proclaimed in
Newry, that on the staunch Presbyterians of Ireland the fate of the
empire is dependent ; and this sentiment ought to be emblazoned
on the front of Buckingham Palace and St. Stephen's."

On Wednesday, the 8th of April, 1840, a special meeting of
the Synod of Ulster was held in May Street Church, for the
purpose of considering the proposed union. The advisability

of union was at once unanimously agreed upon; and the Synod proceeded to discuss the details. On one of the points laid down as a basis there was some difference of opinion. It was this :—" That all Ruling Elders shall produce documentary evidence of their subscription to the Confession of Faith." Many argued that it would be wrong to require elders, who were often, though pious and devoted, yet men of limited education, to sign a creed so long, and in many respects so profound, as the Confession. It was, therefore, moved, as an amendment, that elders should only be required to sign the Shorter Catechism. Dr. Cooke advocated full subscription. His speech was racy and eloquent. He strongly repudiated the idea that the elders of the Presbyterian Church were unable to comprehend the Westminster Standards.

" It is reported, Moderator, that a friend once visited Sir Isaac Newton, and observing two holes in the door of his study, one large, the other small, inquired their object. ' The large one,' replied the philosopher, ' is for the cat, and the small one for the kittens.' Now, like Sir Isaac, our friends here would have two doors of entrance to office in this Church, one for teaching, another for ruling elders— the large one for the cat, the small one for the kittens. Truly philosophers have strange fancies ; and why not divines ? Never was such an unhappy compliment paid to any body of men as is now proposed to be paid to the elders of the Synod of Ulster. They are to be required, in token of special favour, only to sign the Shorter Catechism. What was the original design of our Catechisms ? I ask. The *Larger* was for those who had made some progress in the grounds of our religion ; the *Shorter*, for ' those of weaker capacity.' Are, then, those elders whom my learned friend so highly and so justly complimented to be classed among those of weaker capacity ? . . . . I have found in real life, that those who have studied few books besides the Bible—who have, perhaps, received all their systematic theology from the Catechisms and Baxter's ' Fourfold State ; ' all their experimental religion from their own hearts and Willison's ' Afflicted Man's Companion '—were first to receive the Confession of Faith, and readiest to defend it by Scripture proofs. Gentlemen imagine that a rural peasantry are uneducated ; but I will not admit that because they are not learned, they are therefore void of education. I will take a class of Ulster mechanics and farmers, and I will take the Larger and Shorter Catechisms with our Confession of Faith; and I will take a class of the learned profession, including physic and law, and examine both on the doctrines contained in these invaluable works; and let the best answerer be the best qualified for the elder's office. When my opponents know the Ulster elders as well as I do, they will renounce at once and for ever their philosophic device of a small hole for the kitten."

The amusing illustration set the house in a roar; while the truth that lay beneath carried their convictions. The law of full subscription was passed by an overwhelming majority.

All barriers to union were now removed, and it was unanimously resolved :—" That this Synod feel deeply grateful to Almighty God for the prospect of a speedy accomplishment of the important measure of a union between the two Synods— that we agree to form this union—and that the committee appointed at the last Synod be now re-appointed to meet the committee of the Seceding Synod, in order to arrange the minor details necessary for perfecting the union."

It was then arranged that the two Synods should meet on the forenoon of Friday, April 10th, at eleven o'clock, for devotional exercises. The meeting was held in May Street Church, which was filled with a deeply-impressed audience. The services were commenced by the Rev. Dr. Hanna, the venerable Professor of Divinity, who read the 17th chapter of John's Gospel. When he came to the words, " That they all may be one; as thou, Father, art in me, and I in thee, that they also may be one in us : that the world may know that thou hast sent me," a fervent " Amen," breathed by many voices, showed how deep was the feeling. Dr. Cooke concluded the solemn services by a prayer, whose earnestness and pathos touched every heart. The most intense emotion was manifested. Sobs were heard in every part of the assembly; the eyes of strong men were suffused with tears; all seemed to realize the presence and power of the Spirit of God. " We believe," says an eye-witness, " that this day will be long remembered for the hallowing tone which it imparted to the minds of all present. The universal feeling during the whole meeting, especially during the concluding prayer, was that of high devotion. All seemed to be lighted up above the earth with its distracting and dividing passions, and to breathe a purer atmosphere—the atmosphere of heaven."

The committees met on the 21st of May. Their proceedings were characterized by the utmost harmony. All minor details necessary for effecting the union were satisfactorily arranged, and a series of resolutions was drawn up to be recommended for adoption at the approaching annual meetings. In prospect of effecting the union, the meeting of the Synod of Ulster was postponed to the first Tuesday of July.

When the Synod of Ulster met, one of the first subjects to which its attention was directed was Church Extension. Dr. Cooke moved the appointment of a committee to devise a proper scheme, and to collect the requisite funds. In his speech he referred in eloquent terms to the spiritual destitution of Ireland, and to the duties of Presbyterians to use all their energies and all their means to meet it. He cheered and stimulated them by examples of Christian munificence set by their brethren in Scotland and England.

" Who has not heard of Robert Barbour of Manchester—Barbour, who never turned a poor Presbyterian pastor empty from his door ? God has blessed him with riches ; but He first blessed him with a heart rich in love to Christ and His cause. Who has forgotten the name of Campbell of Glasgow—a man who brings back to memory the best days of Argyll ? In London we have James Nisbet of Berners Street, with a heart as wide as the world, and as liberal of his means as if they were wide as his heart. Gordon, too, is another name at the mention of which Presbyterian gratitude will flow forth spontaneously. Of Mr. Ferrier of Dublin, who is present, I also speak as one of our best friends. . . . . There is Mr. Collins of Glasgow, who resolved some time since that twenty new churches should be erected. He set the scheme on foot, and the greater number are already built. Have we not a Collins in Belfast ? I believe we shall find one. . . . . I trust that by the warmth of

Orthodox truth, we shall be able to melt the icebergs of Arianism, and that we shall now in safety navigate those intricate passages which error placed in former days between us and the haven of that Christian union, peace, and enjoyment, which are promised to the Church."

On Friday, the 10th of July, the two Synods left their respective places of meeting, and having united in the street, marched in one body to Rosemary Street Church, headed by their Moderators, the Rev. James Elder and the Rev. Dr. Rentoul. The streets were crowded with spectators, and in a few minutes the spacious church was filled to overflowing. The two Moderators sat, side by side, in the pulpit. On an elevated platform in front, were the leading members of the United Church, with the Rev. Patrick Macfarlane, the Rev. James Begg, the Rev. R. M. McCheyne, and Maitland Makgill Crighton, Esq., Deputies from the Church of Scotland. The Moderator of the Secession Synod read the 133rd Psalm, which was sung by the vast assembly. The Moderator of the Synod of Ulster then read the 17th chapter of the Gospel of John. When devotional exercises were concluded, Dr. Seaton Reid, Clerk of the Synod of Ulster, submitted the Act of Union, which, after detailing the leading events of the history of Presbyterianism in Ireland, thus recited the terms and Act of Union :—

" It is hereby resolved and agreed upon, in the name of the Lord Jesus Christ, the Great Head of the Church, by the said General Synod of Ulster, and the said Presbyterian Synod of Ireland, distinguished by the name of Seceders, on this the 10th day of July, in the year of our Lord 1840, duly assembled together, that they do now, and in all times hereafter shall, constitute one united Church, professing the same common faith, as set forth in the Standards as aforesaid ; and in all matters ecclesiastical exercising, and subject to, the same government and discipline. . . . .

" And it is hereby farther resolved and agreed upon, that the said United Church shall henceforth bear the name and designation of ' The Presbyterian Church in Ireland ;' and that its Supreme Court shall be styled ' THE GENERAL ASSEMBLY OF THE PRESBYTERIAN CHURCH IN IRELAND.' "

The Act having been read, the Moderators put the question to the House, whether the members of the Churches present approved of, and considered themselves bound by, it.   The whole body immediately rose and held up their right hands in token of assent.

Thus was consummated one of the most important acts in the history of the Presbyterian Church in Ireland.   It was the crowning result of Dr. Cooke's long and noble struggles.   His triumphant advocacy of evangelical truth had compelled eighteen Arians to leave the Synod of Ulster.   But in eleven years nearly eighty new congregations had been added to it by evangelistic work ; and now one hundred and fifty more had joined it, confessing the same doctrines, and animated by the same spirit.

Dr. Hanna was elected first Moderator of the General Assembly.   It was a graceful tribute to his age, and his valuable services.   When he had formally constituted the Assembly, Dr. Cooke rose to introduce the Deputies from the Church of Scotland.   He spoke in terms of glowing eulogium of Messrs. Macfarlane and Begg.

" Mr. McCheyne," he continued, " is almost the only man in the world whom I could envy.   He is the bringer of good tidings from the land which has been trodden by the feet of Jesus.   He has stood in Jerusalem, upon the foundation stones of the Church apostolic and universal.   He is here to-day as an apostolic messenger to bid God-speed to our propitious union.   Makgill Crighton is here, too, with the spirit and the courage of our covenanted forefathers. He is now lifting up the banner of the old Kirk of Scotland in the face of difficulty and persecution ; and he will not quail even before another Claverhouse."

The first public act of the General Assembly showed the new spirit which animated the Presbyterian Church, and gave bright promise of that success which has since attended her labours.   It was the setting apart of two Missionaries, the Rev. James Glasgow and the Rev. Alexander Kerr, to labour among the heathen of India—they were the first foreign

missionaries ever sent out by Irish Presbyterians. In bygone
years Dr. Cooke had been often warned—warned, too, by
Orthodox men—of the fatal effects that must follow the rending
of the Church by his opposition to Arianism. He was not
alarmed; he was not even influenced by such gloomy fore-
bodings. With a stronger faith and a clearer perception, he
felt confident in the triumph of truth. He had more than
once predicted the success of a purified and reformed Church.
He had himself inaugurated missionary effort at home; and he
had eloquently advocated its extension to foreign lands. Now
he saw his brightest hopes realized. Heresy found no place
within the walls of his beloved Church. New life quickened
her ministry. A spirit of unexampled liberality was displayed
by the whole body of her people. From her little island home
she was, in the true spirit of Apostolic times, about to send
the Gospel to all nations. The state of the United Church,
and the result of Dr. Cooke's labours and triumphs, cannot be
better described than in the words of a distinguished member
of the Church of Scotland, who was present at that first
meeting of the General Assembly :—" By the union which has
been effected between the two orthodox Presbyterian Churches
in Ireland, 600,000 souls have come under the joint spiritual
superintendence of men, a large proportion of whom are
eminently distinguished by all the qualities which should
adorn the ministers of the Gospel of Christ; and new and
increased vigour has been given to their praiseworthy effort for
arresting the progress of Romanism, and for diffusing the
knowledge of pure Christianity among our fellow-subjects in
Ireland. The missionary zeal of the Presbyterian Church in
Ireland is not less the ground of joy and thanksgiving.
Though the cry for help is continually addressed to them
by their benighted and perishing countrymen, and is listened
to with feelings of the most enlarged and active beneficence,
they are not forgetful of the still darker places of the earth—
the habitations of horrid cruelty, or of the command of their
Divine Master, ' Go preach the Gospel to every creature.'

The Christian love which led to the formation of their Home Mission has prompted the efforts which they have begun to make on behalf of the heathen. The cause of Presbytery also has gained accession of strength. Its efficacy as an instrument of spiritual and moral improvement, and, we may add, of civilization and temporal prosperity, is nowhere, perhaps, more strikingly illustrated than in Ulster, where it stands in perpetual contrast with the baneful and depressing influence of Popery. The Church of Scotland has cause to rejoice in the additional energy which, we trust, has been imparted, by the events which have been mentioned, to her most powerful ally, in the contest in which she is now engaged in defence of her liberties, and the liberties of her people."

The writer was not disappointed. The Irish General Assembly aided the Church of Scotland in her struggle for freedom. And none manifested a deeper interest in the question than Dr. Cooke. He thoroughly sympathized with those who laboured to abolish patronage, and to release the Church from State control in all matters ecclesiastical. Yet he was most anxious to preserve the integrity of the Church of Scotland. He loved her with a true filial love. He was equally anxious to preserve, in all its integrity, the Constitution of the empire; and he believed the Churches of Scotland and England to be integral parts of that Constitution. He, therefore, deprecated rash and hasty measures. He would counsel no decisive step, until all means had been tried to obtain redress. He exerted his own powerful influence to induce the Conservative leaders to renounce their dangerous policy of attempting to control the Church in the legitimate exercise of her spiritual functions. He was grieved to find the political party to which he had ever been, and was still, conscientiously attached, acting in a way so dangerous to their own ultimate stability, and to the liberties of the Church of Scotland. His position became one of great difficulty and delicacy: but his course of action was, as it had always been, bold and straightforward. He saw his duty plainly; and where duty called, he would not

permit private feeling, or political influence, or the ties of
party, to turn him aside from the straight and honourable
path.

On Wednesday evening, February 26th, 1840, a great
meeting assembled in May Street Church, to express sympathy
with the Church of Scotland, and to petition Parliament in
favour of *Non-intrusion.* The chair was occupied by Dr.
Hanna; and addresses were delivered by Dr. Seaton Reid,
Mr. Morgan and others. It was known that Dr. Cooke was
ill. He had been confined to his room for several days by
acute influenza. His medical attendant and his friends had
warned him that should he go to the meeting it would be at
the risk of his life. But Dr. Cooke had a will of his own;
and no power could bend that iron will. Dr. Reid was in the
midst of his speech, when he was suddenly interrupted by an
enthusiastic burst of applause from the audience. It was
caused by the appearance of Dr. Cooke. The cheering was
renewed several times ere the speaker was permitted to
proceed.

In moving a resolution to the effect that " The national
endowment of a Christian Church does not imply a surrender
to the State of the spiritual liberties either of ministers or
people," Dr. Cooke said :—

" Labouring, as I am, under an affection of the voice that renders
me, as you hear, nearly incapable of speaking, I should not have
attended the meeting at all, or attending, I had remained silent,
were it not that my silence might be construed, either here or .else-
where, into coldness or neglect in the cause of our Mother Church.
' But if I forget Thee, O Jerusalem, let my right hand forget its
cunning, and my tongue cleave to the roof of my mouth.'

" Before entering, however, upon the motion entrusted to me,
permit me to offer a word of explanation in reference to an observation that fell from my Rev. brother, Mr. Morgan, in relation to the
headship of Christ over the Church ; and which, by those who
do not understand the subject, as my Rev. brother does, might be
readily construed into, what he never intended, an attack upon the
Church of England and Ireland. Now, by certain acts of Henry VIII.,

and Elizabeth, the king or queen, as the case may be, is constituted the only supreme head on earth of the Church of England and Ireland, invested with power to call and dissolve the Convocation, and to sit in Chancery as the *dernier ressort* in all causes ecclesiastical. But let it not for a moment be imagined, that the Church of England thereby intends to set aside those supreme, providential, and mediatorial rights of Christ, wherewith the Father has invested Him as ' Head over all things to the Church, which is His body; the fulness of Him that filleth all in all.' I judge it my duty to make this observation, lest in defining and asserting our own views of the extent of Christ's headship in the Church of Scotland, we should be suspected of a covert attack upon the Church of England. No doubt that Church gives a title to the king the Church of Scotland never has conceded; and she yields to him certain rights of nomination and appointment to her offices, which the Church of Scotland labours to preserve to her people and Church Courts. Still does the Church of England recoil from being supposed to yield one jot or tittle of the Spiritual Headship of the Lord Jesus Christ; and, in every point of view, but so far as I have stated from law authority, does the Church of England assert and maintain it in a manner as ample and unlimited as the Church of Scotland. In stating and defending our own views of the doctrine of Christ's Headship, we make no ungenerous insinuation, calculated *ad captandum*; we make no attack upon others, where the ostensible object is simply to defend ourselves. God knows each of the Protestant Churches in these lands has enough to do in defending doctrinal truth, without pausing to quarrel on governmental detail; and each, alas! has mote large enough in her own eye to teach her charity and forbearance for the beam in her neighbour's."

He then proceeded to reply to the arguments by which the majority in the Court of Session had attempted to justify their decision in regard to patronage; and also to Lord Brougham's celebrated exposition and defence of the law of patronage in the House of Lords. He laid down three fundamental principles. The first was that "Protestant Christianity is the law of the empire." This he proved from Blackstone; adding to that proof the following argument:—

" I do not rest my cause upon a mere general principle expounded by a lawyer. I establish it by an oath prescribed by the entire

nation, and solemnly sworn by the Queen. Christianity is the law
of the land, the essence, the spirit of our glorious Constitution. By
1 William & Mary, chap. 6, settling the coronation oath, the third
paragraph asks, ' Will you, to the utmost of your power, maintain
the laws of God, the true profession of the gospel, and the Protestant Reformed religion established by law ?'—the Queen swears,
' All this I promise to do.' Here I take my stand, not as an interpreter of repealable Acts of Parliament—though from that part of
the task I shall not shrink—but as an interpreter of the irrever-
sible statutes of Heaven, which, so far as human understanding goes,
our Queen has sworn to maintain. Here I take my stand, not as a
builder of an Established Church on the sand of a fluctuating expediency, but as the assertor and enforcer of the bounden duty of
rulers to be ' nursing fathers and nursing mothers ' to the Church."

The second principle he laid down was, that "The Westminster Confession, so far as the Church is concerned, is the
law of Scotland ; " the third was, that " No man can divest
himself of the rights God has bestowed upon him, nor can any
man righteously divest him of them by force, or even purchase
them at any price."

" The grand error in the majority of the Court of Session, and
Lords Brougham and Cottenham, arises from their total neglect of
the first and fundamental principles of constitutional and statute
law. I dare not challenge, but I respectfully propose, that they
examine my three propositions, and tell me if they can discern a
single legal flaw. . . . Now if they grant me these principles—
and I say it respectfully but advisedly, let them deny them at their
peril—then do I affirm that their arguments and their decisions
against the spiritual independence of the Church of Scotland, are
not worth the parchment on which they are recorded."

The speech was a master-piece of argument. It exhibited
not merely marvellous legal acuteness, but an extent of legal
knowledge, and a profundity of legal research, which astonished all who heard it. It has often been said that had
Dr. Cooke been a lawyer he would have reached the wool-
sack ; and, unquestionably, if it can be reached by logical
acumen, stirring eloquence, and commanding genius, he must

have reached it. Be that as it may, his reply to Lord Brougham was triumphant. He showed that his Lordship had misread Scotch history, that he misunderstood Scotch law, and that, therefore, he grievously wronged the Scotch Church. Comparing his conduct to the Church, in trying to tyrannize over the many at the dictation of a few, Dr. Cooke said:—

" Is not this, my Lord, the very counterpart, the very twin-brother, ay, and Esau-like, the bad twin-brother, of that very system of borough-mongering policy, against which in other days you were wont to utter your bitterest anathemas ? And is it now to force such a system upon the Church of Scotland, that you waste your study, and enkindle your eloquence, and devote your legal character ? "

His definition of an Established Church, the distinction he drew between it and an Endowed Church, and his exposition of the inherent rights of both, are clear and sound. They have a permanent interest, whatever changes necessary policy or cowardly expediency may effect in the British Constitution.

" What is the difference between an Endowed Church and an Established Church ? The Endowed Church, I suppose I will be told, is merely supported by the State; the Established Church is adopted by the State. The Endowed Church is acknowledged only in her individual ministers; the Established Church in her cor-porate capacity. The Endowed Church is left to enforce her laws on those who choose to obey, by the sole virtue of her own authority ; the Established Church has her laws enforced by the additional authority of the State. Nay, perhaps, I may be told, on the autho-rity of the Legal Bench, that an Established Church is the mere creature of the State. Now, that all this may be a just description of a Church established on Erastian principles, I do not deny ; but that all this is at direct variance with the scriptural doctrine of an establishment, with the coronation oath, with the Westminster Con-fession, and with the essential principle of inalienable liberty, a brief argument will determine. Do the Scriptures originally invest the Church with the power of internal self-government ? This my Lord Brougham will not venture to deny. Then were the Church even willing, can she sell this power, or transfer it to the king, or the parliament, or the judges ? Can the State legitimately take away and refuse to restore, any right originally belonging to the Church and derived from Christ? Surely establishment is the taking of a Christian Church into the protection of the State, not the creating of a new corporation. Surely establishment is the bestowment of civil rights, not the infliction of civil chains. The State may endow, not enslave. The Jews, under Ezra and Nehemiah, received with a good conscience and with God's approbation, a state endowment, even from a heathen emperor; but even that heathen sought no intrusive patronage over her priesthood, nor did the Church barter away one jot or tittle of her inalienable rights."

His apology for the blunders of Lord Brougham and the Court of Session was admirable; and through it he administered a sharp, but deserved, reproof to a Church which had been long and largely, though not universally, unfaithful to its duties and its Head:—

" I look with great tenderness on what I believe to be the legal mistakes of the Court of Session and Lord Brougham. They were all nourished on the breast and cradled in the arms of Moderatism. But what was Moderatism? I acknowledge my insufficiency for the definition; but for lack of a better interpreter, I attempt her description. In doctrine, she did not deny the Articles of the Confession, but she sometimes signed them as mere 'bonds of peace.' In preaching, she did not often contradict them, but she turned some of the most important into abeyance, and substituted in their room a cold and paralytic philosophy—miserable substitute for the warmth and activity of the gospel. When any were accused of teaching erroneous doctrines she threw the shield of her protection over them, and accepted explanations and apologies, in place of inflicting censures or removing the false teachers from the office they had abused; and, on the contrary, when any came forward to recommend and circulate works on the freeness and fulness of grace, she issued her caveats to the public against them, and promulgated legality for gospel. In government she was all compliance to power, all tyranny to the people she would enslave. She planted her nominees at the point of the bayonet, and she ejected the faithful men that testified against her enormities."

He concluded in the following stirring words:—

" I look to the Court of Session with the profound respect due to their extended learning, their unsullied character, their exalted rank.

But I would that my voice could reach them, to warn them of the sin of their interdicts and threats of imprisonment for disobedience to their will, out of obedience to God. Interdicts against preaching the gospel without their leave ! The first interdict of which I read is in Acts v. 17, 18, 28, 40. To all which Peter answered in the words which the Church of Scotland will employ, should the utmost threat be carried into effect :—' We ought to obey God rather than man.' I do remember of a certain judge who threatened a prisoner arraigned before him, and who, in reply to the prisoner's defence, exclaimed—' Silence, sir, or I'll commit you.' ' If you do,' coolly replied the prisoner, ' you'll commit yourself.' Yes, the eloquence of Chalmers may be silenced in the dungeon. The venerable Gordon, who looks a sermon before he utters it, may be removed from people's sight ; and all that warms the younger hearts of Scotland's ministers may be chilled in penury and exile. Yes, they may deal with Scotland's ministers as in the days of Lauderdale—send them to the Bass ! They may send them to the Bass as they sent their fathers, and the wild birds of the ocean may again sing their nightly requiem, and the troubled waters of the Forth may again become the emblems and the wafters of their sorrows ; but there is no interdict between their prayers and Heaven ; and there is no interdict between them and the hearts of the Scottish people ; and there is no interdict between Christ and His Church. He may adjudge her to be purified by oppression, and prove His love by the chastisement by which He prepares her for glory."

It is utterly impossible, says one who was present, to describe the effect produced upon the vast audience by these thrilling words, especially when he said, in a voice which rung through the house, " Send them to the Bass." It was like an electric shock. Every heart felt its power, and throbbed responsive to the genius of the orator. That speech largely served to awaken the sympathies of Ulster for the suffering Church of Scotland.

Immediately after the meeting of the General Assembly Dr. Cooke went as a deputy to London, on behalf of the cause he had so eloquently advocated. It was well known that he had been largely instrumental, through his influence with the Conservative party, in arresting the progress of Lord Aber-

deen's obnoxious Bill. His object now was to put the leaders
of the party in possession of the true facts of the case. They
were being studiously misled as to the state of public opinion
and as to the effect the enforcement of patronage would produce. Lord Londonderry, for instance, had been informed,
and had stated openly in Parliament, that Lord Aberdeen's
Bill was universally approved by the Presbyterians of Ireland.
Dr. Cooke put him right, by assuring him there were not
ten Presbyterians in the country in favour of it. Sir James
Graham had been assured, by a distinguished Scotch divine,
that should a disruption be attempted, not forty ministers would
follow Chalmers. Dr. Cooke had interviews with Lord Aberdeen, Sir Robert Peel, Lords Downshire, Castlereagh, and
Londonderry. Among Irish peers and members of Parliament
his success was complete. He soon found, however, that strong
opposing agencies were at work with Sir Robert Peel and Lord
Aberdeen; yet he did not despair even of them.

" Of my Lord Aberdeen I must say, I found him greatly different
from what I had expected from the apparent asperity with which I
had heard him speak on the question in the House of Lords. With
the utmost patience he listened, replied, explained, or defended his
Bill; and though I am not able to say I either shook or modified
his opinions, I must express my decided conviction that his mind is
perfectly open to argument."

Had the Church of Scotland been united, had wrong impressions not been, carefully and studiously, made upon the
minds of leading statesmen, by members of the Church itself,
the cause of liberty would have triumphed. Another species
of opposition was at work. The feeling of the High Church
party in England was adverse to the claims of the non-intrusionists. Theirs was a foolish and a fatal policy. Dr.
Cooke saw it and lamented it. He was frequently heard to
say that those measures of the Legislature which forced on the
disruption of the Church of Scotland struck the first deadly
blow at the root of all establishments in the empire.

On Monday evening, the 14th of July, another great non-intrusion meeting was held in May Street Church. The chair was again occupied by Dr. Hanna, Moderator of the General Assembly. Speeches were delivered by Dr. Stewart, of Broughshane, and the deputies from Scotland, the Rev. Messrs. Begg and McCheyne, and Maitland Makgill Crighton, Esq. Dr. Cooke also spoke, and discussed the question in its political bearings.

"I have been specially gratified with the declaration of my friend Mr. Begg, that as patronage and freedom can never be reconciled, no quarter should be given to the system . . . . So long as patronage submitted to be mollified by the veto Act, the minds of the Christian people and of Church Courts had a portion of independence and freedom ; but when the voice of the Christian people is silenced, and the ecclesiastical authority is, in things ecclesiastical, superseded by the civil power, independence and freedom are no more, and nothing remains but the tame submission of slaves, the struggle of freemen, or the endurance of martyrs . . . . The modifiers or opponents of patronage in Scotland have a thousand difficulties to encounter from which we are free. The Church of Scotland is divided on the question ; the Ulster Presbyterians are united to a man."

Referring to the opposition which unfortunately now began to be too clearly manifested to the just claims of the Church of Scotland by the leaders of the Conservative party, he uttered these noble sentiments :—

"One of my friends has contemplated the possibility of being driven to change his party. This is a course I can neither commend nor practise. Let us stand by our principles and party, as the sailor by his ship in the storm or in the shock of battle. Ah ! these are dangerous times for a party man, especially if he be a clergyman ; for every sentimental young lady shudders at the thought of a political parson. Now, in spite of this sentimentalism, I confess I am a party man. If a party man be a party to truth and justice, I am one. If it be a party man to be a party to Presbyterianism, I am one. If it be a party man to belong to the anti-Popery party, with Luther, with Knox, with Cranmer, with Ridley—then I am a Protestant-Presbyterian party man. Some there are who cry woe to a political parson, but only when he is not on their side. As long as he does their work, what a delightful, liberal, independent man he is ; but when he refuses to do their work, they can no longer endure a political parson. . . . . If I renounce my politics, I must renounce my religion. I have not learned them from Whig, or Tory, or Radical ; I have got them from the Bible—I have got them from that mysterious warning revealed to us to be a guide to our feet in these latter days :—' Babylon the great is fallen, is fallen, and is become the habitation of devils, and the hold of every foul spirit. Come out of her my people, that ye be not partakers of her sins, and that ye receive not of her plagues.' My politics are inseparable from my religion. To my party I still adhere, because they are our best barrier against fierce democracy on the one hand and more terrible Popery on the other. Between Protestantism and Popery there is still an impassable wall. But if we passively lie down in the ditch, our bodies will be the bridges for Popery to pass over ; or, if we in anger forsake the garrison, it may soon be compelled to surrender to our common foe. We will not forsake our friends ; and I trust our friends, better instructed, will not forsake us. Now, lest it should be supposed, that by adhering still to the party which other friends of the Church of Scotland are nearly prepared to give up, I would be injuring the holy cause I am labouring and bound to maintain, I reply, that in doing my utmost to maintain that cause, the blue banner of the Covenant is not more unchangeable than I am. As a minister of God, I will reason from the Scriptures with the heads of my party. If they will not listen, I will in secret shed tears over their errors and delinquencies. I will appeal to their judgments and their fears ; and, if that won't do to drive the Ahithophel counsel from among them, I will neither change my principles nor forsake my party ; but I will retire from every activity ; and if it were in the power of my single tongue to raise them to political supremacy, I dare not utter one word in their behalf; for if they will join in oppressing the Church of Scotland, we have no alternative but to stand aloof from the men we cannot persuade, yet will not forsake ; and be forced at last to what, perhaps, we have too long neglected, the distinct formation, not of a party of Presbyterians (that I deprecate as too narrow a basis for so great a political building), but a Presbyterian party of men thoroughly informed in our principles, and thoroughly devoted to our religious interests, by whom the Church of Scotland will be sufficiently protected, and her freedom speedily achieved. I would press upon my friends of the deputation, and upon the Church of Scotland, and upon this meeting, the words of Scripture—'Trust not in princes.' Employ all means of persuasion and entreaty, but still hold by your first principles, and depend upon no one but the living God."

At a banquet given in Glasgow to the Marquis of Breadalbane, Dr. Cooke again spoke on the question of non-intrusion. After referring to the deep sympathy felt for the suffering Church of Scotland by Irish Presbyterians, and their readiness to give all the help in their power, he strongly urged the necessity of pressing the claims of the Church upon higher ground than had hitherto generally been attempted.

" In the discussion of this great question, it has never, except in a few cases, been placed on the ground of divine right—the divine right of a Christian people to elect their own ministers. I regard this as a far higher point than any other element that has generally mingled in our argumentation on this subject. The great thing wanting in the minds of those whom we conceive to be opposed to us—the great object to be attained in dealing with such persons is, to take possession of their minds with the principles of divine right. I have frequently had occasion to employ that argument when in London, and the answer I generally got was, that is not the argument used by the Church of Scotland. This, I maintain, is the true Biblical argument. It clearly appears from the very first election recorded in the Acts of the Apostles, that the people were consulted —that it was not the choice of patrons, nor the choice of the Apostles even ; but the choice of the whole brethren of the Church. . . . This is the groundwork of the argument ; and I counsel you to base all your appeals to Parliament and the country on the ground that it is the divine right of the people to choose their own pastors ; and that whatever interferes with that right is interfering with the privilege which Jesus Christ, the King and Head of the Church, has given to His people. . . . . Will men who talk of, and contend for, the civil rights of the people, take away the franchise from the people of the living God—that franchise which was neither theirs to confer upon them, nor to deprive them of ; but which was granted to them as their inalienable privilege by the Great King and Head of the Church ? The people are allowed to choose the men who go between them and their Queen ; is it to be tolerated that they shall not be allowed to choose the men who go between them and their God ? "

While the struggle on behalf of freedom in the Church of Scotland continued with still increasing ardour and interest, another struggle arose which called forth all the power and courage of Dr. Cooke, and led to one of the most memorable achievements of his whole career. To the Repeal Conflict a new chapter must be devoted.

CHAPTER XVI.

1840—1841.

THE Repeal agitation moved the British Empire to its centre. Ireland is never without some real grievance, and when a clever man lays hold upon it, he can so rouse the passions of its excitable people, that in the hope of calming them, an English Parliament will consent to almost any measure, if it affect Ireland alone. Protestant principle has not always been proof, in the Cabinet or in the Senate, against Irish clamour and outrage. Fear, too, it must be admitted, has not unfrequently wrung from a reluctant British Parliament, what justice had long sought in vain. O'Connell found in the government of his native country more than one grievance ; and with a skill and a determination never surpassed in the prosecution of any cause, good or bad, he used them for the accomplishment of his own purposes. Parliament trembled before his fierce invectives. For a time he almost attained the place of Dictator. When success had won for him, in the estimation of Irishmen, the title of Liberator, he represented Repeal of the Legislative Union as the sovereign remedy for all his country's ills. Five-sixths of the nation believed him ; for however divided they may be on other points, in this they are united—intense hatred of English rule. O'Connell's progress through the south and west, as Repeal agitator, was a continuous triumph. On the Hill of Tara, the seat of ancient sovereignty, and in Dublin, the modern capital, he was alike hailed as Patriot-chief. He was the virtual ruler of the Roman Catholic population. They followed him almost to a man in his demand for repeal. Had Ireland been unanimous, or had its Protestant population remained passive, England could not have resisted that demand except by force of arms. A new conquest would have been necessary. But there was fortunately one party in Ireland which gave to Repeal and to O'Connell a determined opposition, and of that party Dr. Cooke was the leader. It was comparatively small in number, but it was great in its traditions, and therefore in its influence, for it represented the noble band of heroes who defended England's liberties in 1688. It was great in moral power, for it represented the enterprise, the education, and the Protestant principle of Ulster. Dr. Cooke had mainly contributed to organise and consolidate the party. He had freed it from the admixture of those revolutionary elements which crept in during the troubles of '98. He had also amalgamated, with singular ability and success, the somewhat discordant elements of Episcopacy and Presbyterianism.

At an early part of his career, O'Connell saw the rising influence of Cooke in Ulster, and he tried to counteract it. His special aim was to attach to his own party those Presbyterians who held Liberal views in politics. He professed to have the good of the entire nation at heart in his plan of repeal. To convince the Protestants of his good will, he actually toasted the "Immortal Memory" of William in a glass of Boyne water. He tried to make it appear that his principles did not differ, fundamentally, from those of the Prince of Orange, whose name has been for nearly two centuries the watchword of Irish Protestants. But the task was too great, even for O'Connell. The scheme was too shallow to deceive thoughtful men. Even the most Radical of Protestants refused to participate in the Repeal movement. New tactics were there-

fore adopted by the Liberator. Advantage was taken of
garbled extracts from Dr. Cooke's parliamentary evidence to
excite the fanaticism of Roman Catholics. He was denounced
as a slanderer and false witness, by a great aggregate meeting
in Dublin.

Hitherto the Protestants and Papists of Ulster had lived
together in peace. Those feelings of brotherly kindness which
Protestantism inculcates, had produced a salutary effect upon
all parties. The enterprise of Protestant manufacturers, the
industry of Protestant agriculturists, and the capital which
they were able to command and willing to invest, gave them the
means of offering lucrative employment, and affording relief
when needed, which they did without distinction. The vast
body of Roman Catholics, therefore, showed no jealousy of
Protestant success. The spirit of fanaticism which generally
characterises their faith had well-nigh disappeared. They even
joined with their Protestant brethren in the celebration of those
national jubilees, the observance of which has of late given rise
to scenes of strife and bloodshed which bring disgrace upon
our country. Under the influence of O'Connell, a system of
agitation was inaugurated which changed the whole tone of
society in Ulster. A newspaper called *The Vindicator* was
established in Belfast, whose chief mission was to inflame sectarian passion, and stir up Roman Catholics against their
Protestant fellow-countrymen. Unfortunately the Roman
Catholic clergy became the tools of O'Connell. Roman
Catholics were reminded of their vast numerical preponder-
ance. They were told that they had a right to proportional influence, power, and representation in all government, local as
well as Imperial. Protestants were denounced as heretics,
usurpers, aliens. It was shown how they had taken Ireland by
the sword ; how they had driven out or murdered its patriotic
native chiefs ; how they had enslaved their brave and attached
subjects. It was a touching picture, and though utterly false,
its effects upon an uneducated and excitable people were
lamentable. Most of them believed it to be literally true.

They groaned in agony when addressed as " Hereditary Bonds-
men." They were inspired with intense hatred of Protestants.
They looked upon them as enemies and oppressors. They
could not as yet drive them from the country, or appropriate
the fruits of their toil and industry; but they could, and they
did eventually, stir up a spirit of enmity which has destroyed
the peace, and materially retarded the prosperity of Ulster.

It must be admitted that a small party of educated and respectable Roman Catholics in Belfast, protested against the
intolerant doctrines of *The Vindicator*. O'Connell and his
ecclesiastical friends, finding they had gone too far, counselled
The Vindicator to assume a more conciliatory tone. It had
already done its work, however. It had not only roused the
indignation of the entire Protestant community, but it had constrained the more moderate Catholics to oppose its fierce
fanaticism. Efforts were made to counteract these evil effects.
Sectarian exclusiveness was ostensibly repudiated, and peace
was preached by the very men who had lately sent round the
fiery cross. This was preparatory to a new act in the Repeal
drama.

When the parliamentary session closed in 1840, O'Connell
announced his intention of visiting the provinces of Ireland, to
organise a universal agitation for Repeal. Belfast was included
in the programme. But Belfast was new ground to the
Liberator. He feared that success there might be doubtful.
He knew there was a strong opposition element. He knew that
the cool, logical Protestants of the North were not so easily influenced by high-sounding oratory as the excitable Celts of
the South. Still he thought he might be able to flatter a few
of the Radical Protestants into acquiescence, while the Roman
Catholics would rally round him in a body. Mr. O'Connell
was entertained at a banquet in Drogheda, on the 19th of
October. A deputation there waited upon him and invited
him to Belfast. He delayed replying. He wished to feel his
way, and calculate the prospects of success. Opposition might
retard; defeat might even ruin his plans. At length, on the

30th of December, he informed his friends of "the extreme satisfaction it would give him to accept their invitation to a public dinner in Belfast." Arrangements were made for his reception. The dinner was fixed for the evening of Monday, January 18th. A Repeal meeting would be held on Tuesday ; while a number of his fair admirers proposed to entertain him at a soirée on the evening of that day. Mr. O'Connell spoke of his approaching visit to the North in glowing terms. He anticipated for Repeal an easy triumph. He wrote to the Roman Catholic Bishop of Dromore, announcing the day and hour when he would pass through Drogheda, Dundalk, and Newry. At each stage processions were to be organised to accompany him. His invasion of Ulster was to have the aspect of a triumph.

In Belfast and Ulster generally, the tidings of O'Connell's visit, and its attendant processions, were received by all the lovers of order with feelings of alarm and indignation. The Protestant population were already excited by the calumnies of *The Vindicator*, and the Roman Catholics by the inflammatory teachings of their clergy. Apprehensions of the most serious character were entertained. A spark might set the whole province in a flame. A religious war, if once kindled, might, under existing circumstances, endanger the integrity of the Empire. The Roman Catholics had a vast numerical majority. If they could, by force or fear, crush the Protestants, Repeal of the Legislative Union could only be prevented by the presence of an overwhelming English army.

Dr. Cooke saw the danger, and resolved to avert it. He determined by a bold stroke to stop the progress of Repeal in the North. He knew the chivalrous nature of the Irish people. He knew how dearly they loved a battle of any kind—physical or intellectual. He knew that through pure love of the conflict they would give a fair field to any combatants, and resist all attempts to withdraw from the gage of battle. He knew that to shrink as a coward, no matter under what pretence, from an open challenge, would largely contribute to shake popular confidence in any man. The merits of Repeal, besides, were disputed in Ulster. Protestants who agreed with O'Connell in his general political principles, differed from him in this. The more enlightened Roman Catholics, though their hearts were with the Liberator, were not quite certain that Repeal was possible, or, if even achieved, that it would prove an unmitigated blessing. The question was fairly open to discussion. It needed fresh light. Dr. Cooke, therefore, resolved to challenge O'Connell to a public discussion, in Belfast, on the " Advantages or disadvantages of a Repeal of the Legislative Union."

On Saturday, January the 2nd, Mr. O'Connell's acceptance of the invitation to Belfast, appeared in *The Vindicator*. In *The Ulster Times* of the following Tuesday, Dr. Cooke announced his intention of challenging him to a discussion; and on Wednesday the challenge appeared in *The Chronicle*:—

" TO DANIEL O'CONNELL, ESQ., M.P.

" SIR,—So long as you confined your Repeal agitation to the South of Ireland, no man dared to meet you. But this want of daring was not want of courage—it was the mere shrinking of gentlemen from such rude and ungenerous treatment as you furnished to your quondam protégé and friend, Mr. Sharman Crawford, when, in the simplicity of confidence, he allowed himself to be inveigled to the Corn Exchange, where a fact was turned aside by a jest, and an argument replied to by an insult.

"But when you invade Ulster, and unfurl the flag of Repeal, you will find yourself in a new climate. And as there never yet was a man who could equal you in ' putting off or on ' to suit his company, I do expect to find you in Belfast as innocent and well-mannered a gentleman as any one could desire in a summer day. And were I sure you would never return to your original nature, and abuse Belfast, when you had fairly got out of it, as lately you did, when, echoing the eructations of a bilious barrister, you pronounced it one of ' the most criminal towns in the kingdom ;' and were I sure that you would not, in Parliament, brag and boast of the progress of Repeal, even in the ' black North,' and were I sure you would not affirm that, ' from Carrickfergus to Cape Clear,' you were received, not only without opposition, but with eyes of admiration and shouts of applause—were I sure on all these points, I must confess I should shrink, as others have done, from venturing or offering to come into conflict with you. But, so far from being sure that you will not do these things, I am fully convinced they are just the very things you would do. You will *blarney* Belfast as long as you are in sight of it, and it will be in your vocabulary a ' great city ' of the ' lovely and the good ;' but once over the border, it will again shrink into ' a village' (you recollect that?), and the ' lovely and the good' town will again become ' the most criminal in the kingdom.' And I know that were you to enter and pass through Ulster in unimpeded triumph, your organs, that at first proclaimed your invasion ' as the most signal triumph ever achieved over bigotry,' but which, on hearing of the possibility of your being met in argument, have lately drawn in their horns, and begun to inculcate peace (rare apostles they of peace who have called Mr. O'Connell into Ulster to proclaim it)—were you once fairly out of the town, full well I know they would soon be at their triumphs once more, and the North and the South would ring with the *hullabaloo* of your unexampled victories ; and as for yourself, I do equally well know you would dare to tell the British Parliament that Repeal was the very life-pulse of the country, and that the ' sturdy Presbyterians of Belfast ' have received you with all their hearts as its mighty organ—the people with morning shouts, the gentlemen with dinners, and the ' lovely and the good' with oceans of evening tea.

"Now it is just because I know you would attempt all this and more, that I, by God's help, will attempt to prevent you ; and that, Mr. O'Connell, not in your own favourite style of ' Sharman my jewelling,' but in calm, deliberate, and logical argument. And to this decision I, perhaps, should never have arrived, but that, being challenged by one of your own entertainers, to meet you, and discuss Repeal ; and acting upon a principle that I have long adopted, that a jest has always some earnest in it, I replied I would meet you, and hoped, by God's blessing on a good cause, literally to make an example of you. And this I said in no vain confidence in my own poor abilities, but literally, and plain truth to speak, because I believe you are a great bad man, engaged in a great bad cause ; and as easily foiled by a weak man, armed with a good cause, as Goliath the giant of Gath was discomfited by the stripling David. I propose accordingly the following plan for your consideration :—

"1. Your proposed Repeal meeting in Belfast, instead of a meeting for harangues, all on one side, shall be a discussion between yourself and your humble servant.

"2. The meeting shall be managed by a committee, composed equally of your friends and mine.

"3. Tickets (free) shall be issued, under their common authority —one half to your friends, one half to mine.

"4. Subject : The advantages or disadvantages of a Repeal of the Union to Ireland, in its bearing on agriculture, manufactures, general trade, safety of the present settlement of all property, and the protection of civil and religious liberty.

"5. Each speaker to confine himself, as far as possible, to two-hour speeches, but no absolute limit beyond the feeling of the speaker ; but, if the opener of the discussion occupies three hours, he shall forfeit his right of reply.

"6. The meeting to be governed by two chairmen, one to be chosen by each discussionist.

"And, now, Mr. O'Connell, let me speak a word very plainly to you. You cannot avoid this discussion. I am the man you have so often reviled behind his back ; can you do less than meet him face to face ? You cannot pronounce me too ignoble for your argument, when you did not judge me too obscure for your abuse. Turn the matter as you will, you can find no excuse or evasion. Let your friends hint that it may endanger the peace : the time to have thought of that was when they invited you to make an experiment upon our Northern patience. But, in point of fact, Mr. O'Connell, the discussion will be the surest mode to preserve the peace, which your presence can never once endanger. Even the recollection of your recent abuse of ' our village,' our ' most criminal village in the kingdom,' could not provoke us to more than a legal *morceau*, which I have provided for your feasts, viz., the " Statistics of Northern Crime," in which, by reference to the records of county gaols and local prisons, I purpose to trace upwards, both before you and the empire, the streams of crime, and inundate the really guilty with the polluted waters they have muddied and embittered at their fountain heads. . . .

"Another secret let me whisper to you. If you refuse this discussion, the ghost of it will haunt you on the benches of St. Stephen's. I grant you that to prostrate me could gain you little credit, but to shrink from me, under any pretence, would ensure you the greater disgrace. You profess to be able, if they would but hear you, to convince the Conservatives of the mischief of the Union. You never before had such an offer of a Conservative audience. Prove, then, your sincerity by appearing before them. . . .

" I have the honour to be, both for truth and peace's sake, your faithful servant,

"H. COOKE."

The news of the challenge sped through Ulster and Ireland. The excitement was unprecedented. Dr. Cooke had hitherto been regarded as the leader of the Conservative party. Whigs and Radicals had opposed him with all their might. Now, however, he touched a chord that vibrated through every loyal heart. Liberal Protestants were almost as enthusiastic in supporting the champion of Union as Conservatives. Even *The Northern Whig* hailed the challenge of Dr. Cooke as an auspicious event, likely to put an end to the Repeal agitation in Ulster. *The Chronicle*, which professed neutrality in politics, came prominently forward against Repeal. *The News-Letter* accompanied its publication of Dr. Cooke's challenge with an editorial article of unusual power and stinging irony.

O'Connell's answer was looked for with intense interest. No man who knew him believed that he would be in haste to reply. He could invent excuses, he could profess to regard the whole as a joke ; but his ultimate resolution would, without doubt, be the result of calm, calculating, and thorough deliberation. The consternation among the Repeal party was manifest. They had never calculated on such a bold stroke. They tried to conceal their fears beneath a cloak of vulgar ridicule and insult. Again *The Vindicator* overdid its work : it stated that O'Connell could not, of course, stoop to meet such a man as Dr. Cooke ; and that, therefore, the Repeal party had selected a " Hercules Street artizan," in other words, a butcher, to take up the challenge. The *ruse* was too absurd. It only excited scornful laughter among Protestants, while it disgusted those of the Repealers themselves who had the least pretensions to respectability. *The Vindicator* was supposed to be inspired by O'Connell. Accordingly, the next issue of *The Chronicle* contained an able letter from the Rev. Daniel M'Afee, Wesleyan minister, a man of high standing and talent, addressed to Mr. O'Connell, in which he told him

plainly that subterfuge would not serve him now,—" Come
you must; you are confidently expected; you are announced
in all the newspapers, and placarded on every wall about town,
as president of the grand soirée to be given by the ladies.
Ulster is now in commotion; the cry of *Repale* is up. . . .
Never did any man enter Ulster under more favourable aus-
pices. High and low, rich and poor, the nobleman and the
beggar, the clergy and the laity, are all of one mind, and say
' Come, Mr. O'Connell, come.' . . . . When you arrive
here you *must* meet Dr. Cooke. There is no alternative but
stay away altogether, or meet your antagonist face to face.
No apology will avail. Read a capital article in *The News-
Letter* to-day, hemming you in on every side. You must
neither take a sore throat at Mullingar, sprain your ankle on
the frost, take ill with gout or toothache, or, returning home,
say you did not receive the Doctor's letter in time, complain of
the shortness of the notice, plan another meeting for yourself,
dread a breach of the peace; nor, above all, affect to despise or
treat with silent contempt the challenge of Dr. Cooke. You
cannot do this : he stands on too high a pedestal for your low
scorn to reach him."

Mr. O'Connell broke silence at a Repeal meeting in Dublin,
on the 9th of January. He attempted, just as had been anticipated, to turn Dr. Cooke's challenge into ridicule; but the
attempt was a failure. He stooped to a style of comment
which would not be tolerated by gentlemen :—

" I must soon be upon my road for Cork ; I am sorry for this, as
it would amuse me to have some leisure to reply to my friend Bully
Cooke, the Cock of the North. He is a comical fellow; he invites
me to a conference, and the mode he takes of conveying that invitation is by writing me the most insulting letter he could possibly
pen. What a way of coaxing me to do the thing ! Why he'd coax
the birds off the bushes. I admire the talent exhibited in his letter.
There is a good deal of talent in it. It amused me exceedingly
when I read it first, and I read it over twice for the pure pleasure of
seeing what a clever Cock of the North he was. But, sir, it came

upon me by surprise. I mentioned to a friend of mine—by the way
of asking an advice, as people do when they have made up their own
minds on the subject—the contents of this letter ; and my friend,
who understood me to say, that not only was the challenge given,
but that I had accepted it, said to me, 'My judgment is this : I
think he was a fool for sending the challenge, and you are a fool for
accepting it.' 'Oh, no,' said I ; 'now, stop a while. You are mistaken ; neither of us are fools. There is more wit about the anger of
Daddy Cooke than you imagine. It is a mere plan of his ; for when
does he send to me ? On Wednesday morning, when I was going
off to Westmeath ; I got a letter on that morning, signed, as I
thought, 'John Cooke.' I won't say positively what the signature
was, but it was challenging me to a political discussion. It was not
half the length of the document that appeared in the newspapers,
nor the one-tenth part of it ; but, when I saw the signature, *I
recollected that I had read an authorised contradiction* in *The Ulster
Times,* that Dr. Cooke had any such intention as that of challenging
me ; that is, *he told them he would not, and yet he afterwards did so.*
Why, he told a lie in his own person, in the first instance ; for the
authorised contradiction was authorised by him, and it was as if he
signed the contradiction one day, and denied the next his having
done so."

Mr. O'Connell then adds :—

" So, by that calculation, my worthy Cock of the North knows I
could not comply with his letter, and therefore he sends to me. Now,
let him crow as much as he pleases—I consent to it. He is entitled to
the benefit of his trick ; and, as it was a good trick, why let him have
the benefit of it. He throws out in his letter an excuse that he is a
theologian, but would introduce no questions of theology. That is
his trade, though it is not mine ; but I challenge him to this—let
him assail my religion in one of the Belfast newspapers, and if he
does not get an answer, let him write me down any name he pleases.
But I won't contend with him, nor am I such a blockhead as to take
up a political question with him. I have no notion to give him that
advantage, which would be this : he is at the head of the Presbyterians of Ulster, and if I was to argue politics with him, it would be
admitting that I was an antagonist of theirs in politics. . . . I
am no antagonist in politics with them ; on the contrary, I am most
desirous to serve the Presbyterians in every way in my power. And

if, in my present struggle, I succeed, it will be as much for their
benefit as for that of the Roman Catholics. Oh, no, Daddy Cooke,
I will not gratify your trick."

In this reply to Dr. Cooke, O'Connell committed one of the
greatest blunders of his life. Dr. Cooke was not a man to be
put down by a sneer or a joke. He was far above the reach of
any shaft of ridicule or vulgar insolence which O'Connell could
direct against him. True, O'Connell was leader of the Roman
Catholics. Among them he was a hero; none could vie with
him in popularity. But Cooke was the leader of a party
far superior in social standing, in education, and in moral
influence. He was as popular in the North as O'Connell was
in the South. He was, besides, the champion of a great constitutional principle, which had been assailed by a revolutionary
faction. He was the representative of loyalty and Protestant
freedom, as opposed to Popish tyranny and rebellion. He could
not, therefore, be ignored; it was worse than folly to make the
attempt. O'Connell was about to invade the North. He was
attempting to kindle among the industrious people of Ulster
the flame of discontent, which had already done so much mischief in the southern provinces. Cooke only stood upon the
defensive. He desired to preserve the peace of Ulster; and
to do so by a fair discussion, in the presence of its thoughtful
people, of the merits and demerits of Repeal. He sought for
no advantage. Fully convinced that he had truth on his side,
and confident in his ability to expound and defend it, he did not
fear to meet the greatest popular orator of the day. The same
could not be said of O'Connell. He manifestly doubted the
justice of his cause. He knew Dr. Cooke of old; and he knew
well that empty declamation and plausible sophistry, such as
deluded an excitable southern mob, would avail nothing against
the incisive logic and cutting irony of such an antagonist. To
meet him, therefore, would be almost certain defeat; to avoid
him, however he might try to cloak it, would betray cowardice.
O'Connell was thus placed in a dilemma, from which all his
tact and his effrontery failed to free him.

As soon as an authentic report of O'Connell's speech reached Dr. Cooke he replied. The reply is dated 14th January. After quoting that part in which O'Connell mentions the private letter, and charges him with lying, he says :—

" You have my entire pardon for all the uncivil epithets you have bestowed upon me ; for, surely, if you, as a gentleman, can use them, I, as a Christian, am much more bound to forgive them. . . . I forgive you for unceremoniously calling me a liar. But while I do so, I feel at liberty, nay, bound to defend myself against the foul imputation, and to warn you against the deadly sin (your own Church being the judge) into which you have plunged. . . . And now, to vary but a little the language of a distinguished ornament of your own profession, ' I will tie you down to the ring of falsehood, and I will bait you at it, till your testimony shall cease to produce a verdict against me, though human nature were as corrupt in my readers as in yourself.'

" In what number of *The Ulster Times* did you ever read any authorised statement that I would not challenge you ? What do you answer, Mr. O'Connell ? . . . You told a lie ! Yes, and you knew it when you told it. But your popularity was at stake, and—I shudder to write it—but—let conscience finish the sentence.

" Was it Mirabeau who boasted that he ruled over eleven millions of Frenchmen ? You have boasted of ruling or representing eight millions of Irishmen. Yet he was an idol of but four years ; you have enjoyed the popular apotheosis of twenty. But your days are numbered. Had you met me like a man, the chivalry—nay, perhaps the condescension—of the act had insured you, in any event, against a diminution of honours. But to skulk from the conflict beneath the meanness of a falsehood ! Ah ! it will pursue you like a shadow —it will haunt your very dreams—like the spirit of the murdered, it will sit heavy on the soul of your eloquence ; and the whisper of my humble name— of the man whom you abused and belied behind his back, but whom you dared not to encounter face to face—will drown in the ears of conscience the loudest shouts of that momentary popularity which you purchased at the expense of every honest man's respect—and, what is worse, at the expense of your own.

" You conclude your pitiable subterfuge by offering to encounter me in a theological discussion. This is a miserable *ruse*, that would disgrace any other man, . . . but . . . I take you at your

word upon one simple condition, to protect myself from your gen-
teel talent of invention. . . . My proposal is this : you obtain
me, in one or more of your own papers, one, two, or more columns
per week, fortnight, or as you please. You take for defence as much
as I am allowed for attack; and thus, by God's blessing, I trust to
open both your eyes, and the eyes of the multitude that shout after
you, to the errors and heresies that disfigure your theology, and the
disloyalties and the cruelties that disgrace your jurisprudence."

He concluded with the following solemn warning :—

" Never yet was there a man who employed his power or popularity, not to enlighten reason, but to inflame the passions of his
country, that did not, sooner or later, kindle a fire that he could not
extinguish, and perish in the flames of his own raising. Beware,
Mr. O'Connell! Your expedition to Belfast perils the peace of the
kingdom. You won't discuss with me, forsooth, because I am a
Presbyterian, and you are not politically opposed to Presbyterians.
I tell you, Mr. O'Connell, there is not, to my knowledge, a Presbyterian Repealer in Ulster—and I bless God that I can proclaim the
glorious news to the empire. Minor political differences there may
be amongst us ; but in opposition to you and Repeal, we present a
united and indissoluble front. Had you agreed to discuss with me
calmly the question of Repeal, the Ulster Presbyterians, in common
with their brother Protestants, would have listened as calmly. I
pay them no compliment when I say they are a thinking people, and
they see clearly through you. They see you can declaim, but dare
not argue ; and they see you want to overawe the Government, and to
terrify the North by processions of physical force. But again I say,
beware! If the peace of the country be disturbed, and if, notwithstanding all the salutary precautions of Government, Belfast
become another Bristol, and property and life be sacrificed to the
insatiable Moloch of your vanity—upon your head and upon your
conscience let all the guilt descend. The very men who, in their
folly, called for you, are standing, like the fabled wizard, terrified at
the apparition their own incantations conjured up ; and, believe me,
I do truly read your own mind, when I tell you you would give a
month of the Repeal Rent that you had never promised your fatal
visit to Belfast. Mark me, Mr. O'Connell, I am not speaking out of
vanity, but I tell you you will never recover the blow inflicted by a
Presbyterian. You have begun to fall before him, and, as sure as

ever Haman fell before Israel, so sure will you continue to fall, unless you cast off your vanity and repent of your sins—which may God grant, I do most sincerely and humbly pray."

It need scarcely be added that the paragraph in *The Ulster Times* was a pure invention of Mr. O'Connell's. No such paragraph had ever appeared. The editor formally contradicted the statement, and offered to place the file of his paper at the disposal of any person who wished to investigate the matter.

Mr. O'Connell still resolved to visit Belfast. In fact, he could not draw back; all arrangements were completed for the banquet, the Repeal meeting, and the soirée. But it was found prudent to change the proposed plan of triumphal progress and entry into the town. When it was publicly announced that Mr. O'Connell would be accompanied by a procession of southern Repealers through Newry, Dromore, Hillsborough, and Lisburn, the Protestants of Down and Antrim resolved to prevent what they considered a disloyal and insulting display. They would permit no such procession. Placards were accordingly issued calling upon all loyal men to assemble at the place marked for invasion :—

" We will be the last to offend the laws of our country, or offer an insult to the public peace ; but this we avow, if there be any unusual excitement caused by the entry of Mr. O'Connell into town, or anything in the shape of a procession to disturb the public peace . . . if there be any insult offered even to a schoolboy . . . we will treat them to a thunder of northern repeal that will astonish the brewers of treason and sedition. . . .

" Protestants of Down and Antrim, show your loyalty to your Sovereign and your cause by attending, on Monday, the 18th instant, to assist the small remnant of Her Majesty's troops, if necessary, and see the defamer of the glorious character of Protestant Ulster pass through in peace, the same way that other travellers do, upon more important matters than Repeal. GOD SAVE THE QUEEN."

The Protestants of Ulster were in earnest. The threatened

triumphal procession of O'Connell made them indignant. The
insult offered to Dr. Cooke had roused them to a state of
uncontrollable excitement. The peace of the province was in
danger. Should a procession of Repealers attempt to march
through Down, no power could prevent a collision between the
parties; and such a collision would, at that period, have set
Ireland in a flame. The Government saw the danger, and
hurried large bodies of troops and police to the North. Belfast
presented the appearance of a besieged city. Strong detach-
ments were posted at Newry, Dromore, Banbridge, and other
towns in the proposed route of O'Connell. The Repealers lost
courage. They felt that any mob they could gather from the
purlieus of Dublin, the lanes of Drogheda, and the mountains
of Louth, could not stand before the sturdy yeomen of Down.
They wisely resolved, therefore, to abandon the procession,
and to adopt a more prudent, if less dignified, mode of progress.
At five o'clock on the morning of Saturday, January 16th,
Mr. O'Connell and a few select friends set out from Dublin in
a private carriage. They travelled in disguise, under fictitious
names, and so secretly that neither friend nor foe heard or
knew of them till they entered the Royal Hotel, Belfast, about
six o'clock on a dark, cold evening. It was a sad fall from the
pompous announcement in the Rotundo; but stern necessity compelled the advocate of sedition and Repeal to steal
into the capital of Ulster Protestantism like a thief in the
night.

The day after his arrival Mr. O'Connell remained in his
hotel. On Monday he also remained within doors, but held a
kind of rough levée, at which the great unwashed presented
themselves. In the evening he was entertained at dinner in an
old wooden theatre, which was fitted up for the occasion, and
dignified by the name " Pavilion." Some eight hundred guests
sat down, among whom were two or three Liberal Protestants.
The Roman Catholic clergy were present in great force. Mr.
O'Connell delivered a characteristic speech. Those present
were praised and flattered, while his political opponents, and

especially Dr. Cooke, were abused in no measured terms :—

"What I want to know is, why I did not come sooner amongst you, for I never met men after my own heart till I came here. Will they call this—have they ever called this—'the black North'? To me it is the bright and brilliant North; no North contains such stars as these (pointing to the ladies in the gallery). This galaxy of beauty would ornament any region upon earth. I am bound to admit there is a factitious appearance given to our present meeting, not so much from the zeal and energy of our friends, as the craft and activity of our enemies; from the boxing buffoon of a divine, up to the truculent threatening of the worst instrument of faction, and a slight bit of hypocrisy amongst it."

In another part of this elegant oration, he said of the Orangemen :—

"I laugh at their opposing my progress, on the ground that that progress was conceived or entered upon in the spirit of religious or sectarian bigotry, or with the intention of insulting any sect or party. I leave such objects to the Cookes of a festivity of a very different description from this. . . . I have lived but for the promotion of freedom, unrestrained freedom of conscience to all classes and sects of the human family; I have lived but to be the advocate of civil and religious liberty all over the world; I have lived only for the advocacy of those exalted objects, and I have not, I think, lived in vain. I have not assumed the attitude of the gladiator, nor of the ferocious divine."

In regard to Dr. Cooke's challenge, he said he was ready to give "not two, but six, or even twenty-six hours, if he wished, on any subject connected with civil and religious liberty." This was a lame excuse. It did not deceive even the obsequious friends who surrounded him; for no sooner were the words uttered than some wag called out, "Don't boast, Dan. Here's Cooke coming."

It was part of the original programme to hold a Repeal meeting in the "Pavilion" at twelve o'clock on Tuesday.

Admission was by ticket; and every precaution was taken that
the tickets should be sold only to friends. Long before the
hour the body of the building was crowded. It was whispered
that Dr. Cooke would be present. Remarks were heard
through the assembly which proved that he had many friends
there. The clerical pioneers on the platform showed symptoms
of alarm. To test the feelings of the audience a green flag was
unfurled inscribed with the word "Repeal." Many shouted
their applause; but a majority preserved a dignified silence,
while some ominous groans were heard. This experiment
decided the fate of the meeting. The public were respectfully
informed that Mr. O'Connell would not appear, but that he
was prepared to address them from the window of his hotel.
The indignation of the meeting was great; but the truth was
now plain to every one,—O'Connell was afraid to venture to
any place where there was a possibility of encountering Dr.
Cooke.

The crowd rushed to the Royal Hotel, which is situated at
the corner of Donegall Place and Donegall Square, having a
large open area both in front and at the side. This was filled
by a motley mob, numbering eight or nine thousand. Some
were Repealers, and shouted lustily, "Dan for ever!" But
the mass seemed to hold different views, and gave expression
to them in such terms as "Hurrah for Dr. Cooke!" "No
Surrender!" The whole scene was strange and suggestive.
A platform or balcony had been constructed before an upper
window of the hotel. In front of it, suspended from a tree in
the square, was a huge placard, inscribed "Dr. Cooke's Challenge." Round it stood a body of stalwart artizans, whose
determined bearing showed that they would suffer no hostile
hand to touch the paper; while clinging to the branches of
the tree, and of others near it, was a crowd of sharp-witted
boys, who ever and anon called attention to the challenge.
When Mr. O'Connell stepped from the window to the platform, he was saluted with a storm of cheers and groans.
Meanwhile the merry boys from the trees cried, "Here's

the challenge; won't you come down and read it?" He tried to speak. It was in vain. His lips moved; his hand was waved; attitude and action proclaimed the orator, but not a word was heard amid the yells of the crowd. The reporters stood close behind him, with heads thrust forward, and papers resting on the speaker's broad shoulders, trying to catch his words. Occasionally there was a momentary lull; and then would be heard some stentorian voice from the crowd—" Come down and meet the Doctor, and we'll give you a fair hearing." The speech was reported; at least a speech appeared in *The Whig*, which purported to be that delivered. It may have been, but so far as the crowd was concerned the whole was a pantomime. The demonstration was a total failure. It was worse; for as Mr. O'Connell withdrew through the window, his retreat was celebrated by a round of Kentish fire, followed by a cheer for Dr. Cooke, which made the welkin ring.

O'Connell and his friends now saw that the invasion of Ulster was a blunder. He thought he might ignore Dr. Cooke, and affect to despise his challenge; but he found, when too late, that Dr. Cooke's power in Belfast was supreme. In fact, O'Connell, from the moment of his arrival, had been virtually a prisoner. He dared not venture to leave his hotel except by stealth, or under escort. The hotel, itself, did not seem safe, after the abortive attempt to address the mob on Tuesday. A demand for protection was addressed to the authorities, and a cordon of troops was drawn round the house. Early on Wednesday morning a close carriage drew up at the door, closely encircled by mounted police with drawn swords. Lines of infantry, and patrols of cavalry kept back the crowds. O'Connell and his friends entered the carriage, which drove rapidly off to Donaghadee, under military escort. The last object O'Connell saw, as he left Belfast, was a huge placard, which some boys waved like a banner before him; it bore the significant legend, DR. COOKE'S CHALLENGE. At Donaghadee fresh indignities awaited the unhappy fugitive. After going on board the steamer, he attempted to address a few words to the

crowd of idlers on the quay; but a Highland piper, who
chanced to be among them, struck up the appropriate air,
"We'll gang nae mair to yon toun;" and the shrill notes of
the pibroch were the last sounds that fell upon the ear of
O'Connell as he left the shores of Ulster.

The effects of his visit did not terminate with his flight. His
boasting in Dublin and elsewhere among his southern friends,
had roused the indignation of the Protestant people of Ireland.
His rash attempt to carry the Repeal agitation into the north,
made them resolve upon counter demonstrations.

The students of Belfast College were the first to give expression to their loyalty. They prepared and published the following resolutions:—

"1st. That, understanding a declaration was made by Mr.
O'Connell, to the effect that the Presbyterian youth of Ulster
would coincide with him in the question of Repeal, but for the
undue influence of Dr. Cooke, we, the students of Belfast Royal
College, feel ourselves called upon, at the present time, publicly to
repudiate the groundless assertion of Mr. O'Connell; and, also, to
profess our decided and conscientious opposition to the political
creed of this gentleman, believing that it is inimical to Protestantism, and subversive of the best interests of our country.

"2nd. That, in common with the Protestants of Ulster, we do
express our admiration of the manner in which Dr. Cooke has
challenged and confounded Mr. O'Connell."

Ere Mr. O'Connell left Belfast, an advertisement appeared
in the newspapers, which shows the state of feeling among the
loyal men of Ireland:—

"The undersigned request a meeting of the nobility, clergy,
gentry, and other friends of the British Constitution, in Antrim,
Down, and contiguous Northern counties, to be held in Belfast,
upon Thursday, the 21st January, at eleven o'clock, for the purpose
of expressing their opinion in opposition to the attempt, now for the
first time undisguisedly made in Ulster, to effect the Repeal of the
Union."

The requisition was signed by 41 Peers, 14 Right Honourables and Honourables, 18 Baronets, 32 Members of Parliament, 11 High Sheriffs, 6 Lieutenants of Counties, 98 Deputy
Lieutenants, 335 Magistrates, and 330 Clergy of various
denominations.

The meeting assembled in the Circus, an immense building,
which was crowded by the rank, wealth, and talent of the
country. No such array had ever been seen in Belfast. Before
the business opened the building rang with " Cheers for Dr.
Cooke." The chair was filled by the Marquess of Downshire ;
and the leading speakers were the Right Hon. G. R. Dawson,
Lord A. Chichester, Colonel Verner, M.P., the Earl of Hillsborough, Lord Newry, Mr. Emerson Tennent, M.P., Mr. G.
Dunbar, M.P., Colonel Close, Sir Robert Bateson, Richard
Davison, Esq., Lord A. Loftus, Rev. Dr. Stewart, &c. Dr.
Cooke's speech was the great attraction. It was mainly a
reply to Mr. O'Connell. He thus gave his reasons for the
challenge :—

" The moment his portentous visit was threatened, my duty
became matter of solemn prayer to Him who can employ the
' weak to confound the mighty.' . . . I did believe that in
1841 I saw the fearful shadow of 1641. I saw the circumstances
merely so far changed, that, in 1641, physical force marched in the
van of rebellion and massacre ; but in 1841 intellect and eloquence,
enlisting argument, prejudice and passion, advanced in the front, to
mask and to cover the array of physical force that fearfully gathered
behind. I judged the spirit of the terrible movement to lie in pretended appeals to reason, intèrest, and facts. And I said in my
heart, Shall we see the sword coming, and will no man give warning,
and grapple with it, ere it come too nigh ? I did believe, and I do
still believe, that this mighty conspiracy may, under Providence, be
met and averted : therefore did I take one step in advance to meet
it. I did not miscalculate when I counted on Mr. O'Connell's abuse
—nay, I did know I was taking my life in my hand ; but I did also
calculate that my life was in the hands of Him who gave it, and
that if one hair of my head were molested, or one drop of my blood
spilled, yet would the event be overruled to unite still more closely
all true Protestant hearts, and that the loss of one humble man

might be the salvation of our Churches and our country. I may not overlook the newspaper statement, that Mr. O'Connell has challenged me to twenty-six hours of a discussion upon civil and religious liberty. I take him at his word. The time, the place, I leave to himself, but London and Exeter Hall I take to be the best ; and I claim but one condition—the issue of half the tickets. And never since truth tore the cloak off hypocrisy, did man stand for such a stripping as awaits you, Daniel O'Connell. . . . There should I exhibit him, sitting this moment in the councils of the land, as the transformed hero of Milton sat at the ear of the sleeping Eve. So sits he whispering his dreams of Repeal into the ear of the people, and infusing the poison of his Popery into the vitals of the Constitution. But as the spear of Ithuriel compelled the foul toad to start into his native Satanic form, so shall the history of the past, and the condition of the present, compel O'Connell to appear in form, what he is in heart—the genius of knavery, the apostle of rebellion."

He concluded as follows :—

" You (Mr. O'Connell) have said, there is no hope of the Presbyterian youth of Ulster so long as ' that loathsome theologue, Dr. Cooke, has influence over them.' Now, that there is no hope of their becoming Repealers is, happily, one truth ; but that I have influence over them, such as you would indicate, is utterly untrue. No! I will tell you what and who has influence over them. The Bible and its principles have influence over them. The Spirit that descended upon John Knox, who never feared the face of man, has influence over them. His mantle has fallen around their manly shoulders, and they will never exchange it for the frieze coat of Repeal. . . . Look at the town of Belfast. When I was a youth it was almost a village. But what a glorious sight does it now present ? The masted grove within our harbour—our mighty warehouses teeming with the wealth of every clime—our giant manufactories lifting themselves on every side—our streets marching on, as it were, with such rapidity, that an absence of a few weeks makes us strangers in the outskirts of our town. And all this we owe to the Union. No, not all—for throned above our fair town, and looking serenely from our mountain's brow, I beheld the genii of Protestantism and Liberty, sitting inseparable in their power, while the genius of Industry which nightly reclines at their feet, starts with every morning in renovated might, and puts forth his energies, and

showers down his blessings, on the fair and smiling lands of a
Chichester, a Conway, and a Hill. Yes, we will guard the Union, as
we will guard our liberties, and advance and secure the prosperity of
our country."

The speech was received with enthusiastic applause ; and a
special vote of thanks to Dr. Cooke was moved by the Dean of
Ross, and seconded by Lord A. Loftus, for the eminent service
he had rendered to his country and to Protestantism in
triumphantly opposing Repeal.

On the succeeding evening the members for Belfast, J. E.
Tennent, Esq., and G. O. Dunbar, Esq., were entertained at a
banquet, in the Music Hall. There Dr. Cooke's health was
proposed, and received with an enthusiasm even greater than
that accorded to the guests of the evening. His speech in
reply was filled with racy humour and cutting sarcasm. It
bore chiefly on Mr. O'Connell, and his recent displays in
Belfast. Referring to the challenge thrown out to discuss the
principles of civil and religious liberty, he said :—

" Hear me, Mr. O'Connell. You challenged me in Belfast. I
challenge you in the face of the empire. I know you are confident
in your abilities; but you feel the rottenness of your cause. *You*
argue for civil and religious liberty ! Like the ' Amen ' in the throat
of Macbeth, the very words would endanger strangulation, and would
so vividly conjure up before you the foul mysteries of the confessional,
and the horrid racks of the Inquisition, that you would shrink from
the cause you had proposed to advocate, and become the convert of
that Protestant liberty you have hitherto laboured to destroy."

He concluded with the following eloquent and stirring
words :—

" It is said of Constantine the Great that, in one of his marches,
in vision he beheld on the sun a cross bearing this motto—*In
hoc signo vinces.* So, also, seizing on the cross of Christ, we will
conquer—not by intellect, or intelligence, or zeal, but by the Spirit
of our God—our fathers' God. The cross represents Union, while it
seals the reconciliation between God and man. . . . And if the

enemy should ever repeat his invasion, the Protestants of Ulster will
stand united, as the parts of the cross, that sad but glorious emblem
of our religion ; and we will united meet him again, as our rock-
bound shores meet the waves of the Atlantic."

Dr. Cooke effectually stopped the Repeal agitation in Ulster.
His bold policy and manly determination brought the boasting, and the predicted processions and triumphs of O'Connell,
alike to an ignominious close. Mr. O'Connell had said he would
enter Ulster at the head of thousands, and that he would pass
through it as a conqueror. He entered it by stealth, and he
fled from it in fear. The reports of the great anti-Repeal
meeting followed him to Scotland, England, and even into his
own dark and deluded Munster. The enthusiastic cheers of
loyal Protestant Ulster, inspired by the eloquence of Dr.
Cooke, rung the death-knell of Repeal. True, Mr. O'Connell
continued to boast, and to talk of past triumphs, and to throw
out fresh challenges to his great adversary; but Dr. Cooke
met him at every point, and replied with such skill and power,
that he converted each fresh challenge and assault into a new
victory.

The enthusiasm excited in Belfast, and over the North of
Ireland by Dr. Cooke's opposition to Repeal was unparalleled.
He was hailed as the saviour of the country. Immediately
after O'Connell's flight, steps were taken to present the victor
with a suitable testimonial. It was known that his life was
threatened, and it was feared that some fanatic might murder
or disable him. It was, therefore, resolved that the testimonial
should take such a form as would, to some extent at least,
secure a provision for his family, should his life fall a sacrifice
to his patriotism. The proposal met with a ready and hearty
response from the Protestants of Ireland. The Dublin *Evening
Mail*, in an able article, advocated the scheme, and paid an
eloquent tribute to Dr. Cooke :—

" If the Union be of any value to the country, the country owes
a proportionate debt to the man who has done more to cripple

and discomfit the principal assailant of that Union than any one else since the time when the Right Honourable Francis Blackburn was Attorney-General. If Mr. O'Connell had succeeded in making a decidedly successful progress through Ulster as the Apostle of Repeal, there can be no doubt that that fact alone would have been a blow, and a serious one, to the stability of the Union. And he had every prospect of making at least such an unresisted progress as his party could have magnified into a gigantic triumph, up to the day when Dr. Cooke stepped forward with his timely—and we may almost say—providential challenge. By that single step Dr. Cooke converted the expected triumphal progress of Mr. O'Connell into a clandestine journey, more like the surreptitious approach of a thief than the bold advent of a political deliverer; and changed the bluster and the confidence of these mischief-makers who awaited his arrival into silent shame and downcast mortification. The challenge was given with the frankness and fearlessness of a man who knew he was in the right; and it was declined with a shrinking timorousness that has satisfied all Britain that Mr. O'Connell feared to meet his adversary, because he knew and felt that he was in the wrong. Believing, as we do, that the preservation of the Union is worth anything, or everything, to this country, we can form no estimate of the value of this great service rendered to both nations by Dr. Cooke, that may not possibly fall under the mark. To the nobility and gentry of Ireland—the owners of those forfeited estates which a Repeal Parliament would reclaim—the preservation of the Union is worth their whole income—ay, probably, worth the heads as well as the lands of the greater number of them. To the mass of the people, who would be plunged into the miseries of intestine war, and of external blockade by the first inevitable difference that would spring up between the rival legislatures, the preservation of the Union is worth all the profits of their home trade and foreign commerce, and all the value that they may set on the blessings of peace and the immunities of social order. To every Protestant in the land the preservation of the Union is worth whatever price liberty of conscience may be estimated at by men who have been educated in the enjoyment of love of freedom. By giving his aid so effectively for the preservation of this inestimable good of the country, Dr. Cooke rendered a momentous service to us all, but more especially to his Protestant fellow-citizens; and we trust that they, at least, throughout all parts of Ireland, will not be slow in acknowledging their sense of its value. With this object, we are glad to observe that an influential committee has been formed in Belfast for the purpose of presenting Dr. Cooke with a suitable testimonial, and we understand that some of the leading merchants and citizens of Dublin are about to second their patriotic exertions, so as to give every one who values the preservation of the Legislative Union here an opportunity of acknowledging his obligation to its successful defender in Belfast."

The munificent sum of two thousand pounds was soon raised and invested. The annual proceeds were applied, under the direction of trustees, to the payment of a life insurance, so that the whole might be available for his family after his death. This was a graceful and appropriate acknowledgment of eminent and successful services.

CHAPTER XVII.

1841—1843.

Dr. Cooke Moderator of the General Assembly—Marble Bust presented to May Street Church—Efforts on behalf of Church of Scotland—Letter to Emerson Tennent, M.P.—Correspondence with Drs. Chalmers and Candlish regarding Non-Intrusion—Dr. Cooke's Views and Policy explained—Letter of Lord Castlereagh—Difficulties of Dr. Cooke's Position—Efforts to obtain a Government Measure thwarted—Injudicious Policy of Non-Intrusionists—Dr. Cooke's Views misrepresented—His unwavering Faithfulness to the Church of Scotland—The Disruption—Dr. Cooke's Speech in the First Free Assembly—Remarkable Letter to Sir Robert Peel.

THE services of Dr. Cooke were as fully appreciated by the ministers of the Presbyterian Church as by the general body of the Protestants of Ireland. At the meeting of the General Assembly in 1841 he was raised by acclamation to the Moderator's chair.

A few days after the Assembly closed, a public meeting was held in May Street Church, to witness the presentation of a marble bust of Dr. Cooke to the congregation. The chair was occupied by A. J. Macrory, Esq. Mr. Emerson Tennent, M.P., in presenting the bust, said—

" Mr. M'Dowal, an artist of distinguished eminence, was employed, at my suggestion, in producing a bust of Dr. Cooke. His success was quite remarkable; and it occurred to me that a work of art, at once so creditable to our town from the talents of the sculptor, and so gratifying to our own feelings from the record which it preserves of Dr. Cooke, should not be allowed to perish in the frail material of clay, but should be transferred to the more lasting marble, and placed in some suitable situation to perpetuate the memory of our friend. I was anxious to have accomplished this at my own expense ; but a few admirers of Dr. Cooke in London, Manchester, and Dublin,

as well as some members of his congregation, had entreated that
they might be permitted to have their names associated with the
object. Amongst the principal of these were Mr. William Henry
and Mr. Ferrier, of Dublin, and Mr. Barbour, of Manchester. By
their aid and co-operation the work was completed, and a request
conveyed that I should this day place it in your hands, and leave it
to your discretion to find a suitable position for its perpetual preservation. . . . Gentlemen, permit me to say, that my first impulse
in suggesting the execution of this monument was esteem for the
man, admiration for his talents, and gratitude for his friendship.
But to you, who have been united so long in the closest intimacy
and the most unreserved communication with him, why should I
dwell upon a feeling which I share in common with you all—
a feeling which the man who knows Dr. Cooke and is yet a
stranger to it, must be unsusceptible of admiration for genius and
appreciation of knowledge, and dead to the charms of every quality
that can shed enjoyment over companionship and society. Nor, as
a public man myself, was I less sensible of the public claims of my
friend upon the gratitude and admiration of Ireland. I cannot forget that whilst, for the last ten years, the flames of party discord in
this unhappy land have been fed by religious rancour, the efforts of
Dr. Cooke have been all directed to the formation and consolidation
of a great national party in defence of the truth, by inculcating the
oblivion of all minor religious differences, which, in less perilous
times, might divide, if they did not alienate, the affections of men
whom he has taught to glory in the one common name of Protestantism. I cannot forget that when the peace of our country was
threatened by the invasion of a man who laid his claim to our confidence by threatening the dismemberment of our empire, it was Dr.
Cooke who went forth to meet him, at the head of compact and consolidated Ulster, and offered him that gage of battle, his refusal of
which involved his suicidal discomfiture, and drove him back to his
accustomed haunts crestfallen and confounded. But, powerful as
were these claims upon our remembrance and recognition, they are
valueless when brought into comparison with his higher and nobler
qualities as a minister of the Gospel—qualities in which he need
acknowledge no superior, and in which he combines, with the
unbending bearing of the ancient Puritan, the dignity and accom-
plishments of the modern divine. . . . Gentlemen," he said, in
conclusion, "to your cause, to your community, and to your minister
I have to offer this humble testimony of my services, my attachment,

and my esteem. In all human probability, the gift will long survive the fleeting existence of the giver; but the marble itself cannot out-live the memory of the man whose noble features it will perpetuate to our descendants; and if, in addition to my ostensible desire to bear my homage to the merits of a great and good man, I have a personal feeling excited by the incident, it is the hope that, at some far distant day, my children may have it recalled to their recollection, by this memorial, that their father was the advocate of Presbyterianism, and the friend of Dr. Cooke."

Mr. Macrory, in accepting the bust, said—

"Allow me, on behalf of the elders, committee, and members of May Street Church, to return you our most grateful thanks for this elegant and suitable present; elegant as a piece of workmanship, and so faithful in its likeness that now, when we have the great and gifted original before us, the most critical eye or fastidious taste cannot discover an omission; suitable, that inasmuch as the church was built expressly for his ministrations, and will hand down his name to posterity, this bust will hand down to posterity the all but breathing likeness of that illustrious divine. . . . His name is now known and appreciated in every country of the globe, and all have testified their united approbation of the man, the scholar, the Christian. Scarcely had America tendered her Degree in Divinity, when Trinity College, Dublin—one of the first seats of learning in the world, and one exceedingly chary of her honours—conferred her Degree in Laws. Municipal favours and city freedoms, of which Dublin and Derry were the foremost, have also joined in goodly array to testify their admiration of the man. Therefore it is that the splendid gift this day deposited within these walls partakes more of a national than a congregational character."

Dr. Cooke, being called upon, said—

"Mr. Chairman, this is the first time in my life I ever appeared with two faces. I believe that, among all the sins which have been laid to my charge, the sin of having two faces has not been included. I have not had two faces for my friends, and surely none will accuse me of having two faces for my enemies."

After a passing reference to his labours and struggles, and

an eloquent tribute to friends who had aided him, he thus
spoke of the great ecclesiastical question which was then
agitating Scotland and Ulster :—

" When the case of the Church of Scotland is brought before
Parliament, I do not hesitate to affirm that the Members for Belfast,
now here before us, will advocate her cause and support her in her
trials. If I have laboured for these gentlemen, or have been in any
way serviceable to them, I hope they will requite it by labouring for
the Church of Scotland. They may tell the Premier that there are
in Ireland seven hundred thousand honest, thinking Presbyterians—
seven hundred thousand hearts, not cold like that marble, but warm
and active, like my own. If the Premier of England think he can
part with the support of the seven hundred thousand, let him be
told we have an alternative. If he do not support us, we will not
support him. You, gentlemen, carry over peace or war. The independence of the Church of Scotland is the question on which our
affections turn. . . . We cannot remain warm to that party that
will not remain warm to our Church. If Scotland's Church be
shackled, and her chains riveted on her, the chains will be riveted
on the Church of this country also."

Dr. Cooke's sympathy with the Non-Intrusion party in the
Church of Scotland never waned. His eloquent advocacy and
powerful influence were never wanting when required, whether
on the platforms of Ulster, England and Scotland, or in the
halls of St. Stephen's. In April, 1841, he went to London, as
a deputy from the General Assembly, to aid the Church of
Scotland in important negotiations with the Government. Dr.
Candlish bore honourable testimony to the services he rendered
on this and other occasions at a public meeting held in Belfast,
on the 13th of July following. Dr. Cooke, being Moderator
of Assembly, was in the chair :—

" You, sir," said Dr. Candlish, " on a former occasion, were the
instrument which caused Lord Aberdeen to abandon his Bill; and if
the Duke of Argyll's be altered so as to be unworthy of acceptance,
we will entreat you to lend us again your powerful assistance, and

we will say to the Government, Give us the Bill, the whole Bill, and nothing but the Bill."

Dr. Cooke watched, with the fidelity of a son, over the interests of the Church of Scotland. He wrote to Mr. Emerson Tennent in terms which showed he was in earnest, and would tolerate no equivocation :—

" Will you support by voice, as God has given you the gift of speech, and by vote, as the Presbyterians have given you a seat ? Will you support the Duke of Argyll's or any similar Bill, founded *bonâ fide* upon any of my three propositions submitted to Sir Robert Peel ?—Yea or nay ? It will be totally in vain to reply you would wish to do it. For my own part I am ready to make full allowance for your situation ; but upon this point I am decided. If the members for Belfast be returned by orthodox Presbyterians, they *must* support the Church of Scotland.

" I know you will say to me, and say with justice, what did the Whigs do for you ? I care not what they did, or what they did not do. I shall neither become Whig nor Radical. But then, so long as God grants me grace, I shall never become a Tory. I stand unshaken in my avowed repudiation of both parties. I alike despise and abhor them both, for one single reason—as parties they have no religion. But I stand by the Conservatism I avowed—by all that is worth conserving. Now, I do believe, that within the empire there is no institution better worth conserving than the Church of Scotland. And I will support neither man nor party by whom the Church of Scotland is either neglected or oppressed. Whigs do for her very little, I admit. With their usual tactics, they promised much and did little. Still, I must not be less than ' thankfu' for sma' mercies,' when they are contrasted with no mercies at all. In a word, the Whigs gave some liberties ; the Tories gave none. The Whigs were civil ; the Tories insulting. The Whigs ruled by sentiment ; the Tories by bayonets. *Solitudinem faciunt, pacem appellant.*

" Nothing so astonishes me as that a mind so perspicacious as that of Sir Robert Peel does not discern how the system of patronage is slowly, but surely, working upon the Scottish mind, and upon Presbyterian Ulster, so as in the end to overthrow both patronage and its supporters. By one ill-omened refusal of any reform, the Duke of Wellington so roused the public mind, that he was overturned, and the whole Conservative party with him. . . . Were Sir Robert Peel to grant even any of the propositions I submitted to him, all Scotland, with a few violent exceptions, would bless him, and Ulster would almost worship him. Let him refuse—and I fear he will refuse—and he not only loses Scotland and Ulster, but he converts them into opponents to his measures and partizans to his enemies. This last result I dread. The vision of it is flitting before me this monent in a kind of second sight. I see in it the elements of revolution in public sentiment and in public institutions, which a little concession—no, a little justice—would avert now, but which, if not granted now, cannot be averted hereafter. In Belfast this process will begin, and no living man could retard it. The Whigs will eventually triumph over us. The Presbyterians will be alienated, and no man will be able to reclaim them. Sir Robert Peel has disappointed my hopes—my confidence hitherto. Tell him so, as I have told him; and tell him too, what I also told him, that such disappointments are calculated eventually to bring about the overthrow of those great national Protestant Institutions which he wishes, and we all wish, to maintain.

" One other point. In writing to your friends, you accuse us and our Scotch friends of agitation. Now, ' no more of this, as you love me.' It is the veriest—no, I won't say what it is; but it is a thing never to be repeated to me. . . . Did not you agitate Belfast ? Was not I with you ? I underlay more obloquy for the sake of peace than most men would endure for me. I sacrificed popularity; and I am repaid with —' Don't agitate !' It was agitation, aided vigorously and widely by myself, as you know, which placed the present ministry where they are. . . . Indeed there must be no more of this."

Dr. Cooke has been charged with preferring the interests of his party to the liberties of the Church of Scotland. The foregoing letter, his public speeches, his public acts, and, above all, his private remonstrances with leading men, of which the foregoing is a specimen, show how unjust the charge was. The propositions referred to in the letter to Mr. Tennent were laid before Sir Robert Peel, and pressed upon him by Dr. Cooke after correspondence with Doctors Chalmers, Cunningham, and Candlish. It would seem that the leaders of the Non-Intrusion party had been led, through private information, got from Liberal friends in Belfast, to entertain doubts as to Dr. Cooke's full sympathy and hearty co-operation. They were warned that his strong political feelings would interfere with his advocacy of the claims of the Church of Scotland. Dr. Cooke heard of this, and wrote to Dr. Candlish expressing his surprise and indignation at such misrepresentations, and asking to be informed explicitly and authoritatively what would satisfy the Non-Intrusion party. Dr. Candlish replied at length on 1st December, 1841, detailing what his party wanted, and what would satisfy them :—" Our principle is, that we must be allowed to reject presentees on the sole and exclusive ground of unacceptableness,—that we must not be compelled to settle a minister against the will, the expressed dissent, or dislike of the congregation." This principle, he stated, might be carried out in three ways:—1st, by the Call; 2nd, by the veto; 3rd, by the *liberum arbitrium*. Each of these he explained. In regard to the last, which Dr. Candlish looked on as the minimum which his party could accept, Dr. Chalmers wrote on the 27th December:—" If the *liberum arbitrium* and the finality of church courts were heartily and unreservedly granted to us, I am clearly of opinion that the Church should acquiesce." He closed his letter as follows:—" How much I long that the patriots and statesmen, to many of whom you have free access, could be made to understand the true policy of sound and admiring Conservatism. Do, my dear sir, take every opportunity of pressing upon them the Duke of Argyll's Bill, nay, even shooting ahead of it. You, of all men, can appeal to the strongest experimental argument which can possibly be given, in the state of Presbyterian Ireland—certainly the most loyal, and manageable, and peaceful of all your provinces. . . . . I do hope to hear of your being in London, feeling, as I do, that we are in the hands of a steady, influential and devoted friend."

These were substantially the very propositions which Dr. Cooke submitted to Sir Robert Peel, and spoke of so firmly and plainly to Mr. Tennent. In placing them before Sir Robert Peel he was fully carrying out the wishes of the Non-Intrusionists, as expressed at the close of Dr. Candlish's letter:—" I have no doubt your private access to Government may avail us much; and if you get a decision on our principle, you will do us an inestimable favour." Dr. Cooke pressed the Government on this point; and he was led to believe, at the close of 1841, that he would be successful. He fully adopted the principles, though he did not quite concur in the policy, of his Scotch friends. His opinion was, they should have agreed upon the minimum of concession which they would or could accept, and then have firmly and unwaveringly pressed it alone upon the Government. Instead of this, they made large demands; and by asking too much they prevented the Government from giving anything. Dr. Cooke was also of opinion that, in speaking to or of statesmen, language conciliatory and respectful, yet firm, should always be used; and that care should be taken not to give offence by strong expressions or irritating insinuations. This wise policy had not been followed. Dr. Cooke sometimes felt himself called upon to defend his political friends from the injudicious and unjust accusations of those who were seeking their aid. The following letter affords an illustration:—

"London, Nov., 1841.

"My dear Dr. Cooke,—When I was at Corunna, on my way home from Gibraltar, a Derry newspaper was put into my hands, with an account of a meeting in the north with reference to the Scottish Church, at which you spoke.

"I think it almost needless to thank you for the kind and warm-hearted manner in which you defended the absent from undeserved censure, because those who are of a fine and generous nature are not slow to attribute good qualities to others; and I think you will believe in my gratitude to you without more extended phrases. At the same time, the feeling was so strong on my mind at the moment, that I determined one of my first acts in England should be to write to you and tell you I had seen your words.

"I shall never disgrace you, or your advocacy of my character. It was not as an election manœuvre that I professed my attachment to the Blue Banner, but an interest deep and sincere in its fortunes, which, when tested, will not be found to have faded away.

"I am,
"Ever sincerely yours,
"Castlereagh."

Dr. Cooke's generous and chivalrous nature, prompting him thus to defend the absent, left him sometimes open to attack on the part of those over-zealous partizans who did not know the whole facts, and who, probably, having party ends to serve, did not wish to know them. No doubt Dr. Cooke trusted the leaders of his party. Perhaps, under the trying circumstances in which they were placed, and in face of the adverse interests set before them, and pressed upon them with extraordinary persistence, he trusted them too far. Be this as it may, he had good ground for trusting them. He had means of knowing their wishes and their purposes, which were entirely unknown to mere onlookers. He was informed, by the highest authority, that the Church of Scotland would be saved. He was unwilling, in the critical position of affairs, to embarrass the Government by calling a meeting of General Assembly. He was repeatedly urged to do so by his brethren, and he ran the risk of a vote of censure by refusing. At the close of 1841 great pressure was brought to bear upon him by zealous, but not over-prudent, friends of the Church of Scotland in Belfast. He knew, however, that should he yield, incautious and irritating language would be used in the heat of debate, and the Assembly would impede rather than further the cause of freedom. To calm increasing clamour, he published the following letter on the 1st of January, 1842 :—" I think it a duty I owe to the ministers, elders, and people of the General Assembly to state that, according to the latest information I have received, my confidence in the settlement of the affairs of the Church of Scotland, in a manner satisfactory to her Non-Intrusion committee, not only remains unchanged, but, in so far as anything human can be called certain, amounts to certainty."

Soon after writing this letter he proceeded to London, by request of a leading member of the Government. He had interviews with Sir Robert Peel, Sir James Graham, and others, and urged the necessity of immediately introducing to Parliament a measure founded upon one or other of his propositions. The reply he got was:—" We are prepared,—we are most anxious to do so; but the demands of the Non-Intrusionists are so large, and the opposition of the moderate party is so intense, that we see no possibility at present of framing any measure which would give satisfaction to both, or at all tend to promote peace." Dr. Cooke replied, that entirely to satisfy both parties was out of the question; but that if a measure, moderate, yet sound and just, were passed, all would acquiesce, and the Church would be saved. Just at that time, while he was pressing his minimum upon Sir Robert Peel, a motion was proposed and carried in the Presbytery of Edinburgh which served largely to increase the difficulties of settlement. It affirmed the propriety of seeking the total abolition of the

Law of Patronage. This, it was seen on all hands, was a new phase of the controversy. It showed the Government how far the Non-Intrusionists were resolved to go; it alienated many of their friends, among whom was the Duke of Argyll; and it stirred up the Moderates to more determined opposition. Dr. Cooke felt his efforts paralyzed by this untimely motion, and he returned to Ireland deeply disappointed. But he did not relax his efforts to bring about a settlement. He tried all possible means. He suggested the propriety of a friendly conference between the leaders of the opposing parties; and he himself volunteered to be the medium of communication. In this he was met by a decided refusal on the part of the Non-Intrusionists; and he was even warned that any attempt to open a correspondence with the Moderates "would inevitably injure the cause, and destroy his own influence." "It is, I assure you," wrote a Non-Intrusion leader, "most delicate ground to attempt to tread."

Every day's delay, and each new phase the controversy assumed, embittered the feelings on both sides, and rendered the prospects of a settlement more and more hopeless. Still Dr. Cooke persevered: he was persuaded, from personal intercourse with Sir Robert Peel, that he and his colleagues were most anxious to introduce a measure which would be generally acceptable. The grand difficulty was to frame such a measure as would meet the conscientious scruples of the Non-Intrusionists on the one hand, and yet not excite the fierce opposition of the Moderates on the other. Government could not, of course, ignore either party. They must make fair allowance for the feelings and conscientious convictions of both. Unfortunately, too, the Non-Intrusionists were not agreed among themselves, and their policy was injudicious. In private they expressed their readiness to accept the simple *liberum arbitrium* rather than leave the Establishment; yet they publicly pressed upon the Cabinet, and urged Dr. Cooke to press, far more comprehensive claims. This tended vastly to complicate all negotiations, and in the end it proved ruinous. Statesmen could not understand the different, and sometimes conflicting, views expressed by different men of the party. They were displeased also, and even indignant, that what were at least intended as honest efforts on their part at a satisfactory settlement, were misrepresented in the heat of debate, and not unfrequently even denounced as attempts at deception.

In March, Sir Robert Peel appeared more anxious than ever to save the Church from impending schism. He was only retarded from immediate legislation by the conflicting views pressed upon him by deputations and letters from Scotland. Through a trusted friend he intimated to Dr. Cooke his desire to be furnished with a statement of the lowest terms of concession which the Non-Intrusionists could conscientiously receive, and which Irish Presbyterians would approve. He proposed to make them the basis of a Government Bill. He required at the same time a pledge that the Irish General Assembly would support him in carrying such a Bill through Parliament. Dr. Cooke, accordingly, stated the minimum, as embodied in the letters of Doctors Chalmers and Candlish. In a private note, Sir Robert Peel thanked Dr. Cooke for the communication, and said :—" The subject is now occupying the attention of the Government. Whatever be the result of this attempt at legislation on the part of the Government, their motives cannot, I think, be called in question—their sole intention being to heal the unhappy differences prevailing in the Church of Scotland."

Meantime, however, a rupture took place in the Non-Intrusion party; and it was affirmed in London that it was breaking up. A section of it, headed by Doctors Simpson and Leishman, made proposals to the Cabinet, which were less exacting than those of Dr. Cooke. They were adopted; and it was announced in the House of Commons in May, that Government were about to introduce a Bill which would satisfactorily settle the question. When, however, its principles were subsequently explained by Sir James Graham, they were found to be of such a kind as the vast body of

Non-Intrusionists could not accept. This was a sad disappointment to Dr. Cooke; and the opposition to the measure seems to have left the impression on the minds of her Majesty's ministers that, in consequence of the divided state of feeling in Scotland, satisfactory legislation was impossible.

Dr. Cooke's attempt failed, but not through any fault of his. Had there been unity of action among the Non-Intrusionists, had the lowest terms which they stated they could conscientiously accept been clearly and firmly pressed, apart from all other claims,—above all, had there been less of acrimony in speaking and writing about statesmen, and had there been more of charity in commenting on their acts and motives,—the result might, and probably would, have been different. Be this as it may, it was admitted by all who saw behind the scenes, and who were not blinded by party feeling, that Dr. Cooke was faithful to the Church of Scotland from first to last; and that, in his attempts to secure her liberty, he had exhausted all his influence.

Even when thus repeatedly baffled, he did not desist. To the very last he continued his efforts to induce the Government to legislate. Sir Robert Peel still professed his anxiety to do so; but such influence was brought to bear upon Sir James Graham by the Moderate party, and such representations were made to him even by professing Non-Intrusionists, that he was led to believe a settlement would eventually be effected on easy terms. At that time, too, unfortunately, owing in part to a slight misunderstanding in London with Dr. Candlish, and in part to a defective report of a speech subsequently delivered in Belfast, Dr. Cooke was represented in Scotland as an apostate from his original principles, and an enemy to the Church's freedom. It was a gross and malicious calumny. In a letter published on the 28th of April, 1843, he indignantly denied it, and set forth anew the views which he had always held, and which he had laid before Sir Robert Peel. But the calumny was persistently affirmed by certain parties in Scotland, because it served a purpose.

In spite of the misrepresentations of enemies, and, it must be added, the strange coldness of professing friends—even when all hope of legislation before the meeting of Assembly was abandoned, and when it was known that the disruption could not be postponed—Dr. Cooke pressed the Church's claims upon the Cabinet; and he was assured, on the highest authority, that such instructions would be given to the Lord High Commissioner as would prevent a schism. But here, again, adverse influence prevailed. One of the leaders of the Moderate party, as Dr. Cooke accidentally discovered, assured Sir Robert Peel that, under any circumstances, not more than twenty or at most thirty ministers would secede, and those extreme men, whom the Church could well spare. Dr. Cooke immediately tried to correct this fatal misrepresentation. He assured Sir Robert Peel that, unless satisfactory legislation were carried out, more than four hundred ministers would leave the Establishment.

When the meeting of Assembly drew near, Dr. Cooke was still sanguine. He had faith in the justice and goodwill of the Premier. He went to Edinburgh in full expectation of a satisfactory settlement. He was sadly disappointed. He was present when Dr. Welsh, the Moderator, in words of solemn import, addressed his Remonstrance to the Lord High Commissioner and the House, laid upon the table the famous Protest, and bowing to the chair, left the Church. He joined the long file of ministers and elders who followed, bidding farewell to an Establishment which he loved with true filial affection. He was not a deputy, and consequently had no claim to a seat in the Free Assembly; but Dr. Chalmers, the new Moderator, did him the high honour of requesting him to address the Court. In a remarkable speech, he expressed his full concurrence in the momentous step the Church had just taken; and, with a clearness which might almost be called prophetic, he sketched her future success :—

" You have been compelled, by a regard to the authority of the

Lord Jesus, by a sense of duty to the memory of your fathers, by a regard to those principles which you subscribed when you received the Confession of Faith, to take this step, the bearings of which upon future events it is impossible to foretell. But, seeing it has been taken in obedience to the great Head of the Church, and for the honour of the great Head of the Church—seeing it has been taken on the ground of the Word of God, and the dictates of conscience—though I do not stand in the shoes of a prophet, yet I believe that from these great principles there will flow results on which will hang a thousand attendant blessings. . . . Though you meet as a diminished band, you will go forth to the spiritual regeneration, not only of Scotland, but of the heathen throughout the world and of God's ancient people."

Referring to the letter of the Lord High Commissioner, and to his own information regarding the proposed acts of the Government, he said—

"Your hearts have been crushed; my expectations have been crushed. I depended on common sense; I depended on common reason; I depended on the views which particular men would take of this question. I have had sleepless nights, and tossings to and fro, for the Church of Scotland. My own heart has been crushed. The heart of Scotland may have been crushed; but, under the Providence of God, great will be the results. It is by compressing the muscles nearest the heart that the blood is propelled to the extremities of the body. The blood of the Church of Scotland has been thus propelled from the heart, and will send its influences to the ends of the earth, and exert a powerful and invigorating effect upon the Protestantism of the world. . . . There is not a corner of Europe to which the heart of the Church of Scotland will not propel the life-blood of religious liberty."

On Thursday, the 18th of May, Dr. Cooke took part in the Disruption; on Saturday, the 20th, he wrote the following remarkable letter to Sir Robert Peel:—

"EDINBURGH, 20th May, 1843.

"My dear Sir Robert Peel.—A solemn sense of accountability to God, and of duty to his Church in these lands,

compels me, once again, to bring before you the affairs of the
Church of Scotland. I formerly ventured to foretell, in the
face of all contrary information which you had received, that at
least four hundred ministers would retire in case no Relief Bill
were conceded. I have this day seen the roll of the Protesters ;
it contains four hundred and twenty-five names, and includes
the greatest and best of Scotland's ministers. The enthusiasm,
though passionless, is great ; and the enthusiasm of Scotchmen
is no bubble of an hour. Would to God you had taken my
humble advice, and prevented this calamity when prevention
was so easy ! Would that I could even yet persuade you to
avert calamities still greater ! I am a Presbyterian by conviction ; yet for my friends and brethren's sake, I am as anxious to
prevent the overthrow of the Established Church of England
and Ireland as I was to prevent the disruption of the Established Church of Scotland. Yet here, I would not be misunderstood. I profess no affection for Prelacy, but I do for
many prelates and godly ministers ; and so long as they do
God's work in upholding true Protestantism, and opposing
Popery in the garb of Puseyism, so long would my ' aversion
of them that are given to change,' lead me to preserve what
is practically settled, rather than incur the fearful risk of
theoretic improvement. But that the disruption of the Church
of Scotland, which is held to be the fault of the Government,
will be followed by the overthrow of the other, I entertain no
more doubt than I do of my own existence. The evil will begin
in Ireland—it matters little where it will end. In Ireland this
disruption is felt by every Presbyterian as an injury inflicted on
himself.

" But can anything now be done ? I know not; but surely
something may be attempted. The remedy I would therefore
propose is this—the total extinction of patronage by purchase,
and the concession of the same spiritual independence to the
Church courts in Scotland as the Presbyterians of Ireland
enjoy. . . .

" I do, even at the eleventh hour, most earnestly entreat you

to consider these things.   Do not listen again to those who at
least attempted to deceive you before.   What now has come
of Dr. Leishman's and Dr. Cook's predictions, against which
I warned both yourself and Sir James Graham ?   They have
been proved worse than nothing, and vanity.   For God's sake,
I beseech you, trust such fallacious prophets no more.   .   .   .

" I fear I shall still continue to speak and prophesy in vain.
But my accuracy in the past ought to gain me some credit for
the future ; and, be the result as it may, I feel that I have
done my duty.

> " I have the honour to be,
> > " My dear Sir Robert Peel,
> > > " Your very obedient servant,
> > > > " H. COOKE."

CHAPTER XVIII.

1842—1849.

Bicentenary of Presbyterianism in Ireland—Presbyterians not Republican—Presbyterian Marriage Question—Special Meeting of Assembly—Exhausting Labours—Marriage Bill passed—Dissenters' Chapels Bill—Literary Labours —Analytical Concordance of Scripture—Notes on Brown's Bible—Hours of Study—Political Resolution passed by the Assembly in 1843—Dr. Cooke's Protest—Withdraws from General Assembly—Queen's Colleges projected— Dr. Cooke's Views—Proposal for a Presbyterian College—Letter to Sir Robert Peel—The Appointment of President to Queen's College, Belfast— Dr. Cooke appointed Agent for Regium Donum—The College Controversy— The Magee Bequest—Establishment of Assembly's College—Dr. Cooke elected Professor of Sacred Rhetoric and PRESIDENT—Resigns May Street Church—Appointed constant Supplier by the Assembly—Testimonial from Congregation—Appointed Dean of Residence in Queen's College—Public Services.

FRIDAY, the 10th of June, 1842, was celebrated as the bicentenary of Presbyterianism in Ireland. On the 10th of June, 1642, the first Presbytery was organized at Carrickfergus. It consisted of only five ministers and four elders. After two centuries the General Assembly of the Presbyterian Church contained thirty-three presbyteries and four hundred and seventy-four ministers; while its people were estimated at seven hundred thousand. Dr. Cooke, as Moderator, took a principal part in the Jubilee. In the morning, at seven o'clock, he led devotional exercises in Rosemary Street Church, Belfast. At twelve o'clock he preached in Carrickfergus, taking as his text Psalm li. 18—" Do good in thy good pleasure unto Zion : build thou the walls of Jerusalem." They were the same words from which the Rev. Mr. Baird had preached at the organization of the first Presbytery in the same place, two hundred years before. In the evening, at seven o'clock, he presided at a public meeting in Belfast, and made an able speech on the rise, progress, and prospects of the Presbyterian Church. Referring to the principles of Presbyterianism in regard to the great question then agitating the parent Church of Scotland, he said—

"Our principles are in opposition to allowing man to model the Church in any other way than that pointed out by the Head of the Church Himself. We feel that there is no antiquity beyond the New Testament, and that no antiquity save that mentioned in Scripture can alter or model our Church. . . . We allow no man to model the Church of Christ ; we allow none to alter or interfere with the New Testament. This is our principle, and this lies at the root of the headship of Christ. Christ, and He alone, is the Head and authority which our Church acknowledges ; and He, in the New Testament, has given us His authoritative acts, which alone, as a Church, we are bound to obey."

Replying to an article which had just appeared in *The Times*, he said—

"It has been said by a writer in that paper, that Presbyterians are essentially Republican. Now, this is both true and false ; and those calumnies are most dangerous which contain a portion of truth. If by Republican it is meant that Presbyterians are in favour of popular rights and liberties, we glory in the name. I hold that the British Government is the only perfect Republican Government this world ever saw. Places mentioned in history as having been Republics, such as Athens and Rome, were no Republics ; they were oligarchies of the rich. . . . If it be meant that Presbyterianism is Republican in the sense in which Republicanism existed in Athens or Rome, I assert that a grosser falsehood never was uttered. . . . If it be meant that we are favourable to the fooleries of a Republic, we deny it. . . . Were our fathers Republicans when the throne of Charles was at stake ? When the liberties of our own island were in danger, were our forefathers Republicans ? No ; they were the first to give the hand to William the Third at Carrickfergus, and the first to acknowledge him in Belfast."

The Bicentenary Jubilee was no mere empty expression of joy : it took a practical form. The Church resolved to place a thankoffering upon God's altar; and the sum of £14,000 was contributed for the promotion of mission-work in Ireland.

While the Church of Scotland controversy was raging, another question suddenly sprang up, and moved the Presbyterian Church of Ireland to its centre. From their earliest settlement in Ulster the clergy had exercised the same rights as their brethren of the Established Church in regard to the solemnization of marriage. In 1840, a dispute having arisen about some property, the Armagh Consistorial Court pronounced a marriage performed by a Presbyterian minister, between a Presbyterian and an Episcopalian, illegal. In the following year a man was tried and convicted of bigamy. His counsel appealed against the verdict, on the ground that the first marriage was illegal, and for the same reason given above. The appeal was heard before the judges in Dublin, and they, by a majority, sustained it. The decision created a tremendous sensation throughout Ulster. Hundred of families were painfully wounded by it. For two centuries such marriages had been of frequent occurrence, and now all were pronounced invalid, and the offspring illegitimate. Property to an immense extent was involved. Presbyterians felt themselves deeply wronged; and as an Episcopal court had first raised the point, they, not unnaturally, regarded the Episcopal Church as the chief cause of their wrong and degradation. The question was carried to the House of Lords. There the six Law Lords who sat upon it were equally divided,—three pronouncing Presbyterian marriages legal, and three illegal. The decision of the Irish Bench, therefore, stood.

The matter, however, could not rest here. Such a foul injustice to the Presbyterians of Ireland could not be tolerated. The excitement was intense. Meetings were held in every part of Ulster. Government, feeling it necessary to interfere, gave notice, on the 24th of February, 1842, that a Bill would be introduced into Parliament to legalize all marriages on which doubts had been thrown. The Bill was merely retrospective; and it was proposed to leave the wider question open for future consideration. On the 15th of March a special meeting of Assembly was convened by Dr. Cooke. Immediately after it was constituted he left the chair, moved a series of resolutions, and pressed them on the House in a speech which the *Belfast News-Letter* characterised, " As one of the most brilliant and eloquent addresses which it has ever been our fortune to listen to." The resolutions condemned the Government Bill, because it embodied an invidious distinction between the ministers of the Established and Presbyterian Churches ; and they affirmed that Presbyterians, as constituting half the Protestant population of Ireland, as being an affiliated branch of the Established Church of Scotland, settled in Ulster on the invitation of the Government, have a just right to be specifically recognized in any Marriage Bill for Ireland.

These resolutions of the General Assembly, the protests of the Presbyterian people, and the energetic remonstrances of Dr. Cooke addressed to Sir Robert Peel, Lord Eliot, and others, had the desired effect. The obnoxious Bill was stayed in the House of Lords, and a special committee appointed to take into consideration the whole subject with a view to full and final legislation. In July, 1843, Dr. Cooke was examined before the committee, and submitted the draft of a Bill which he had prepared. It was not adopted by the Government, and nothing was done during the session. Again in April, 1844, he was recalled to London. A Bill was then drawn up by the Government, of which he wrote to Mrs. Cooke :—" We have now seen the proposed Marriage Bill ; and I have simply to say that worse is impossible. I have no doubt I shall upset it ; so I must stay here and fight the monster. The ministry seem to me to be mad. . . . The bishops are secretly opposing us. In this they are playing a foolish game ; for the day is not distant when they will need our help." On the 21st of June he again wrote :—" The Bill is in a tolerably promising state. Indeed it is satisfactory for Presbyterians ; but it leaves Methodists, Independents, Baptists, &c., in the same oalition with the English Dissenters. I have, therefore, put

forward their claims to equality with Presbyterians, as we
claim equality with the Established Church." Eventually he
succeeded in effecting such changes as secured, if not entirely,
yet to a very large extent, the rights of the Presbyterian
Church and of the Nonconformists of Ireland.

During the parliamentary session of 1843-44, Dr. Cooke
opposed another Bill which was then being pressed through
the House, and which largely affected the property of the
Presbyterian Church. The Arians, who had withdrawn from
the Synod of Ulster, and their co-religionists in England,
claimed and held possession of churches and endowments
originally designed for Trinitarians. Attempts were made to
dispossess them, and suits, instituted in the law courts, were
in several cases successful. The Dissenters' Chapels Bill
was, therefore, introduced into Parliament. It had for its
object to secure Unitarians in the possession of all ecclesiastical
property which had been in their occupation for a period of
twenty-five years. It was opposed by the Evangelical Dissenters in England and Ireland; but, unfortunately, in their
opposition they extended their claims too far. Dr. Cooke
proposed to Sir Robert Peel a compromise on a just and
equitable basis; and there is reason to believe that, had
he been left to himself, had there been no mismanagement on
the part of some with whom he was associated, and had others
not pressed claims which, in the opinion of the Government,
and in Dr. Cooke's own opinion, were extravagant, his compromise would have been accepted. Such, at least, was the
opinion he expressed in a letter to Mrs. Cooke :—" Though in
the estimation of some it might seem to savour of vanity, yet I
do boldly affirm that, had I been left to myself, I should have
seen a different result of the Chapels Bill from what we have
seen." The Bill passed the Legislature, and a large amount
of property was appropriated by men who held and propagated
doctrines which would have been repudiated by the original
donors.

Those important public affairs, as well political as ecclesiastical, in which Dr. Cooke took a leading part, though they seriously interfered with, did not, by any means, wholly interrupt literary labours. His reading was most extensive, embracing chiefly theology and history, with his favourite sciences, geology and chemistry. His pulpit discourses and speeches were as brilliant and powerful as ever. His lectures in the class-room, which, at the urgent request of the Assembly, he still continued during each collegiate session, evidenced the same careful and profound research. In addition, he com- menced, about the year 1834, the preparation of an Analytical Concordance of Scripture, on a new and original plan, so as to facilitate reference to the subject-matter. For the successful execution of such a work his acute logical mind, his long controversial training, and his minute knowledge of the Bible eminently qualified him. For seven years, nearly the whole of his spare hours were spent on the work. In 1841 the manu- script was complete, and he took it to London to arrange for its publication. Here, however, a sad misfortune happened. His hotel was burned while he was attending a meeting of the friends of the Church of Scotland. Writing to Mrs. Cooke on the 1st of May, he thus mentions the calamity :—" Our hotel was burned, happily while we were all out. I came home just in time to see the last of it. My clothes, money, books, sermons, and, worst of all, my manuscript, which cost me so many years of toil, are all in cinders." His labour was entirely lost. He had no copy, and he never found time to resume the task.

In 1839, he undertook to edit, with additional notes and introductions, a new edition of Brown's Family Bible. That it might not interfere in any way with his ordinary and official duties, he resolved to devote to it two hours each morning— from four o'clock till six; and this resolution he rigidly adhered to until the work was finished. When writing to Mrs. Cooke, in 1844, and through her giving advice and counsel to his son Henry, he stated incidentally how this habit of early rising was formed, and how it was made to operate in moulding

his character :—" During my solitary walks, from four o'clock
on summer mornings, in boyhood and early manhood, away
among the hills miles from home, my character and habits of
study were formed. There I first learned to commune with
God, with my own heart, with the mighty dead. There, in
morning cool, I read Young's *Night Thoughts*, Hervey's
Meditations, and many other such works. Far away from
human habitation, with no company save the wild birds and
the trees, hearing no sound save the shrill note of the lark and
the sighing of the wind among rocks and mountains."

In the midst of his labours sorrow visited his home. Two
of his sons, youths of great intellectual promise, died within a
few months of each other. This sad bereavement cast a
shadow over his joyous nature, which was never completely
dispelled. Amid the labours and excitement of the outer
world strangers would scarcely observe it ; but in private, and
especially in his family circle, the suppressed sigh, the quivering lip, the gathering tear-drop, have often betrayed to close
observers the deep sadness of a bleeding heart. Years afterwards, writing to Mrs. Cooke, he says :—" Oh ! my poor heart.
Time heals none of its wounds. Last night I thought my
dead Thomas was alive in my arms. May the Lord sanctify
me by these means !" The deaths in his family had been
many. Of thirteen children, only six now remained. Well,
therefore, might he use language of such touching pathos.

During the sittings of the General Assembly in 1843, a
resolution was passed which deeply moved him. He was
doubtless rendered more keenly sensitive by family bereavements. Many of the members of Assembly had felt, while the
struggle in the Church of Scotland was raging, that the
Presbyterian interest, especially in the north of Ireland, was
not sufficiently represented in the House of Commons. The
Presbyterians constituted fully one-half of the Protestant voters
of Ulster, and yet, at that time, there was only one Irish Presbyterian Member in Parliament. It was freely admitted that
Dr. Cooke's influence with the Protestant Members of Ulster,

though they belonged to another communion, was paramount in all matters affecting the Presbyterian Church. But it was argued, and with justice, that he could not be always by their side, and that, through their ignorance of the policy and principles of Presbyterianism, and through conflicting claims, grave mistakes were sometimes committed, and the interests of the Church compromised. It was well known that Dr. Cooke had consolidated the Conservative party, that he was its virtual head, and that largely through his exertions Conservative Members gained and retained their seats. It was therefore moved in the Assembly—

"That the difficulty which has been often experienced in having the wishes and interests of Presbyterians efficiently represented in Parliament—a difficulty powerfully manifested during the recent struggles of the Scottish Church—and the serious injury which, from the aspect of the times, we have reason to fear may arise from a similar course, warrant this Assembly in recommending the adoption of measures for securing a more adequate representation of the principles and interests of Presbyterians in the Legislature of the country."

Dr. Cooke felt that the motion was virtually a condemnation of his own acts, and a reflection on the conduct and policy of his political friends. He admitted, as fully as any of his brethren, that the Presbyterian Church ought to be represented in proportion to its numbers and position in the country. He had no objection to any member of the Church using whatever influence he possessed in endeavouring to return Presbyterian representatives. He had done so himself wherever and whenever he could find a suitable man. But he deprecated any resolution which would, by implication, condemn those who, as he well knew, had been honest and zealous· in their efforts to advance Presbyterian interests. Above all, he protested against the Church enacting a law, and assuming an attitude, which would give it the appearance and the place, before the world, of an electioneering club. He, therefore, resisted the adoption of a purely and exclusively political resolution in a court of the Church of Christ. His views were supported by many of the older and more experienced ministers of the Assembly, including some of his political opponents. The debate on the motion was long and bitter. Party spirit triumphed. Dr. Cooke was rudely assailed by men who were not old enough to remember his great services, nor sagacious enough to comprehend the wisdom of his policy. For once the great leader was chafed and dispirited. His heart, bleeding under the sharp stroke of private sorrows, felt all the more keenly the injustice and ingratitude of brethren. He stated his objections to the motion with his wonted clearness and power, not stooping to notice personal abuse. He then retired from the Assembly, and addressed the following letter to the Moderator :—

"Belfast, 12th July, 1843.

"Rev. Sir,—Having taken the opportunity upon Monday, the 10th inst., of bearing my testimony against the political resolution proposed to the Assembly, I felt constrained to absent myself from its discussion yesterday ; and now, finding that it has been carried, though by a small majority, I beg leave by this letter (the insertion of which in your Minutes I respectfully request) to record my solemn protest, with reasons, and to withdraw (which, in the Lord's name, I hereby do) from the jurisdiction of the General Assembly, so long as said resolution remains unrescinded.

"1. I protest against the adoption of a resolution involving so many permanent interests, at a period of the sitting when the whole Assembly was reduced to ninety-six members, and the elders almost totally withdrawn.

"2. I protest, because a resolution so novel and unprecedented, which adds a totally new field to the Church's operations—which upon ministers, and elders, and people imposes, by ecclesiastical authority, an entirely new class of duties—involves all the principles of an enacting overture, goes far to revolutionize the whole constitution of the Church, and should not have been introduced without passing a Committee of Overtures, nor passed into a law without notice of a year.

" 3. I protest, consequently, because the act of the majority, by which said resolution was passed, is a palpable infraction of the constitution of the Assembly.

" 4. I protest—not because I question or deny the right or the Assembly, as such, to express a political opinion upon any given subject, occurrence, or measure,—nor because I deny the right of ministers of the gospel to exercise, either singly or in combination, their legitimate influence in political matters (nay, those rights, which are often duties, I solemnly maintain),—but I protest against a church court, as such, pledging themselves to the struggles of political partizanship, to the use of means undefined, which the very patrons of the resolution, when called upon, can neither specify nor explain.

" 5. I protest, because the only means directly stated, or indirectly admitted, by any of the supporters of the resolution involve all the possible turmoil of agrarian excitement, tend to bring into conflict a peaceful and industrious tenantry with landlords, who, with few exceptions, are considerate, kind, and indulgent, and to whom, with scarcely any exception, our Presbyterian congregations are deeply indebted for sites for their churches, and liberal subscriptions for their erection.

" 6. I protest, not because I would inculcate that any amount of kindness and patronage should purchase a surrender of our Presbyterian principles, but because I am convinced from Holy Scripture that the means there admitted are utterly forbidden; from all human history, that they are utterly inadequate to the ends proposed; and from the living condition of a large portion of the kingdom, that they are followed by consequences alike deplorable to the secular and spiritual interests of the people.

" 7. I protest, because the Word of God warns me that ' the beginning of strife is as when one letteth out water ; therefore, leave off contention before it be meddled with.'

" I offer this protest, and I make this severance from my brethren, with intense pain of mind ; but, for the foregoing and not a few other reasons, I make it with a determination that will not be shaken.

" Believe me, dear brother in the Lord,

"Yours faithfully,

"H. COOKE,

" Moderator of the General Synod of Ulster."

" The Rev. Dr. Stewart,

" Moderator of the General Assembly."

Dr. Cooke carried out his determination. For a period of four years he did not enter the General Assembly. He considered himself a member of the Synod of Ulster, which, though amalgamated with the Assembly, was still obliged to maintain a separate jurisdiction. He had been chosen Moderator of the Synod in 1842, and that office he retained. It was not until 1847, when the political resolution was rescinded by the Assembly, that Dr. Cooke again took his place in the Supreme Court of his Church.

The conflicts between the Synod of Ulster and the Belfast Institution have been detailed. They became more serious as Arian influence increased in the Board of Management and among the professorial staff. The Synod at length found it necessary to withdraw its students from three of the classes, and to refuse to acknowledge the General Certificate, which had hitherto been received as equivalent to a Degree in Arts. Under these circumstances a special meeting of the General Assembly was convened, " to consider the propriety of applying to her Majesty's Government for aid in the erection and endowment of a college for the education of candidates for the ministry, under the superintendence and control of the Church." It was there agreed to empower the College Committee " to take such steps as to them may appear expedient, for the erection and endowment of a college for this Assembly ;" and it was further agreed to appeal to the Presbyterian people for aid. The appeal was made, and within a month 3,000*l.* were subscribed. A deputation waited upon Sir Robert Peel, who stated that the Government had determined not to endow any denominational college ; but he announced the intention of her Majesty to establish in Ireland a fully equipped collegiate system upon a non-sectarian basis.

When the scheme was explained in Parliament, many of the Presbyterian clergy regarded it with dissatisfaction; but Dr. Cooke saw in it from the first the elements of success. He saw the advantages which a national institute must possess over one merely denominational. He saw that it could command the services of the talent and learning of the empire. He saw the prestige that must attach to a college patronized by royalty and supported by the State. He was most anxious that the Presbyterian clergy should have the best available training. To secure this he was prepared to cast aside all the trammels of sect and party, and to commit the students to the care of the ablest men the nation could furnish. But experience had taught him the necessity of certain safeguards in the departments of Ethics, Hebrew, and Greek. These, he felt assured, a wise Government would concede.

Though he still absented himself from the Assembly, his opinions were known, and his advice was asked upon all important questions. In February, 1845, he accompanied a deputation to London, to negotiate with Government, if possible, for the establishment of a complete college under the control of the Assembly. He knew the application would be vain ; yet he considered it his duty to give the deputation his countenance and aid. When a definitive refusal was given, he wrote to Sir Robert Peel :—" I beg again to state my conviction that the erection of a complete literary, scientific, and theological college would be considered a great boon, and would confer extensive benefits upon the Presbyterian community ; and to such an establishment, I humbly conceive, the Presbyterians have a reasonable claim, founded not merely upon their status in the country and their services to the Crown,

but also upon repeated promises and pledges given by the
British Government. But still, if the mind of the Government be now made up against the erection of a complete
college on distinctive religious principles, and if they resolve
to establish a great national institution, thoroughly unsectarian—that is, fully equipped in all branches of secular
knowledge, and systematically avoiding all interference with
doctrinal truths, directly and indirectly, as well against as in
support of them—then I shall regard this as a boon to the
whole people of Ireland. If constructed on a sound basis, and
carried out in a liberal spirit, it will give a new impulse to
education, and, I believe, also to social peace in this country.

" At the same time, it must be evident to you, that such a
collegiate system, however perfect in plan and detail, could not
meet all the wants of the Presbyterian Church. Candidates
for the ministry must have, in addition to a literary and
scientific, a distinct theological training, under professors
appointed and controlled by the Church. I would, therefore,
beg leave again, most respectfully and earnestly, to urge our
claims to the endowment of a separate Theological College,
upon such liberal principles as will enable us to raise the
standard of education by the stimulus of bursaries to the more
diligent and distinguished students.

" This mere department of a college will not, I am aware, be
satisfactory to some of my brethren; but there are others, and
not the least influential, who agree with me that a Theological
College is as much as the temper of the times will, perhaps,
allow any Government to grant."

In reply, Sir Robert Peel said, after explaining the plan of
collegiate education he had in view :—" I wish, for the present,
to limit myself to the expression of an earnest hope, that an
arrangement in regard to collegiate education with a special
view to the ministry, satisfactory to the great body with which
you are connected, and for which I have always entertained
the highest respect and most friendly feelings, may be concluded." Sir Robert Peel, at the same time, informed Dr.

Cooke, during a personal interview, of his readiness to propose to Parliament the endowment of a complete Theological College, so soon as a formal application to that effect should be made by the General Assembly. Sir James Graham inquired whether, and upon what terms, the Assembly's Theological Faculty could be connected with the Government College.

Dr. Cooke's views, as stated to Sir Robert Peel, proved to be correct. The General Assembly met in June, 1845, and, after hearing the report of the deputation, resolved to abandon the proposed plan of a complete college, and to endeavour to obtain such changes and modifications in the constitution of the new Government Colleges as would make them available for the literary and scientific training of Presbyterian students. The way was thus open for a satisfactory solution of the collegiate education question.

When it was officially announced, in 1845, that one of the Queen's Colleges would be located in Belfast, the belief became general throughout Ulster that Dr. Cooke would be placed at its head. His services to the State, his high position in the Church, his popularity with all classes of evangelical Protestants, his literary abilities, gave him, it was supposed, pre-eminent claims. His friends and admirers did not rest satisfied with the expression of hopes and wishes upon this subject. Numerous petitions were forwarded to Government, praying for his appointment, and pressing upon the Ministry this fact, that such an appointment would not only be popular in Ulster, but would give a prestige to the College which would be a certain guarantee of success. Dr. Cooke was not chosen; and the *Belfast News-Letter* said, with some truth :—" In passing over the claims of Dr. Cooke—claims not urged by himself, but by those who know him, and love him, as the great arbiter of the Protestant peace of this province—the Government has done itself irreparable injury with those who were hitherto but too willing to pass over its indiscretions and to excuse its inconsistencies."

The Government seemed to feel this, and resolved, as far as
possible, to allay the general irritation. The Rev. Dr. Henry
received the appointment of President on the 29th of November,
and on the same day the important office of Agent for the
Regium Donum, which he had held, was, without any solicita-
tion, conferred by the Lord Lieutenant on Dr. Cooke. " We
need not say," writes the *Belfast News-Letter*, " how much
gratified we are in being enabled to give this information to
our readers. The appointment, which is worth £320 *per
annum*, is not indeed, by any means, to the admirers of Dr.
Cooke, a sufficient recompense for their disappointment in not
seeing him the President of the new college ; but it is nevertheless an index of the high estimation in which he is held by
the Government." Dr. Cooke continued to fill this responsible
office till his death.

The important question of collegiate education occupied
much of the time and attention of the General Assembly
from the year 1845 to 1849. Some of the members wished
a complete college, literary as well as theological, under
the exclusive control of the Church. Others thought that
Queen's College might with safety and advantage be used for
the undergraduate course: they believed that the association
of Presbyterian students with the members of other communions would exercise a beneficial influence upon their minds,
and better fit them for the duties of public life. The discussions were protracted, and not unfrequently stormy. In 1846
it was announced to the Assembly that the late Mrs. Magee, of
Dublin, had bequeathed the sum of £20,000 for the erection
and endowment of a Presbyterian College. This bequest
tended largely to increase the difficulties of an amicable settlement. The advocates of a complete Presbyterian College
thought the way was now clear to the attainment of their
object ; but a majority of the Assembly thought otherwise, and
wisely resolved to take full advantage of Queen's College. Dr.
Cooke was one of the most strenuous advocates of this policy.
He argued that the new collegiate scheme of the Government

would be free from the evils necessarily connected with the Belfast Institution. There Ethics, New Testament Greek, and Hebrew formed part of the curriculum; and those branches could not be taught satisfactorily without trenching on the foundations of religious belief. When Infidel, Socinian, or Arian professors held such chairs, the Assembly could not safely entrust to their training candidates for the ministry. From the curriculum of Queen's College these branches were excluded. The training in them would be purely literary and scientific. It was provided in the Charter that no subject connected with Christian doctrine should be touched upon by any professor, and that no statement should be made in any department opposed to the truths of revealed religion. The alumni of Queen's College were thus guarded from erroneous teaching; and in order to provide for sound instruction in those branches necessarily excluded from the scheme, her Majesty's Government agreed, as Dr. Cooke had requested of Sir Robert Peel, to endow chairs of Ethics, Hebrew, and Ecclesiastical Greek, in Assembly's College. This plan was satisfactory to Dr. Cooke, and through his influence mainly the Assembly was led finally to adopt it. He endeavoured also to induce the trustees of the Magee Bequest to place their funds in the hands of the Assembly, so as to build and equip a Theological College in some measure adequate to the wants, and worthy of the status, of the Church. In this he was unsuccessful; but most men will now admit that it might have been better for the general interests of the Church had his counsel been followed.

When the General Assembly agreed to sanction Queen's College, as a place of training for the Presbyterian clergy, her Majesty's Government resolved to place the existing professors of Assembly's College on an equality, in regard to endowment, with the professors of Queen's; and also to endow, in the same ratio, as many additional chairs as might be shown to be necessary for a full theological course. At a special meeting, held in August, 1846, the Assembly established four additional chairs, namely, Ethics, Hebrew, New Testament and Eccle-

siastical Greek, Sacred Rhetoric and Catechetics; all of
which were endowed by Government. Government acted
wisely in endowing a Theological College in Belfast. It was
needed by the Presbyterian Church, which had strong and
very peculiar claims upon the State. It was a necessary
appendage, besides, to Queen's College. Indeed, it was
absolutely necessary to its success; for at least three-fourths
of the arts' students in Queen's are Presbyterians, and
most of them candidates for the Ministry. Had it not been
for the patronage of the Assembly, and the existence of
Assembly's College, Queen's College, Belfast, would have been
a failure, like its sisters in Cork and Galway.

On the 14th of September, 1847, a meeting of the General
Assembly was held to elect professors to the new chairs. It
was there unanimously resolved, " as a tribute of justly deserved esteem and respect, to give Dr. Cooke the privilege to
say whether he would prefer " the chair of Ethics or of Sacred
Rhetoric. He declared his preference for the latter, and was
at once elected. The Assembly afterwards incorporated the
theological professors into a Faculty, and Dr. Cooke was appointed PRESIDENT. Both these offices he held to his death.

The high honours conferred upon him were not accepted
without regret. The law of the Assembly made it necessary
for a professor to resign the pastoral office. It was a severe
trial for Dr. Cooke to leave a church which had been built for
him, and to resign the oversight of an attached people. The
congregation of May Street were very unwilling to part with
their minister. They, therefore, presented a memorial to the
Presbytery of Belfast, praying that Dr. Cooke should be continued constant supplier of the pulpit until the appointment of
a successor; and that he should also have the right to preach
to the students in May Street once each Lord's Day, until
another place were provided. The Presbytery transmitted the
memorial to the Assembly, which, at its meeting in 1848,
resolved that its prayer be granted. Dr. Cooke was thus, by
the act of the Supreme Court of the Church, continued constant

supplier of May Street. It is right, however, to state, that from the time of his election to the Professorship, he resigned all the emoluments connected with the congregation, including the Royal Bounty of £100 a year. It was his anxious wish that the congregation should at once proceed to elect a successor. With this view he invited some of the most distinguished young ministers of the Church to preach in his pulpit, and he urged his people to make choice of a pastor. It was in vain. So long as he would, or could officiate, they would have no other. It was not until within a few months of his death, twenty years afterwards, that the congregation consented to elect a man to occupy that pulpit which the genius and elo-quence of Dr. Cooke had made celebrated over Britain.

The congregation felt deeply indebted to Dr. Cooke for his generous labours. In June, 1849, they resolved to give him a substantial token of their gratitude and attachment. They accordingly presented him with a horse and car, accompanied by an address which recited his services to the congregation, to the Presbyterian Church, and to the country. His reply was chaste, eloquent, and affectionate. Referring to his struggle in the Arian controversy, he said, with that modesty which is a characteristic of genius :—

" I must, in truth and justice, look beyond myself to others whose names have been less public than my own, but to whose prayers, encouragement, decision, and zeal, the results of our reformation are, under Providence, mainly due. Of these some remain, and of them I may not further speak. Others are gone to their rest, and amongst them I may not fail to record in the first place, as nearest to my knowledge and affection, the dear and respected name of Sydney Hamilton Rowan ; as also our common friend, William Duncan Stewart, to whom I must add Henry Henry, Francis and Samuel Dill, James Elder, the late father of our Assembly. . . . Nor can I omit Henry Kydd, who, while modestly shrinking from public view, was yet, by his piety and his talents, an unwearied contributor to the evangelical cause.

" With respect to the gratuitous services I have been enabled to

render to the congregation, I neither desire nor deserve your thanks.
You have furnished me with a permanent pulpit in which to preach,
and a congregation to hear the Gospel. A silent minister I could
not have been."

When Queen's College was opened, in 1849, Dr. Cooke was
appointed by the Crown to the office of Dean of Residence for
the Presbyterian Church. The letter of Sir Thomas Reding-
ton, conveying to him the official notice, was particularly gratifying from its cordial acknowledgment of his services.

Dr. Cooke's official duties were now extremely onerous, yet
he discharged them all with unabating faithfulness and distinguished success. His catechetical classes in Assembly's
College were usually attended by about one hundred and fifty
students. With them he was an especial favourite. They
honoured him as a laborious professor, and they loved him as
a friend and father. His eloquence stirred their hearts. His
care over them was not confined to the class-room, or to the
bare routine of academic instruction. He gave them counsel
as strangers in Belfast; he taught them how they should
deport themselves in their new spheres, and amid the temptations of a large town, as candidates for the Christian ministry;
he even gave them, in private, with the affectionate solicitude
of a parent, advice and direction for their guidance in society.
And his interest in his students did not cease when they
passed from under him. He never forgot them. He would
recount with pride and pleasure every success they attained
in life. And many a time, by encouraging word, by friendly
interest, and by generous act, has he cheered and aided
them.

His multitudinous professional duties did not prevent
him from taking a leading part in public matters, whether
connected with his Church or his country. The great
controversies which had agitated the Presbyterian Church
in his earlier days were now settled. He had driven out
Arianism; he had triumphed over Voluntaryism; he had

so moulded the National system of Education, that Presbyterians could, with a safe conscience, take advantage of
it for the support of their schools. He had thus, by the
Divine blessing on his long-continued labours, inaugurated
an era of new life and peaceful progress for the Presbyterian
Church. He lived to see its development, and to rejoice
in its abundant fruits. He still continued, down to the very
close of his life, by his eloquence, his wisdom, his experience,
and his influence, to advance the cause of evangelical truth
over Ireland, and indeed over the world. At least three-
fourths of the new Presbyterian Churches in Ireland, besides
many in England and Scotland, were opened by him. When
appeals were to be made for aid towards any great Christian
work, Dr. Cooke was the man generally applied to. His
charity sermons were almost innumerable, and the amount
of money he was the means of raising, if calculated, would
appear fabulous. His desire to give all his brethren, however remote their position, however obscure their station,
the benefit of his powerful advocacy, never abated. No
amount of fatigue in travelling, or of labour in preaching and
lecturing, could daunt him. His public sermons usually came
in groups. When it was announced that he had consented to
officiate in any locality, other applications from the district, or
from the line of his route, showered in upon him; and he
has been known, for two or three weeks together, to preach
every day, travelling great distances often in the most un-
comfortable conveyances. Even when old age came on,
and his iron frame was bowed beneath the weight of years,
the Protestant people of Ireland seemed more desirous than
ever to hear the great divine; and he was equally desirous
to gratify them, and serve to the last that Master whom
he had served so long and loved so well.

CHAPTER XIX.

1850—1865.

Lecture on "The Present Aspect and Future Prospects of Popery"—Letter from Dr. M'Crie—Election of Mr. Cairns as Member for Belfast—Death of Dr. Stewart—Sketch of his Character—Magee College Controversy—Merle D'Aubigne opens Assembly's College—Portrait of Dr. Cooke, by Macnee—Cooke and D'Aubigne in the Free-Church Assembly—Hugh Miller's Sketch of Dr. Cooke—Labours in England—Journal-letters to Mrs. Cooke and others—Thirst for knowledge—Leadership of the General Assembly—Professor Witherow's description — Professor Wilson on his business habits—Dr. Murray ("Kirwan") in the General Assembly—Letter from Dr. Murray— Dr. Cox on Dr. Cooke's projected visit to America—Sir J. Napier, Professor Wilson, and Dr. Blackwood on Dr. Cooke's pulpit oratory—Beauty of his Illustrations—Character of his later Sermons—Secret of his Popularity— Striking example—A third time Moderator--Death of his daughter—Public Testimonial—Address and Reply.

FROM the period of his settlement in Belfast, Dr. Cooke took a leading part in all political and ecclesiastical movements affecting the town and the empire. In 1850, the subtle advances of Popery began again to be felt and feared in England. Dr. Cooke was among the first to observe the danger and sound a note of alarm. On the evening of Tuesday, 4th December, he delivered a lecture in his Church " On the Present Aspect and Future Prospects of Popery." The Mayor of Belfast presided, and the house was crowded to excess with the rank and wealth of the town and surrounding country. The lecture occupied three hours and a half in delivery, and was characterised by searching argument and stirring eloquence. It was printed, and obtained a wide circulation. A profound impression was made by it upon the Protestant community, and Dr. Cooke was hailed anew as the Champion of Bible Christianity.

A few months afterwards, he received the following letter from Dr. McCrie, of Edinburgh :—

" MY DEAR DR. COOKE,—Permit me to send you a copy of the *Sunderland Herald*. The paper has been sent to me by some unknown friend, who has directed my attention to the discourse and dinner-speech of Cardinal Wiseman. I feel the force of the appeal; but what can I do ? . . .

" Must this emissary of Rome, who seems so well qualified for his mission, be permitted to march in triumph through the length and breadth of this Christian land, spreading moral contagion around through the agency of the press; gulling the natives of England, so ill-informed on the subject, with his affected charity and pietism ; imposing on the unwary with his angelic-looking sophistries ; following up the Romanizing mania produced by the tawdry sentimentalism and mediæval fooleries of Oxford ; distorting truth, and throwing the halo of a seducing sensual devotion around the putrid superstition of Rome ? And is not a voice to be raised against him ?

" Looking around for one willing and able to take up the gauntlet against this Goliath of our day—one who could prove a match for him in the power of popular address, and more than a match for him, in virtue of being clothed with the armour of truth on the right hand and on the left—I can discover none, unless it be yourself; and, having spoken on the subject with some of my friends on whose judgment I rely, and whom you would respect, they agree with me in this opinion, and have requested me, in the meantime, to express my sentiments to you. . . ."

Dr. Cooke did not see his way to enter on such a gigantic undertaking. He considered it enough for him to defend Protestantism in Ireland, and to further that mission work which his own Church was so vigorously and successfully prosecuting in the South and West.

At the general election in 1852, he induced the son of his

old and esteemed friend and parishioner, William Cairns, to become a candidate for the borough of Belfast; and, by his influence and eloquent advocacy, he succeeded in returning both him and his fellow-candidate, Mr. Richard Davison, as members to Parliament. He had known Hugh McCalmont Cairns from boyhood. He had watched with feelings of honest pride his brilliant talents and indomitable industry. After the election he wrote to me : — " Probably you may take some interest, even in your Eastern Paradise, in the public affairs of this Isle of the West. We have just passed through a great political struggle, and our principles have been triumphant. We have returned Messrs. Richard Davison and Hugh Cairns as members for Belfast. The former I think you know, and of him I need say nothing. To know is to respect him. Mr. Cairns is a young man of the highest promise. A bright future is before him. If God only spare him health, I firmly believe he will attain to the highest honours England can bestow. He possesses all the elements of greatness—intellectual grasp, logical acumen, rare analytical power, accuracy and force of expression, and, best of all, thorough Christian principle. I feel proud of him, for he is the son of my oldest friend, and I have intently watched, and to some small extent, helped to guide his career."

On the 27th of September, 1852, Mrs. Cooke received the following sad letter from her husband :—" Dr. Stewart died yesterday about seven p.m. . . . Poor Mrs. Stewart is in great distress. Only think of three widows in one house ! We, too, must one day part. God only knows who must go first. No matter as to that; God's time will be best. The Lord make us ready that we may be found waiting for his coming." Dr. Cooke visited him on his death-bed. Next to family bereavements, this was one of his severest trials. I have related how they first met at Glasgow College, and how for nearly half a century they had lived and laboured as brethren. Dr. Stewart lacked the fervour of his friend. He did not, therefore, show the same enthusiasm in his early crusade against error. He was calm, acute, and logical. At first he rather endeavoured to retard the impetuosity of his distinguished associate. He often counselled moderation; he sometimes even offered direct opposition; but when the final struggle came Stewart and Cooke stood shoulder to shoulder. They were necessary to each other. The acute analytical power, and searching logic of the one, prepared the way for the over-whelming torrent of the other's eloquence. When the victory for truth was achieved, their friendship seemed to be cemented anew, and it continued unbroken till death severed the earthly bond.

On Sunday, the 31st of October, Dr. Cooke preached a funeral Sermon. May Street Church was densely crowded. His text was 2 Timothy iv. 7, 8: " I have fought a good fight, I have finished my course, I have kept the faith; hence-forth there is laid up for me a crown of righteousness which the Lord, the righteous Judge, shall give me at that day." During the delivery of the discourse the preacher was frequently overcome by emotion, and the audience was almost as deeply affected as he was himself. Speaking of Dr. Stewart's life and character, he said :—

" Forty-eight years have rolled past, on this very day and this very hour, since our intimacy commenced in a neighbouring sea-port. We were on our way to College ; I in my third year, he in his second. An adverse wind would not permit the vessel to sail, and every place where we sought a residence in the town was occupied ; but by searching we found a place for the night. . . . There were six of us, and we constituted ourselves into a society. . . . My departed friend proposed a series of subjects for study, and a large portion of my future studies was commenced and carried on according to that arrangement—in particular that of the composition and derivation of words. . . . From that time onward my inti-macy with my departed friend became still more strict, and until death interrupted it, it never was broken for a day or for an hour. . . . Touching his education for the ministry, he was nearly eighteen years of age before he commenced it. . . . He was but a short time at a Classical school before he came to College ; but he

began with a matured mind. He applied himself to his studies with
his whole heart and his mighty genius—for his was a mighty genius
—and though he did not read the same length of course which many
of our students do, he understood what he read much better than
the greater number do. . . . With regard to the mind of my
departed friend, I may say that there were few minds so thoroughly
stored with knowledge in every department of human acquirement—
I can add, a mind so transparent, clear, and perspicacious in seeing through the most difficult subject—a mind so expert in disen-
tangling the most intricate question—has seldom or never been
known. . . . A mind like his needed no aid from books or
manuscripts. I never knew any one who could so rapidly arrange
a subject. I have, on more occasions than one, seen him take up ten
or twenty arguments, and, without pen or paper, reduce them to two
or three, and proceed instantaneously, without any aid save that of
memory and judgment, to answer and overturn them."

His closing words were deeply affecting; and those who
heard them can never forget the effect they produced on the
assemblage :—

" The Church may forget him—the world may forget him . . .
but there is one who never will forget him as long as he lives. It is
not because my compatriots are dying around me—it is not because
I am fast coming to the top of the tree of life, of which the branches
that grew along with me are nearly all lopped off—but because I
feel the loss of a second self that I now mourn. . . . I, my friend
Dr. Stewart, and the late Dr. Reid, of Glasgow, had often occasion to
form opinions on great public questions, when separated. We used
to meet together to compare our resolutions, and we never arrived at
contrary conclusions. . . . It is not strange, therefore, that I
should feel the loss of my friend and fellow-soldier—that in the
world which becomes a wilderness to an old man, I should miss the
company of my fellow-traveller—that, where to keep the faith is so
difficult, I should miss the supporting arm of a fellow strengthener.
Yet, though he has left me, he has gone to his glory, and has
exchanged the troubles of the Church and the world for the repose
of that place where there is no more sickness, sorrow, or death."

The controversy regarding the Magee Bequest agitated the

General Assembly for years. Dr. Cooke from the first considered that it would be for the interests of the Church to devote
the funds to the establishment of a thoroughly equipped Theological College in Belfast; but the trustees determined otherwise. They resolved to erect a college, literary, as well as
theological, in Derry, under the care of the General Assembly.
Dr. Cooke then insisted that, as the Assembly would be
held responsible for the whole course of training, the professors should be required to subscribe the Standards of the
Church. On this point being finally conceded, the Magee
College was sanctioned, though it was not opened till the year
1865.

Dr. Cooke had the satisfaction of seeing the buildings of
Assembly's College, Belfast, so far advanced as to be ready for
the reception of students in November, 1853. In conjunction
with the Faculty, he resolved to invite Merle D'Aubigne to
deliver the opening address. Accordingly, on the 5th of
December, the Historian of the Reformation formally opened
the College, in presence of a vast assembly of the nobility,
clergy, and gentry of Ulster. His reception was enthusiastic;
and his address was worthy of the man and the ocasion. President Cooke, in presenting him, said :—

"I beg to introduce our distinguished friend, who has come at
great inconvenience, and from a great distance, to speak to us words
of brotherly kindness and encouragement. . . . When I introduce Dr. D'Aubigne I do not require to say one word. He is known
wherever Protestantism is known ; he is known wherever sacred
literature is known ; he is known in every land in which the glorious
Reformation lifts her banner, wherever victory still abides with her,
and wherever her hopes of going forth conquering and to conquer
encourage the rising generation."

Soon after the opening of the College a number of Dr.
Cooke's friends resolved to place in the Common Hall a
portrait of its first President. A committee was appointed,
with the Rev. Dr. Gibson, Professor of Christian Ethics, at its

head. Guided by his fine taste, Macnee was selected as
the artist. In the autumn of 1856 President Cooke was
induced to accompany Dr. Gibson to Glasgow, so as to give
the requisite sittings. While there he was not permitted
to remain idle. On Monday, October 20th, he wrote Mrs.
Cooke:—"I preached three times yesterday, and was nothing
the worse. Indeed I was all the better for it. . . . The
portrait gets on well, and I expect to be off on Friday. Give
my love to little Nora (his granddaughter), and tell her to be
very good till my return. Speak a loving word and give a kiss
to Selim from his grandpapa. Teach him what a holy child
he ought to be, having been born in the Holy Land." On the
day following he again wrote in his gay, easy style:—"I have
just been sitting, and standing, and trying to think of Nora
and everything nice and joyous. I wish I had Harry Porter
here; his Arabic prattle would rejoice my heart. I am to
return at two. I am quite sure you will all be hopelessly in
love with the portrait, and will find that you never before
knew what a charming man your husband was. I know it
is possible to make a beautiful likeness without making an
exact fac-simile. However, in due time you shall see what
you shall behold."

"I have been back. Macnee is a glorious fellow. He is the
very soul of humour. He has been making me split my sides
with laughter. And just when I succeed in screwing up
my features into such composure as befits a venerable personage, who is to be transferred to canvas for the adorning
of college halls, he begins another story, and in a moment I
am in convulsions. Gibson is in high glee. He seems to
enjoy the whole scene amazingly. I never saw his bright,
genial nature till now.

"I go out on to-morrow evening to Loudon Castle, and
shall be there on Thursday. On Friday I appear again to the
painter; and you may expect me on Saturday."

The painting was a great success. The artist confessed he
had a noble subject, and he treated it in his usual masterly

style. It was exhibited at the Royal Academy in 1857 ; and it afterwards formed one of the most striking portraits in the Great Exhibitions of London and Dublin. On April 28th, 1858, a public meeting was held at the close of the College session, and the portrait was presented to the Faculty. The chair was occupied, in the unavoidable absence of the Mayor of Belfast, by Colonel Macpherson. Dr. Gibson, after a brief history of the portrait, said :—" It has at length found its proper resting-place in the Irish Presbyterian College—a college identified with a Church which owes its life and liberty, to a great extent, to the distinguished individual whom the painter has so ably portrayed."

An address was read by Samuel Gelston, Esq., one of Dr. Cooke's oldest friends. He spoke of his eminent services, and then referred as follows to the special time of presentation :—" The occasion on which we are met reminds us that the public life and labours of Dr. Cooke have now extended over the lengthened period of fifty years, and how can we more becomingly signalise the event than by affixing this pictorial tribute upon the walls of the Assembly's College. This splendid hall is the befitting receptacle of such a memorial of one who throughout his entire career has been identified with the Presbyterian Church, and who is so intimately connected with an Institution dedicated to the training of the future ministry."

In 1856 Dr. Cooke was specially invited, in company with Merle D'Aubigne, to address the General Assembly of the Free Church of Scotland. He reached Edinburgh on Saturday, the 31st of May, and, as usual, wrote immediately to Mrs. Cooke :—" I find I am to preach for Doctors Candlish and Guthrie to-morrow. On Tuesday, it is advertised, that D'Aubigne and I will address the Assembly. The programme has been arranged for me, and there is nothing left but to go through it in the best way I can."

" On the evening of June 3rd," says *The Witness*, " The Assembly

Hall was crowded to excess. On the entrance of Doctors Cooke and
D'Aubigne, the whole of the vast assemblage rose to their feet, and
greeted them with prolonged applause. Dr. Cooke referred to the
solidity and progress of the Sustentation Fund ; to the remarkable
success of the Debt Extinction Fund ; to Colleges, and the subjects
proper to be carried on in them. He described with considerable
minuteness his own method with the students under his care. He
occasionally gave a lecture, but he acted almost entirely as a catechist
or tutor. . . . Referring to the temporal prosperity with which
Scotland was blessed, he reminded them, in a singularly humorous
and telling manner, of their duty to the vast numbers of Scotchmen
now settled in Ireland. He concluded amidst loud, repeated, and
enthusiastic applause."

Dr. M'Crie, the Moderator, in conveying the thanks of the
Assembly, to Dr. Cooke, said :—

" It has often been remarked that God has raised up men fitted for
the exigencies of his Church, qualified exactly for the duties and trials
allotted to them ; and never has this remark been more signally
verified than in the history of Dr. Henry Cooke. Endowed with no
ordinary talent, and with that trenchant wit and pungent satire,
without which the highest talent might have proved among his keen-
witted countrymen of small avail ; he was able, in the days of his
prime, to assail the ranks of the enemy with irresistible effect, and
we are glad to find that, after age has begun to silver his hair in the
service of his Master, Jesus Christ, he has lost none of his pristine
vigour and manly eloquence."

The distinguished editor of the *Witness*, Hugh Miller,
added the following graphic sketch of Dr. Cooke's personal
appearance :—

"If the reader has not happened to see Dr. Cooke, he may figure to
himself a tall and distinguished-looking man, touched, rather than
stricken with years. The profile is a very fine aquiline ; the forehead
is spacious, the cheek is denuded of whisker, and the chin is of that
square and massive mould, which those who have examined the casts
of the skull of the Bruce will remember. The depth of stock and

collar, and the coat-sleeve reaching to the knuckle of the thumb, give him a somewhat American look. He spoke with a very quiet manner, and used extremely little gesture of any kind. His native humour, however, welled out continually, and without effort, and he wielded his vast audience with the practised ease of a master."

Dr. Cooke's labours in opening Churches, preaching charity sermons, and delivering public lectures and addresses, increased with his years. During the whole College recess he had scarcely a day to himself. Even when he went on his annual visit to Harrogate, his time was portioned out by exacting friends, and every Sunday was occupied. Sheffield, Leeds, Manchester, Hanley, Dudley, Birmingham, Cheltenham, Plymouth, and Newcastle, pressed their wants and their claims, and were favoured in turn. During his journeys he wrote regularly to Mrs. Cooke, giving graphic sketches of the districts he passed through, the people he met, the congregations to which he preached, and frequently the subjects of his discourses. His letters form a diary of his life and work while from home on the Church's service, and they show an amount of both mental and bodily labour, such as few men could have undertaken. The good he accomplished, and the money he was instrumental in obtaining for evangelistic objects throughout the empire, could not be calculated.

Some idea may be formed of the character of these evangelistic tours from the following extracts of letters written during one of them, in the summer of 1858 :—

"DEVONPORT, 31st July.

"MY DEAREST ELLEN,—I think it best to write you a small journal, which, if it do not prove my work an approach to the labours of Hercules, will at least prove me an indefatigable traveller.

"Monday, 26th, at home. Tuesday, Dublin. Saw the Lord Lieutenant on the subject of the second *Regium Domum* for Mary's Abbey, and think we shall get it. No other Church is so entitled. . . . Dined with hospitable Drury, and his

most amiable wife and excellent children. Saw dear Mrs. Miller.
Johnston, the Moderator, carried off my hat, which fitted him
as mine did Mr. —— in days of old; that is, as an ex-
tinguisher fits a candle. Got a headache by wearing Johnston's
hat till half-past seven on Wednesday morning. Crossed
the Channel in five hours. Arrived at Dudley at nine—not
wearied, but weary of a carriage. Thursday, the 29th.
Sauntered in the morning into the most romantic old quarries,
now green and overgrown with bushes. Lay on the grass.
Talked of many things, and thought of you, wishing you had
been there to see. Heard from this paradise the sound of the
almost infernal regions to the east—then got up, and went to
see from the castle's brow; but all I could see was smoke,
intermixed here and there with lurid flames. Preached to a
good congregation. Sir James Murray saw me announced in
Wolverhampton, and came to Dudley. Stayed with Lewis for
supper—as pleasant as ever. Started at nine for Plymouth.
What a country I traversed! wide plains—undulating hills—
all cultivated and blooming like a garden.

" 3rd August. Yesterday I visited the Queen's Steam-
Yard. It adjoins vast floating and dry-docks, in one of which
is an immense Turkish ship in the process of conversion into
a screw-steamer. Here I saw the wonderful power of the
wedge. By props attached to the sides of the ship, and
wooden wedges under the lower end—perhaps five or six hundred in number—a man with a sledge at each wedge, the
whole company hitting at the same instant, the ship was
raised off her keel high enough to have a new one introduced.
I have no doubt the ship was heavier than the great stones of
Baalbek—60 feet long, 14 broad, and 11 deep; or than the
Menai tube, which is some tons heavier than the great stones;
yet this ship was raised by a number of insignificant wedges.
So if the ancients did not know the secret of the hydraulic-
press, the stones of Baalbek, or of Solomon's temple, could
have been raised by this process alone, though there still
seems a difficulty of sliding them off into their beds on the

wall. No doubt I see, at last I think I see, how this could be effected; viz., when raised higher than the bed, slide them off on oiled iron ways; then raise them again by wedges, take out the ways, and extract the wedges, and the stone is laid. . . . .

" Next I went to the Breakwater. This wonderful work is about three-quarters of a mile in length, crossing the entrance of the outer harbour. It was begun by merely throwing in the largest stones, commingled with smaller, until it rose some feet above high water. Then it got a coat of cut stone of various kinds—granite, clay-slate, and marble. The commixture, I guess, will be found a great blunder. The slate and some of the marble are perishable—especially the former, and will, in the course of years, be worn away. But, after all, it may last as long as the throne and power of England. It is melancholy to be thus prophetical of evil days. But they come to all empires; and why should England be an exception? Yet that exception she might be, if she turned and adhered to the Lord. Does she? Will she? God grant it! I fear, however, she will not. . . . .

" From the Breakwater we went to Mount Edgecombe, one of the finest places, for its extent, in England. There is a noble house, yet the noble owner lives in a cottage on the other side of the bay, a martyr to rheumatic gout. Rank and wealth cannot free from suffering or death; nor can they open the gates of Paradise. The Lord give us all the rank and spiritual wealth of saints! . . . Spent a delightful day with three Presbyterian families at the Victualling Yard—an immense place, where they turn out fifty tons of biscuits in a few hours, and grind thirty-six tons of coffee in the fragment of an afternoon. The coffee destroys the mill-stones rapidly. The granite cannot grind it; the oil renders it so smooth. The stone employed is a kind of freestone, which rubs off and will not polish. The quantity of biscuits sent to Ireland during the famine is astonishing; yet the Popery of Ireland is, and ever will be, rebel to England, unless England, from infantile

Puseyism, advance into full-grown Romanism; or, what is more
hopeful, until England, and all her Protestantism, stir herself
and it into faithful exertion for the true emancipation of the
bodies and souls of men from the slavery of all that is anti-
christian.   God can do this—none else.

"I can, as yet, say little of our prospect of a church here,
except this, that it is very encouraging.   I never saw a better
staff for an infant congregation; and the 'staff' is nothing the
less hopeful that, if not held by the hand of women, it is
polished by them.   I have met several of them : they have fine
hearts; they are indeed 'Ladies of the Covenant.'" . . .

So he runs on, in an easy, instructive, affectionate style,
relating what he saw and did in Plymouth, Bristol, Birmingham,
and other places on his line of route.   Not an hour was wasted.
While doing church-work, and doing it with unparalleled success, he was improving his own mind by observation and
inquiry on every possible subject.   Nothing escaped his
watchful eye.   Nothing was too minute for intelligent notice.
He questioned a Birmingham button-maker as to his reason
for making two holes in each button, instead of, as formerly,
four.   And in the very same letter in which he tells Mrs.
Cooke all about buttons, he details the grand theory developed
by Stevenson, that the sun is the real source of the mineral
wealth of the earth, and therefore of the achievements of iron
and the triumphs of steam.   His power of mental abstraction,
his facility in adapting himself to circumstances, his tact and
skill in eliciting information from philosopher, mechanic, and
peasant, and his ability to communicate the knowledge gleaned,
in a most attractive form, to others, were perhaps scarcely ever
equalled.   He was especially and profoundly versed in the
workings of the human heart.   His delineations of character
were life-pictures; and his exhibitions of the influence of guilty
passion in moulding the lives of men were often appalling.

In addition to his letters to Mrs. Cooke and other members
of his family, he wrote to me at least once every month, during
the period of my residence abroad, from 1849 to 1859.   These

letters were all most instructive. He seemed to know, as if by instinct, the questions in which I felt special interest, and the very points on which I needed information. But that which mainly characterized them was depth of feeling and intensity of affection. His love for his children and grand-children was almost beyond conception. His first letter to me, after I left England, was most touching :—

" You will scarcely think it credible that I have made many attempts to write to you since you went away, but have hitherto felt utterly incapable of proceeding. Whenever I attempt it my heart is like to break with the thought of my child—especially the thought that I may never see her. When I have written this, I confess I am weeping like a child. I have to keep my head back from the paper, that I may not spoil it. I acknowledge the weakness, and, perhaps, I should add, the sin, of all this. I am, however, unable to help it. God help me! I am here alone in my vestry—but my heart is with you. . . I hope you will be able to make full proof of your ministry. ' Lo, I am with you alway,' is the Christian's consolation, whether at home or abroad. The Comforter is never withheld from them that ask. Live near to God, and He will live near to you. His grace is sufficient for you; and every quality without grace is vain. . . .

" Only think of poor M'Keown, of Ballymena,—dead and buried a week ago! My favourite pupil—my great hope—gone; gone! My name was on his lips to the last. ' I will go and die beside Dr. Cooke,' he said. Noble fellow! he died beside a better; he died in Christ. Perhaps you may have lost some cherished friend; if so, you can measure my feelings. He stood alone in many points of excellence. God has taken him."

With equal tenderness, and sometimes with still more touching pathos, he wrote from month to month. When a mail chanced to be missed, the next was certain to bring a letter, with some such apology as the following :—

"My dear Porter,—On the 12th May I set out for the south-west on a preaching excursion, carrying this very paper, in the full determination of writing to you before the 17th, our post day by Southampton. On that day I reached Athlone. Preached twice on the 13th. On the 14th visited an estate rendered famous by certain evictions of savages, and the introduction of civilized agriculture. The savages deprived of an average of four acres of uncultivated land, left in their cabins till new ones could be erected, and enabled to earn seven shillings per week *vice* seven pence! But this was quite sufficient for an Irish grievance; and Mr. Pollock was denounced in Parliament as the enemy of God, and man, and Ireland! He was, however, able to defend himself by statistics, showing that the estate now maintained twenty-five per cent. more people than before his evictions. But the priests and the patriots lied on, and will to the end of their chapter. Would that we had many such enemies to poor Ireland!

"I preached in the evening in Ballinasloe. We have a noble representative there. Started early next day for Ennis, partly by rail, partly by coach—a coach of the olden time; and after a weary day reached the city, the head-quarters of Jesuitism—open and avowed by engravings on stone in front of their chapel. Here I opened a new church with some prospects of usefulness. Next day set out by long-car for Limerick, which I reached in time to enable me to visit Garryowen and the 'Stone of the Violated Treaty.' I preached twice on ·Sunday. Wilson is doing a good work in Limerick. He is an ornament to our Church. On Monday I had a seven hours' sail on the Shannon: saw many of its ancient glories and modern beauties. Reached Moate in the evening, in time to preach. Next day I went to Tully, and attended a soirée; the day after, Moyvore, and preached. Returned to Tully, and preached next day. Thence travelled to Cavan, and rested there; next morning to Drumkeen, Monaghan, and preached there; and so home by the aid of a horse that brought me to the railway at the rate of ten miles an hour. On reaching home, found letters from friends in the Free Church Assembly urging me to visit them as I had been appointed, but, by reason of my western journey, had not been able to join our deputation. I wrote that I should go, and set out the moment I had finished unavoidable duties at home. I need not say how kindly I was received. To this visit I gave eight days, and so came home again; but only to set out on the 9th of June to Tyrone and Fermanagh, to preach in three distant congregations—Tempo, Dromore, and New-townparry. Two days were given to travel *viâ* Derry, as there was not continuous rail on the nearer line.

" I have given you this history to account for my not having written by the 17th ultimo, as I had purposed, nor by Marseilles, as I had also purposed; for from the 12th ultimo till now I have hardly enjoyed an hour of rest from preaching and travelling. . . . Now for news of the dear children. Satisfactory reports have just reached me of Henry and Selim from their mamma, who has arrived on a too brief visit. Nora is here, but, alas! is to be taken from us to-night. She is strong as a young horse, and as red in the cheeks as a rose. . . . .

" To-day I have been reading Taylor's book on the Dead Sea and Cities of the Plain, and find he mainly relies on De Saulcy. Can De Saulcy be depended upon in this case? He represents the ruins of Gomorrah as very extensive; but a certain abbé who was with him affirmed that he could see no ruins at all. Write me your opinion. I do believe that geographical and archæological researches are not only strong pillars of the Divine Records, but that the wisdom of God intended to employ them progressively for that very purpose; so that as infidelity should assume its new phases, so should a new source of evidence be opened to correspond to and counteract each of them, and leave cavillers without excuse."

Such were all his letters—full of instruction, and full of affection. His racy, genial humour, too, was ever welling out.

Toil and weariness could not repress it, and even sorrow was not able to prevent its perennial flow.

Dr. Cooke's thirst for knowledge, capacity for study, and wonderful facility in communicating truth, continued unimpaired. Long after he had passed his seventieth year it could be said of him, " his eye was not dim, nor was his natural strength abated." In the lecture-hall, on the platform, in the pulpit, he displayed much of the vigour and eloquence of his best days. To the very close of his life he was the most prominent figure, and confessedly the leading spirit, in the General Assembly. He was scarcely ever absent from its sittings. When it met at six in the morning he was the first in his place ; when the debates were protracted, as was sometimes the case, till two in the morning, he was there to the last. He has often advised the true friends of the Church, especially those who, from their talents and business habits, are qualified for the position of leaders, to be regular and constant in their attendance on meetings of Presbytery, Synod, and Assembly. " Rash and dangerous measures," he was wont to say, " are usually introduced and passed when the house is thin and exhausted with work."

It was in the Assemblies of 1848 and 1849 I had my first opportunities of personally witnessing his tact and power in debate. As an almost total stranger, at that time, both to him and his brethren, I was able to watch, without prejudice or personal feeling, the character of the discussions. They were generally conducted with great ability, but they occasionally degenerated into storms of invective. The leading subject in 1848 was the College question. That in 1849 was of purely local interest, but it was of such a kind as to create, both among clergy and laity, intense excitement. Dr. Cooke's mastery at once struck me. At every step of the debate he retained command of the house. In the midst of wild confusion he would rise, and by a brilliant sally of wit, or a sparkling repartee, restore good humour and order. The secret of his power consisted partly in his readiness to meet every assailant and every assault; partly in the skill he displayed in analysing arguments, detecting fallacy and exposing sophistry; partly also in the facility with which, by a flash of wit, or a touch of satire, or a humorous anecdote, or a piece of admirable mimicry, he made his auditors laugh at both his opponents and their arguments. Add to these a logical faculty of unsurpassed acuteness; an eloquence which like a torrent carried all before it; a transparent honesty which friends and foes alike admitted; a courage and an earnestness which never faltered; and an all-pervading bonhomie which shone like a sunbeam through a thunder-cloud, revealing the grand aims of a pure and noble spirit;—such was Dr. Cooke in the General Assembly of the Presbyterian Church in Ireland.

Professor Witherow has sketched him with his customary felicity and success :—

"The great strength of Dr. Cooke as a public man lies in his powers of debate. His extemporaneous ability is of the highest order. He has great moral courage, great self-possession, great fluency of speech, a clearness of expression, and a vigour of conception, that can find few parallels. He is never unprepared, and the very commonest remark from him falls with such emphasis as invests it with importance. . . . His speeches, read in the newspapers, do not seem at all so superior to the speeches of other men, thus proving how much of the impression is produced by his fine delivery. In matter he may have superiors, but in manner he has none. His voice is full and deep . . . and is capable of every variety of intonation, from the low whisper that makes an audience hold its breath, up to the thunder-clap by which he electrifies a multitude. Every word falls with power. He can reason or appeal, entreat or declaim, as the occasion demands. He can be serious or severe, merry or sarcastic, as he pleases. Words and ideas flow at will. A fact, that he once knows, is never forgotten, and, when there is necessity to use it, it is ever within call. The tragic and the comic are both alike to him : he speaks at times with such pathos that the tears start into your eyes ; the very next moment and he flings forth some flash of merriment that sets the audience in a roar. The mechanism of the human heart is open to his eye, and he can strike whatever chord and produce whatever tone he pleases. At ordinary times he does not consider it necessary to put forth his strength, but he rises with the occasion. Give him only a crisis for the exhibition of his splendid powers—give him the excitement of some great cause, a worthy antagonist, and a large assembly, and you will never be disappointed in Dr. Cooke.

"Four-fifths of the five hundred members who usually take their seats in the annual gathering of the Presbyterian clergy have received a university education ; the General Assembly, therefore, comprises in it more intelligence and cultivated intellect than any other meeting that usually assembles in Ulster. It is our ecclesiastical Parliament, and numbers on its roll many able men, but among them Dr. Cooke is most prominent of all. He is great by contrast with the great. What was physically true of the son of Kish, is intellectually true of him—from his shoulders and upwards he is higher than any of the people. When he rises to address the chair, he is listened to like an oracle. His opinion goes very far to decide the question. Sometimes, indeed, the Court takes a fit of independence, and leaves him in a minority ; but soon afterwards, pleased with having shown that it is not in bondage to any man, it lays aside its fitful humour, relapses from its eccentricities into its old course, and becomes placid and governable as ever. Even to a stranger, it is evident that ' the old man eloquent ' is the star of the house. Though it is sometimes but too obvious that he is not free from human infirmity and passions, yet constantly his talents overtop his failings and dwarf them into littleness. The Assembly never looks like itself when Cooke is not there. His figure is the first we look for when we enter the house. His presence makes us feel at home. And every returning season we regard the veteran ecclesiastic with deeper interest, for that venerable head, blanched with the storms of years and battles, reminds us that we are not to have him with us for ever ; and the sad reflection follows after, that when Henry Cooke is gone, the Presbyterian Church of Ireland shall have lost the foremost man that has risen in it for two hundred years."

" But though renowned as a polemic, and invincible in debate," writes Professor Wilson, " it would do Dr. Cooke flagrant injustice to represent him as shining merely amid the strife and the struggle of theological or general discussion. In the committees of the Church, far from the excitement of a public auditory, his words are weighty and wise. In her judicatories he has been observed as the first to arrive and the last to depart—patiently and vigorously transacting her business through the most protracted sederunts. Nor are the instances few in which he has proved himself possessed of a heart to feel, as well as of a head to plan and hands to execute. Let a legitimate demand be made upon the Church's tender sympathies, and what bosom will heave with purer, stronger emotion; and from what spirit will the generous fellow-feeling gush forth with equal power to soften and subdue?"

Dr. Murray, the celebrated "Kirwan," was a friend and admirer of Dr. Cooke. He happened to be in Ireland in 1851, and was present during one of the stormiest debates in the General Assembly on the Magee College question. He soon afterwards published a graphic sketch of the exciting and somewhat extraordinary scene. His description of Dr. Cooke was admirable; but some others of the more prominent orators and actors on that occasion were drawn with a touch so vivid, so true to life, that great offence was given to them and their friends. Dr. Murray was annoyed and grieved, and wrote as follows to Dr. Cooke :—

"ELIZABETHTOWN, Oct. 10, 1854.

"MY DEAR DR. COOKE,—By the hand that carries this, I send a note to Dr. Edgar, in reference to the attacks made on me because of my reference to —— in my notice of the Assembly at which I was present in Belfast. . . . I really meant my notice to be laudatory and exculpatory. . . . I put my defence into your hand and that of Dr. Edgar.

"But I write this note for another purpose. There is a report that you are about making a visit to this country. And I say by all means come. There are thousands here to greet you; and many houses to give you a home. Come in March or April, and, if you cannot prolong your visit, return in August. This would give you the pleasant part of the year here, and would enable you to see all our great ecclesiastical gatherings.

"My house is open for you, and any of your family you may bring with you. And just now your visit would have a great effect, as the Papal controversy is rife, and the country is full

of it. Do, by all means, come, and I will do all in my power
to make your reception here as hearty and as useful as possible.
You need not fear the passage. The steamers have converted
the Atlantic into a ferry, as we say here.

" With the highest consideration,

" I remain, yours sincerely,

" N. MURRAY."

Dr. Cooke was requested by his Church to visit America, but
was unable to go ; and in reference to this Dr. Cox, of Ingham
University, wrote as follows :—" Dr. Cooke, though designated,
as I understand, came not with Dr. Edgar and his companions.
His years are more, his cares many, and his detention allow-
able as well as reconcilable, without forgetting our loss and his
own, in omitting this perhaps only opportunity of ever visiting
America, instead of allowing his friends here to do him honour
and service, as a veteran so worthy in the cause of our common
and glorious Lord. For one, I cannot suppress my regret
that such a chieftain, in his venerable age, could not make a
personal acquaintance, to mutual gratification, with Christians,
and scholars, and friends of rational liberty on our side of the
Atlantic. May his terminal years of life be as tranquil and as
happy as his nobility of conduct and influence has been conspicuous and superior through its previous stages ! There are
few like him. His person is tall and stately ; his countenance
and manner in public demonstrative of the orator, the theologian, the sage ; his self-command and copious wisdom were
always anticipated by a select audience, as well as a large one,
whenever and wherever he was announced to speak or preach,
in Ireland, Scotland, England ; and this especially when called
to meet some rare and grave occasion. As a master of debate
in public, he is said to have no superior ; and the highest compliment O'Connell could pay him was never intentionally
withheld—it was to effectuate a personal *alibi* when Cooke was
there."

Dr. Murray revisited Ireland in 1860. The Assembly was

sitting; and, after slyly asking Dr. Cooke whether it was safe for him to venture, he entered the court. It was somewhat singular that another college question, and one, too, which caused much excitement—the election to a professorship—was the first taken up. When it was over Dr. Murray congratulated Dr. Cooke on the dignity and great ability which had characterized the whole proceedings. He and his friend George H. Stewart, with a number of others, dined with Dr. Cooke that evening. The conversation was interesting and brilliant. It was a meeting of kindred spirits; and those who were present will not soon forget it. It was the last time Doctors Cooke and Murray met on earth.

It is difficult to say whether Dr. Cooke excelled in the pulpit, on the platform, or in the arena of debate. He had gifts which shone preeminently in each. In a recent letter Sir Joseph Napier says:—" The late Bishop of Limerick (Dr. Griffin, formerly Fellow of Trinity College) went to hear Dr. Cooke preach, and he told me that he seldom, if ever, heard a more able and powerful sermon. I remember to have heard some one ask the late Archdeacon Irwin whether he had ever met Dr. Cooke. He said, ' I did; I met him on a platform at a public meeting.' ' What did you think of him ? ' ' I would not have liked to have provoked him,' was the reply." The late Professor Wilson has given the following description of Dr. Cooke's pulpit ministrations :—

" As a pulpit orator he is so widely known and so thoroughly appreciated over the United Kingdom, that a minute description or critique were superfluous. We have always considered him greatest and happiest in the public ministrations of the sanctuary, particularly in the department of exposition. In the illustration of Scripture he lays all nature, all history, all the arts and sciences, under varied and heavy contribution. As he proceeds with his discourse, the meaning of God's Word assumes a distinctive form, and is made to stand out in attractive or terrible self-manifestation—wooing or warning the hearts of a riveted audience. Sinai clothes itself in the thunders of old: the soft whisper of mercy is heard from Mount Zion. The

preacher evinces deep insight into the mind of God and the soul of
man—unfolding the inexhaustible treasures of revelation, and morally
extorting from the hearer the admission of their perfect and exclusive fitness to enrich our bankrupt humanity ' with all spiritual
blessings, in heavenly places, in Christ Jesus.' Tearing to shreds
every cloak of hypocrisy, and pitilessly storming the refuges of lies
by which men strive to screen conscience in the neglect of Christian
duty, he fails not to urge home the claims of the truth, by mingled
motives of awful and alluring enforcement. His pulpit addresses
partake plentifully of the strong, argumentative, sometimes scathing
eloquence of John Knox ; yet are they not wanting in tones of sweet,
affectionate tenderness, characteristic of ' the man that had seen
affliction,' and whose soul melts for the stricken and bereaved of his
flock. On more public and exciting occasions, his preaching realises
the boldest flights of sacred oratory, displaying peculiar brilliancy,
and expatiating in extensive ranges of thought, while depth and
massiveness are never sacrificed on the altar of popular effect. It was
the observation of an able and learned clergyman of the Established
Church, in reference to one of his own brethren—' In the discourse
of Mr. ——, you have no doubt enjoyed the A, B, C of Gospel
simplicity ; but had you come to the service of Dr. Cooke, you would
have been feasted with the X, Y, Z of Christian philosophy.' We
merely add that the utterance of the Doctor is seldom marked by
rapidity : the onward march of his eloquence commonly suggests the
idea of a slow and measured tread ; but it is the tread of the
honoured veteran on the field of his fame.''

Another friend, the Rev. Dr. Blackwood, who was intimately
associated with Dr. Cooke during a part of his public career,
has depicted in eloquent terms some characteristics of his
most splendid efforts :—

" His style was in accordance with the majestic contour of the
outward man. Clear in his thinking, and nervous in his words, a
perfect master of language, he ever had the right word in the right
place. There was a rhythm and flow in his sentences that fell with
wondrous power on every musical ear that heard him. When precision demanded, his sentences were short, sharp, and incisive; but
anon he would stretch out into longer periods, and with an affluence
of riches scatter flowers as he went along, that showed the un

wonted fertility of his mind. We have hearkened to many men of great power, of whom some were logical and didactic ; to others, whose style was flowing, lucid, and yet adorned with flowers of poetic imagery. Like the phosphorescence of the fire-fly in the calmness of the summer eve, these gleams and momentary scintillations were attractive from their beauty ; but the sparkling was only for an instant, and the brilliancy was quickly gone. Not so was it with him. The match when applied to the rocket enkindles it, and forthwith it begins to ascend. Higher and higher it rises, while it gilds its pathway with light and brightness. At length it reaches the summit of its range, when, bursting in an efflorescence of gorgeous hues, it fills the vast empyrean with a diadem of beauty. So was it with his wondrous spoken style. How often have we seen the largest audiences spell-bound and rapt in admiration as he ascended in thought, adding member after member to the expanding sentence, until the climax was complete, and the whole was finished by a burst of effulgent beauty, when the pent-up breath of the audience would find its way, and again his hearers would prepare for a repetition of the scene. Few men ever lived who more readily discerned analogies and relations in things. So vivid was this faculty of mind, that at times the fertility of his fancy had to be held in restraint ; especially when expounding the typology and symbolism of the Old Testament, a department of Scripture study in which he had special delight."

Dr. Cooke's illustrations and figures were remarkable for their appropriateness and beauty. The finest of them were extemporaneous—they were the offspring of a momentary inspiration. Few of them, therefore, were recorded; and none with that fulness which would make them dazzle and delight as when they flowed from the lips of the living orator. A friend* has supplied one. The preacher was drawing a distinction between the Law and the Gospel. Of the former he said :— " The Law is powerless to save. It only warns of danger. It is the beacon-light that within its hard and stony ribs contains no heart of sympathy to beat for the perishing mariner ; and when he sinks beneath the waves, it sends forth no sigh

* William Hamilton, Esq., to whom we are also indebted for the most striking photograph ever taken of Dr. Cooke.

of sorrow, nor dims its twinkling with any tear of regret."
Those who have heard his sermons on Ecclesiastes ix. 10:
"Whatsoever thy hand findeth to do, do it with thy might;"
1 John i. 3: "And truly our fellowship is with the Father,
and with His Son Jesus Christ;" 1 John v. 12: "He that
hath the Son hath life;" Isaiah xl. 28—31; or the lecture on
"The Good Samaritan," can never forget the unrivalled
splendours of that imagery with which he illustrated those
magnificent specimens of pulpit oratory.

The first time I heard him preach was in 1848. His
subject was "The Lord's Prayer." I was especially struck
with the depth and originality of thought and the power of
application in that wonderful discourse. It formed a complete
treasury of theology and Christian ethics, yet expressed in
language so clear as to be intelligible to all classes. From
1859 till the close of his active ministerial career in 1867, I
was a member of his church, and heard him almost constantly. At that period his pulpit services had undergone
considerable change. They lacked much of the fire and
lofty oratorical flights of earlier years; but there was more
unction—there was more uniform and earnest effort to press
a living Saviour, and a finished work of salvation, upon the
acceptance of his hearers. It almost seemed as if he felt
each sermon might be his last. But, at the same time, all
the original power of intellect was there. His expositions
were, if possible, more full and striking than ever. They
showed that he not only kept abreast of the theological and
critical literature of the time, but that, from longer and
closer communion with God and His Word, he had so
entirely caught the spirit of the sacred writers, that his
mind could grasp their sublime truths, and his heart
feel their power. His knowledge of Scripture was not
merely intellectual; it was also experimental. The deep
well-springs of love which had always gushed forth in his
familiar conversation and correspondence with members of
his family, now flowed with equal copiousness in his pulpit

ministrations. His loving, generous nature was now also shown, as it never had been before, in his intercourse with the world, but especially with his brethren in the ministry. He was ready to bear and forbear. He ever counselled peace and charity. It was the ripening of the Christian character— the gradual triumph of grace over intellect and heart. He consequently became more and more endeared to the whole circle of his acquaintances, and more and more revered by his Church as years passed on.

The respect and honour accorded him had probably no parallel. The first place was assigned to him wherever he went. When he chanced to enter a public meeting or church-court, after it had opened, no matter what business was being transacted, or what speaker was addressing the house, the Doctor's presence was hailed with hearty and general greetings. This was a matter of course. Everybody understood—everybody sympathised with it. On one occasion, during the meeting of the General Assembly in Dublin, in 1867, a deputy from the United States was addressing the house. He had been received, as deputies from America always are received, with an enthusiastic welcome. The crowded audience were giving breathless attention to his speech, when suddenly, and, so far as he could see, without any cause, a burst of applause proceeded from the whole House. The deputy was amazed. He faltered; and, as the applause continued, he stopped, and turned to the Moderator for an explanation. The Moderator pointed to the venerable figure of Dr. Cooke walking up the aisle of the church, with every eye intently and affectionately bent upon him. Until he had taken a front seat, which was at once vacated for him, the honoured deputy was forced to remain a silent spectator. He had never seen the like before; and it showed him, and through him it showed the great Western Continent, what a high place in the heart of the Irish nation, and in the esteem of the Presbyterian Church, had been won by Henry Cooke.

In 1862, Dr. Cooke was, for the third time, raised to the Moderator's chair, in the highest court of his Church. No other instance of such distinction had ever occurred in its history. His brethren felt that there was no honour too great to bestow on one whose services had been so eminent and so successful.

But Dr. Cooke felt, as many another has felt, that the esteem of brethren, the love of friends, and the admiration of a grateful country, cannot avert bereavement, or heal the wounds of a bleeding heart. A beloved daughter died in May, 1863, after a long and painful illness. He never recovered that blow. She was a treasure to him. Her filial devotion, her noble nature, her pure and loving heart, her cordial sympathy in his trials, her just appreciation of his triumphs, bound her to him by a very tender and a very special tie. When she was taken, it seemed as if one of the stays of his life had been removed. It was a sad picture to see the old man sit and weep in silence. It was sadder still to hear the sob, as that sweet name, " Elizabeth," trembled on his lips. Writing to an old friend—the Rev. J. Burns—he says :— " My dear daughter's death has left me all but a solitary man. After my God and her dear mother, she was all the world to me ; and it is now to me, and will remain to me, a blank. After the salvation of the souls in my charge, there is nothing that interests me. . . . My days and nights are spent in tears. I am not striving with my Maker. He gave, and He has taken away. Blessed be the name of the Lord ! She lived full of grace ; she died in the full assurance of faith. Her end was peace." In another letter he says, in reference to the sad bereavement :—" How miserable were man if deprived of immortality ! How glorious the hope of meeting Him who brought life and immortality to light in the gospel ; and with Him, too, meeting those who were so dear to us here, but from whom death has severed us !"

The Presbyterian Church in Ireland had conferred on Dr. Cooke the highest offices and honours in her gift. His

Protestant fellow-countrymen of all classes resolved to unite once more in presenting him with a tribute of their esteem. For this purpose a meeting was held in the Music Hall, Belfast, on Thursday, July 6th, 1865. The presentation was no ordinary compliment. The chair was occupied by the Marquess of Downshire; and John Lytle, Esq., Mayor of Belfast, read the following address, which was drawn up by the Right Hon. Sir J. Napier :—

" Rev. and dear Sir.—In the name of a large number of your Protestant countrymen, we have the honour this day to ask your acceptance of a testimonial, expressive of our high personal esteem, and in acknowledgment of the great and invaluable services which you have rendered to the cause of civil liberty, social progress, and Divine Truth.

" For nearly half a century your name has been pre-eminently conspicuous throughout the empire as a distinguished and successful champion of Protestantism—the uncompromising, powerful advocate of the imperishable principles of our evangelical faith—the invincible defender of our national religious establishments, and as the eloquent and ardent supporter of Christian brotherhood and co-operation amongst the various sections of the great Protestant community.

" On several remarkable occasions, when the peculiar circumstances of the nation called you to stand forward, you have nobly upheld the cause of loyalty, advocating allegiance to our Sovereign and to the Constitution of this realm, not as a mere passion, but as a principle— a sacred duty. You have ever taught that true patriotism is not more distinguished by its energy than by its calmness ; that a fervent zeal for religion is a profound and tranquil feeling.

" Amongst the intelligent people of Ulster you have always faithfully inculcated, without fear or favour, the rights and duties of property. You have not failed to impress on them that the landed proprietors and their industrious tenants have a common interest in the conscientious discharge of their mutual obligations, and that the maintenance of friendly and cordial relations between them is essential to their mutual prosperity.

" We rejoice to see that the unceasing efforts of an unusually laborious public life have not impaired the great mental vigour and moral energy which God has given you. Be assured of our profound regard ; of our veneration for your exalted character and worth ; and of our thorough appreciation of your life-long services to the community to which we belong, and to the sacred cause of Protestantism.

"Permit us to add the expression of our heartfelt sympathy with you and your family under the bereavement which we know has pressed so heavily upon you ; but we are aware that you 'sorrow not even as others which have no hope.'

"May your declining days be peaceful and happy, your faith sustained, and your hope unclouded! Long may your loved and honoured name, now so dear and precious to your countrymen, be a household word in the homes and in the hearts of Protestant Ulster !

"Downshire, Chairman."

Dr. Cooke replied :—

"My Lord,—I beg leave to return my best thanks to ' the large number of my Protestant fellow-countrymen' who have, through your Lordship's hands, presented to me such a substantial testimonial of their good-will ; and if, as their address declares, I have been able to render any service to the great cause of 'civil liberty, social progress, and Divine Truth,' I appropriate it not to myself, but ascribe it to the grace of Almighty God.

"A Presbyterian by birth, education, and conviction, my inter-course with my fellow-Protestants of other denominations long ago convinced me that pure and undefiled religion was not limited to forms of Church government, but that the power of Gospel truth was common to them all ; and in public and in private life I uniformly stated my conviction, that, while the Gospel is legitimately compared to a lamp, it matters much less what is the shape of the lamp than what is the amount and purity of the light which it furnishes. And if I have been assailed on account of this concession, still I stand by it, and am not ashamed to avow it in the face of all the Evan-gelical Churches. Acting upon this principle, I have, through the greater part of a long life, felt opposed to polemical controversies upon minor points of difference, and have continued to inculcate among the Churches the brotherly watchword of ' Protestant peace.'

"A pupil of the school of Knox, an inheritor of the principles of the early Puritans, when the lawfulness of national establishments of religion was assailed, I stood up in their defence ; and, when the

Throne and the Protestant institutions of the country were threatened, I took my humble part on the side of law, liberty, and order, not ashamed of the glorious Revolution of 1688—nor of the memorable charge against my fathers—' They are Presbyterians and Hanoverians.' Your Address recalls these memories of other days : the days are dead, but the principles are immortal.

"For the sympathetic reference to my sorrows of bereavement I return my melancholy thanks, while I rejoice to say that I sorrow not as the hopeless. As a father my heart has been wounded ; but the hand of the great Healer can bind up the wound it has inflicted.

"And, now that I am drawing nigh to the close of a long life battle, I trust I shall be enabled to maintain to the end the same unchanging principles of Protestant truth and brotherhood by which I have hitherto been characterised, and which have gathered around me so many of those numerous friends who have this day (and formerly) so liberally contributed to my own and my family's comforts.

"H. COOKE."

During one part of the interesting proceedings, the scene was most affecting. When referring to the death of his daughter he burst into tears, and was for some time unable to proceed. So touching was the sorrow of the old man, and so deep was the sympathy of all, that the entire audience appeared almost as much overcome as he was himself. The Testimonial consisted of a cheque for sixteen hundred guineas, and a magnificently illuminated volume, containing the Address and names of the subscribers.

CHAPTER XX.

1866—1868.

Closing Scenes—Present from the Marquess of Downshire—Affecting Interview—
Secret of his Influence and Popularity—Protestant Meeting in the Botanic
Gardens—Hillsborough Demonstration—Dr. Cooke's last Speech—Farewell
to his Congregation—Death of Mrs. Cooke—Visit to Harrogate and last
Illness—"Address to the Protestant Electors of Ireland"—His Principles
unchanged—On his Death-bed—Favourite Portions of Scripture—Dr.
Morgan's Visits—Faith Triumphant—A last Interview—His Death—Public
Funeral.

THE close of a long, laborious, and honoured life was now
manifestly approaching. Dr. Cooke's step became feeble, and
his noble voice lost much of its power. Belfast and Ulster
were proud of him. His name had been a household word for
half a century. His old opponents, political and ecclesiastical,
almost forgot their defeats as they joined in according to him at
life's close the tribute of their admiration. All parties regarded
him as the very embodiment of chivalrous honour and high
Christian principle. The respect, the veneration, which he inspired were unparalleled. As he walked slowly along the streets,
now generally leaning on the arm of some relative, every eye followed him with wistful look, as if he might never be seen again.
When he entered any public meeting he was received with a
subdued enthusiasm—a hearty yet touching welcome, which
showed how deep and tender were the feelings with which he
was regarded.

On the 12th of February, 1866, Lord Downshire called at
his house, and, on taking leave, handed him a small parcel,
begging his acceptance of it as a *souvenir* from an old friend.
It contained Queen Elizabeth's Prayer Book, exquisitely
bound, with the inscription :—" To my dear and revered

friend, Dr. Cooke, from his sincere and attached, DOWNSHIRE."
Beneath was written " *Placetne ?*" Enclosed was the following
letter :—

"HILLSBOROUGH, Feb. 12, 1866.

" MY DEAR DR. COOKE,—I wanted often to try to find some
little present to offer you, but up till now without success. I
lately found what is called Queen Elizabeth's Prayer Book.
It is very nicely printed and got up, and I hope you will
accept of it. My wife and children lately were only too happy
to accept of it from me, and I do hope that it may find equal
favour in your sight.

" May God long preserve you to your own Church, and to
the Established Church, of which you have been for so many
years such a candid and sincere friend. You are the man
with whom all my early feelings have been associated, and I
am only too glad of this opportunity of expressing my deep
feelings of attachment to and admiration for you. Believe
me, my dear Dr. Cooke,
                        " Your most sincere and attached,
                                        " DOWNSHIRE."

Lord Downshire died suddenly in 1868, a few months before
Dr. Cooke.

One morning, a short time after the above occurrence, it
was announced to Dr. Cooke that a stranger wished to see him.
He was engaged, and requested me to ascertain his business. I found at the door a fine-looking young man of about
twenty, apparently a mechanic in holiday dress. I asked what
he wanted. His reply was, " I wish to see the Doctor."
" Can I not act for him ?" I inquired. " No," he said ;
"nobody but the Doctor." " But," said I, " he is busy, and
it is unusual for visitors to call at such an early hour. We
are unwilling to disturb him. Can you not call at another
time ?" " No, that's impossible," he said, with a strong Scotch
accent. " I came from Greenock by last night's boat, and I

must go back to-night. I just came on purpose to see the
Doctor. I have heard of him from my mother; I have read
of him in the papers ever since I was a lad; I know all he has
done; and I just want to see him and speak to him. I may
never be here again in his time—can I no' see him?" The
last words he spoke with intense earnestness. The appeal was
irresistible; so I took him in. But still I had some doubts
and misgivings. I could scarcely believe the youth was sincere, though his mien and look were honest and straightforward. I remained to watch the issue. On entering, he
stood for a moment looking at the venerable figure of the old
man sitting in his chair—his long hair, and the full beard which
he now wore, white as the snow-drift. Then he advanced and
took the outstretched hand, while I briefly explained the cause
of the visit. He raised the hand gradually and hesitatingly to
his lips, as if afraid to give offence. "I have come from
Scotland to see you," he said at length. "Then you see an
old man going home—you see a great sinner saved by Divine
grace—you see a frail mortal about to put on immortality." "I
am satisfied now," the youth said. "My mother will be satisfied—thank God for this!" Then, still holding the Doctor's
hand, he put the other arm fondly round his neck, stooped,
kissed his forehead, muttered "God bless you! Farewell!" and
walked out of the house, the tears streaming down his cheeks.

These are but illustrations of that wonderful love and
veneration which Dr. Cooke kindled in the hearts of his
countrymen.

His broad Christian sympathies, his thorough liberal spirit,
contributed largely to make Dr. Cooke the idol of all sects
of evangelical Protestants. When necessary, no man maintained with greater power the distinctive doctrines and forms
of his own Church; but he always deprecated petty controversies and disputes about trifles. He delighted in uniting
with members of other Churches in the defence of a fundamental doctrine, or the promotion of a grand principle. In
this respect he never changed. Whatever others did or said,

he was the same. Personal interest, calumny, misrepresentation, even the reproaches of cherished friends, could not shake him. An intimate and influential friend once said to him, in my presence, " Rest assured, Dr. Cooke, they (certain persons whom he named) only wish to use your name and your influence to secure their own objects; and when they are secured, they will cast both you and your Church overboard." " Be it so," he replied; " that does not affect my duty. If an act be right, the bad motive of the man who asks me to do it cannot impart to it any moral taint. God forbid I should judge so of any men; but even though it were the case, and I knew it, my course would be the same."

One leading aim of his life and labours was Protestant peace, so as, if possible, to secure Protestant union against a common foe. This was known to all his friends—indeed, to the whole nation. Sir Joseph Napier writes to me :—" He had a truly catholic heart. He once said to me he did not so much look to comprehension as to brotherhood. The bond of brotherhood was what he longed for amongst all who profess and call themselves Christians." Chief Justice Whiteside said of him, in 1865 :—" God raised up Dr. Cooke for great and noble purposes, and nobly has he fulfilled them. Every Church in the land is indebted to him for his unsectarian advocacy of Protestant principles, his evangelical charity towards all parties."

In 1862, during his year of office as Moderator, a great Protestant meeting was held in the Botanic Gardens, Belfast. He was one of the speakers, and he advocated the very same principles which he imbibed in youth, and which he developed with so much eloquence at Hillsborough, in 1834. As usual, he was blamed by some of his brethren. They imagined that, as Moderator, he represented the Church, and that some of the statements he made were calculated to compromise them. He thought it necessary, on account of his official status, to publish a defence. He satisfactorily explained all the statements he had made, and he showed that he had in his speech most carefully repudiated all idea of representation; that he had spoken as an individual, and not as Moderator of the General Assembly.

Dr. Cooke's last appearance before the public, and his last speech upon a platform, were made at the Hillsborough Protestant Demonstration, on the 30th of October, 1867. The object of that Demonstration was to resist the attacks then being vigorously commenced against the Protestant Institutions and endowments of Ireland. The vast bulk of the Protestants of Ulster believed that their rights and liberties were in danger, and they resolved to make a united effort to defend them. It was not a mere political assemblage. No attack was made, or intended, on any Church or party. It was a Protestant coalition, on a broad and liberal basis, to resist the overthrow of national endowments. Dr. Cooke took a leading part in its organization. From the first he gave it all the weight of his name and influence. He was present at every meeting of committee; and the energy, zeal, and profound wisdom of the veteran inspired some, who, considering the signs of the times and the almost hopelessness of the cause, were inclined to stand aside. "If we have truth with us," he said, "as I believe and you believe we have, it is our duty to use all lawful means, and leave the result in God's hands."

The meeting was held in the open air, and on the same spot as that of 1834. Thirty thousand people were present. Dr. Cooke was surrounded on the platform by many of his old and faithful friends—Lords Roden, Downshire, Erne, Hill-Trevor, Templeton, Sir Thomas Bateson, Sir J. M. Stronge. The first resolution was moved by the Rev. William (now Lord) O'Neill. Dr. Cooke, on rising to second it, was hailed with an outburst of applause from the vast assemblage so enthusiastic and so prolonged that it fairly unmanned him. His whole frame trembled, and his eyes filled with tears. I was obliged for a time to give him the support of my arm. It was with the greatest difficulty he could speak at all. Nothing but a strong sense of duty, and an invincible determination to advocate to the very last the great principles for which he had so nobly struggled through a long life, would have induced him to be present, or to attempt to raise his voice on that day. It was a grand and yet a sad sight. The great orator, the great political leader, the great Protestant chieftain, inspired by the same truths, animated by the same noble aspirations, with all the old vigour of intellect, yet with feeble voice and trembling lips, trying to address a few parting words to the tens of thousands who eagerly bent forward, and, with a silence as of death, hung upon his lips. All felt and mourned the change which four-score years had wrought in that prince of men, and none more keenly than himself. He spoke as follows :—

" My Lord Downshire, and you my brother Protestants, you will pardon me while I discharge the pleasing duty assigned to me. And, first, you may say why did I come here to-day, when I am not able to make myself heard even by a few of the vast multitude which I see before me ? Years ago I was able to make you hear me when I stood on this spot to address you upon a subject then, as now, dear to us all. But the snows of eighty years are upon my brow, and the progress of years has taken away my voice, and, as you may see, diminished my strength. The only change that has not come over me is a change in my views : my heart is unchanged. It is Protestant—universal to the core. I hold the same sentiments with regard to the Church Establishment that I held when, thirty-three years ago, I addressed a great assemblage from this place. Perhaps I may be allowed to state, in a few words, why I have not receded from my opinions as then expressed, so that I may not be misunderstood. I will tell you why I stand by the Church Establishment of this country, although I do not belong to it. . . . It is because I recognise in her a noble branch of the great Protestant tree planted in Europe by the hands of the Reformers ; because I hear in her the living voice of the primitive evangelical teachers, and the dying testimony of that glorious company of martyrs and confessors, by whom liberty of conscience, the right of private judgment, and unrestricted access to the Sacred Scriptures have been asserted, recovered, and secured. . . . It is now more than thirty years since I stood on a platform in this very field, and proclaimed the banns of holy marriage, intellectual and spiritual, between the Presbyterian Church and the Established Church. I am glad, at the end of thirty years, to see this glorious progeny—to witness the extent of our numbers to-day, amongst whom, I have no doubt, a very large body of our Presbyterian people are to be found. I regret, indeed, that I cannot do the resolution justice—that I am not able to make myself heard by you all. But you will overlook such shortcomings in a man of eighty years, feeble in voice, feeble in body, but strong in spirit, and strong in his original attachment to the great Protestant cause."

His farewell to his congregation was not less affecting. On Sunday, the 5th of May, 1867, he announced, after dispensing the Sacrament of the Lord's Supper, that it was the last time he would preside. He delivered a brief but touching address. He spoke to some who had been members of the Church from the first; he spoke to others whom he had baptized, and who had been trained under his ministry, and with an earnestness and a pathos that thrilled every heart, and brought tears to all eyes, he besought them to prepare for that heavenly home which, he said, he hoped soon to enter. The solemn services of that day left a deep and indelible impress on many a heart. Their effects were felt far beyond the bounds of the congregation. Sir Joseph Napier, on hearing of them, thus wrote to his friend, Mr. James Torrens, of Belfast:—"I can well conceive the effect that must have been produced by Dr. Cooke's last Communion on the 5th, when he announced his intention of not presiding again. He is the last of the mighty men of old whom I remember in the North. I have always had a most sincere affection for him, and the greatest respect for his talents and his virtues. From him I have heard some of the best expositions of Holy Scripture and the wisest lessons of Christian duty."

During the collegiate session of 1867-68, Dr. Cooke found himself unable to fulfil the laborious duties of his professorship, and he requested me to assist him. None mourned his declining health more deeply than his students.

In the beginning of the summer of 1868 his health improved,

and he regained some portion of his wonted vigour. But in June a bereavement came, which seemed to break the last link that bound him to the world. Mrs. Cooke died on the 30th, after a few days' illness. He was entirely unprepared for this terrible stroke. He had always supposed she would outlive him. For fifty-five years she had been by his side. In latter days especially he had leaned more and more on her tender care and self-sacrificing devotion. He could not fully realize the mournful fact that she was gone. He seemed like a man stunned. He could not eat; he could not sleep; he could not rest. Reading of Scripture and prayer were the only exercises that appeared to excite in him any interest. It was thought an entire change of scene might rouse and strengthen him, and Harrogate was recommended, being the place where, for a quarter of a century, he had been in the habit of spending a few weeks each summer. He went to it in the beginning of August, and was accompanied by his son and daughter, and his attached friend, the Rev. John Meneely. During the first few days he revived, and sanguine hopes were entertained of his recovery. But on Saturday, the 15th, I received a telegram stating that he had become suddenly and alarmingly ill. I reached Harrogate at noon on the following day, and found him very weak. There was no apparent disease—only complete physical prostration. His medical attendant could hold out no hope of recovery, and, as it was Dr. Cooke's own wish, we set out for Belfast on the 20th. The scene at the railway station was very touching. He was wheeled into it in a Bath-chair, and placed in the carriage. There, a number of his old and attached friends from Belfast, including the Mayor, S. McCausland, Esq., and Alderman Lytle, gathered round him and bade him farewell, scarcely hoping they would ever again see him alive. He bore the journey well, and rallied considerably when he found himself in his own home.

After his return he occasionally sat for an hour or two in his favourite chair; but he generally lay on a couch in his dining-room reading, or being read to by one of his daughters.

During the month of October he partially recovered strength; and for a time his family fondly hoped he would be able to move about again. He spoke of his returning vigour; and more than once told me he might yet worship one Sabbath in May Street ere he died. During all this time, and indeed during the whole of his illness, he showed great unwillingness to receive visitors. He even objected to see those to whom he had been much attached through life. He made only two exceptions—Mr. Meneely and Dr. Morgan. He requested them to come each once or twice a week; and he looked for their visits with great pleasure. He had usually some short passage of Scripture which he would ask them to read; he then generally gave a brief exposition, and prayed, or asked them to pray.

His great intellect remained unimpaired to the last. It was acute, ready, profound as ever. He was mainly occupied with Divine things; but he still continued to take a lively interest in public affairs. He saw the newspapers every day, and often spoke with me of passing events. When the excitement of the general election came on, he was almost as eager as he had been in the prime of manhood. This will not be thought strange when it is remembered how closely associated were his political and religious principles. He believed that it is righteousness alone which exalteth a nation; and he therefore deemed it a solemn duty to use every effort to have men imbued with sound and righteous principles elected to the Legislature. It was for this reason he issued that Address which created so much sensation throughout the Empire—

"To the Protestant Electors of Ireland.

"Dear Friends and Brethren,—You will hear my voice no more; but I am so deeply impressed with the solemnity of the present crisis, that I cannot refrain from addressing to you a few parting words.

"I have lived a Presbyterian, and I shall die devotedly attached to the Church of my fathers. I have, however, during a long life laboured and prayed for Protestant unity and peace. I could never agree with the government or forms of the Church of England. I lament the abuses and errors that have crept into her. But I bless God that I have always been able to overlook the minor and non-essential points on which we differ, and to recognise in her a noble branch of the great Protestant tree planted by the hands of the Reformers. I have been able to hear, in the living voice of her teachers, the testimony of that glorious company of martyrs and confessors, by whom a free Bible and liberty of conscience were secured to my country. For these reasons I stand by her.

" The Established Church, and all the Protestant Institutions in the land are now in danger. Their overthrow, as National Institutions, is the policy of one party ; their defence, of another. There can, therefore, be no neutral men in this struggle.

" I call upon you, Protestant electors, as you value your faith, as you love your country, to demand of those for whom you would vote a full and explicit declaration of their policy. Tolerate no indefiniteness or equivocation. Vote for no man, however respected or honoured, who attempts to cloak his views on the great question of the day. *Principles, and not men*, must now be your motto.

" Fellow Protestants, be faithful to your country, to your religion, and to your God. Be watchful against the insidious advances of Popish error and despotism ; be united in defence of liberty and truth ; and He who ruleth King of nations will bless and prosper your cause. Farewell !

" H. COOKE.

" Ormeau Road, Belfast,
" 24th Oct., 1868."

" The letter which Dr. Cooke has written to the Protestant Electors of Ireland," says a local paper, " comes upon us like the last sustained notes of some grand old anthem. The strain is familiar ; but we never weary of listening. The sentiments have long been impressed upon the memory, yet the words fall upon the ear with a charm which does not belong to novelty. For they are words of eloquence and truth—words eloquent not merely for their rhetoric and cadence, but because of the associations they recall. On the very threshold of the grave Henry Cooke has paused to lift his voice once more in the cause of Protestant union and political honesty. Of old, he stood erect on many a platform, fired with the ardour of genius, warm with the enthusiasm of youth, strong with active courage, and confident, because he fought under the banner of the Cross. To-day the snows of more than eighty winters rest upon him. No more shall we see his majestic form, defiant and erect—no more shall the flashes of his eagle eye kindle the sympathies of astonished multitudes—no more shall his ringing voice resound in the halls of debate, or his tone of scorn drive the pigmies of Voluntaryism from his presence like frighted sheep. Too truly, in his own pathetic words, we shall ' hear his voice no more;' and yet from the silence of his chamber he speaks, and tens of thousands will not merely listen, but will write his address upon their hearts, and acknowledge that once more, and for the last time, they have heard weighty words of counsel and of wisdom from one who never spoke in haste, and seldom spoke in vain."

Dr. Cooke was consistent to the last. The very same principles which he adopted in 1798, when his country was torn by revolution, he enunciated in 1868, when, from his deathbed, with the eye of a seer, he saw the dark clouds again gathering round her. " Be faithful to your country, to your religion, and to your God." These were noble words, and they were worthy of one of whom it may truly be said that he lived for his country, for his religion, and for his God.

When the excitement passed he relapsed into his former weak state. He now seldom rose from his couch, yet there was no diminution of mental power and activity. Several times each day he had a portion of Scripture read to him by one of his daughters. He delighted in the Psalms, and he frequently asked for the 51st, the 71st, and the 103rd. In the New Testament he appeared to derive special comfort and encouragement from our Lord's prayer in John xvii.; also from the fifth and eighth chapters of the Epistle to the Romans, and from the eleventh and twelfth of the Hebrews. I saw him every day from the time of my arrival in Harrogate;

and he had always some text on which to speak with me, and
some special point in it either to call to my attention or to ask
my views upon.   Our conversations were almost uniformly
closed by a short prayer, offered up by him, and bearing on the
subject of which we had spoken.   His expositions were characterised by wonderful depth of thought and clearness of insight.
It seemed as if his spirit were, through the Word, holding
direct converse with the enlightening Spirit of God—so pure,
so profound, so spiritual were his remarks.   He often spoke of
death ; but no shade of fear for an instant dimmed his vision.
He explained how the Omnipotent Saviour had robbed death
of its sting.   He spoke of his own approaching dissolution
with joy.   He seemed to long for it.   He often repeated Paul's
words, " To me to live is Christ, and to die is gain."   Then,
as was customary with him in former years, he would explain
the passage—showing how death to the Christian is gain.   Not
death in itself, for it is a curse ; but death as a passage to
glory, while it is a relief, and the only effectual and final relief,
from sin and suffering.

The moments I thus spent with him I felt to be very precious.   There was a strength of faith, a brightness of spiritual
vision, and a ripeness of Christian experience, such as I had
never witnessed.   Yet there was no excitement.   Truth was so
clearly apprehended, and Christ so fully trusted, that his mind
was in perfect peace.   He waited patiently, hopefully, for his
appointed time.   God's time, he said, was his time.   On
entering one day I found him thoughtful, and apparently
troubled.   " I have been thinking all night," he said, " what
purpose my God can have to serve with me now.   I feel my
work is done.   My physical strength is exhausted ; the mind
cannot act here independent of the body.   I can, therefore,
labour no more for Him on earth.   I cannot solve the mystery,
why He detains me.   Yet I believe there must be some purpose, for He is infinitely wise."   A few days afterwards he
again introduced the subject, and I was then able to relate a
fact which afforded him much gratification.   I had just met a

leading member of his congregation, who asked me very
earnestly about the Doctor's state of mind in the near prospect of death. He told me many of his former hearers were
most anxious to learn whether the great gospel doctrines which
he had preached with so much clearness and power were now,
in his last moments, able to give comfort and peace to his own
soul. I told him all; and I told him about the Doctor's
anxiety regarding God's gracious purposes in keeping him so
long in weakness, when he desired to depart. " Oh ! go and
say to him," said Mr. M., " that the tidings of his faith and
hope, and joy, which you have now told me, will, when conveyed to his people, have a more blessed effect than any sermon he ever preached." Verily his death-bed was a sermon,
which those who were present can never forget.

Dr. Morgan and Mr. Meneely were unremitting in their attention to the last. None saw, or could see, better than they
the triumphs of faith. Dr. Morgan has left on record a brief
but cheering account of his closing interviews with his early
and revered friend :—

" His exercises were those of a servant of God, who was conscious
he was soon to give an account of his stewardship. The Psalms
of David had been long his delight, but latterly that delight had
become an insatiable passion. These sweet compositions, with the
Epistle of Paul to the Romans, absorbed his attention. It has
been my custom, for the last three or four months, to make a
weekly visit to his sick chamber. His mind was uniformly clear
and placid. As he expected me, he had usually some texts of
Scripture of which he asked me to give him an exposition, and when
I did so he followed with his own. These were still such as I had
been used to hear from him, remarkable for their correctness, and
beauty, and ingenuity. To the last he continued to have his family
round him for their daily worship. The Scriptures were read, and he
then generally offered some observations upon the passage that had
been selected, concluding the exercise with an appropriate prayer.
From what I have been told of these precious hours, I felt it must
have been a great privilege to have spent them with him. A few
days ago, he said, ' I die in the full assurance of understanding ; in

the full assurance of faith, and in the full assurance of hope.' Let this be our last lesson from his bed of death, to understand, and appropriate, and speak the same words. Surely, we may well say as we think of him—'Mark the perfect man, and behold the upright, for the end of that man is peace'—'Let me die the death of the righteous, and let my last end be like his.'"

My last visit to Dr. Cooke was on Saturday, December 12th. I had a public engagement for the following day, which made it necessary for me to leave Belfast that evening. He knew of it, and told me it was my duty to go. Before leaving he requested me to read Hebrews xii. 18—24. When I had finished, he offered up a short prayer. Then, holding out his hand, he said :—" What a prospect ! Jesus the Mediator. The blood of sprinkling ! Farewell." They were his last words to me. I saw him no more. Early on Monday morning the news of his death reached me at Castle Ward.

He slept during the greater part of Saturday night. On Sunday morning he was in his usual state, his mind clear and vigorous. He requested Miss Cooke to read, as his morning portion, the story of Gideon in the seventh chapter of Judges. After it, he engaged in prayer. During the day he spoke little, but he prayed frequently. About five o'clock in the evening it was observed that he was sinking. The members of his family —his son Henry, and his three surviving daughters, Miss Cooke, Mrs. Gordon, and Mrs. Porter—with the servants, assembled round him. He spoke no more. He appeared to be asleep. He breathed gently, but very slowly. Not a muscle moved ; and in a few moments his breathing entirely ceased. His spirit passed peacefully away.

With the speed of lightning the sad tidings flashed over Ulster and Ireland. His death had been long expected, and yet, since the death of Prince Albert, no event created such a profound sensation throughout the country.

Dr. Cooke had expressed a wish that his funeral should be as private as possible. He named those brethren of his own Church who were to be requested to conduct the religious services; he also named a few gentlemen whom he should like to follow his body to the tomb.*

His wishes in these respects could only in part be carried out. The people of Ulster resolved that "in deference to his life and labours, and as a mark of respect to his character and work, there should be a public funeral." When his family were informed of this resolution they were unwilling to oppose the strongly expressed desire of the people whom Dr. Cooke had loved so well, and from whom he had received so many favours. Accordingly, on Friday, the 18th of December, the funeral took place. It was a day long to be remembered in Belfast. It was cloudless; but the sun shone with the subdued light of mid-winter. At noon the solemn procession formed in the Park of Ormeau. Long files of students, headed by the Presidents and Professors of their respective colleges, were there. The clergy, of all denominations, were there. The young minister and the members of May Street Church were there. The Corporation of Belfast and the representatives of almost every corporate body in Ulster were there. Among the pall-bearers were the Primate of Ireland, the Moderator of the General Assembly, the Bishop of the Diocese, the Mayor of Belfast, and the Members of Parliament for the borough and county. The procession, which was fully two miles in length, was made up of all ranks, sects, and parties. From an early hour business was suspended in the town.† The leading shops and warehouses along the line of route were draped in mourning. The streets were lined with tens of thousands. Every available spot was occupied—windows, doors, roofs, balconies, parapets, and even trees. Yet there was no noise, no confusion. Every voice was hushed; every countenance was sad. As the plumed hearse moved slowly on, men and boys uncovered, and the dense throng bent forward, moved by deep, irrepressible, universal emotion. Many an eye in that vast crowd was dimmed,

* Appendix A.   † Appendix B.

and many a cheek wet with tears. Few, indeed, were they who could look unmoved on that wonderful funeral. Never had Ulster seen the like. Well might the mourning poet—himself a friend of the departed—write in sadness :

> "Tread—tread, slow with the dead—
>   Was he a king who hath fallen to-day ?
> Was he a prince whose spirit hath fled ?
>   Who is't that thus they are bearing away—
> Where the white moon lampeth the lonely bed,
>   And the earth-worm rules the kingdom of clay ?
> A prince in all holier senses of sway—
>   Yea, verily, yea !
> And never, methinks, did the crowds evince,
> For a sceptred king, or a jewelled prince,
> A deeper, or holier reverence
>   Than these display,
>   For the Chief whose rest
>   Is so little opprest
> With the gloom of their long array—
> The long—long, sad array,
>   That, with low, slow tread,
>   To the place of the dead,
> The great man beareth away !"*

It was not a king, nor a prince, in respect for whose memory that grand pageant was held—in sorrow for whose death those vast multitudes wept. It was a bereaved people, a mourning country, rendering the last sad tribute of honour to the remains of HENRY COOKE.†

---

* Appendix C.   † Appendix D.

APPENDIX.

---◆---

A.

The ministers named by Dr. Cooke, as those who should be requested to take part in the religious services at his funeral, were, the Rev. James Morgan, D.D.; the Rev. John Meneely; the Rev. William Craig; and the Rev. Henry Henderson. The gentlemen whom he wished to be invited to follow his body to the grave were, James Kennedy, Esq., J.P., and A. J. Macrory, Esq., his trustees; James Torrens, Esq., and Hugh Porter, Esq., as representatives of his congregation; John Preston, Esq., J.P., as representative of the laity of the Church of England; and Alderman John Lytle, J.P., as representative of his friends in the Corporation of Belfast. These gentlemen were mentioned at different times, and to different members of his family. He spoke of them to myself; and he named several others; but he added, better omit them, and let my funeral be as private as possible.

B.

The following account of the funeral is abridged from the local newspapers.

"PUBLIC FUNERAL. Yesterday, at twelve o'clock, a town meeting, convened by the mayor, in accordance with a requisition numerously signed by the leading gentry and merchants, was held in the Town Hall, for the purpose of considering the propriety of having a public funeral for the interment of the remains of the late Rev. Henry Cooke, D.D., LL.D., as a mark of public respect and esteem for his memory. The meeting was exceedingly large, the Town Hall being crowded to excess." . . . . The Mayor of Belfast was called to the chair. . . . . The Lord Bishop of Down and Connor moved,

" That, in deference to the life and labours of the late Dr. Cooke, and as a mark of respect to his public character and worth, there shall be a Public Funeral on Friday next." The resolution was seconded by Wm. Johnston, Esq., M.P.

The appointment of a committee to carry out the arrangements was moved by Sir Charles Lanyon, and seconded by James Hamilton, Esq., J.P., Chairman of the Harbour Commissioners.

The funeral was fixed for twelve o'clock, but at eleven a great company had assembled in Ormeau Park, adjoining the residence of Dr. Cooke. " The Rev. Wm. Johnston acted as secretary, and arranged the procession with consummate skill. He was ably se-conded by the marshal of the day, Head-Constable Rankin. Mr. Commissioner Bailey and Mr. Sub-Inspector Harvey were energetic in facilitating the arrangements. The streets were kept clear by mounted police, and the foot force guided the march.

" The members of the public bodies met in the Park shortly after eleven. The students of the different colleges led the way, in cap and gown—the white of the Bachelors, and the blue of the Masters' hoods, forming a good contrast to the black of the general body of mourners. The President of Queen's College, tall and stately in his Doctor's robes, followed, surrounded by the Professors and Staff. The Rev. William Arthur, President of the Wesleyan College, accom-panied by the Head-Master and the Professors, went next in order. Then the President, the Secretary, and the Professors of Magee College, Derry. The Faculty of the Assembly's College, without its President, who was being carried to the tomb, and without its Secretary, who, as chief mourner, followed the hearse, moved sadly on. Then came the clergy of the different Churches—the Episcopal and Covenanting clergymen, the United Presbyterians and the Wesleyans, the Inde-pendents, the Baptists, and the Unitarians—moving together in a body. The ministers of the General Assembly went immediately before the hearse. The hearse, simply caparisoned, was in the centre of the procession. On one side went the Moderator of the General Assembly ; after him in order, the Primate, the Bishop of Down, William Johnston, Esq., M.P., James Kennedy, Esq., J. P., and James Torrens, Esq. On the other side went the Mayor of Belfast (Samuel McCausland, Esq.), the Hon. Edward O'Neill, M.P. (as representing his father, Lord O'Neill), Thomas M'Clure, Esq., M.P., A. J. Macrory, Esq., John Preston, Esq., J.P., and Hugh Porter, Esq. The son of the deceased, Henry H. Cooke, Esq., the tall forms of his two sons-in-law, the Rev. William Gordon, and th

Rev. J. L. Porter, D.D., LL.D., with his grandson, Master Selim L. A. Porter, followed as chief mourners. Then the young minister of May Street, with the Session and Committee, followed in procession. The Town Council followed ; and then the Harbour Commissioners, the Poor Law Board, the Water Commissioners, the Governors of the Belfast District Asylum, the Belfast Charitable Society, and the Chamber of Commerce. The Staff of the Ulster Institution for the Deaf and Dumb, the Oddfellows, the representatives of the Town Commissioners of Armagh and Ballymoney, and other public bodies, closed the long procession. Then came the mourning coaches and the long line of 154 carriages of the nobility and gentry, that of Dr. Dorian, the Roman Catholic Bishop, being among the number."

The procession passed through the leading streets of Belfast, and along the Lisburn Road to Malone cemetery. The coffin was taken into the Presbyterian church. The Rev. Dr. Morgan ascended the pulpit, and the 90th Psalm was sung. He then delivered the funeral discourse, selecting as his text the words of David, "Know ye not that there is a prince and a great man fallen this day in Israel ? " The Rev. Henry Henderson closed with prayer. The coffin was then carried to the grave, where the Rev. William Craig, of Dromara, the senior minister of the General Assembly, conducted the closing religious exercises.

C.

The stanzas quoted are from a very touching and spirited Poem, written in memory of Dr. Cooke, and entitled " FUNERAL VOICES." Its author is Mr. Francis Davis, of Belfast, well known for his contributions to our poetical literature.

D.

MEMORIALS TO THE LATE DR. COOKE.

" On the day after his body was consigned, amid a nation's tears, to its last earthly home, a public meeting was called to consider what was due to his memory. Men of all classes and creeds came to this meeting. There was but one feeling dominant in every heart—

that the life and character, and, as far as possible, the person of Henry Cooke should be enshrined in some public memorial, in which he would speak to posterity, and show to the generations that are to follow, how the men of his own time loved and honoured him. A large and influential committee was appointed to consider the most appropriate form of this memorial."

After due deliberation it was resolved to erect a statue of the deceased in bronze, to be placed on an appropriate pedestal, in one of the leading thoroughfares of Belfast. The work is now being executed by Samuel F. Lynn, Esq., of London. The statue itself is nine feet high, and the pedestal fifteen feet. By the kindness of the sculptor, I have been able to give an engraving of the monument, taken from the model.

It was further resolved to erect, by public subscription, a still more splendid testimonial to Dr. Cooke, in the form of a HALL, adapted for the Meetings of the General Assembly of the Presbyterian Church in Ireland. The Assembly Hall is to be built in Belfast, and large subscriptions have been received; but the building is delayed on account of the difficulty of securing a suitable site.

The members of Dr. Cooke's congregation also determined to place in that Church which had been built for him, and in which he had ministered for nearly forty years, a suitable monument. It has now been completed. It is a splendid Portal of the Corinthian order, corresponding to the style of the building, and opening from the inner vestibule to the central aisle. It is of white Italian marble, on a massive plinth of polished Aberdeen granite, and is chastely ornamented with carvings and sculpture. The effect is very beautiful.

The remains of Dr. Cooke lie in Malone Cemetery, two miles from Belfast. His tomb, erected by his three surviving daughters, Miss Cooke, Mrs. Gordon, of Gilford, and Mrs. Porter, of College Park, Belfast, is a massive Sarcophagus of polished granite, resting upon a granite pedestal. On one side, as represented in the engraving, it bears the name of the deceased, and on the opposite side the date of his birth and of his death.

THE END.